Baseball

An Astrological

Sightline

by César Love

23ʀᴅ Street Books

© César Love 2019

ISBN 978-1-7339978-0-5

23rd Street Books
San Francisco, CA

Typeset by Chris Carlsson
Book and cover design by Marco Moura

Printed in the USA

To everyone who has written about baseball.

Acknowledgements

I wish to thank my father and mother who brought me to baseball games; Jake who encouraged me and taught me so much; the staff at the Hall of Fame Library in Cooperstown, especially Bill Dean, who helped me with my research; and Sheila, who took the trip with me to Cooperstown.

Table of Contents

A. A Note on the Text 7
B. Introduction 8

Part I: Foundation

1. Archeology 9
2. Cycles and Stars: The Basics of Astrology 17
3. The Correspondences of Signs and Positions................... 35
4. The Hero's Journey 44
5. Saturn, Time and Space 49

Part II: The Birthcharts of Teams

Introduction to the birthcharts of teams 59
Reds 63
Cubs 70
Braves 82
Dodgers 92
Tigers 102
Pirates 111
Cardinals 119
Giants 132
Phillies 145
The Western League 155
White Sox 159
Browns/ Orioles 169
Senators/ Twins 179
Indians 190
Athletics 199
Yankees 211
Red Sox 218
The Expansion Era 231
Mets 232
Astros 237
Senators/ Rangers 243
Angels 251

Pilots/ Brewers	258
Royals	262
Padres	267
Expos/ Nationals	273
Mariners	280
Blue Jays	286
Rockies	291
Marlins	294
Rays	299
Diamondbacks	304

Part III: Transits

Transits in Games	310
Orbs	311
Aspects	312
Examples of Transits from History	312
Axes Conjunct to the Planets	317
Transits to the Seasons	318
Hitters Years and Pitchers Years	319
The Months	320
Saturn in the Post-Season	321
Transits to the Birthcharts of Pitchers	327
No-Hitters	330
The Double No-Hitter of 1917	332
Combined No-Hitters	334
Birthcharts of Position Players	338
Injuries	339
Famous Games	342
Cubs 26 – Phillies 23	342
Whiz Kids Win the Pennant	344
The Sixth Game	347
Blue Jays 15 – Phillies 14	350
Following a Game	353

Bibliography 355

Index 362

A Note on the Text

This book is intended for both those with little or no astrological knowledge and for those well-versed in astrology. When an author writes a book for both experts and beginners, he or she faces the question of how much introductory information to incorporate into the text. Initially, I sought to assist the novice by parenthetically including astrological theories and principles where they were needed within the text. This proved too cumbersome. I chose, instead, to add a chapter on the fundamentals of astrology. This chapter is not thorough, but it does provide a foundation upon which to follow the developments of this book. If you are already knowledgeable with signs, planets, houses, aspects, and transits, feel free to skip Chapter 2. You may, of course, use this chapter for reference or review. In contrast, I have no chapter that explains the basics of baseball. I assume each reader to have knowledge of its rules and its lore.

INTRODUCTION

How is it possible that the game of baseball, something so seemingly mundane, embodies and reveals the astrological signs and the planets of the solar system?

Poets and filmmakers attribute spiritual qualities to the game of baseball. A genre of literature describes its pantheistic flavor. Movies such as *Field of Dreams* and *Damn Yankees* speculate upon the metaphysical elements of the game. But our literature and film have yet to provide a framework that discerns and expounds upon the spiritual aspects of baseball in a rigorous and analytical manner. At our most illuminative, we can only use descriptive phrases such as "that nostalgic feeling of youth and renewal that comes every spring when we smell the fresh grass and hear the news of Opening Day." But there is so much more to be said.

This book demonstrates the spiritual and transcendental nature of baseball through the methodology of astrology. The game of baseball embodies the universal archetypes of the astrological signs; elements of the game are representations of the twelve astrological signs and of the planets of the solar system. This is demonstrated through an examination of the history of the game, from its origins as a pagan fertility ritual to its current status as a spectator sport.

This book also introduces the astrological birthcharts of the 30 Major League teams currently playing in the United States. The history and tendencies of these teams become quite lucid when viewed from an astrological perspective. Furthermore, this book presents methods through which the transits of each game and each baseball season can be witnessed. Transits and planetary positions affect the course of every Major League baseball game. Astronomical factors also affect the course of every baseball season, from Spring Training to the World Series.

The mysteries and legends of baseball become intelligible through the methods of astrology presented in this book. Why did the Chicago Cubs keep losing for so long? Why did the Boston Red Sox hold their myth that to come just short of championship victory was sweeter than complete victory itself? Why do the Yankees excel in post-season play? Why did so many pitchers excel in 1968? What was the miracle of the 1969 Mets? These questions are answered here through the lens of astrology.

Archeology

Baseball, and games similar too it, have been played for millennia in Europe, Africa and Asia. The Iroquois tribes played a game in which a ball was hit with a bat,[1] but baseball is not a uniquely American artifact. The game has deep roots in the American soil, yet baseball flourished on ball fields all over the planet long before it became the national pastime in the United States. Some scholars link the African and Asian versions of baseball to the migrations of Aryan tribes,[2] while others state that all baseball-like games are descended from the Ancient Egyptians.[3] The thesis of this book advances a universality of baseball that will be demonstrated by its astrological elements. Baseball, like the stars and planets, exists outside of cultural and geographical influences. Yet, regardless of this book's bias towards a universality of baseball, an examination of the cultural and historical influences on the game is illuminating. It enlightens our study to learn how other cultures view the phenomenon of baseball. It is also useful to untangle the current misconceptions surrounding the origins of baseball.

The belief that Abner Doubleday, a Civil War general, invented baseball has been disproved by historians. This story was created to increase the game's popularity. It was Albert Spaulding who lodged this myth into the popular mind. Spaulding, who founded the sporting-goods company that bears his name, was also a player and owner of the Chicago White Stockings.[4] At the turn of the Twentieth Century, baseball was experiencing a surge in popularity within the United States, and Albert Spaulding used nationalism to further promote the game. Harold Peterson, author of *The Man who Invented Baseball* writes, "Spaulding so hated the idea that any part of the sport might have started outside the United States that he virtually drafted as inventor the poor general (Doubleday), who would have much preferred to be remembered for his military exploits but who, having died in 1893, was helpless to defend himself." [5] In 1907,

---

1. Vlasich, James: *A Legend for the Legendary*, p. 5
2. Peterson, Harold: *The Man Who Invented Baseball* pp. 41-49
3. Henderson, Robert: *Ball, Bat and Bishop* (p. 4) Egyptian drawings from the time of the Pharaohs show men hitting balls with clubs. See the figures between pages 28 and 29 and the text description on pages 19-20.
4. In the 19th Century, the team now known as the Chicago Cubs was called the Chicago White Stockings.
5. Peterson, Harold: *The Man who Invented Baseball*, p. 5

Major League Baseball assigned a group to determine the origins of the game. This group would be known as the Mills Commission. Under Albert Spaulding's influence, the Mills Commission would seal the myth that Abner Doubleday had invented baseball.[6]

A more recent myth credits Alexander Cartwright, a New York bank clerk, for establishing the structure of baseball as it is now known. Cartwright was inducted into the National Baseball Hall of Fame in 1938. His plaque in Cooperstown calls him the "Father of Modern Base Ball" and states that he "set bases 90 feet apart" and "established 9 innings as game and 9 players as team." Cartwright's contributions would become further embellished with the publication of Harold Peterson's book, *The Man Who Invented Baseball*, in 1973. Peterson claimed that sometime around 1845 Cartwright made the definitive adjustments to the games of Townball and Rounders to give us what we now know as baseball. But research by Monica Nucciarone, author of *Alexander Cartwright: The Life Behind the Baseball Legend*, would prove that many of the claims made on Cartwright's behalf were erroneous and based on a diary forged by his grandson. David Block, author of *Baseball Before We Knew It*, also confronts the assertions that Alexander Cartwright and his team, the Knickerbockers, originated many of the elements of modern baseball. Block debunks the declaration that Cartwright established the nine-inning game and the 90-foot distances between bases.[7] Yet he leaves in place the claim that the Knickerbockers introduced putting out a runner by throwing to the base rather than at the runner.[8]

The seminal work on the history of bat and ball games is *Ball, Bat and Bishop* by Robert Henderson. Henderson's work, published in 1947, includes descriptions of the French game Poison Ball and the English game of Stoolball.[9] Peterson's book, although it advances the eroneous Cartwright myth, does provide an important survey of baseball-like games in earlier eras and on other continents. Peterson's work ventures to lands farther away than France and England and includes depictions of baseball-like games played in Germany, Scandinavia, Russia, India, and Libya.[10] David Block's history of the game elaborates on the research of Harold Peterson and William Henderson. Block also demonstrates that

---

6. Peterson, Harold: *The Man who Invented Baseball*, pp. 5-6
7. The 90-foot distance between bases was formalized at the first baseball convention on Feb. 25, 1857.
8. Block, p. 87
9. Henderson: Stoolball pp. 70-78; Poisoned Ball pp. 140-149
10. Peterson: The German game, p. 37; the Russian game, p. 40; the Indian game p. 41

the game of baseball was not born fully formed, as the proponents of the Cartwright and Doubleday myths claim, but rather that it developed through an evolutionary process with influences from a number of games, including Stoolball, Cat, and the New York Game.[11] Block hypothesizes, "Baseball did not spring from a single linear evolutionary path but is the ultimate product of a common cultural memory extending back thousands of years." [12]

The most striking of the games described by both Peterson and Block exists in Libya.[13] This game is played by a Berber tribe in the area of Jadum in the Gebel Nefusa, a desert plateau of western Tripolitania. The game is called *Ta kurt om el mahag*, which translates to "The Ball of the Mother of the Pilgrim." The Berber game is very similar to our version of baseball. The captain of the team in the field pitches a ball towards the batter of the team at bat. The batter has two tries to hit the ball. If the batter is the captain, he is allowed three swings at the ball. Once the batter hits the ball, he runs to the base in the field. If he hits the ball far enough, he attempts to run back to the base from which he batted. The Berber game has only two bases, and the distance between these bases can vary from 70 to 90 feet. Players slide into the bases. The Berbers call the base they bat from "home." They call the base in the field "the pilgrim's base."

The Berber tribe that plays this game has a blond strain in its gene pool. Corrado Gini, an Italian population specialist, who observed the game in 1937, believed this strain to descend from the Northern Europeans who migrated to Africa between 6000 and 3000 BC. Soon after Gini published his findings, a Danish scholar named Per Maigaard, pointed out that *Ta kurt om el mahag* is almost an exact match to the ballgame played in Scandinavian countries called "Long Ball."[14] Gini and Maigaard agreed that baseball was brought to North Africa by Northern European tribes during their migrations to Africa millennia ago. [15]

Maigaard pointed out that the players of both games, be they Berbers or Northern Europeans, use similar language to describe players who are out. Both describe a player who is out as "rotten." In addition, the Northern Europeans refer to a player who is safe as "fresh.[16]" Within these words,

---

11. Block provides a genealogical diagram on p. 153
12. Block, p. 104
13. Peterson, pp. 42-46
14. Miagaard, Per: "Battingball Games" (reprinted by David Block) originally published in *Genus*, Rome, Italy, Vol. 5, N.1-2, 1941, pp. 57-72
15. Peterson, p. 43. (John Thorn reprinted Gini's article in 2012) *https://ourgame.mlblogs.com/rural-ritual-games-in-libya-berber-baseball-and-shinny-d17cf72c8ed9*
16. Peterson, p. 46

"rotten" and "fresh," exists a clue towards comprehending a profound meaning of baseball, one that has endured for thousands of years. On a symbolic level, the duality between fresh and rotten represents the battle between burgeoning spring and dying winter. Plants live, grow, and thrive in spring and summer: they are fresh. Vegetation becomes rotten and dies in fall and winter. Green leaves become brown. Connie Mack, the founder of the Athletics franchise, used similar language to open his autobiography when he equated dying with being called out. "Whether I make it (to age 100) depends on the decision of the Great Umpire who sooner or later calls us 'out.'"[17]

Baseball and baseball-like games are fundamentally rooted to the changes of the seasons. In these games, a ritualistic and symbolic battle is performed between emerging spring and passing winter. Such games are generally played in the season of spring when the plants are sprouting. Winter has just ended. The land is becoming green again.

Henderson states that all modern games in which balls are hit with stick-like objects descended from the fertility rites of the Ancient Egyptians.[18] Not only baseball and cricket, but golf, tennis and croquet derive from these ancient fertility rituals. All these sports, according to Henderson, share a lineage to the Egypt of the Pharaohs. The Egyptian myths most relevant to the fertility games of Ancient Egypt are those of Osiris and Seth. In the Egyptian pantheon of gods, Osiris and Seth were brothers. The goddess Isis was sister to them both, but she was also the wife of Osiris. According to myth, Osiris brought many of the elements of civilization to Egypt. He gave the Egyptians agriculture, metal-work and the rule of law. Together, Osiris and Isis ruled over Egypt. But Seth, their brother, would bring trouble. Seth envied Osiris for his throne. After a few attempts by Osiris to usurp him, Seth eventually killed Osiris and seized the throne. Seth then sealed the body of Osiris in a coffin and threw it into the Nile River.

The grieving Isis searched downriver for her husband's body. She found Osiris' body far away in the land of Byblos, where it was hidden within a trunk of a tree. Isis brought the body back to Egypt and hid it. However, one night, Seth found the body of Osiris. This time, Seth cut Osiris' body into fourteen pieces, scattering them throughout Egypt. Once again, Isis went on a search for her murdered husband's body. In time, she found all the pieces of the body except for the phallus which had been eaten by a fish. Isis assembled the remaining pieces of the corpse together,

---

17. Mack, Connie: *My 66 Years in the Big Leagues*, p. 1
18. Henderson, p. 4

substituting a rod of sycamore wood for Osiris' penis. Isis then performed magic ceremonies that brought Osiris back to life. Once reborn, Osiris did not return to his previous throne. Instead, he became king of the "Western Region" wherein Osiris presided over the souls of the dead.

Osiris was a god of vegetation. His story is one of death and rebirth. The death and rebirth of Osiris echoes the continuity of vegetation dying then reemerging as the seasons shift. His myth embodies the cycle of death and renewal that comes with the seasons. Seth was a god of the desert. Seth was also the god of winter. Both the desert and winter are associated with barrenness and an absence of vegetation. Seth is a god of death and negation. For the Ancient Egyptians, the conflict between Osiris and Seth embodied the opposition of life and death. But most relevant to baseball, Osiris and Seth embody the opposition between the seasons of spring and fall.

Rituals were performed by the Egyptians to ensure that spring would follow winter. For spring to return and for the season's crops to be plentiful, it was necessary for Osiris to be successful in his resurrection and to win his battle with Seth. The Egyptians performed ceremonies to assist the deity Osiris in his return from the dead. These rites were a symbolic reenactment of the battle between Osiris and Seth. In these rituals, balls were hit with bats.[19]

The Egyptian myth of Osiris and Seth is similar to the more familiar Greek myth of Persephone and Hades. Both myths embody the dualism of Spring versus Fall. Hades, the god of death and the underworld, abducted Persephone, the goddess of Spring. Hades brought Persephone to his underworld kingdom and made her his queen. The balance of the seasons exists because Persephone resides half the year above ground and half the year in the underworld with Hades. Vegetation does not grow in the six months of the year in which Persephone lives with Hades. The Christian holiday of Easter also embodies the oppositions of death and life, fall and spring. Easter commemorates the death and resurrection of Jesus. This holiday occurs in the season of spring when the plants are sprouting. The hunt for eggs, a symbol of life and fertility, is an Easter ritual.

The conflict between Osiris and Seth is also expressed in the astrological signs of Taurus and Scorpio. Taurus, whose constellation is prominent in spring, is the sign of vegetation and farming. Scorpio, a constellation of the fall, is the sign of death. Taurus and Scorpio occupy opposite positions in the zodiac wheel. The baseball season begins in spring with the sun

---

19. Henderson, p. 4

near the sign of Taurus. The baseball season also begins at the time of planting. After passing through spring and summer, the baseball season ends in fall. The World Series is played in October with the sun in Scorpio. The crops have been harvested. It is time to put away the bats and balls. The weather is chilly. Leaves are brown and falling from the trees. Seth and Hades now rule.

Another symbolic distinction exists between the fielding team and the batting team. Eugene Piasecki, a Slavic games scholar, describes these games as contests between the "father's side"—the batters, and the "mother's side"—the fielders. In the Slavic game, the captain of the fielding team was called "mother."[20] The Freudian symbolism is obvious on both sides. The father's team hits the ball with a long phallic object, a bat. The mother's team fields the ball with vaginal objects: fielding mitts or cupped hands.

The ball symbolizes an egg. As an egg is normally cared for by a mother, the ball is handled by the mother's team, the defense. The ball becomes symbolically fertilized as the game is played. As the father hits the ball with his bat, he symbolically inseminates the egg. The mother's team also represents the earth in which the seed will be planted. The father's team represents the Sun that will energize the seed in order for it to grow sufficiently to feed the tribe.

The name of the Berber game, "the Ball of the Mother of the Pilgrim," is also highly relevant to this study. The names of games that are played with balls are usually compound nouns that end with *ball*: *baseball, football* and *basketball*. Before the word *ball*, there exists a word that provides a description of the game. *Basket* means the ball is put through a basket. *Foot* indicates that the ball will be kicked. But the Berber game is called *The Ball of the Mother of the Pilgrim*. The ball belongs to the mother of the pilgrim. This name begs deciphering. Whose mother? What pilgrim? The side in the field, the defense, is called the *mother's side*. This mother is symbolically linked to the earth, which waits to be fertilized. Fertility rites are generally linked to the earth: to nature and mother goddesses. An earth-mother goddess is honored in this game. This mother also has a son. Who is he? Why is he called a pilgrim?

The base in the field for the Berbers is called the "pilgrim's base." Consider the dictionary definitions of "pilgrim:" 1: one who journeys in foreign lands 2: one who travels to a shrine or holy place as a devotee. The batter is not only symbolic of the inseminating father, but he is also

---

20. Peterson, p. 49

symbolic of a voyaging son. The batter is a pilgrim who leaves home on a religious quest. If he is successful, the son will return home, bringing home a spiritual boon to his tribe.[21]

Leo Frobenius is a German anthropologist who studied non-Western cultures early in the Twentieth Century. Frobenius theorized that primitive people play in response to natural and celestial phenomenon.[22] Play and rituals occur not only in response to animals and vegetation, but in response to the Sun, the Moon and the stars. Natural and celestial phenomena are echoed in games, performances, and religious rituals. Primitive people perform games and ceremonies that "recreate" natural and celestial events. Frobenius theorized that primitive people believe such ceremonies assist to maintain the cosmic order. Such rites are performed not only to induce the growth of vegetation, but to assist celestial events to happen. Events such as eclipses, planetary convergences, and the rising and setting of the Sun and Moon are supported by rituals.

The theories of Leo Frobenius are now suspect. He is considered a biased Westerner who imposed his interpretations onto cultures that were not his own. Frobenius, like many Western intellectuals, imposed Garden of Eden projections onto primitive tribes. Such theories and writings conceal a yearning for a long ago "innocent time."[23] Primitive people become idealized. The natives are viewed as childlike and at one with nature. Today, such noble savage myths are politically incorrect and can even be dismissed as back-to-the-womb fantasies. I propose, however, that something similar to Frobenius' theory of play goes on in *our* sports, in the play of modern people within the industrialized Western World, even though we lack the consciousness to understand it. We do not play to assist the growth of crops or the movement of the planets. We do not believe the crops will fail or that the solar system will stop when the players go on strike. Yet, the cosmic order, the placements and alignments of planets, is embodied in our games. Our games do not influence the cosmic order, as Frobenius' natives believed; rather, the cosmic order influences our games. The following chapters demonstrate how the planets of the Solar System and the zodiac constellations are represented in baseball and how their influences are manifest in the outcome of games.

---

21. The symbolic content of the batter is further explored in "Chapter Five: The Hero's Journey."
22. Huizinga, Johan, *Homo Ludens*, pp. 15-16
23. Describing an African tribe, Frobenius wrote, "They are all children of an ever luxurious, ever generous Mother Nature, never late with the growth of the year. They grow as Nature grows." (*Voices of Africa, Vol. II* (pp. 395-396).

Cycles and Stars

This chapter reviews the basics of astrology. The field of astrology is quite vast, but this chapter is contained. Its purpose is to ground the following chapters and to provide an introduction to astrology for those with little knowledge of the field. If its discussion is too brief for you, there are many in-depth astrology books available. Browse a bookstore or library.

Many facets of our lives display themselves in reoccurring cycles. As the earth rotates on its axis, we witness the Sun rise and set. We wake, eat, work, and sleep at set times of day and night. A day ends, the following day begins, and the cycle repeats itself. The years operate similarly. As the Earth revolves around the Sun, the months and the seasons arrive, depart, and return. We celebrate holidays at particular days within the cycle of the year. We participate in certain sports depending on the time of year: baseball is played in spring and summer; football is played in fall and winter.

As human beings, we are in tune with the cycles of the solar system. The Moon revolves around the earth in 28 days, approximating the same duration as a woman's menstrual cycle. After thousands of years of observing the cycles of the solar system and the cycles of life, human beings learned that events occur in repeating and predictable patterns. Humans learned to anticipate what would occur within the cycles they were experiencing.

The understandings of astrology emerge from observing the moving bodies of the solar system as they repeat their cycles. The planets, the Sun, and the Moon are in continuous movement. They appear in different locations of the sky from night to night. In contrast, the stars serve as a still backdrop to the moving bodies of the sky. Against the constellations, astrologers chart the movement of the planets, the Sun, and the Moon. The stars are also in motion, but, for the purposes of astrology, they are generally considered as fixed points in space.[24]

The constellations that are most relevant to astrology exist within a narrow 15-degree belt within the sky called the "zodiac." When we observe the sky on a clear night, the planets and our Moon are positioned within this band of constellations. The Zodiac Band and its set of constellations are also called the *ecliptic*. The zodiac is divided into twelve segments. Each of these twelve segments contains 30 degrees and is referred to as

---

24. Astrologers engage in a rich discussion on the gradual movement of the stars and its implications for astrology.

"a sign." Each of these 30 degree segments—each of these signs—has a constellation of the zodiac within it or nearby.

The Zodiac Band, like any ellipse, is divided into 360 degrees. Ellipses, like circles, are measured geometrically by degrees. Both consist of 360 degrees. Furthermore, each degree consists of 60 minutes, and each of these minutes contains 60 seconds. The 360 degrees of the Zodiac Band divide into 12 equally sized segments of 30 degrees. Each contains a constellation of the zodiac that represents an astrological sign. The twelve signs of the zodiac divide the 360 degrees into 12 equal segments of 30 degrees. Each degree has a number from 0 to 29 and the name of its sign, such as 20 degrees Cancer. Astrologers pinpoint the locations of a planet by naming the degree through which it is passing, such as in the finding that, at a particular time, "Mercury is located at 14 degrees Libra."

The planets travel through all 360 degrees and through all the signs of the Zodiac Belt. They do this over and over within courses that are predictable. Following mathematical formulae, astrologers know when planets reach specific points in the sky. Following their associated lore, derived from thousands of years of observations, astrologers know which events to expect when planets reach certain points in the sky.

THE SIGNS

Each sign holds a distinct current of the flow of life energy, and each sign of the zodiac is manifest in a symbol, usually the figure of an animal. The twelve signs are commonly presented in an order that begins with Aries, the first spring sign, and ends with Pisces, the final winter sign. Each sign has multiple manifestations that include a part of the body and a position on a baseball team.

The first spring sign, **ARIES**, has the symbol of the ram. Aries represents life, pure and unrestrainted. After the cold and freeze of winter, life reemerges in spring. The ram embodies the energy of life as it charges head and horns first. A football lineman performs a similar act, charging into the opposing line. Those born under the sign of Aries are known to be enthusiastic, courageous, willful, and headstrong. An Aries excels at getting things started. An impulsive Aries swings at the first pitch, not bothering to wait for a walk. An Aries begins a project with a full head of steam, yet often has difficulty following through or sustaining an effort. Mars is the ruling planet of Aries. The part of the body that corresponds to the sign of Aries is the head.

TAURUS, whose symbol is the bull, is the second sign. The bull of the zodiac is not a threatening figure, but a docile, luxuriating, and sensual animal. His activities are eating, making love, and just existing. The leisurely pace of baseball is closer to the sensibility of Taurus than to any other sign. Lacking the contact and aggression of Arian football, baseball takes its time. Like a bovine slowly chewing its cud, the game waits for a batter to swing, and the ball to be hit in play. Unlike the previous sign Aries, a Taurus has tenacity. A Taurus is stable and sturdy but can also be slow and inflexible. The ruling planet of Taurus is Venus. The parts of the body ruled by Taurus are the neck and shoulders.

The third sign is **GEMINI**, whose symbol is the twins. Gemini is a mental sign. The dexterous mind of Gemini is inquisitive and communicative. The dual nature of the twins sharpens the Gemini mind by allowing one to perceive subjects from multiple perspectives. A Gemini is witty, eloquent, clever, and well-informed. But the abuse of Gemini intelligence can lead to over-intellectualization, to thought that is out of touch with relevant purposes. A Gemini can also indulge in excessive chatter. The planet of Gemini is Mercury. The parts of the body associated with Gemini are the hands, arms, lungs, and nervous system.

CANCER, the first summer sign, has the symbol of the crab. A crab has claws and a shell exterior. Its claws are used to grasp things and hold them into close contact. To understand something or someone, a Cancer embraces them in personal contact. A Cancer will relate to others primarily through feeling and emotion. Cancers like to hug. Homes are important to Cancers. Like the shell of a crab, a house protects one from the outside world. A Cancer invites someone into his or her home to nurture and feed them. Cancer is the sign of mothers and cooks. The Cancer tendencies, when expressed negatively, become over-possessiveness of family and friends, insulation from the outside world, and emotional instability. The celestial body associated with Cancer is the Moon. The parts of the body associated with this sign are the breasts and the stomach.

LEO, whose symbol is the lion, is the fifth sign. The lion is the mighty "King of the Beasts." Those born under the sign of Leo radiate authority and possess a regal quality. Leo is the sign of kings and queens. Leos are magnets for attention and adoration. Many become stars of movies and sports. The Leo bearing, when expressed negatively, becomes vanity, egoism, or bossiness. A Leo may be unwilling to share the stage with others. One may grandstand for attention, becoming a hotdog and a showboat. The celestial body associated with the sign of Leo is the Sun, the center of the solar system. The planets, naturally, revolve around the

Sun's regal presence, as do those associating with a Leo. The part of the body associated with the sign of Leo is the heart.

The sixth sign is **VIRGO**, whose symbol is a harvest maiden. Like Gemini, Virgo is a mental sign. The Virgo mind excels at analysis. Whereas the Gemini mind is attracted to new information, the Virgo mind concentrates on the data in hand, analyzing and organizing it. Like the maiden separating the wheat from the chaff, the Virgo mind separates the useful from the disposable. Virgos make order from disorder, placing things into categories and rightful places. They enjoy cleaning. When their energy is expressed negatively, Virgos become nitpicky and hypercritical. Many are cleanfreaks and workaholics. As with Gemini, the planet of Virgo is Mercury. The parts of the body associated with Virgo are the intestines.

LIBRA, whose symbol is the scale, is the seventh sign and the first fall sign. The purpose of the Libra scale is not to weigh but to balance. A Libra seeks balance, harmony, and justice. Evenhanded, fair, and conciliatory, Libras make good mediators, negotiators, and partners. They are gracious and charming, ever concerned with another person's well-being. Libra is the sign of marriage and partnerships, social interactions that balance the needs and desires of two people. Since they are naturally in tune with principles of beauty and harmony, many Libras become artists. When expressed negatively, Libra energy can be wishy-washy, rendering them at times unable to take a firm stance or make a decision. They can be codependent, in constant need of a partner. Libras may swing back and forth between extreme positions and lifestyles, attempting to balance their scale by tipping an end with a ton of bricks, then countering with another ton on the opposite extreme. The planet of Libra is Venus. The parts of the body associated with Libra are the buttocks and the ribs.

The eighth sign is **SCORPIO** whose symbol is the scorpion. A scorpion is a hard-shelled creature that keeps to itself in dark places. It stings only when it is disturbed. A Scorpio is willful and powerful. One holds the power of creation, destruction, and regeneration. As the energies of sex and death come together in this sign, a Scorpio can alternately create and destroy. The power of Scorpio is highly pressurized, like one's fluids verging on orgasm. Scorpios are secretive; they know that projects develop best in dark isolation. Some become adept at occult practices. A well-developed Scorpio is highly disciplined, creative, and resourceful, while a less evolved Scorpio can be power-hungry, oversexed, and destructive. The planets of Scorpio are Pluto and Mars. The parts of the body identified with Scorpio are the sex organs and the excretory system.

The ninth sign is **SAGITTARIUS**, the centaur. Centaurs are a mythical race of beasts, half horse and half human. They are skillful at archery. The centaur of the zodiac aims an arrow at a star, a symbol of upward aspiration. The half animal and half human centaur is evolving from its lower animal side to its higher nature. A Sagittarius seeks a divine consciousness that is beyond the animal and the human. The Sagittarius mind quickly leaps from small matters to larger pictures. A Sagittarius is concerned with large philosophical matters. Many excel as philosophers and teachers. Their temperament is usually joyous and enthusiastic. They can be awkward in the face of small details, as the absent-minded professor is a Sagittarius manifestation. They are generally honest to the point of bluntness. Similarly, they can be self-righteous, judgmental, and imperialistic. A person who thinks he or she has attained the truth often feels free to impose it upon others. Crusaders, missionaries and conquerors, whether on horseback or ringing doorbells, are Sagittarian manifestations. The planet of Sagittarius is Jupiter. Its corresponding body parts are the hips and thighs.

CAPRICORN, whose symbol is a mountain goat, is the first winter sign and the tenth sign of the zodiac. Capricorns are goal-oriented. Like the goat that slowly climbs up a mountain, a Capricorn stays focused on its goal. Its concentration is highly refined. A mountain goat is sure-footed and cautious as it ascends the mountain. A goat must carefully look where it steps or it will fall off the mountain; therefore, a Capricorn observes carefully, perceiving beyond common delusions and sentimentality. A Capricorn recognizes imperfections and smells the coffee. But such a realistic outlook can leave one with a self-assured cynicism. An evolved Capricorn is organized, ambitious, and civil. A less-evolved Capricorn can be stodgy, pessimistic, and suspicious. The planet of Capricorn is Saturn. Its parts of the body are the knees, back, bones, and teeth.

The eleventh sign is **AQUARIUS**, whose symbol is the Water Bearer, a man or woman carrying a large container of water. The water within the jug is symbolic of consciousness. An Aquarius captures the water of consciousness from the sky and serves it to humanity. An Aquarius is ever concerned with the universals of truth, brotherhood, love, and freedom. An Aquarius struggles to bring people into unity with these principles. Their attunement with universal laws enables Aquarians to tap the energies of the cosmos for new purposes. Many are scientists and inventors such as Thomas Edison and Nikola Tesla. Other Aquarians become revolutionaries. They act and dress contrary to the social norm, engaging in battles for the causes of individuality and freedom. Many remain Bohemian to their grave. An Aquarius usually has many friends, but one's loyalty may be less to each friend as individuals than to the principle of friendship. People of this sign can become needlessly eccentric or dogmatic, unwilling to compromise their lifestyle or vision with the clay of reality. The planets of Aquarius are Uranus and Saturn. The parts of the body associated with Aquarius are the ankles and the blood.

PISCES is the twelfth and last sign of the zodiac. Its symbol is two fishes. One fish swims upriver to spawn, while the other swims towards the ocean. Whether in a stream, lake or ocean, a fish is sensitive to everything within its body of water. A Pisces relates to others through the realm of feeling. Like a fish sensitive to the currents, a Pisces feels what others feel—joy, sadness, anger, laughter—all the sentiments flowing nearby. Their capacity for empathy makes them good listeners. Highly impressionable, Pisces can easily become absorbed and overwhelmed by forces outside of themselves. Their innate fluidity draws many toward the mystical realms. Others take a lower road through drugs and alcohol. The planets of Pisces are Neptune and Jupiter. Its parts of the body are the feet.

The twelve signs of the zodiac are grouped by element. They are also classified by modality.

The Elements

The four elements are fire, earth, air, and water. The three fire signs are Aries, Leo and Sagittarius. Fire signs are naturally dynamic, creative, and exuberant. Fire signs are also lively and highly spirited. The earth signs are Taurus, Virgo, and Capricorn. Earth signs are practical and grounded. Highly dependable, they function well with the demands of the real world. The three air signs are Gemini, Libra, and Aquarius. Air si gns are thoughtful and social. They generate and distribute information. They also serve as catalysts to bring people and groups together. The water signs are Cancer, Scorpio and Pisces. The nature of water is feeling. Water signs are empathetic and sensitive to the nuances of emotions.

The Modalities

The three modalities of the signs are cardinal, fixed, and mutable. The four cardinal signs are Aries, Cancer, Libra, and Capricorn. Cardinal signs are dynamic. They initiate action. Cardinal signs have a quality of motion to them. The four fixed signs are Taurus, Leo, Scorpio, and Aquarius.

Stable and determined, the fixed signs concentrate energy. The mutable si
gns are Gemini, Virgo, Sagittarius and Pisces. The mutable signs transfer
and disseminate energy. They are versatile and adaptable.

THE PLANETS

As the planets revolve through the Zodiac Belt, they act as dynamic forces. Each planet has a unique energy. Each behaves as a catalyst. As they travel through the signs, the planets stimulate activity. Most systems of astrology employ ten planets. The Sun, Moon, and Pluto, although not generally thought of as planets, are considered planets within the field of astrology. The planet Earth is generally not included as a planet in astrological systems. Instead, the Earth is the fixed point from which we observe the other planets and their influences.[25] The ten planets discussed in this chapter are the Sun, Moon, Mercury, Venus, Mars, Jupiter, Saturn, Uranus, Neptune ,and Pluto. The Nodes of the Moon are also discussed. In addition to the planets, there are other heavenly bodies that behave as catalysts, including comets and asteroids.

The SUN's energy is radiant, vital, and life-affirming. The Sun represents a person's center of consciousness, individuality, will, and volition. What most individuals know to be their "sign," is more accurately called one's "Sun sign." This is the sign of the zodiac through which the Sun was traveling on the day of one's birth. A person knows oneself as an Aries, for example, because he or she was born between March 21 and April 21, the days the Sun travels through the segment of the zodiac belonging to the sign of Aries. The Sun travels through all twelve signs in one year. Its ruling sign is Leo.

The MOON's energy is cool and moist. It is receptive and reflective. The Moon manifests in a person's emotions, memories, family, and ethnic origins. The Moon rules over our domestic life and our family relations. Maternal and nurturing, the Moon also manifests in motherhood. As the Moon revolves around the Earth, it passes through the twelve signs in 28 days. The Moon's ruling sign is Cancer.

The energy of MERCURY is quick and mental. Mercury represents intellect and rationality. It also governs sense perception and communication. Mercury rules over two signs, Gemini and Virgo,

---

25. A system of astrology that takes the Earth as the vantage point of the planets and the Zodiac Belt, is called "geocentric." In contrast, a "heliocentric" system of astrology views the location of the planets in the Zodiac Belt from the vantage point of the Sun.

manifesting in the inquiring and communicative functions of Gemini and in the analytic abilities of Virgo. Mercury revolves around the Sun in 88 days.

The nature of **VENUS** is receptive and feminine. Venus rules matters of attraction. In social realms, it governs attractions between people in matters of romance, diplomacy, and commerce. Venus also governs material possessions, ruling over money and property. Venus brings us the arts and other refinements such as social manners. The planet lords over the material sign of Taurus and the artistic sign of Libra. Venus revolves around the Sun in 225 days.

In contrast with Venus, the planet **MARS** is masculine, energetic, and outgoing. Mars stands for action and assertiveness. While Venus brings the qualities of compromise and diplomacy, Mars would rather hold its ground or go to war. Mars is represented in muscle and strength, the courage and energy for battle. Mars rules over the signs of Aries and Scorpio. Mars revolves around the Sun in 2 ½ years.

In keeping with its large size, **JUPITER**'s energy is about expansion. Jupiter brings the instinct to grow and expand oneself, mentally and spiritually. In the mental realms, Jupiter is embodied in wisdom and philosophy, extending one's viewpoint beyond personal concerns into the views and interests of others. Jupiter brings the urge to travel, to expand one's horizons. Jupiter also expands into the realms of religion, benevolence, and hope, embodying the bigness and generosity of our highest values. Jupiter's signs are aspiring Sagittarius and mystical Pisces. Jupiter takes 12 years to revolve around the Sun.

SATURN's energy is concentrated, restrictive, and paternal. While Jupiter provides expansion, Saturn brings limitation. Saturn concentrates energies, solidifying them. It is a builder who provides structure and frameworks. Saturn pours the concrete that makes things solid. Saturn's energy is authoritarian, setting rules and assigning responsibilities. Saturn is also the planet of time. The signs ruled by Saturn are Capricorn and Aquarius. Saturn revolves around the Sun in 28 years.

The outer planets—Uranus, Neptune and Pluto—take human lifetimes to revolve around the Sun. Since they can remain in a single sign for decades or longer, their effects are felt collectively on generations. Astrologers refer to the Baby Boomers, for example, as "the Pluto in Leo Generation."

The energy of **URANUS** is electric and revolutionary. Uranus is called "the higher octave of Mercury" since it brings an extreme rationality.

Original and inventive, Uranus brings technology. Discovered in 1781, during the period of the French and American revolutions, Uranus has a political dimension. The planet is ever insistent on freedom. Uranus is most in tune with the sign of Aquarius. Uranus revolves around the Sun in 82 years.

NEPTUNE's energy is sensitive and mystical. Neptune is called "the higher octave of Venus." While Venus emphasizes a love shared between two people, the love of Neptune is universal. The planet brings a sensitivity and concern for all beings. The idealism of saints is a Neptunian quality. Mystics and psychics are led by this planet. Neptune rules the sign of Pisces. Neptune takes 165 years to revolve around the Sun.

The energy of PLUTO is dark, powerful, and transformative. Pluto is called "the higher octave of Mars" because both planets share an aggressive nature. Pluto serves to transform and to metamorphose. Pluto is named for the god of death and the underworld. Pluto brings death but also allows for regeneration and rebirth. Alan Oken states, "Pluto is the force which transforms the atomic structure of life so that the various energy patterns can regroup into their new forms."[26] Pluto rules the sign of Scorpio. Pluto completes its orbit around the Sun in 248 years.

The LUNAR NODES consist of two points in the zodiac that are 180 degrees apart from each other. They exist where the Moon crosses the ecliptic. The South Node is represented in one's past and inheritance. In contrast, the North Node is one's path of growth in this life, including challenges to be met.

BIRTHCHARTS

At the moment of birth, each person becomes marked with the pattern of signs and planets present in the sky at that instant. An indelible imprint is made. An astrologer reconstructs these patterns of stars and planets when he or she casts a "birthchart." For millennia, astrologers cast these charts using compasses and mathematical formulae. But current astrologers use computer programs.

The outlines of a life are present in a birthchart. The tendencies, opportunities, and struggles of each person are written in this birthchart. It is both a science and an art to interpret a birthchart. Astrologers draw upon a body of lore to guide their interpretations. Much of this knowledge, which is based upon centuries of observations, is available in astrology

---

26. Oken, Alan: *The Horoscope, the Road and its Travelers*, p. 62

texts. On the following page, Pete Rose's birthchart is displayed. By applying astrology's body of knowledge, one can make generally accurate statements about his life, character, and future.

Astrological birthcharts are also cast for group entities, such as nations, corporations, and teams. Social organisms have a discernible life beyond that of their individual members. Any thriving organization consists of more than the sum of its members. It also consists of a birth, a history, and a culture. Corporations are often described as having cultures: their unique values and customs. When baseball pundits discuss "the Dodger way" or "the Yankee way," they describe the culture of a team. The birthchart for the United States is printed on the following page. The cultural and political tendencies of the U.S. are inherent in its birthchart.

Pete Rose
Monday, April 14, 1941 5:15:00 AM
Cincinnati, Ohio
Time Zone: 05:00 (EST)
Longitude: 084° W 29' 54"
Latitude: 39° N 08' 48"

Houses

Astrological birthcharts are divided into twelve sections called "houses." These divisions are present as displayed in Pete Rose's birthchart and in the United States' birthchart. Each house is a theater for particular experiences. Each house also has a correspondence to a sign of the zodiac. The twelve Houses parallel the twelve signs. The First House bears an association with the first sign, Aries. The Second House is kin to the second sign, Taurus. The Third House matches the third sign, Gemini. The correspondences of houses to signs proceeds in this numerical sequence. The number of the house (its numerical placement) is matched to the number associated with the sign (the sign's numerical place in the order of signs).

The distinction between the signs and the houses is subtler than the distinction between signs and planets. Dane Rudhyar wrote, "The

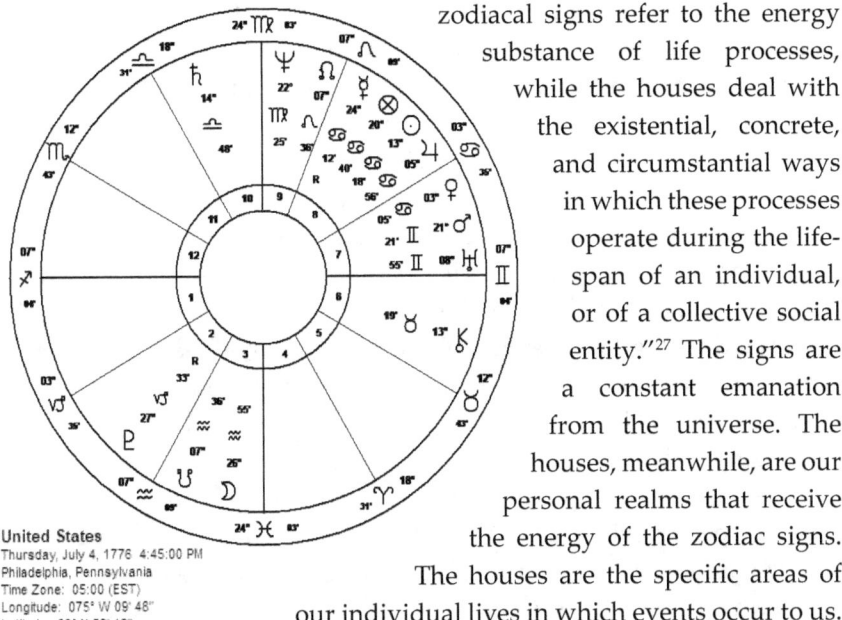

United States
Thursday, July 4, 1776 4:45:00 PM
Philadelphia, Pennsylvania
Time Zone: 05:00 (EST)
Longitude: 075° W 09' 48"
Latitude: 39° N 59' 18"

zodiacal signs refer to the energy substance of life processes, while the houses deal with the existential, concrete, and circumstantial ways in which these processes operate during the lifespan of an individual, or of a collective social entity."[27] The signs are a constant emanation from the universe. The houses, meanwhile, are our personal realms that receive the energy of the zodiac signs. The houses are the specific areas of our individual lives in which events occur to us.

When we separate our life into its various segments — our work life, our social life, our family life, etc. — our life divides along lines very similar to the astrological houses.

Astrological houses are arranged in a counter-clockwise order. (See Figure 3.) The sky within them divides into six sections above the horizon and another six sections below the horizon. The lines that divide the 12 houses stay fixed, while the stars and planets within the houses steadily move in response to the Earth's rotation. The constellations on the horizon keep shifting. Eventually the Sun, Moon, and the planets all rise and set. About every two hours, a different zodiac sign rises on the eastern horizon. In the course of 24 hours, all 12 signs and all 360 degrees of the Zodiac Belt pass through the eastern horizon. The lines dividing the houses, however, remain in their places while the stars and planets shift with the rotation of the Earth.

Various systems exist to determine the house divisions. The Equal House System divides the 360 degrees of the zodiac into 12 equal segments. The Placidus House System divides the sky into segments that appear of equal size from the viewpoint of the location for where the chart is cast. The houses in a chart with the Placidus system can vary greatly in size, depending on the longitude of the location for which the chart is cast.

The Ascendant-Descendant axis and the MC-IC axis are important components to every birthchart. The Ascendant-Descendent axis is the horizontal line that identifies the degrees of the zodiac on the eastern and western horizons. The degree and sign on the eastern horizon are known as the Ascendant.[28] The MC-IC axis runs vertically from the top of the chart to the very bottom. MC stands for *Medium Coli*. The MC is not the zenith, not the point in the sky directly vertical and overhead. Instead, the MC is the degree within the Zodiac Band closest to the zenith. The IC, its opposite, is the lowest point in the Zodiac Band. IC stands for *Imun Coeli*.[29]

The dividing lines between the houses are known as "cusps." Each cusp is named for the house that succeeds it. For example, the dividing line between the Fourth and Fifth Houses is called the Fifth House cusp. The sign on the cusp greatly affects the environment of the succeeding house. Activity in a specific house takes on the nature of the sign at its cusp. A person with Aries on the Fifth House cusp will have an Aries tone to his or her Fifth House activities. Every sign in the zodiac is placed somewhere in every birthchart. One can observe the cusps to find where each sign is manifest in the birthchart.[30]

The **First House** shows one's outward personality and how one primarily interacts with the world. The First House also reflects how one is perceived by others. The First House begins with the Ascendant, also called the "Rising Sign." This is the sign on the eastern horizon. The First House and the Ascendant have an affinity with the sign Aries and the planet Mars.

The **Second House** establishes values and possessions. The Second House includes matters of finance. Here is the stuff we own, whether bank accounts, commodities, or baseball cards. The sign and planet that correspond to the Second House are Taurus and Venus.

The **Third House** includes one's immediate environment, the neighborhood, and matters of communication. Brothers and sisters are also found in the Third House, along with short trips. Its sign is Gemini, and its ruling planet is Mercury.

The **Fourth House** and its cusp, the IC, is the place of our emotions, our memories, and our past. The Fourth House includes domestic matters:

---

28. The Ascendant determines a large part of one's personality and will be discussed with the First House.
29. The MC and the IC are further discussed with the Tenth House and the Fourth House.
30. Some signs do not appear on cusps but are "intercepted" within a house. This happens when all the sign's degrees fall between the cusps of two houses. Intercepted signs still manifest their energy within their houses.

the family, the home, and the nurturing parent. Its related sign is Cancer and its planet is the Moon.

The *Fifth House* is the house of leisure. The Fifth House encompasses sports, games, creative projects, love affairs, recreational activities, and artistic pursuits. It is also the house of children. The sign and planet associated with the Fifth House are Leo and the Sun.

The *Sixth House* includes matters of work, service, health, and animals. Cleaning and organizing are Sixth House activities. The sign akin to the Sixth House is Virgo, and its planet is Mercury.

The *Seventh House* is the stage of partners, be they partners in love, marriage, or business. Enemies are also found in the Seventh House. Its related sign is Libra and its planet is Venus.

The *Eighth House* includes the realms of sex, death, and the occult. Inheritances and taxes also fall in the Eighth House. Scorpio is the sign associated with the Eighth House. Pluto and Mars are its ruling planets.

The *Ninth House* includes education, religion, and values. Journeys to distant lands, especially religious pilgrimages, are Ninth House pursuits. The planet Jupiter and the sign of Sagittarius are associated with the Ninth House.

The *Tenth House* and its cusp, the MC, reflect one's public persona and career. The parent with the authoritarian role is found in the Tenth House. The sign Capricorn and the planet Saturn are associated with the Tenth House.

The *Eleventh House* contains friends, clubs, and social activity. A person's hopes and wishes are also included in the Eleventh House. Its ruling sign is Aquarius. Its planets are Uranus and Saturn.

The *Twelfth House* is the realm of hidden things. Mental states such as sleep and psychic activity are Twelfth House activities. The places where people are separated from society—prisons, asylums, and monasteries—are found in the Twelfth House. The Twelfth House's corresponding sign is Pisces. Its planets are Neptune and Jupiter.

Rulerships and Affinities

Each house has a planet and a sign that are its natural correspondents. For example, the Tenth House has a natural affinity to Capricorn and Saturn. Capricorn and Saturn are said to *rule* the Tenth House. The columns of the following chart group the signs, planets and houses by their natural affinities.

sign	planet	house
Aries ♈	Mars	1
Taurus ♉	Venus ♀	2
Gemini ♊	Mercury ☿	3
Cancer ♋	Moon ☽	4
Leo ♌	Sun ☉	5
Virgo ♍	Mercury ☿	6
Libra ♎	Venus ♀	7
Scorpio ♏	Pluto ♇	8
Sagittarius	Jupiter ♃	9
Capricorn ♑	Saturn ♄	10
Aquarius ♒	Uranus ♅	11
Pisces ♓	Neptune ♆	12

Aspects

Aspects are the geometric relationships between planets. Aspects between planets affect the flow of each planet's energy. Some aspects increase a planet's strength, while other aspects restrict the flow of a planet's energy. Within the 360 degrees of the Zodiac Belt, the planets are continuously creating and dissolving angles with each other. In Pete Rose's birthchart, for example, his Mercury and Pluto are 119 degrees apart. This aspect, and any aspect near 120 degrees, is considered a *trine*. Most astrologers employ the following aspects when analyzing a birthchart.

The aspect of the *conjunction* occurs when two or more planets are near to each other. Planets in conjunction are close to the same degree of the zodiac. In some conjunctions, the planets will actually occupy the same degree. This aspect unites the energies of both planets. The conjunction usually increases the power of both planets, but it may also weaken one planet by making it subservient to the stronger one.

The aspect of the *opposition* exists when planets are 180 degrees apart from each other. The opposition is a challenging aspect, as planets in opposition generally serve contrary purposes. If an opposition operates crudely, the individual experiences it by swinging back and forth between the opposing planets: preferring the state of one and denying the other, then reversing the preference. If an individual grows with this aspect, he or she gains an awareness of multiple perspectives. A harmony between the opposing planets can also develop for that person.

The aspect of the *square* occurs when planets are separated by a 90 degree angle. Planets in square tend to operate at cross purposes. Both planets suffer when their energies are in square. The square is considered the most difficult of aspects, as it will interfere with normal functions of one's life unless its challenges are met. The square requires one to address the energies of both affected planets so that each becomes understood and strengthened. Once mature, squares become the strongest aspects of our birthcharts. Mature squares are like solid blocks, providing strong foundations and support.

The aspect of the *trine* separates planets by 120 degrees. Since planets in trine usually share the same element (fire, earth, air or water), they have a natural harmony. Planets in trine easily express themselves because both planets are complimented by the natural flow. This aspect brings talents that emerge without difficulty. Although the trine is considered a beneficial aspect, too many trines in a birthchart can make a person lazy. Without sufficient challenges, a person becomes corrupted by a life of ease.

Planets that are 60 degrees apart have the aspect of the *sextile*. Planets in sextile also combine their efforts, but, unlike with the trine, the sextile does not bring easily accessed talents. The sextile represents potential and opportunity, but an effort is required before this aspect will bear fruit.

The *quincunx*, also called an *inconjuction*, is an aspect of 150 degrees. This aspect is somewhat challenging, but not as difficult as the square. Some adjustment is necessary for a quincunx to function to one's benefit.

The *semi-square* is formed when planets are 45 degrees apart. Alan Oken describes the semi-square as energy that is activated but not yet mature. This "energy can be said to be in its adolescence, for the individual, although aware of the planets in the semi-square, is not quite certain how to properly channel this energy interchange to his or her best advantage."[31] The semi-square brings a tendency towards rashness and misplaced judgments.

Aspects do not need to be the exact number of degrees specified. An orb of 8 degrees is allowed for the conjunction, square, trine and opposition. For astrology's purposes, an angle of 82 degrees is still considered a square, but the orb narrows to 4 degrees for the minor angles of the quincunx, sextile and semi-square. An aspect involving the Sun or Moon, however, has a wider orb of 10 degrees.

Progressions

Potentials latent within a human being reveal themselves in time. A birthchart is a static picture of the sky, yet it also has a kinetic quality. With the passage of time, different features of the birthchart unfold, just as an individual who, over the years of her or his life shows new traits, talents, or interests. The potentials within an individual or a group entity are realized as components of the birthchart that reveal themselves in time. Astrologers calculate the time required for potentials to manifest themselves through the use of "progressions." Although one's original birthchart remains for life, a "progressed chart" can be calculated for each year. In the progressed chart, the planets shift and form new aspects with the planets of the original chart.

There are various methods of calculating the progressed chart.

---

31. Oken, Alan: *The Horoscope, the Road and its Travelers*, p. 207

The easiest method is to advance the chart elements 1 degree for every year since one's birth. For example, if you are 30 years old, simply add 30 degrees to the planetary bodies and house cusps in your birthchart. Another method of calculating progressions uses the number of years one has lived as the number of days to count ahead from the date of one's birth. If you were born on January 1, 1970, your progressed chart for you at age 20 would be the same as that for January 21, 1970.

Pete Rose's birthchart shows how a progression manifested into a marriage. In his original natal chart, the Moon is positioned at 0 degrees Sagittarius. When he married in 1964 at the age of 22, his 0 degrees Sagittarius Moon had progressed to 22 degrees Sagittarius. That year, his progressed Moon was exactly trine to his Venus of 22 degrees Aries. Venus is the planet of marriage. The progression of his Moon into a trine with Venus brought Pete Rose his marriage at age 22.

TRANSITS

While a birthchart contains fixed points within the zodiac, the planets in the sky maintain continuous motion through the signs and the degrees of the zodiac. The fixed points of a birthchart that include the planets, the Ascendant, the MC and the houses are sensitive to the celestial bodies in motion. When a moving planet forms an aspect to a point within a person's birthchart, that person undergoes a transit.

A planet in one's birthchart acts as a net or vessel, catching the energy of the planet in transit, as it forms an aspect. When this happens, the energy of the planet in the birthchart reacts with the energy of the planet in transit. Each time a planet in the sky forms a conjunction, square, trine or other aspect to an important degree in your birthchart, that component of your chart is activated. The energy of the planet in transit combines with the energy of the stationary planet in the birthchart. The result is activity within the part of your life indicated by the planet in your birthchart. A planet in transit does not need to form an aspect to a planet in our birthchart to cause an effect. Planets also cause effects when they enter the houses of our birthcharts.

Transits have various effects and durations. Each planet brings its unique qualities. The transits of fast-moving planets such as Mercury and the Moon pass quickly. Mercury may bring a quick insight. The Moon can bring a sudden change of emotion. The transits of slower moving planets are of longer duration. A transit of Saturn may sustain a long project such as building a house or writing a book.

Astrology, as it is commonly practiced today in North America, observes the effects of transits and progressions on the lives of individuals. When a person consults an astrologer, the astrologer will analyze the client's birthchart and the transits or progressions that the client is undergoing. The astrologer clarifies the underlying issues that the transits brought to the surface. The client is often experiencing a period of internal psychological change. Transits and progressions are what bring such periods of growth and change. One's inner changes are generally reflected in the external events of one's life. The significant moments of our lives, whether comfortable or challenging, are triggered by transits and progressions.

Astrologers perform most of their predictions with an understanding of transits. The paths of the planets are mathematically calculated years in advance. This data makes the anticipation of transits quite easy. With a birthchart and an ephemeris,[32] one can mark in advance the dates that one's transits will occur. Transits become manifest in the realms of life represented by the planets involved. For example, a transit to one's natal Mars affects one's drive towards action or one's feelings of anger. A transit to one's Mercury manifests in the Mercury realms of communication, work, or health. Astrology texts describe in detail how the transits of each planet affect individuals.

Part Three of this book describes how transits affect baseball teams.

---

32. An ephemeris is an astrological text that lists the locations of the planets for periods of a year or longer.

The Correspondences of Signs and Positions

A correspondence exists between the positions of a baseball team and the signs of the zodiac and their ruling planets. Each of the signs is represented in a position. A baseball team is generally considered to consist of nine positions. The number nine, of course, does not equal the number of zodiac signs, twelve. but this incongruity is resolvable. When we add the batter and manager to the nine defensive positions, we have the sum of eleven. The pitcher, meanwhile, is counted twice because it is embodied in two signs, Gemini and Virgo. These additions give us a sum of twelve positions, equal to the number of twelve zodiac signs.

The sign of **Aries** and the planet **Mars** correspond to the **shortstop**. A shortstop requires quick short bursts of energy. The ram, the animal symbol of Aries, charges towards its target, crashing against it with head and horns. A shortstop often charges, ram-like, towards the ball. When fielding a slow grounder, the shortstop must run forward to confront the ball. This play exemplifies Aries energy, charging forward, unrestrained. The other infield positions can usually wait for the ball to come to them. But the shortstop is the infielder furthest away from the batter. The shortstop's throw to first base is generally longer than the throws of the second baseman and the third baseman, since one is often set on the edge of the outfield grass. A shortstop has little time to make the play and must act as quickly as possible, especially on the slow grounder or the ball hit to the hole.

The sign of Aries, the first spring sign, is associated with beginnings. Two shortstops who have contributed to the lore of Opening Day are Ozzie Smith and Lou Boudreau. Ozzie Smith, the St Louis Cardinals shortstop, would perform a backflip on each Opening Day. Lou Boudreau, the Indians' shortstop and manager, once said that, on Opening Day, the world is all future and there is no past.[33]

The birthchart of Luke Appling has the Sun in Aries. The birthchart of Honus Wagner has Mars in Aries.

Taurus and the planet **Venus** are embodied in the position of the

---

33. Halberstam, David: *Summer of '49*, p. 70

center fielder. The position of center field carries a special mystique. Baseball fans hold center field on a pedestal exalted above the other positions. This exaltation is deserved. Center field is the position whose energy is closest to the sensibility of the game. Taurus is the sign of plants and vegetation. Baseball is a game tied to both land and nature. The center fielder stands with a wide expanse of green to one's left and one's right.

Taurus is a sign of fertility. In the grass of center field, we witness the renewal of spring and the life-affirming nature of the game. In the 21th Century, the game of baseball is no longer performed as a fertility ritual. However, baseball does function as a rite of spring. With baseball, we celebrate the return of spring. The cold and hardship of winter has ended. Spring and baseball bring a renewal of life and a communion with nature.

Taurus is also the sign of farmers. Duke Snider, a center fielder for the Brooklyn Dodgers, left baseball to become a farmer. Snyder explained his leaving baseball for the farm in *The Boys of Summer*: "Last fall in the World Series, I'm out there. Big bat. Seventy thousand watching. Great catch. You know what I'm dreaming then? About being a farmer."[34]

Taurus is the sign of sensual indulgences. Baseball fans appreciate the game's sensual pleasures, such as the smell of the grass, and the sound of the bat hitting the ball. Fans recline in the stands, indulging in sunshine, relishing hot dogs and beer. Willie Mays has the Sun and Mercury in the sign of Taurus.

The sign of **Gemini** corresponds to the **pitcher**. More encompassing, the planet **Mercury** also corresponds to the **pitcher**. The birthcharts of Nolan Ryan, Sandy Koufax, and Carl Hubbell all have the Sun conjunct to Mercury. Mercury rules two signs, Gemini and Virgo. Both Gemini and Virgo are the pitcher's signs. The parts of the body that the sign Gemini is associated with are the arms and the hands, both essential for the pitcher to throw the ball.

Gemini is a mental sign. In battle, a Gemini's best weapon is an ability to cleverly outsmart an opponent. The pitcher engages in a mental, as well as physical, battle with the batter. A pitcher's intent is to outwit his opponent, the batter, by throwing the ball past him with a variety of trajectories, velocities, and placements. The pitcher fools the batter into thinking the ball will cross the plate in a location other than where it is ultimately placed.

The sign of **Cancer** and the **Moon** correspond to the **catcher**. The symbol for Cancer is the crab. The catcher wears a chest protector,

---

34. Kahn, Roger: *Boys of Summer*, p. 343

shin guards, and a mask, equipment that is shell-like and reminiscent of a crab. Cancer is the sign of home and domesticity. The catcher's perch is homeplate. With his Cancerian protective and defensive instincts, a catcher guards homeplate against hostile invaders from the opposing team. As Cancer is a mother and a nurturer, the catcher is a nurturer to the pitcher. When a pitcher becomes anxious, the catcher will walk to the mound to soothe the pitcher.

Cancer and the Moon are also embodied in the fans. The Moon is represented in the masses of humanity, the people in their non-individual, mass sentiments and actions. A water sign, Cancer is highly emotional. Fans who closely follow a team experience a full range of emotions during a baseball season: hope, joy, sorrow, anger, and excitement.

A team becomes a family. Cancer and the Moon represent the team as a family unit, the emotional bonds of the players with one another. Like all group entities, a baseball team has collective emotions. A team of players, *en masse*, feels happy, angry or sad. Cancer is the sign of homes, the places in which we dwell. For a baseball team, the home is the city it represents. A team's home is also its homefield and its stadium.

Cancer is a cardinal sign. The cardinal signs initiate action. The catcher signals the pitches that the pitcher will throw. Mutable signs, such as the pitcher's signs of Gemini and Virgo, respond, rather than lead.

The birthchart of Roy Campanella has the Moon in Cancer. Mike "King" Kelly's birthchart has the Moon and Saturn in Cancer. Gary Carter's birthchart also has the Moon in Cancer.

Leo and the **Sun** are represented in the **right fielder**. Baseball stadiums are usually planned so that right field is the sunniest section of the playing field. As a day game proceeds into the late innings, the sun moving across the sky casts shadows onto the field. The afternoon shadows from the grandstands will enclose left field and center field, but right field remains in sunlight longer than the other parts of the field.

In sandlot games, right field receives the least action. Most balls hit beyond the infield go into left field or center field. The least-gifted fielders are positioned in right field, where they have fewer chances to make errors. To be stuck in right field, however, does not diminish a right fielder's visibility. A right fielder clowns and banters for attention. A Leo makes right field into a stage. Showboat personalities like Reggie Jackson, comfortable in the Sun and relishing the adoration, become right fielders. Roberto Clemente had the Sun in Leo. Jay Buhner also has the Sun in Leo. Reggie Jackson has Mars in Leo.

The sign **Virgo**, like the sign Gemini, corresponds to the **pitcher**. Both **Virgo** and **Gemini** are ruled by the planet **Mercury**. Virgo is the sign of the analytical mind. Virgo is also the sign of work. The pitcher, in Virgo mode, is a laborer. The pitcher exerts more physical and mental energy than does any other player on the field. As a laborer engages himself in the object of his labor, the pitcher is the player most focused on the game. An outfielder can daydream or banter with fans, but the pitcher must concentrate, if the job is to be performed effectively.

As a Virgo strives for perfection, a Virgo pitcher will refine his control. Virgo pitchers are finesse pitchers more so than are Gemini pitchers, who rely on velocity. Virgo pitchers are the nibblers who slice the corners of the plate.

The birthchart of Oral Hershiser has the Sun, Mercury, Venus and Pluto in Virgo. Randy Johnson has the Sun, Venus, Uranus, and Pluto in Virgo. Jim Abbot has the Sun in Virgo. Hideo Nomo has the Sun, Mercury Venus, Jupiter, Uranus, and Pluto in Virgo.

Libra and the planet **Venus** correspond to the **second baseman**. The symbol of Libra is the scale. Libras are adept at matters that require balance. Second base is the balancing point of the infield. It symmetrically divides the left and right sides of the diamond.

The second baseman's quintessential act is the performance of the double play. To make the double play, the second baseman must perform a Libran balancing act. One positions the body to receive the throw. Upon catching the ball, the second baseman quickly shifts the body to throw the ball to first base. The body's weight is directed to one's right to receive the throw, then the weight is shifted to one's left when dispatching the throw. The double play is complicated when the runner from first base is close by, rapidly approaching the base. The runner attempts to break up the double play by making contact with the second baseman, preventing the throw from being made. The second baseman, intent on avoiding a collision with the oncoming runner, may throw too hastily. One may also be forced by the barreling baserunner into making a weak or unbalanced throw. The double play is performed in its most spectacular manner when the second baseman avoids the runner by leaping straight into the air. From the air, with his or her feet off the ground, the second baseman throws the ball to first base, completing the play. This act requires a highly refined equilibrium. A second baseman can accomplish this throw without the anchor of one's feet touching the ground because of one's Libran sense of balance.

Libras are masters of beauty. The most beautiful plays in baseball

The Correspondences of Signs and Positions

are made by second baseman. One leaps to catch line drives headed for right field. Second basemen also regularly make diving stops of ground balls. The second baseman's throw to first is shorter than the throw of the shortstop. This shorter distance allows the second baseman more time in which to make the play. After knocking down the ground ball, one has the time to collect oneself and make the throw to first base, putting out the runner.

On any team, the chemistry between the second baseman and the shortstop is important for the infield to function smoothly. Since the second baseman embodies Venus and the shortstop is an embodiment of Mars, the relationship between the shortstop to the second baseman contains a male and female dynamic.

The birthchart of Bill Mazeroski has Venus and Mercury in Libra. Joe Morgan has Mercury and Neptune in Libra. Rod Carew has the Sun, Mercury, Jupiter and Neptune in Libra.

The sign of **Scorpio** and the planet **Pluto** are embodied in the position of the **third baseman**. Scorpio is a highly pressurized water sign. This sign is known for quick responses to assaults and slights. Revenge is a Scorpionic act. The third baseman is similar to a person who waits for someone else to begin a fight so that he or she can finish it. The ball is hit to the third baseman quickly and with tremendous force, especially when a right-handed batter pulls the ball. The ball also advances towards the third baseman from a shorter distance than it does to the shortstop or the second baseman. The third baseman does not have a large area of ground to cover, but the third baseman must react very quickly because of the speed of the ball passing through their territory.

The quick reactions of the third baseman originate from the intense concentration for which third basemen and Scorpios are known. One gets in position to receive the impact of the batted ball. Scorpio is a fixed sign. A Scorpio is stationary, yet poised, alert, and waiting. The third baseman becomes set and waits for the ball to come at him or her. One receives the blow of the ball and rapidly returns it, firing it back, putting the runner out.

Brooks Robinson's birthchart has Mars in the sign of Scorpio. The birthchart of Mike Schmidt has Mars conjunct to Pluto.

The sign **Sagittarius** and the planet **Jupiter** correspond to the **batter**.[35] Like an archer pulling a bow to shoot an arrow, the batter swings

---

35. The relationship between the batter and the pitcher is a reflection of the relationship between their respective signs, Sagittarius and Gemini. Sagittarius and Gemini are opposite signs, occupying opposite positions in the wheel of the Zodiac. Gemini

a bat. The centaur shoots an arrow, aiming, aspiring for a star; the batter swings a bat at a ball, aiming, aspiring to hit the ball to an auspicious place. Once one hits the ball, a journey begins.[36] The hope and optimism of Sagittarius are present in the batter. One's fans and teammates hope that the at-bat of each player will prove fortunate and lead to a run or a rally.

The birthcharts of both Ty Cobb and Joe DiMaggio have the Sun in Sagittarius.

Capricorn and the planet **Saturn** are embodied in the **manager**, the owners of the team, and the front office executives. Capricorn and Saturn are also embodied in the umpires and the rules of the game.[37] The sign of Capricorn has the qualities of age, wisdom, and decisiveness. Capricorn corresponds to the manager who makes the decisions. The manager sets the line-ups, makes the pitching changes, and calls for pinch hitters.

Managers often have both the positive and negative qualities of the sign Capricorn. A manager can be a wise father figure, the sage who guides the players and gives them the advice of his experience. A manager can also be an out-of-touch tyrant, a barrier in the way of a player's freedom, fun, or development.

Capricorn and Saturn, when embodied as the owner and the front office executives, represent the business people who function in the world of hard realities outside of the game. Capricorn is the sign of gritty reality. Players on the field are insulated from the "real world." Baseball games proceed in a world separate from real life. The owners, with their Capricorn abilities, maintain the structures needed for the insulated reality of the game to continue. The owner tends to the mundane concerns of schedules, finance, and politics, the real world duties necessary for the game to be played, a season to continue, and a team to thrive.

The birthchart of Harry Wright has the Sun in Capricorn. Ban Johnson

---

rules the "lower mind" of sense perceptions and communication, and Sagittarius rules the "higher mind" of values and philosophy. The Gemini mind queries and perceives, then challenges the higher Sagittarius faculties to make meaning from the information that the Gemini senses have gathered. A call and response ritual is performed by the pitcher and the batter, much like that between the Gemini and Sagittarius minds. The pitcher asks the question by throwing the ball, and the batter responds by swinging the bat. The relationship between politicians and reporters is sometimes described in the language of the batter and the pitcher. The reporter plays the role of the pitcher while the politician plays the role of the batter. A reporter is said to "throw a curve ball" when one asks a difficult question with a hidden meaning. He or she will "lob an easy one" or throw "a fat pitch" when asking a question that is easy for the politician to answer. The politician, meanwhile, can "hit a home run" by answering a question in a manner that greatly pleases the audience.

36. The batter's journey around the bases as an embodiment of the Hero's Journey is explored in Chapter 5.
37. These manifestations of Saturn are explored in Chapter 6.

also had the Sun in Capricorn. The birthchart of Connie Mack has the Sun, Moon and Mercury in Capricorn. Gene Mauch's birthchart has the Sun conjunct Saturn. Dick Williams' birthchart has the Moon conjunct Saturn.

The sign of **Aquarius** and the planet **Uranus** correspond with the **left fielder**. The mind of an Aquarius strives to be objective and detached. Aquarius is the sign most able to see the big picture. The left fielder needs this ability to track the trajectory of an object in flight. He or she is assisted by a capacity to sense air currents affecting the flight of the ball. The skill to pursue and catch a fly ball is similar to that of an air traffic controller, an Aquarian profession, guiding an airplane to its landing.

Aquarius and its ruling planet Uranus also correspond with the home run. The arc of a home run, a ball hit a long distance and over a fence, has the Aquarian quality of air travel. Like the sign of Aquarius, a home run is fixed and solid, high and all-encompassing. George Will remarked that the home run represents the do-it-yourself, individualist side of American character.[38] Fittingly, the birthchart of the United States has the Moon in Aquarius. A batter who completes a home run does not need the help from his teammates to reach home. This individualism is an embodiment of Aquarius.

Hank Aaron and Babe Ruth both have the Sun in Aquarius. Barry Bonds has the Moon in Aquarius. Roy Hobbs, the hero and home run hitter of *The Natural*, also played left field. The novel contains extraordinary Uranian symbolism. Roy Hobbs' bat, Wonderboy, is carved from a tree that had been struck by lightning. Lighting and electricity are manifestations of Uranus. When his bat is finally broken, Roy Hobbs ceremoniously buries Wonderboy in left field.[39]

When Uranus entered its own sign of Aquarius in 1911, the home run totals rose significantly. Home run totals again inflated when Uranus entered the sign of Aquarius in 1995. This transit of Uranus through Aquarius saw the fall of Roger Maris' single-season home run record and of Hank Aaron's lifetime home run record. The spread of steroid use also occurred under this transit. Uranus also rules technological innovations such as aluminum bats and steroids.[40]

Aquariuses are known for being eccentrics. Many an Aquarius has been told, "You're out in left field."

---

38. Will, George: *Men at Work*, p. 239
39. Malamud, Bernard: *The Natural*, pp. 187-188
40. See Giants Chapter

The sign of **Pisces** and the planet **Neptune** correspond with the **first baseman**. Pisces is a receptive water sign. A Pisces absorbs emotional and psychic vibrations. Similarly, a first baseman's primary function is to receive and absorb. The first baseman receives the throws of the other infielders that put out runners. One requires a receptive ability to gather and absorb all manner of throws made towards one's base. Errant throws will skid in the dirt, fly over one's head, or stray wide to the side. The first baseman, like a fisherman with a large net, is ready to catch all manner of throws.

Each sign corresponds to a specific part of the human body, and the sign of Pisces is associated with the feet. To record an out, the first baseman must makes contact with the first base bag. This is done with one's foot. A first baseman requires agile feet to perform this job. Also, when the first baseman leaves one's base to snare a wayward throw, one must regain contact with the base to record the out. With the runner charging down the baseline, the first baseman often lacks the time to visually search for the base. One employs Piscean psychic abilities to sense the location of the base without the use of one's eyes.

Plays most often end at first base. As the zodiac ends with the sign of Pisces, a play finishes with the ball in the first baseman's mitt. The first baseman then tosses the ball to the pitcher or the umpire, and the next play begins. The first baseman absorbs the play at its completion and makes the field ready for the next play. Similarly, a player often ends his career in the position of first baseman. Older players who lose their speed or agility often finish their careers as first basemen. Veteran catchers are often converted to first basemen to extend their careers. Pisces is the last and oldest sign of the zodiac. Fittingly, the oldest players are often playing first base.

The symbol for Pisces is the fish. The first baseman's mitt has a distinct rounded edge that makes it resemble the gill of a fish. Gills are unique to fishes, the animal symbol of Pisces.

The birthchart of Lou Gehrig has the Sun conjunct to Neptune. Willie McCovey has Mars in Pisces. Will Clark has the Sun, Moon, Mars, and Mercury in Pisces.

Certain players are naturals at their positions. The birthcharts of these players reveal that they were born to play the positions in which they excel. In the birthchart of such a player, the sign or the planet that corresponds to his position is emphasized. Many shortstops have the Sun, or other planets, in Aries, the sign of the shortstop. A player's natural position can also be indicated by an aspect between a personal planet[41] and the ruling planet of the position. The birthcharts of many pitchers have the Sun in a conjunction with Mercury, the planet of the pitcher. Many first basemen have a personal planet in conjunction with Neptune, the planet of first base. A player may also have Saturn in aspect to the ruling planet of his position, as aspects to Saturn often indicate a career or a position of responsibility. For example, some catchers have Saturn in aspect to the Moon or have the Moon in Capricorn.

---

41. The personal planets are the Sun, Moon, Mercury, Venus, and Mars.

The Hero's Journey

A batter's appearance at the plate and his[42] subsequent journey around the bases are a representation of the archetype of the hero's journey. The hero's sign is Sagittarius, which is also the sign of the batter. The hero and the batter also share the ruling planet of Jupiter. Sagittarius and Jupiter rule the domains of travel, religion, and education. The batter's sojourn around the bases is a journey in the Sagittarian sense. Symbolically, it is a pilgrimage, a metaphoric journey with a religious purpose in which the traveler grows in knowledge of the spirit.

Joseph Campbell explores the mythologies of the hero archetype in his work *The Hero with a Thousand Faces*. Campbell outlines the hero myths in the following passage:

> *A hero ventures forth from the world of common day into a region of supernatural wonder: fabulous forces are there encountered and a decisive victory is won: the hero comes back from this mysterious adventure with the power to bestow boons to his fellow man.*[43]

The batter leaves home and embarks on an adventure. He battles hostile opponents who attempt to kill him by putting him out. He encounters relative safety on a base, but he needs to continue. His adventure continues until he either dies by being called out or left stranded as his team is retired, or until he returns safely to home by scoring a run. Each base has its own guardian. Each base also holds its unique trials and lessons.

To Step to the Plate: The batter, stepping up to the plate, attempts to leave home. He rises from the safety and security of the dugout and walks to the plate. A player spends most of his time in the dugout or engaged in his defensive duties on the field. Once at bat, a player departs from these female states. A player at his or her defensive position in the field is in a female mode. The dugout, meanwhile, is a Cancer-like nest, cozy and comfortable. The shelter of the dugout is like the safety and security of being at home with his mother. The batter at the plate attempts to sever himself from the regressive pull of the mother and the stagnancy of remaining at home. At bat, holding a large phallic object, a player is in a male mode. A batter

---

42. The genders in this chapter are employed consciously. See Chapter One for an exploration of the gender characteristics of defense and offense. Both female and male principles are active in astrology and in the game of baseball.
43. Campbell, Joseph: *The Hero with a Thousand Faces*, p. 30

employs the male qualities of initiative and daring. He stands at homeplate, a symbol of hearth, safety and comfort, yet he attempts to leave it. To do so, he must confront the hostile persona of the pitcher.

The pitcher stands on a mound, which makes him or her taller and more authoritative than the batter. The pitcher is akin to a parent or teacher putting down an adolescent, criticizing him and challenging his competence to act on his own. Each pitch thrown at the batter is an attack on his adulthood. It is a challenge of youth to find confidence, to gain a sense of self-volition, and to leave home. In parallel, it is the batter's mission to respond to the challenges and taunts of the pitcher in a manner that will enable him to commence his journey. If he strikes out, grounds out, flies out or cannot otherwise reach first base, his response to the parent or teacher is inadequate. The batter returns to the dugout. He is unable to begin his journey and must stay home. But if he answers the pitcher's challenges with a hit, he successfully leaves home and the adventure has begun.

First Base: First Base is about hearing one's own inner call and about initiation. First Base is governed by Pisces and Neptune. The oceanic waters of Neptune are the unconscious realms, those places we reach in sleep, dreams and mystic states, the hidden parts of our psyche that share the amniotic fluid of creation. The hero will become submerged, for the journey begins by water.

The *Old Testament* adventure of Joseph began when his brothers threw him into a well.[44] Water is also the necessary element in the story of Jonah. In this Bible story, Jonah was called by God to go to Ninevah, where God wanted him to preach. But Jonah did not wish to travel to Ninevah. Instead, he fled from his mission and boarded a ship to Tarshish. While Jonah was asleep in the bottom of the ship, a violent storm threatened its safety. The ship's crew drew lots to detect who had brought the plague upon them. When they discovered it was Jonah, the crew tossed him into the sea. Soon a large whale came and swallowed him. Jonah spent three days and nights inside the belly of the whale. Only then, did Jonah face the necessity of his mission. When he finally heeded the message that God had called him to Nineveh, the whale spat Jonah out onto dry land.[45]

Pisces is the sign of solitude. First Base is an isolation tank of water where one listens to oneself. On First Base, one hears the call to adventure. Every person's calling is unique. The challenge is to hear one's calling and to accept it.

---

44. *Genesis* 37
45. *Jonah* 1-3

First Base is also an initiation. Moments of initiation occur at times of transition such as unemployment, relocation, divorce, or when someone depended upon dies. Initiations serve the purpose of preparing one for the next stage of life. Old modes of being and behaving no longer suit the individual. The hero needs a new maturity and new skills to proceed successfully. New ideas, methods, or beliefs need to be trusted.

A runner on First Base is generally not in control of his fate. To proceed further around the bases, he is largely dependent on the other batters of his team's lineup. During periods of transition, one's sense of control is weak. Our life and environment no longer function as we knew them. We feel like the child who cannot swim, yet is dropped in the deep end of a swimming pool and told he will "sink or swim." The Hanged Man of the Tarot deck depicts such a loss of power. The figure of the card is a man hanging upside down from a tree by his foot. He dangles in the wind with no means of volition, for his feet and hands do not touch the ground.[46]

These periods of initiation are difficult to endure. They are times of anxiety, for one has lost control and feels powerless, but eventually the fog recedes. New abilities to perceive emerge from the subconscious waters. New values and priorities are forged. When this process of solidification is complete, an individual regains a sense of volition. However, he is different from before. The hero is now certain of his mission, having been baptized in the Neptunian waters of First Base.

Second Base: Second Base represents the sign Libra, whose planet is Venus. Libra and Venus are associated with the realms of love and marriage. The hero, approaching Second Base, will encounter its goddess. He falls in love with her. If he succeeds at courting her, he is safe at Second. The lessons of second base are to love and to join with the world.

Until now, the hero's journey has been a solitary one. At bat, he needed to prove his independence from his parents. On First Base, he needed solitude to hear his inner call. But on Second Base, the hero is married. There, he leaves his isolation and unites his life with the life of another. The world was formerly external to the hero. Now, through his marriage to the goddess, he is joined with the world.

Second Base is a wonderful place, but the hero will have to return to the road. If he can take his bride with him, leaving Second Base will be easy. However, she may not understand the excitement and necessity of his journey. If she is unwilling or unable to leave her native land, the hero

---

46. The First Step of Alcoholics Anonymous states, "We admitted we were powerless over alcohol—that our lives had become unmanageable." This is an admission of a loss of volition.

will experience a difficult conflict. If his bride is not willing to travel, she will not want him to leave. Leaving Second Base can be more difficult than arriving there.

Ulysses shipwrecked on Calypso's island. Calypso nourished him, restored his health, and became his lover. But when Ulysses was ready to leave her island and continue the *Odyssey*, she would not let him go. Only with the intervention of the gods was Calypso persuaded to allow Ulysses his freedom. Even if the hero cannot bring his bride with him as he continues the journey, he will bring the lessons he learned from her, to love and to join with the world.

Third Base: The majority of batters are out long before they reach Third Base and its challenges. The hero, resting on third base, is 90 feet from Home. The distance between Third and Home is the most treacherous crossing in the journey. Third Base is ruled by the sign Scorpio and the planet Pluto. The hero, on Third Base, must confront death. Death belongs to the domain of Scorpio and Pluto. Death has been a hazard all along the journey, but now its challenge is intensified. The lessons of Third Base include the mysteries of life and death, letting go, regeneration, and will.

Third Base is Hades. On Third, the hero descends into the underworld. He daringly crosses the river Styx and eludes the three-headed dog that guards the entrance. In Hades, the hero finds what he needs, then attempts to escape. But the greatest difficulty is leaving. Orpheus descended into Hades to find Eurydice and bring her back to the world of the living. Although he escaped, Orpheus failed to bring back his bride. Aeneas visited the Underworld, where he spoke to his dead father who gave him the prophesy of the founding of Rome. Aeneas' guide, the Sybil, knew the way back from the Underworld. The Mayan twins of the *Popol Vuh* endured several ordeals in the Underworld before they were able to leave. Their trials included matches of the sacred ballgame against the Lords of the Underworld.

On Third Base, the hero may need to jettison his baggage, to cut free from old habits or heavy memories, patterns of living that no longer suit him. Sentimentality makes such partings difficult. Old habits are comfortable, but he must separate from those parts of him that weigh him and slow him. To rid oneself of unnecessary weight is part of the life cycle. In November, when the Sun is in the sign of Scorpio, the leaves of trees die and fall off their branches. The snake, an animal with a Scorpionic nature, regularly sheds its skin, parting from the old that is no longer essential.

Similar to death is dismemberment, when our limbs and organs are torn from each other, separated and scattered. When we feel as if this has happened to us, we wait for healing and regeneration. In time, we feel whole again. We become reborn or resurrected. Often, we are transformed radically. A caterpillar metamorphoses into a butterfly. Someone at such a stage in life may undergo a drastic change of personality or appearance. But such a regeneration also brings the infusion of energy needed to continue the journey.

Throughout these difficult ordeals, the hero must maintain his determination and his will to survive. Exhausted and depleted, yet determined to persevere, the hero taps resources dormant or unknown. Like a marathon runner who "hits the wall" and continues on, the hero locates reserves of strength and will. To make it the final 90 feet is an act of extraordinary Plutonic power. The hero on Third breaks for the plate on a shallow fly, or he performs the most daring act in baseball, the steal of home.

Coming Home: The hero crosses the plate and scores a run. Safe at home, the hero's journey is complete. His mission accomplished, he is greeted and welcomed with cheers and applause. To home, from which he took pains to leave, he now returns triumphantly.

The hero brings a life-restoring gift to his family and his city. His gains become the gains of the community. Jason and the Argonauts returned to Greece with the Golden Fleece. Moses brought the Ten Commandments from Mount Sinai. The monk Tripitaka brought the Buddhist scriptures home to China. Olympic athletes return home with medals.

The homecoming of the hero fills the community with a new life-enhancing energy. Life is renewed. Faith is restored. The renewal comes not only from the knowledge and the gifts that the hero bestows, but from the very act of his return. A hero has triumphed in a fantastic adventure. The greatness of his deed is shared by all. His story will be told and retold, as it affirms the triumph of the spirit.

Saturn, Time and Space

The planet Saturn governs structures, and it governs time. The structure of baseball includes the standardization of its rules, the procession of outs and innings, and the diamond with its foul lines and 90-foot distances between the bases. It is within this framework that the energies of the zodiac and the planets are channeled and manifest. The planet is also manifest in the way the game contains the passage of time. The umpires are another embodiment of Saturn. A game of baseball begins when the Saturnian figure on the field, the Umpire, gives the indication. He or she commands, "Play ball!" The umpire is the guardian of the rules, and the one who judges fair or foul, out or safe. The umpire is also the keeper of time. Requests for timeouts must be made to him or her.

Saturn manifests in structures and processes. As the planet Saturn provides the skeletal system for the human body and other vertebrates, it also provides structure for institutions. The structure of a nation is its constitution, laws, and values. For a genre of art, the structure (or form) is a set of images and techniques that are accepted and comprehended by a group of artists and its audience. Such a form serves as both a framework and a set of limitations. A framework directs activity within a prescribed design. Limitations, meanwhile, prohibit activity beyond prescribed boundaries: they prohibit one from proceeding "outside the lines" or "off the path." Frameworks and limitations are tied to each other like a statue and its mold or a photograph and its negative.

A form maintains activity within a constrictive design. Energy is given a channel when such a form is in place. Energy that has such a channel flows in a meaningful and intelligible manner that can be received and understood. The structure of music includes the organization of sounds into tones, scales, and rhythmic sequences. The use of these structures transforms random sounds into discernible and patterned music. Similarly, the structures of language (vocabulary and grammar) channel chaotic jabber into intelligible speech. Without an intelligible form, energy moves in patterns that cannot be understood by the human mind.

This chapter divides structures into those of time and those of space. In the medium of theater, time is structured by the sequence of acts and by the story that proceeds through an introduction, development, climax and resolution. The structure of theater dictates that the parts proceed in this accepted order. Theater's structure of space, meanwhile, prescribes that action take place on a stage visible to an audience. Occasionally, such conventions are broken. The structure of time is challenged when, in an unconventional production, the final act is performed first. Similarly, the spatial structure is defied when actors recite their lines from off stage or from the audience.

Structures of performances have various intentions. Forms such as the symphony and the theater intend to convey intellectual or cultural experiences to their audience. Other forms such as the circus aim merely to amuse or entertain. The structures of religious ceremonies seek to bestow an experience of the divine on their participants. Baseball is a curious form in that it has the potential to reach people in their elevated states, their spiritual dimensions. Yet baseball reaches most of its observers on the level of competitive entertainment or as participation in a tribal gathering. Some fans contemplate the game in a more intellectual state by analyzing statistics or studying its history.

Time

Baseball does not proceed by the pace of a clock. The game proceeds differently than football and basketball, sports in which timeouts and the ticking of minutes and seconds are vitally important. Baseball time is measured, not in the standard units of hours, minutes and seconds, but in outs and innings. George Will remarks that the pace of baseball relates to the pre-industrial agrarian era.[47] Today, in our industrial age, time is broken into small units in which specific tasks are done. We must "clock in" at work at a specified hour. Television programs are set in "time slots." The word "slot" implies a designated location into which something firmly fits. Prior to the Industrial Revolution, when the economy was based on agriculture and the majority of people were farmers, time had a more amorphous quality. Time was not rigid and compartmentalized. Sundials, not clocks, were used to mark the passage of the hours. It was of little concern that the inaccuracy of sundials lengthened certain hours of the day and shortened others.

Baseball's sense of time has a striking connection to our notions of eternity. With extra innings, each game has the theoretical potential to go on forever. Likewise, each inning and each at-bat, especially with foul balls, can also theoretically go on forever. Baseball time, however, does not only stretch into the future, it also harkens backward. Nostalgia surrounds

---

47. Will, George: *Men at Work*, p. 130

the game. The sentiments of baseball call us back to our childhood, or to a romanticized bucolic past, a lost Golden Age. In no other sport is the past so venerated. Records are carefully maintained and evaluated. Stars of past eras become semi-mythical figures. In the Major Leagues, wooden bats are preferred to aluminum bats not only for the sake of tradition, but because wooden bats feel old and genuine. The aesthetic of wooden bats protects us from the discomforts of the current metallic and digital age.

Baseball appears as both immemorially old and forever young. The game possesses the crusty wisdom of age and the hopeful enthusiasm of youth. It relates to both Father Time and to the baby of the New Year. The game reaches both backward and forward in time.

This duality of past and future leads us to another consideration. Baseball has been described as timeless, in existence beyond the procession of years, outside of time. The movie *Field of Dreams* portrays baseball played in such a timeless realm. W. P. Kinsella's novel *The Iowa Baseball Confederacy* [48] depicts a journey back in time to 1908 and a game played for more than 2000 innings between the Chicago Cubs and an amateur all-star team. In baseball, our basic mechanism of time is altered. Time is one of the most essential of "real world" constraints, yet baseball allows us to step outside the demands of alarm clocks and deadlines.

The game's connection to an eternal sense of time is also mirrored in the images we have of baseball played in an afterlife. A spiritual goal of Buddhists and Hindus is to step beyond the recurrent cycles of time, thereby reaching the timeless state of Nirvana. In Christianity, this state is called Heaven and is considered the reward of eternal life. Baseball fans have images of their game played in Heaven. A. Bartlett Giamatti titled his book *Take Time for Paradise*. Alexander Cartwright and his team the Knickerbockers played in a park called the Elysian Fields, a name that alludes to the Roman afterlife for heroes fallen in battle.

Although baseball time is not measured by the standard clock, time does pass as the outs and innings are counted. The advance of time brings a tension and an excitement to both the ending of a game and the close of a season. Time cannot be eluded. Moreover, time eventually brings death.[49] Chapter One discusses an early meaning of the game as a ritual battle between burgeoning spring and dying winter. Those living on earth die with the passing of time. To quote at length the opening of Connie Mack's

---

48. Kinsella, W. P. *The Iowa Baseball Confederacy*, 1986
49. The lyrics of the song "Take me out to the Ballpark" contains the haunting refrain, "I don't care if I never get back." But eventually the game ends, and we must leave the ballpark and return to the "real world" with real-world time and its considerations.

autobiography:

> By the grace of God, if he so wills it, I enter my nineteeth year on December 23, 1952, with only ten years to go to cross the homeplate of the century mark. Whether I make it depends on the decision of the Great Umpire who sooner or later calls us "out." The scoreboard at the moment says: "Two strikes - three balls." Father Time is in the pitcher's box.[50]

There is a finality when the last out is recorded and a game ends. Similarly, there is a millennial quality to a game that ends in a final at bat, a walk-off win or loss. A game ends in a sudden and final manner. An outcome is suddenly manifest. Football uses the phrase "sudden death overtime" to describe the tie broken in an added quarter by the first team to score. Baseball seasons end on such millennial codas when contending teams are eliminated and championship teams win pennants and their World Series.

Along with millennial endings, there are the waits for such climaxes. A fan waits and endures the trials of a long season. The baseball season, lasting from March into October or November, is longer than the seasons of football and basketball. There are also waits that exist beyond a season. Fans endure periods longer than a year for a promising young team to develop into a contender. To wait through such periods requires faith. For some fan bases, such waits extend through generations. The fans of the Cubs and Red Sox waited faithfully through multiple generations for their teams to win the World Series. As of this writing, fans of the Cleveland Indians and Texas Rangers are waiting through more than two generations for their teams to win a World Series. The faith of such fans resembles that of a millennial sect that patiently endures the travails of life on Earth. Such followers are braced and nourished by their belief that eventually their team will win the World Series, as sure as God's Kingdom will someday arrive.

SPACE

An examination of spatial forms in baseball leads us to a body of knowledge known as Sacred Geometry and to the age-old puzzle of how to square the circle.

Sacred Geometry assigns spiritual and philosophical meaning to

---

50. Mack, Connie, *My 66 Years in the Big Leagues*, p. 1

the principles of mathematics and geometry. The philosophers who have sought meaning in geometry and numbers include Pythagoras and Leonardo DaVinci. To these thinkers, numbers and geometric forms have specific significances. For example, the number one represents unity and God; number two represents duality and multiplicity; number three stands for creation; and the number four represents materiality.[51] Contemporary physics describes matter as wave phenomena that are understood through the use of numbers and mathematics. Similar to the field of physics, which employs numbers to define matter, the field of Sacred Geometry defines "reality" as numbers and geometric forms. Such numbers and geometric forms hold meaning beyond their uses for quantification. Robert Lawlor, author of *Sacred Geometry: Philosophy and Practice*, writes, "The primary geometric forms are considered to be the crystallizations of the creative thoughts of God." [52]

The practice of squaring the circle is an attempt to construct a square that is the same size in area as a given circle by using only a compass and a straight-edge. Another approach, using these same tools, is to try to construct a square that has the same length in perimeter as the circumference of a given circle. One is only allowed a finite number of attempts, as formulae with infinite numbers of attempts are disallowed. The problem was attempted by mathematicians of the ancient civilizations of Babylonia, Egypt, and Greece. More recently, it was attempted by mathematicians in Victorian England. To those not in the know, seeking to square the circle, like asking how many angels can dance on the head of a pin, is an example of useless and medieval thought. However, for those who pursue it, squaring the circle is not merely a geometry problem but a spiritual endeavor, as well.

The spiritual aspect of the problem is apparent within the symbolism of the circle and the symbolism of the square. The circle is symbolic of Heaven, God, and divine energy; while the square is symbolic of Earth and life on the material plane. Here is an example from Masonic iconography.

In this familiar symbol, the compass and the square are less about what they do than what they symbolize. The compass and the circle it draws represent the sky, the heavens,

---

51   Lawlor, Robert: *Sacred Geometry: Philosophy and Practice*, p. 12
52   Lawlor, p. 17

and divine realms. The square, meanwhile, symbolizes the earth, and the material plane. When placed together, its significance is nothing less than the connection between Heaven and Earth and the mystery of creation. The circle symbolizes the ideal, heavenly realm, and the square symbolizes earthly reality. A passage of Joseph Campbell describes it like this:

> The dome of heaven rests on the quarters of the earth, sometimes supported by four caryatidal kings, dwarfs, giants, elephants, or turtles. Hence, the traditional importance of the mathematical problem of the quadrature of the circle: it contains the secret of the transformation of heavenly into earthly forms.[53]

The transformation of energy through a circle of heaven into an earthly square can also be described as creation.

A baseball diamond is nothing less than a circle that has been squared. Not only does the game connect the realms of Heaven and Earth by manifesting the energy of the zodiac, but the diamond itself is a manifestation of a circle squared.[54] The baseball diamond is, of course, also a square. The distance of 90-feet between the bases has been recognized as a kind of wonder. It is the perfect distance for a contest between the runner and the fielders. Were the distance between bases longer than ninety feet, the fielders would have too great an advantage. Likewise, if the distance were shorter than 90 feet, the runner would have too much of an advantage. Red Smith, the sports columnist, wrote:

> Ninety feet between bases represents man's closest approach to absolute truth. The world's fastest man can not run to first base ahead of a sharply hit ball that is cleanly handled by an infielder; he will get there only half a step too late. Let the fielder juggle the ball for one moment or delay his throw an instant and the runner will be safe. Ninety feet demands perfection. It accurately measures the cunning, speed and finesse of a base stealer against the velocity of a thrown ball. It dictates the placement of infielders. That single dimension makes baseball a fine art—and nobody knows for sure how it came to be.[55]

---

53. Campbell, Joseph: *The Hero with a Thousand Faces*, p. 42
54. A letter by Alexander Cartwright's grandson describes a moment when his grandfather may have held this mystery: "I remember seeing him draw a circle in the dust with his umbrella and then draw a cross through the circle. He then explained to the crowd who had gathered how he divided the "Baseball Square." (Nucciarone, Monica *Alexander Cartwright: The Life Behind the Baseball Legend*. p. 219)
55. Will, George: *Men at Work*, p. 259

SATURN, TIME AND SPACE

Red Smith pondered the marvel of the baseball diamond but described its origins as close to unknowable. [56] Illumination of the mystery, however, is provided by considering the circle squared.

When the 90-foot distances between all the bases, the four sides of the square, are added, the sum is 360 feet. Remarkably, this number of 360 matches the number of degrees in a circle. The 360 feet around the bases matches the number of degrees of a circle. A circle is measured mathematically by degrees; the total number of degrees for every circle is 360. This number *360* is indelibly associated with the circle, and this number *360* is manifest in the length of the perimeter of the baseball diamond, which is also a square. I ask the reader to consider the significance of the number 360 as both the number of degrees in a circle and as the sum of the distances of the base paths of the diamond.

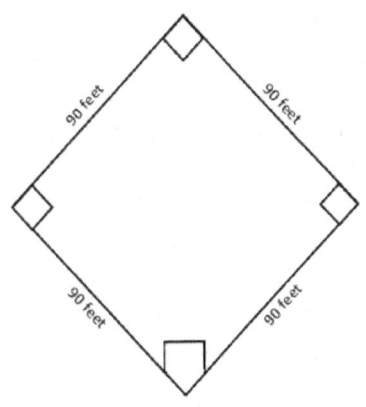

360 degrees: 90 + 90 + 90 + 90 = 360 feet.

These numbers beg us to examine the units of measurement we are using. From where do the units of degrees and feet come? Are they not randomly chosen units, whose only authority derives from convention? The assignment of 360 degrees to the circle has been handed down to us by the Chaldeans of Ancient Mesopotamia. The number 360 corresponds roughly to the 365 days that it takes for the Earth to go around the Sun. In the history of geometry, perhaps its most practical application has been for building. Ninety-degree right angles, which are quarter divisions of the circle, are necessary for

---

56. The baseball convention of Feb. 25, 1857 codified the 90-foot distances between bases into an official rulebook. (Block, p. 82) (*Baseball in the Garden of Eden*, John Thorn, pp. 52, 72) The discussion or debate that took place before the rule was agreed upon remains a mystery.

construction. Square corners need to be measured for buildings to stand upright. We measure such angles by degrees of the circle.

An examination of the unit of the foot begins with a consideration of the human body. The foot is an "anthropometric" unit, which means that it uses a feature of human anatomy as a measurement. Other anthropometric measures include: "an arm's length" for an intermediate distance; and "the blink of an eye" for a short span of time. Anthropometric measurements are not just folksy usages but significant elements within humanistic thought. These measurements are echoes of the declaration by Pythagoras that "Man is the measure of all things." Philosophers from various ages and cultures have stated that each human being is a microcosm of the universe, and that he and she are created in the image of God. The features of the human body all have divine significance. Chapter Three notes the relationship of the parts of the body with the signs of the zodiac.

The unit of the foot, of course, originates from our two feet that hold our weight and allow us to walk on the Earth. Our feet are that part of us designed for intimate contact with the Earth. We stand on two feet, instead of on four feet like most mammals. Our head and spinal column aspire upward to the heavens, but our feet remain down with the ground. They keep us joined to nature and the Earth: that which is manifest, tangible and palpably real.

The unit of the foot has not been a consistent length through history. Researchers trace the unit of the foot to Ancient Egypt where it had a length of 12.4 of our current inches. In Medieval England, a longer foot of 13.2 inches was in use. The current 12-inch foot would be introduced in England before 950 AD. A different standard was used after the Norman Conquest, but the 12-inch foot would re-emerge. Its official sanction was issued by Parliament in 1760.[57] Close to 100 years later, the Baseball Convention of 1857, would employ the 12-inch foot when it institutionalized the 90-foot base distances.

It is convenient to conclude that anthropomorphic units are arbitrary. Man may be the measure of all things, but human beings are varied. Men and women have feet of different sizes. But when one contemplates the baseball diamond and the precision of the 90-foot distances between bases, one realizes that the diamond is not arbitrary, nor is it relative. It is exact. So, too, must be its components, the 360 degrees of the circle and the 12-inch foot.

Saturn is often unappreciated by astrologers. The planet is called a

---

57. Feather, Norman: *Mass, Length and Time*, p.11

"malefic," a bearer of bad fortune, and human beings generally chafe when limitations are imposed upon them. Saturn is the umpire who insists on play within the limitations of the rules. He will eject those who disrespect him. Rebellious youth seek to explore beyond the limits imposed on them by parents and society. To do so, one must defy Saturn, who, in the guise of a parent or authority figure, seeks to contain and discipline. A person's relationship with Saturn changes as one grows older. Rebellious youth become upholders of mainstream values. At times, our politics demand that we disobey the standards of Saturn. People of any age may be seized by a purpose higher than the rules. One may follow a political or ethical impulse to disobey the laws and standards of society. While human beings often voice their dislike for rules and restrictions, it ought to be acknowledged that the rules and boundaries of Saturn do create beauty. Marvelous things, like baseball, happen within limitations.

PART II

Introduction to the Birthcharts of Teams

This section introduces the astrological birthcharts of the 30 major league baseball teams currently playing in the United States. Each chapter of this section contains the birthchart of a team and a brief history from an astrological prospective. These chapters tell the history of our baseball teams and the history of baseball in the United States from the perspective of the theories introduced in Section One. The birthcharts of these teams are presented in the chronological order of their birth—beginning with the Cincinnati Reds, the oldest professional team, and ending with the expansion era Arizona Diamondbacks and Tampa Bay Rays. I ask the reader to resist the impulse to jump to the chapter of your favorite team. Please read the chapters of this section in their order to fully enjoy the history of the game.

The identities and tendencies of these teams become quite lucid once their birthcharts are known. Until 1960, only 16 major league teams existed. These original 16 teams have amassed long and rich histories, and each of their birthcharts deserves a book rather than a chapter. The scope of this book, however, only allows one chapter for each team, but the chapters of this section do address the most significant events in each team's history. As noted in Chapter 6, the game of baseball venerates its past, and the histories of the older teams are the stuff of legends. Our younger teams, those born since 1960, have less lore, and their past is less revered. The newest expansion era teams, those born in the 1990s, are still establishing their identities.

For dates of birth, I have used the dates in which the franchises were organized. I found most of these dates in secondary sources and newspaper accounts. One date of birth that proved elusive belongs to the Chicago Cubs. My search for a documented birth date has been unsuccessful. I was, however, able to deduce their date of birth. It is documented that the Cubs franchise was organized during the winter of 1869-70.[58] Given this general time frame and knowing enough tendencies of the team, I boiled down their birth date by reviewing dates of this period in an ephemeris. These findings and my methods are explained at length in the Cubs'

---

58. WPA, *Baseball in Old Chicago*

chapter. For times of birth, I have used rectifications.[59] All the birthcharts of these teams are rectified.

Several teams have more than one birthchart. The Braves and Athletics have three different birthcharts, one for each city in which they were located. Likewise, the Dodgers have two birthcharts, one set in Brooklyn and one located in Los Angeles. When a team moves from one city to another, a different birthchart is cast for the new home city. The new birthchart keeps the same date and time of birth as the original chart, but replaces the longitude and latitude of the vacated city with the longitude and latitude of the new home city. The degrees of the zodiac within which the planets are placed, remain the same, but the house placements of the planets change when the longitude and latitude are adjusted. The MC-IC axis and the Ascendant-Descendant axis also change. When a team relocates, new tendencies emerge that are reflections of the new birthchart.

Multiple births of baseball teams are common. Often, when a league chooses to expand, two cities are simultaneously given franchises. The New York Giants and the Philadelphia Phillies were both born on Dec 7, 1882. Their rectified charts show they were both born at 1:36 p.m. EST. These birthcharts, however, are not identical because they are cast for different locations with different longitude and latitude. The most striking case of a multiple birth occurred on Nov. 20, 1893. On that date, the Western League, the antecedent of the American League, was founded. Seven franchises were born on this day, although only four survived until 1901. Those four teams are thriving to this day as the Chicago White Sox, Minnesota Twins, Cleveland Indians, and Baltimore Orioles.

Both the San Diego Padres and the Washington Nationals were born May 27, 1968. But the Nationals, for many years known as the Expos, were born several hours later than the Padres. These teams have their planets in the same degrees of the zodiac, except for their Moons.[60] In 1991, the cities of Denver and Miami were given expansion franchises by the National League. These two teams were not born on the same day. The Marlins and Rockies were born 12 days apart. Their birthcharts, however, show similar features. Both have the Sun in Gemini and Uranus conjunct to Neptune.

The birthcharts of baseball teams have similarities with the birthcharts of nations and corporations. A mundane astrologer can, with these

---

59. A birthchart is "rectified" when the time of birth is reconstructed with the aid of astrological factors such as solar arc progressions and transits to the axes.

60. The Moon is the fastest moving of the planetary bodies. Between the birth of the Padres and the birth of the Expos, the Moon advanced more than two degrees of the zodiac. The Padres' Moon is located at 12 degrees, 14 minutes of Gemini, whereas the Expos' Moon is positioned at 14 degrees, 27 minutes of Gemini.

birthcharts, analyze issues such as labor relations and the strength of the executive. These teams are also businesses. Similarly, the methods of financial astrologers can be used to analyze their strengths and weaknesses as businesses. I occasionally refer to the political and financial matters of the teams in their histories.

The positions of a baseball team are manifestations of the planets and astrological signs within that team's birthchart. Chapter 3 explains the relationship between signs, planets, and the positions of a baseball team. The tendencies of each position of a team are revealed within its birthchart through its signs, planets, and aspects. The character, history and tendencies of a team's shortstop position are evident by the placement of its Mars, its planets within the sign of Aries, and their aspects to these planets. Likewise, the placement of Venus, planets within the sign of Taurus, and their aspects reflect the nature of a team's center fielder. In this manner, each position of a team is revealed within its birthchart.

The houses within these birthcharts correspond with the positions in a pattern that is parallel to the correspondences between those positions and the planets and signs. Traditional astrology assigns a rulership to each of the twelve houses. Each house has a ruling planet and a sign. For example, the First House is ruled by the first sign, Aries, and the planet Mars. In baseball, the First House corresponds with the shortstop position,[61] which is the position associated with Aries, the first sign. Each house in a baseball team's birthchart corresponds with the position of its corresponding sign:

First House: shortstop

Second House: the center fielder

Third House: the pitching staff

Fourth House and IC: the catcher, fans, and home ballpark

Fifth House: the right fielder

Sixth House: the pitching staff

Seventh House: the second baseman

Eighth House: the third baseman

Ninth House: the batters

Tenth House and MC: the manager, coaches and owner

Eleventh House: the left fielder

Twelfth House: the first baseman

---

61. The First House of a baseball team also relates to the traditional First House rulerships of appearance and outer personality.

A team's strengths and weaknesses at each position are revealed in these birthcharts. The Cubs, whose birthchart has a Pisces emphasis, tend to be strong at the first base position. Teams that tend to excel in pitching have birthcharts that emphasize the signs of Gemini and Virgo. They may also have well-aspected Mercurys or favorable planets in their Third and Sixth Houses. The Padres, who have the Sun and Mercury in the sign of Gemini, tend to excel in pitching. Teams whose pitching is often weak, meanwhile, have afflictions with such planets, signs, or houses. The San Francisco Giants, who have a Third House Saturn, have a history of weak pitching. The Oakland Athletics, who often have injuries to their second basemen, have afflictions to their Venus.

Each chapter of this section includes birthcharts of players who are identified with their teams. The birthcharts of these individuals demonstrate the affinities between them and their teams. The birthchart of Pete Rose shows he was born to play for the Reds. Most of these birthcharts of players do not have birth times and are cast for noon in the city of the player's birth. Some of these birthcharts of players, however, do have times of birth. These have been rectified by the author.

The Cincinnati Reds

The Reds franchise was born on September 9, 1868[62] at 3:23 pm EST.[63] The team was originally called the Red Stockings.[64] Unlike many franchises that have relocated between cities, the Reds have always made Cincinnati their home. The birthchart of the Reds has the Sun and Mercury in the sign of Virgo, a feature that is embodied in their professionalism. The Reds' Capricorn Ascendant is reflected in their conservative appearance. Mars and Uranus are conjunct in the sign of Cancer, an aspect that has given the Reds their inventiveness. Their aspect of Jupiter and Neptune conjunct in Aries has brought the Reds their gambling scandals.

The Reds' Virgo Sun became distinguished right at the team's debut. It was the Reds franchise that brought the Virgo and Sixth House values of work to baseball and to sports. The 1869 Cincinnati Red Stockings were the first all-professional team. Each of the Red Stockings'

Cincinnati Reds
Wednesday, September 9, 1868 3:23:00 PM
Cincinnati, Ohio
Time Zone: 05:00 (EST)
Longitude: 084° W 29' 54"
Latitude: 39° N 08' 48"

---

62. Ellard, Harry: *Baseball in Cincinnati: A History* (Chapter 4); Sept. 9, 1868, is the date the franchise chose to field an all-professional team.

63. Rectification Note: The Reds' Neptune of 16 Aries, progressed by solar arc, becomes conjunct an IC of 2 degrees Taurus in 1884, the year they moved into League Park. An IC of 2 degrees Taurus, progressed by solar arc, becomes conjunct the Reds' Moon of 16 Gemini in 1912, the year the team moved into Crosley Field. An IC of 2 degrees Taurus, progressed by solar arc, becomes conjunct the Reds' Sun in 2003, the year they moved into Great American Ball Park.

64. Two other major league baseball teams have also in the past been called the Red Stockings—the franchises currently known as the Atlanta Braves and the Boston Red Sox.

players was signed to a contract and paid for his services. This team was the leader of a social trend that transformed sports from a gentlemanly pursuit, one performed in leisure, into a paid activity, a job. Prior to the Reds, baseball was under the influence of the aristocratic Leo and Fifth House values of leisure and recreation. Sports, to the upper class of the 19th Century, were a leisure activity performed by gentlemen in their free time. Wealthy men, who had ample time on their hands, pursued sports. The notion of a paid team offended the sensibilities of the upper classes of the day.[65] Although a few baseball players had been paid prior to 1869, the notion of a paid athlete was considered vulgar.

The early Red Stockings were a powerhouse team that won 129 straight games[66] before finally losing to the Brooklyn Atlantics in their second season. The streak was stunning not only for its length, but for the fact that a team from an upstart Western city could defeat every East Coast team. Aaron Champion was the man who paid the Cincinnati players. Harry Wright was the team's first manager. The success of the early Reds was due, not only to Aaron Champion's ability to maintain quality players by paying them, but by the embrace of the Virgo values of hard work and discipline. These Red Stockings had a work ethic that would make George Will proud.

The superior training of the Cincinnati team made their team a consistent winner.[67] The Reds exercised and practiced regularly. Harry Wright, the team's first manager, kept his team well-trained. He also held them to professional standards. Today, scheduled practices and standards of play are the norm, but in the 1860s, such systematic approaches were new, not only to baseball, but to the nation. The Industrial Revolution was transforming the United States from an agrarian-based culture into one based on wage labor. The all-professional Reds were a reflection of this historical change. Like paid employees, the Reds became held to "professional" standards. More than a century later, the Reds of the Big Red Machine also performed in a methodical and professional manner. The Reds of the 1970s maintained a "let's take care of business" approach. Their nickname, "The Big Red Machine," describes an automatic machine-like Virgo approach.

Mercury and its signs of Virgo and Gemini rule the pitcher. The Reds' Virgo Sun and Gemini Moon are embodied in a team that has excelled at

---

65. Allen, Lee: *The National League*, p. 205
66. Historians disagree as to the exact number of games won in this streak. See *The Cincinnati Game*, p. 30
67. Voight, *American Baseball: Volume I*, p. 26

pitching. Johnny Van der Meer, the only player to pitch consecutive no-hitters, played for the Reds. The famous double no-hitter of 1917 was won by the Reds' Fred Toney.[68]

The Reds' excess of Mercury energy has also brought afflictions. Their Sun and Moon are in a challenging square to one another, which has manifested in the more problematic qualities of both Gemini and Virgo. Asa Brainard,[69] the pitcher of the 1869 Red Stockings, embodied afflictions from both of the Mercury signs. Virgos are generally health conscious, but Asa Brainard was obsessive about his health, suffering from hypochondria and often complaining of imaginary illnesses. Indeed, hypochondria is a Virgo affliction. The sign of Virgo governs the analytical mind, and an unrestrained Virgo often overanalyzes, even self-diagnosing mild symptoms as major ailments.

Brainard's Gemini afflictions have handed down a comical story. Gemini governs the sense perceptions. Like an overwhelmed Gemini, Asa Brainard would became easily distracted. Once, as he was poised to deliver a pitch, a rabbit scampered in front of the mound. Forgetting all about the batter and the runners on the base, Brainard took aim, then threw the baseball at the rabbit. Two runners scored as the ball rolled into the crowd.[70] More than 100 years later, the Reds' Gemini afflictions would manifest as excessive verbiage when owner Marge Schotz allowed her racist views to be known to the press. A Gemini often speaks when it is wise to be silent.

The Reds' Capricorn Ascendant gives them their conservative appearance. When a Capricorn chooses clothes, he prefers the staid to the flashy. The Reds' conservative style was on conspicuous display in the 1972 World Series, which matched the Reds against the Oakland Athletics. Their conservative uniforms and short hair contrasted with the A's moustaches and brightly colored uniforms. While the A's were in synch with the polyester 1970s, the Reds kept their traditional look. The Reds have a Middle America appeal. They share the values of the mainstream American. In 1956, amidst the anti-communist hysteria of the Cold War, the team even changed its name in order to not be associated with Communists. The name "Reds" had become appropriated by Communists, so the team changed its name to "Redlegs."

The sign of Capricorn rules the manager and owner. A Capricorn

---

68. The double no-hitter of 1917 is analyzed in Section III.
69. His name, *Brain*ard, has a Mercury suggestion to it.
70. Voight, p. 31

Ascendant will place the team's manager or owner in a very visible position. Managers and owners of the Reds have not sat in the background. Harry Wright, the manager of the original 1869 team, maintained a high profile. Pete Rose, as a player manager, was the most visible member of the team. The controversial Marge Schotz was also a conspicuous owner.

The Reds have Mars and Uranus conjunct in the sign of Cancer. This aspect is a very inventive one, as the innovative genius of Uranus merges with the can-do energy of Mars. Both planets are in the sign of Cancer, a fertile womb for the ideas of Uranus and the energy of Mars to germinate. The history of the Reds illustrates that they have been one of the most innovative teams in sports. In addition to beginning professional sports, the Reds' long list of inventions includes the following innovations: the fielder's glove (1869), the 7th inning stretch (1869), the baseball beat writer (1869), Spring Training (1870), the doubleheader (1876), the catchers squat (Buck Ewing 1880), Ladies Day (1886), the farm system (1887), the catcher's mitt (1890), season tickets (1934), air travel by a baseball team (1934), big league night baseball (May 24, 1935 at Crosley Field), and televised baseball (Reds at Brooklyn, Aug 26, 1939).[71]

Aside from becoming the first professional club, the Reds' innovations have generally not been social or political. They are inventors of technique rather than crusaders for social causes. Capricorn Rising is not comfortable in taking a stand against the social mores. However, the first Latino player to become a star pitcher, Adolfo Luque, played for the Reds in 1919.[72] The Reds also employed a deaf outfielder, William "Dummy" Hoy, in the 1890s.

The Reds birthchart has Jupiter conjunct Neptune in the sign of Aries, two planets that can bring out the worst in each other. Jupiter is usually considered a benefic for its buoyancy and expansiveness, but, when poorly aspected, Jupiter loses a sense of proper limits. Even under the best of circumstances, Jupiter does not like to be restrained. Jupiter is also the planet of gamblers. Neptune, while usually inspirational and sympathetic, has a murky and sinister side. A poorly aspected Neptune can cloud one's ethics. Simple questions of right and wrong become fuzzy and gray under the influence of an afflicted Neptune. Lies and scandals become commonplace. Drugs and alcohol are often involved.

---

71. Bjarkman, pp. 181-2; Allen, Lee, *The National League*, p. 201
72. Bjarkman, p. 195

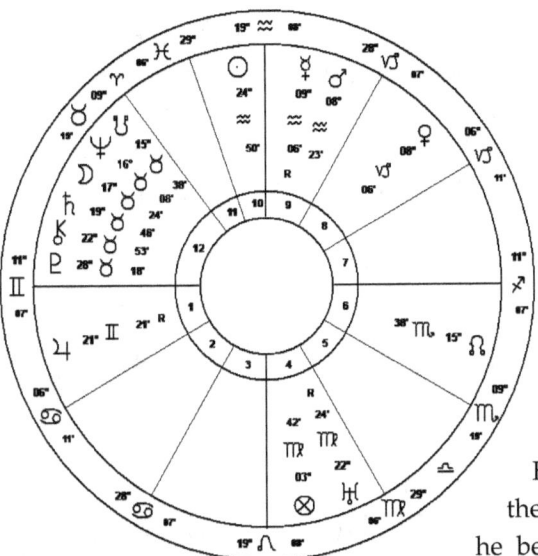

Hal Chase
Tuesday, February 13, 1883 12:00:00 PM
Current Day and Time
Los Gatos, California
Time Zone: 08:00 (PST)
Longitude: 121° W 57'
Latitude: 37° N 14'

The Reds' Jupiter-Neptune conjunction was active, not only in the Pete Rose scandal of 1989, but in the Hal Chase suspension of 1918. Hal Chase played first base, the Neptune position. When he began playing for the Reds on April 16, 1916, Jupiter was in transit at 15 degrees Aries. The Reds had just undergone a Jupiter return,[73] and transiting Jupiter was in a conjunction of a little more than one degree to the Reds' Neptune of 16 degrees Aries. The excess of Jupiter and Neptune energy set this chapter of Reds history. Chase had previously worn the uniforms of the Yankees, the Giants, and the White Sox. In his day, he was considered one of the best hitters in baseball. However, by the time he joined the Reds, there were doubts about Hal Chase's character. In August of 1918, after careful observation, manager Christy Mathewson suspended him. The charge was withholding his best effort in order to influence the outcome of games for the benefit of gamblers.

The Reds' second baseman Lee Magee was implicated as Chase's conspirator. As the Descendant rules second base, Jupiter and Pluto were conjunct the Reds' Descendent of 9 degrees Cancer for much of 1918. Pluto and Jupiter are another dubious combination. When the ruthlessness of Pluto teams up with the excesses of Jupiter, bad things can happen.

Hal Chase would be exonerated in the following winter and play the 1919 season with the Giants, but new evidence would emerge that Chase had bet on Reds' games while wearing their uniform. He would also be implicated for having prior knowledge of the 1919 World Series fix. Eventually, he became banned for life from Major League baseball. After he left the majors, Chase went west and played in semi-pro leagues. Hal

---

73. A "return" occurs when a natal planet within one's birthchart undergoes the transit of the conjunction from the same planet.

Chase eventually succumbed to alcoholism, another affliction of Neptune.[74] Hal Chase's birthchart has a conjunction between Moon, Saturn, South Node, and Neptune. The Moon and Saturn are indicators of one's mother and father. With these planets conjunct to Neptune, Hal Chase was likely influenced by alcoholic or deceitful parents. These planets are also square to a Sun in Aquarius, a sign with a libertine attitude.

Pete Rose
Monday, April 14, 1941 5:15:00 AM
Cincinnati, Ohio
Time Zone: 05:00 (EST)
Longitude: 084° W 29' 54"
Latitude: 39° N 08' 48"

The Jupiter-Neptune conjunction within the Reds birthchart also set the stage for the tragedy of Pete Rose. Rose's serious gambling troubles began in 1987 during another Jupiter return of the Reds. As Jupiter traveled through Aries in 1987, it made conjunctions not only to the Reds' natal Jupiter but to the many Aries planets in Pete Rose's own birthchart. His gambling became publicly known in the spring and summer of 1989, as transiting Neptune and Saturn were both conjunct the Reds Capricorn Ascendant. During the Hal Chase scandal, transiting Neptune was conjunct the Reds Descendent. Seventy-one years later, Neptune would be 180 degrees farther in the zodiac. Instead of dragging in the Descendant's second baseman, Neptune conjunct the Ascendant brought down the most visible player on the team, the face of the franchise. With Capricorn Rising, the scandal's central figure became the manager. A clean-cut native son of Cincinnati, Rose was a much more respected figure than Hal Chase. Although Chase was popular with fans, he was disliked by his fellow players for his arrogant manner.

Pete Rose's rectified birthchart[75] shows an Aries Ascendant with a

---

74. Allen, Lee, *The Cincinnati Reds*, p. 128
75. Rectification note: in his autobiography, *Pete Rose: My Story*, Rose states that he was born "sometime in the morning" (p. 41). An Ascendant of 2 Aries, progressed by solar arc, becomes conjunct Rose's Sun of 24 Aries at age 22, when he made his Major League debut. When he broke Ty Cobb's hitting record on Sept 11, 1985, Neptune was conjunct his MC of 2 degrees Capricorn. When he was banned from baseball in

conjunction to Mercury. His Sun and Venus are also in the sign of Aries and in his First House. His abundance of Aries energy would manifest in his intense head-first-slide style of play. Rose habitually sprinted to First Base on a walk. His birthchart also has Pluto in the Fifth House of sports, a placement which reflects his fierce competitive nature. One of the best hitters ever to play the game, Pete Rose broke Ty Cobb's record for most career hits. His natural ability as a hitter is a manifestation of his Moon in Sagittarius, the sign of the batter. Rose's Jupiter, the planet of the batter, is well-aspected with conjunctions to Uranus and Saturn. While he was quite gifted in the Jupiter art of batting, he was brought down by another manifestation of Jupiter: gambling.

Surprisingly, the Reds won only five pennants between 1871 and 1969. One would expect that, given their long history, the Reds would have won more championships, but there is fragility to the Reds' birthchart. The Reds have had several seasons in which a solid winning campaign, even one with a pennant or World Series victory, is followed by a steep plunge to a losing record the following year. These years include 1921, 1941, 1971, 1982 and 1991. The Reds' Sun and Moon are both in mutable signs, which respond adversely to transits from challenging aspects. Mercury, the depositor of both their Sun and Moon, is ever important to the Reds. However, transits from challenging aspects to the Reds' Mercury disrupt the functioning of the team.

A Virgo is a fine machine that can be easily thrown out of whack, yet the standard of Virgo professionalism set by the Reds continues to endure.

1989, his Saturn of 14 Taurus, progressed by solar arc, was square an Ascendant of 2 Aries.

The Chicago Cubs

The Cubs franchise was born on March 8, 1870[76] at 7:35 am.[77] They were the second professional baseball team to be born. After the Cincinnati Red Stockings defeated every opponent in 1869, the Chicago Baseball Association was formed to field a team of paid players who could combat the upstarts from Cincinnati.[78] In an interesting way, the Cubs are the antithesis of the Reds. While

Chicago Cubs
Tuesday, March 8, 1870 7:35:00 AM
Chicago, Illinois
Time Zone: 06:00 (CST)
Longitude: 087° W 39' 42"
Latitude: 41° N 51' 54"

---

76. I have no documentation for the birth date of the Cubs. *Baseball in Old Chicago* states that the team was assembled during the winter of 1869-70 yet remained unincorporated through the 1870 season (p. 21). The organization was formally incorporated after its first season in January 1871. I arrived at the birth date of March 8, 1870 upon reflecting on two features of the team. Wrigley Field, with its bucolic atmosphere, would indicate a Taurus moon. The wispy quality of the Cubs would indicate a Pisces/Neptune emphasis. Using an ephemeris, I searched through the dates of the winter of 1869-70 for days with a Neptune and Taurus emphasis. The date of March 8, 1970 has a Pisces Sun matched with a Taurus Moon. I became convinced that this was the correct date for the birth of the franchise after comparing the birthchart of this date with the charts of key players and events in Cubs history.

77. I rectified this chart using solar arc progressions involving the IC and moves to new stadiums. In 1877, the year the team moved to the Lake Park Grounds, a progressed IC of 11 degrees Cancer became conjunct the Cubs' natal Uranus of 18 degrees Cancer. In 1884, when the team moved to the Loomis Street Grounds, a progressed IC of 11 Cancer became conjunct to the team's North Node of 25 degrees Cancer. In 1916, the Cubs Moon of 25 degrees became progressed to 11 degrees Cancer and conjunct the MC. That year, the team moved into Weegham Park, which eventually became known as Wrigley Field.

78. *Baseball in Old Chicago* "The Early Years." Additionally, the "College of Coaches" experiment, in which managers and coaches would be rotated for the 1961 season, was announced on December 20, 1960 while Jupiter at 11 degrees Capricorn was conjunct a Cubs MC of 11 Capricorn. (Hazacha, Andrew, *Educating Wrigley: The Failed Experiment of the College of Coaches"* and *Northsiders: Essays on the History and Culture of the Chicago Cubs.*

the Reds' Sun is positioned at 17 degrees Virgo, the Cubs' Sun is located at 17 degrees Pisces, the exact opposite degree of the zodiac wheel. This tight opposition between the Cubs' Sun and the Sun of the Reds mirrors how the Chicago team was assembled in response to the Reds. It also demonstrates how Virgo energy is often countered by the appearance of Piscean energy. The birthchart of the Chicago Cubs has a strong Pisces and Neptune emphasis. The Sun and Mars are conjunct in Pisces, while Neptune is conjunct the Ascendant. This Pisces-Neptune prominence has brought the Cubs depressive tendencies and a legacy of losing seasons, but it also gave them the hopefulness that was finally fulfilled in 2016 when the Cubs ended their 108-season wait for a World Series win.

With Neptune conjunct the Ascendant and the Sun and Mars conjunct in Pisces, the Cubs are thoroughly soaked in Piscean energy. For generations, the Cubs were known for last place finishes, pennant-race collapses, and the Curse. Pisces, the last sign in of the zodiac, rules last place. However, early in their history, the Cubs were not losers. Their 19th Century record is glorious. The Chicago White Stockings, as they were then called, were the dominant team of the 1880s, winning five pennants from 1880 to 1886. The Cubs of that decade featured Hall of Fame players Cap Anson, Mike "King" Kelly, and John Clarkson. Cap Anson played first base and managed. King Kelly, the catcher, was a tremendous *bon vivant* and the most popular player of his era. Pitcher John Clarkson won 326 games in a brief twelve-year career, including 52 wins in 1885.

In the 1880s, the team's Pisces-Neptune emphasis was embodied in drunkenness, more so than in last place. Manager Cap Anson often fined and berated his players for drinking. Anson's birthchart has the Sun and Saturn conjunct in Aries. Both

Mike "King" Kelly
Thursday, December 31, 1857 12:00:00 PM
Troy, New York
Time Zone: 05:00 (EST)
Longitude: 073° W 40' 00"
Latitude: 42° N 44' 24"

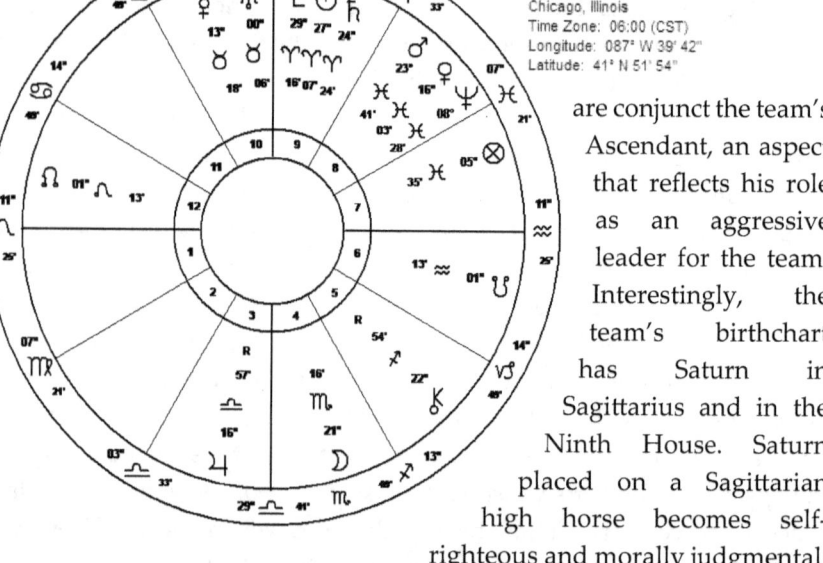

Cap Anson
Thursday, April 17, 1851 12:00:00 PM
Chicago, Illinois
Time Zone: 06:00 (CST)
Longitude: 087° W 39' 42"
Latitude: 41° N 51' 54"

are conjunct the team's Ascendant, an aspect that reflects his role as an aggressive leader for the team. Interestingly, the team's birthchart has Saturn in Sagittarius and in the Ninth House. Saturn placed on a Sagittarian high horse becomes self-righteous and morally judgmental. Their manager, embodying this Saturn, responded to his team's partying ways with condemnation.

The Cubs allegedly lost the 1886 World Series against St Louis because they were drunk when they took the field. Owner Albert Spaulding, a Virgo, made this charge.[79] A review of the transits for the 1886 World Series supports Spaulding's accusation, as Neptune was heavily aspected during the Series. Neptune, in transit at 27 degrees Taurus throughout the Series, formed a square to the White Stockings' natal Venus and an inconjunction to the White Stockings' Saturn. Transiting Jupiter in Libra,

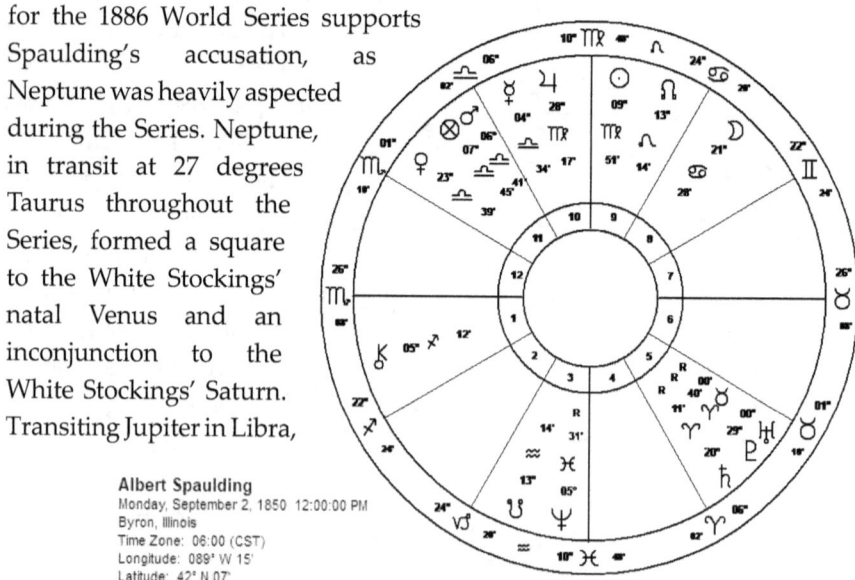

Albert Spaulding
Monday, September 2, 1850 12:00:00 PM
Byron, Illinois
Time Zone: 06:00 (CST)
Longitude: 089° W 15'
Latitude: 42° N 07'

---

79. Virgo, the sign of cleanliness and sobriety is opposite to Pisces in the zodiac wheel.

Chicago Cubs

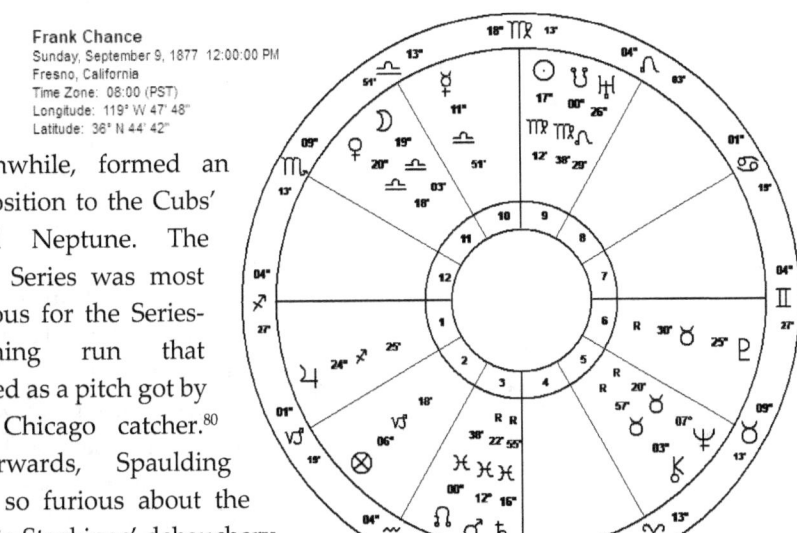

Frank Chance
Sunday, September 9, 1877 12:00:00 PM
Fresno, California
Time Zone: 08:00 (PST)
Longitude: 119° W 47' 48"
Latitude: 36° N 44' 42"

meanwhile, formed an opposition to the Cubs' natal Neptune. The 1886 Series was most famous for the Series-winning run that scored as a pitch got by the Chicago catcher.[80] Afterwards, Spaulding was so furious about the White Stockings' debauchery that he dismantled his team. He sold off his star players: "King" Kelly, pitcher Jim McCormick, and outfielder George Gore. Spaulding's sobriety sale cost the White Stockings the glory of future pennants. Their dynasty of the 1880s ended, and the Cubs would not win another pennant until 1906.

Since the Cubs are accustomed to Pisces and Neptune energy, they respond quite well to transits from Neptune. In their dynasty of the 1880s, Neptune transited through the sign of Taurus, making conjunctions to the Cubs' Pluto, Jupiter, and Moon. During this period, Neptune would also form squares to the Cubs' natal Mercury and Venus in Aquarius. The Cubs next era of greatness occurred in the 1900s. The famous infield that consisted of shortstop Joe Tinker, second baseman Johnny Evers, and first baseman Frank Chance brought home three consecutive World Series victories from 1906 to 1908. During these seasons, Neptune, transiting through Cancer, made frequent conjunctions with the Cubs Cancer IC and regular trines to the Cubs' Sun in Pisces. The 1984 Cubs, who won the Eastern Division, had transiting Neptune in Sagittarius in conjunction to their natal Saturn. The 1989 Division winners were assisted by Neptune and Saturn in conjunction to the Cubs' Capricorn MC for much of the season. Then, when the Cubs won the World Series in 2016, Neptune was trine to the Cubs IC from its own sign of Pisces.

The Cubs have excelled at the Pisces position of first base. Four Cubs

---

80. Game 6 occurred on October 23, 1886 in St. Louis, as Venus and Jupiter were conjunct near 20 degrees Libra and square to Saturn at 22 degrees Cancer.

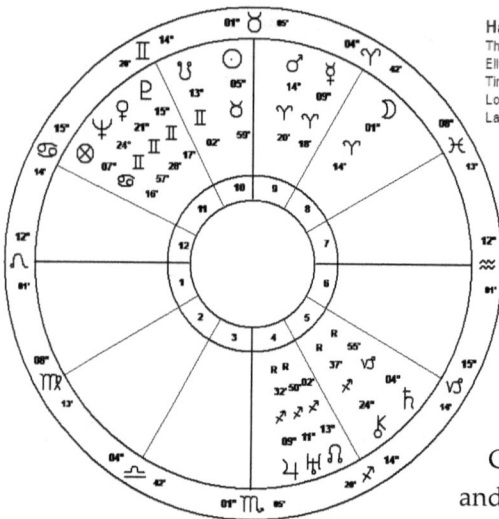

Hack Wilson
Thursday, April 26, 1900 12:00:00 PM
Ellwood City, Pennsylvania
Time Zone: 05:00 (EST)
Longitude: 080° W 17'
Latitude: 40° N 51'

first basemen are in the Hall of Fame: Cap Anson, Frank Chance, Hack Wilson, and Ernie Banks.[81] Cap Anson's birthchart has Neptune, Venus, and Mars all in Pisces, indicating he was a natural first baseman. Frank Chance's birthchart has Mars and Saturn conjunct in Pisces. In 1930, Hack Wilson set the record for RBIs in a season, with 190. Unfortunately, Wilson's career was cut short by alcoholism, the Pisces disease. He would play only 12 major league seasons and die at the young age of 48. Ernie Banks, who hit 512 home runs, has his North Node in Aries conjunct to the Cubs' Neptune.

Wrigley Field very much embodies the Cubs' Taurus Moon. Taurus is the sign of nature and vegetation. Wrigley Field, with its dangling ivy and thick grass, is a park lush with Taurus splendor. Taurus, a fixed sign, is also conservative and resistant to change. A Taurus prefers the old established way. The ballpark known as "the Friendly Confines" is very resistant to change. Lights were not installed there until 1988. Interestingly, the Cubs have Uranus in the Fourth House, the house of home and stadiums. Uranus is the planet of electricity and technology, but

Ernie Banks
Saturday, January 31, 1931 12:00:00 PM
Dallas, Texas
Time Zone: 06:00 (CST)
Longitude: 096° W 48' 12"
Latitude: 32° N 47' 24"

---

81. Ernie Banks played shortstop in the early years of his career, then became a first baseman. This transition was a natural one for a team with Mars, the planet of shortstop, in Pisces, the sign of first base.

the Cubs' Uranus has avoided technological changes. Instead, the planet has instilled an individualistic attitude to the Fourth House. Wrigley Field is Uranian, not in the modern technological sense, but by insisting on its uniqueness and individuality. The ballpark expresses a freedom to be as it wants to be, much like a cantankerous old man who refuses to change with the times. Uranus also rules the homerun, and its placement in the Cubs' Fourth House has made Wrigley Field a homerun park. Wind, so prominent at Wrigley Field and a catalyst for homeruns, is also governed by Uranus.

The Cubs have Mercury and Venus conjunct in the sign of Aquarius and in the Eleventh House, an aspect that has made the Cubs leaders in communications media. Mercury rules media, and Aquarius brings innovation and technology. The Cubs have broken ground in media throughout their history. In 1877, Cubs' owner Albert Spaulding published *Spaulding's Base Ball Guide*, a periodical that contained news and information about professional baseball. Eventually, it became an official voice of the National League. In 1925, the Cubs were the fist team to regularly broadcast all their games on radio. To do so took courage, since it was widely believed that radio broadcasts diminished ballpark attendance. In 1948, the Cubs began television broadcasts of all their home games on WGM.[82] Then, in 1981, the Cubs were purchased by the Chicago Tribune Media Group. Soon afterward, television viewing of the all Cubs games became available across the nation on cable stations. Many teams followed the Cubs' leadership in both radio and TV when they too began broadcasting all their games on radio and national cable TV.

The current name of "Cubs" is a suitable mascot for a team with an Aries Ascendant. The name was proposed by the *Chicago Daily News* on March 27, 1902 for the many young players on the team that year.[83] Previously, the team had been called the "Colts," for the same reason: the youth of the players.[84] Aries, the youngest sign of the zodiac, associates with rookies and youth. Mascots of young animals, Colts and Cubs, are fitting names for their Aries Ascendant. Interestingly, the team's 19th Century name, "White Stockings," was a Piscean one. Stockings are a garment worn on the feet, which are ruled by the sign of Pisces. The name White Stockings emerged from Neptune's conjunction to the team's Ascendant.

---

82. *https://sabrmedia.org/2015/04/29/cubswhite-sox-play-first-mlb-game-on-wgn-tv-in-1948/*
83. Dewey and Acocella, p. 125. On that day, the Sun and Mars were conjunct at 6 degrees Aries, making a 15-degree aspect to their Ascendant. Also, the Cubs natal Mars of 18 Pisces, progressed by solar arc, became conjunct their Ascendant in 1902.
84. Dewey and Acocella, p. 123

The Cubs are known for fast starts, a manifestation of their Aries Ascendant. The first sign of the zodiac gets a quick jump. The Cubs have not only Aries Rising, but two planets in the First House, Jupiter and Pluto conjunct at 16 degrees Taurus. Nearby, on the cusp of the Second House, is their Moon of 25 degrees Taurus. When the baseball season begins in April, the Sun is traveling through Aries. Soon it enters the sign of Taurus. Alongside the Sun are Mercury and Venus, which are always in close proximity. The spring transits from the Sun, and the inner planets form conjunctions to the planets in the Cubs' First House, assisting them with early season victories. It is the abundance of Aries and Taurus planets in the Cubs' birthchart that allows them to generally play well early in the season.

An Aries Ascendant and a loaded First House, however, lack tenacity. An Aries has difficulty conserving energy: difficulty in pacing oneself. He or she is likely to squander all their energy at the beginning of a project or the start of the race. The full head of steam enjoyed in April is spent long before the home stretch of September. In the parable of the tortoise and the hare, Aries is like the hare. At the finish line, an Aries is generally beaten by the tortoise-like contenders who pace themselves for a long season. Baseball seasons in which the Cubs began the season strongly but faded down the stretch include 1955, 1969, 1973, and 1975.

When the Cubs do survive into October, they often lose in post-season play. Losses in the playoffs and World Series are the flipside to their fast starts. The 1969 Cubs, who were beaten by the "Miracle Mets," led the race for the pennant most of the season, but collapsed in September. The Cubs became tired down the stretch. Cubs manager Leo Durocher was criticized for not resting his regular players often enough.[85] In September and October, not only is an Aries likely to be tired, but one has the added hardship of playing with planets in the fall signs of Libra and Scorpio. The Cubs Pisces' planets will be opposed by transits from planets in Virgo in late August and early September. The signs of Libra and Scorpio are in natural oppositions to the signs of Aries and Taurus, which are so prominent in the Cubs chart. Similarly, when the pennant race heats up in the regular late months of August and September, the Cubs Pisces' planets are opposed by transits from planets in the sign of Virgo.

Aries Rising has another expression, that of a brawler, an aggressive in-your-face type of player. The early White Stockings were a rough bunch. Cap Anson engaged in fights with both opponents and umpires. Anson's birthchart shows the Sun, Pluto and Saturn in Aries. Frank Chance, who

---

85. Dewey and Acocella, p. 137

both managed and played first base for the Cubs early in the Twentieth Century, was a similarly aggressive leader. As a manager, Chance was a stern disciplinarian who would use his fists to discipline unruly players. As a player himself, he was fanatical to the point of allowing himself to be hit by beanballs in order to reach first base.[86] Chance's birthchart has Mars conjunct to Saturn in the sign of Pisces, indicating a willingness to sacrifice, to endure the pain of being hit by a pitch to help the team.

Although the Cubs' Pisces and Neptune energy gives them an image of self-sacrifice, their history and their astrological chart show they have a birthright to a tougher style. Not only does the team have an Aries Ascendant, but their Sun is conjunct to Mars, the planet of the warrior. Leo Durocher, with his aggressive style, could have inspired the Cubs to reclaim their Mars persona. Durocher's own Mars in Scorpio is trine to the Cubs' Mars and Sun. But Durocher's Mars was also opposite to the Cubs' Pluto in Taurus. This opposition became embodied in a conflict between Durocher and Cub third baseman Ron Santo.[87] Pundits claim the hostility between Durocher and Santo distracted the team just enough for them to lose the 1969 pennant.[88] The Cubs' Sun and Mars, however, are afflicted. Each is hidden away in the Twelfth House. When Mars is turned inwardly like this, it can lead to self-inflicted wounds. This placement can also make one highly susceptible to others' negative energy, including curses upon the team. In the Cubs' case, it manifested in The Curse.

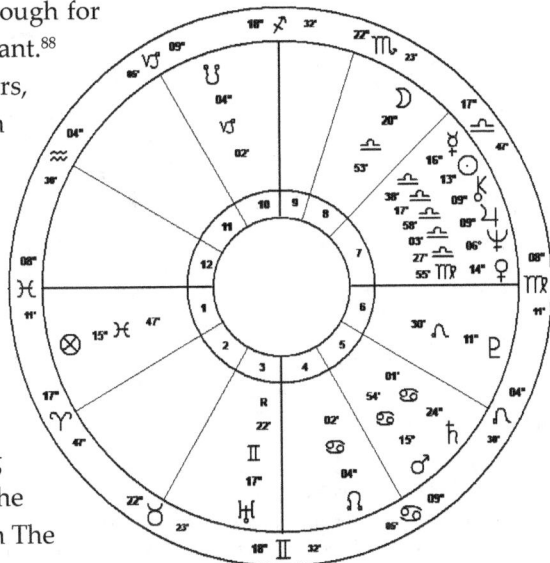

Curse of the Goat
Saturday, October 6, 1945 4:00:00 PM
Chicago, Illinois
Time Zone: 06:00 (CST)
Longitude: 087° W 39' 42"
Latitude: 41° N 51' 54"

---

86. Ahrens, Art, p. 144
87. Aspects between planets within a teams's birthchart often reflect the harmony or conflict between the players who embody those planets. A team with a Mars-Saturn opposition will likely have conflicts between its shortstop and manager. (See Indians and White Sox chapters.) But here, Durocher's natal Mars was opposite the Cubs' Pluto.
88. Dewey and Acocella, p. 137

The infamous Curse of the Goat was placed on the Cubs on October 6, 1945[89], during Game Four of the 1945 World Series. The game was attended by Billy Sianis, a tavern owner who brought along his pet goat. Ushers, acting on orders from the team owner, kicked Sianis and his goat out of the stadium.[90] As he was leaving Wrigley Field, Sianis cursed the Cubs, yelling that a World Series would never again be played in Wrigley Field. The Cubs subsequently lost the 1945 Series to the Tigers. The Curse would endure for 71 years, as the Cubs did not return to the World Series until 2016. Transits for the afternoon strongly suggest dark energy thrown towards the Cubs. In examining the transits of the Curse of the Goat, obviously one must look to Saturn, since Saturn and Capricorn rule goats. During the game, the Sun at 13 degrees Libra[91] was semiquincunx (75 degrees) to the Cubs natal Saturn of 27 degrees Sagittarius. Transiting Saturn at 24 degrees Cancer was conjunct to the Cubs North Node in Cancer of 25 degrees 26 minutes Cancer. At 4:00 in the afternoon, the Moon was at 21 degrees, 51 minutes Libra, square to transiting Saturn and the Cubs North Node, but also conjunct to the Cubs Descendant of 21 Libra.[92] A curse thrown by a fan corresponds to the square from the Moon, as the Moon rules fans. This fan also took an oppositional enemy-like stance

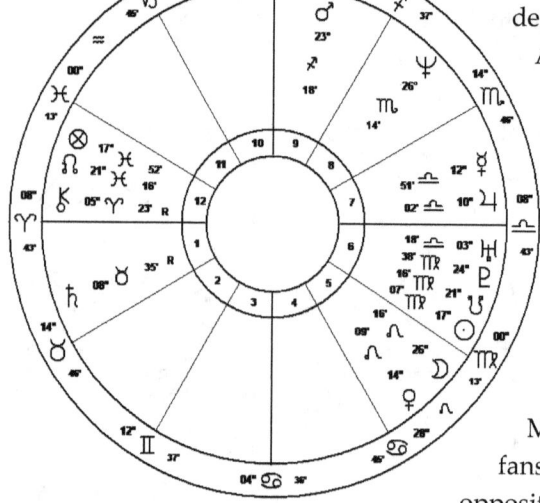

Black Cat Incident
Tuesday, September 9, 1969 8:00:00 PM
Flushing, New York
Time Zone: 04:00 (EDT)
Longitude: 073° W 50'
Latitude: 40° N 45' 12"

---

89. www.thisdayinchicagocubshistory.com/Cubs-curse.html
90. Conflicting versions of the story have been handed down. One version states that Sianis and his goat were never allowed to enter Wrigley Field, while another maintains that Sianis and his goat paraded on the field before the game. The most likely version is that the goat was kicked out during the seventh inning.
91. 13 degrees Libra is also the antiscion of 17 Pisces, the degree of the Cubs Sun and Mars. An antiscion is an indicator of a planet's shadow and hidden energies at odds with the planet. An antiscion is located on the point that is the same number of degrees to the 0 Cancer/ 0 Capricorn axis as the planet but on the axis' opposite side.
92. The exact time that the curse was placed is not currently available. I am proceeding with the assumption that the curse occurred in the seventh inning near 4:00 in the afternoon.

against the team, which corresponds with the conjunction of the Moon to the Cubs' Descendant. The Descendant, like the Seventh House, is a place of enemies and opponents.

Cub fans would point to late season collapses and various incidents in their history as proof of the endurance of The Curse. Two incidents are analyzed here: the Black Cat of 1969, and the 2003 fan interference in Game Six of the 2003 LCS. On September 9, 1969[93], the Cubs were enjoying a robust lead in the NL East and appeared to be on their way to the playoffs. Then, during one game at Shea Stadium, a black cat mysteriously appeared and circled Ron Santo as he stood in the on-deck circle. That night, Mercury was positioned at 13 degrees Libra, semiquincunx to the Cubs Saturn and in the same degree occupied by the Sun when the curse had been thrown in 1945. The Cubs lost 17 of 25 games that September. They were eventually overtaken by the Miracle Mets and finished out of the playoffs.

In Game Six of the 2003 League Championship Series against Florida, a fan named Steve Bartman interfered with left fielder Moises Alou as he attempted to catch a ball from a Marlin batter. When Bartman got in the way of Alou, the Cubs were five outs away from advancing to the World Series, but, instead, the Marlin batter reached base, and a rally ensued. The Cubs eventually lost the game and would lose the pennant in the next game. Transits for this incident also echo those of the original curse. Game Six occurred on October 14, with the Sun positioned at 21 degrees Libra, conjunct the Cubs Descendant, and at the same degree occupied by the Moon when the curse had been placed back in 1945. Moreover, just as in the Black Cat Incident, Mercury was positioned at 13 degrees Libra, the same degree of the Sun from

Fan Interference
Tuesday, October 14, 2003 9:25:00 PM
Chicago, Illinois
Time Zone: 05:00 (CDT)
Longitude: 087° W 39' 42"
Latitude: 41° N 51' 54"

---

93. http://www.cubbiesbaseball.com/chicago-cubs-curses

when the curse was thrown and semiquincunx to the Cubs' natal Saturn.

The interference occurred at 9:25 pm, CDT[94] while the MC was positioned at 29 degrees Aquarius and exactly conjunct to Uranus in transit at 29 degrees Aquarius. Significantly, Uranus rules the left fielder, the position played by Moises Alou, whose play was interfered with. Moreover, Uranus was conjunct to the Cubs' Venus of 28 degrees Aquarius and Mercury of 21 Aquarius, both of which are square to the Cubs' Moon. Interestingly, Bartman was wearing radio earphones when he interfered with the play and entered Cubs history. As their history shows, a radio is a manifestation of the Cubs' Mercury in Aquarius. Although radio connected Bartman to the game, it also disconnected him from awareness of the situation he entered. The square from the Cubs' Mercury to their Moon helped bring down the Cubs that evening. It also added Steve Bartman to baseball's pantheon of goats.

The Curse would endure for 71 years and then be broken when they won the World Series in 2016. The Curse was largely broken under strong transits from Uranus. A key to their World Series victory was the hiring of Joe Maddon as manager at the end of the 2014 season. Maddon's birthchart has the Sun and Venus conjunct at 19 and 21 degrees Aquarius. These planets are conjunct to the Cubs' Venus and Mercury in Aquarius. Maddon brought new Aquarian and Uranian energy to the Cubs. He brought defensive shifts he had developed and experimented with as the manager of the Tampa Bay Rays (see Rays chapter). He also employed the advanced use of computer models for platoons. In Tampa Bay, his thick glasses contributed to his persona as a nerd scientist. In Chicago, this persona persisted, and he was often referred to as a mad scientist.

For much of 2016, the year the Curse would be broken, Uranus in Aries was conjunct the Cubs Ascendant, with an orb of less than one degree. A key game towards understanding the benevolent influence of Uranus in the Cubs 2016 season was an extra-inning win that occurred in Cincinnati on June 28. That evening, the Moon in Aries was conjunct Uranus. In the late innings of this 15-inning game, Joe Maddon had employed the highly unusual strategy of having pitchers switch back and forth between playing left field and pitching. Before the game was won by a Javier Baez grand slam, three different pitchers had played in left field. A game played while the Moon is conjunct Uranus will bring especially strong Uranian energy. That night, Joe Maddon employed a strategy that emphasized the Uranus position of left field. It is also relevant that the game was won with

---

94. FOX Sports broadcast

a homerun, a Uranian tool, and that the homerun was hit by Javiar Baez as he was playing shortstop, the position of Aries, the sign in which the Moon and Uranus were conjunct that night.

The 2016 World Series would be played with Uranus retrograde in Aries, between 22 and 21 degrees Aries, conjunct to the Cubs' Ascendant within less than one degree. Ben Zobrist, who had played various positions for the Cubs in the regular season but only the Uranian position of left field in the World Series, would best manifest the energy of this transit. Zobrist not only won the World Series MVP title but made the most important hit of the Series. An epic Game Seven would be played in Cleveland on November 2nd. In the 10th inning of Game Seven, Zobrist hit a double that scored the go-ahead run.[95] Interestingly, in that final game of the season, Chicago would score eight runs with RBI's credited to eight different batters. Uranus likes team efforts

The lifting of the Curse demonstrates how the Cubs were responsive to strong Uranus energy, even though, for many years, they had been mired in the Neptune energy of losing and last place.

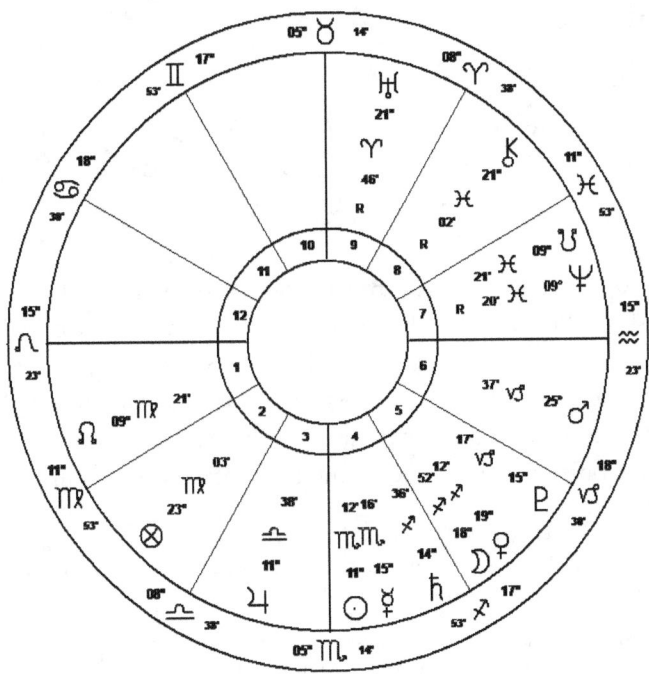

Cubs Win World Series
Wednesday, November 2, 2016 9:47:00 PM
Cleveland, Ohio
Time Zone: 07:00 (PDT)
Longitude: 081° W 40' 42"
Latitude: 41° N 28' 24"

THE BRAVES

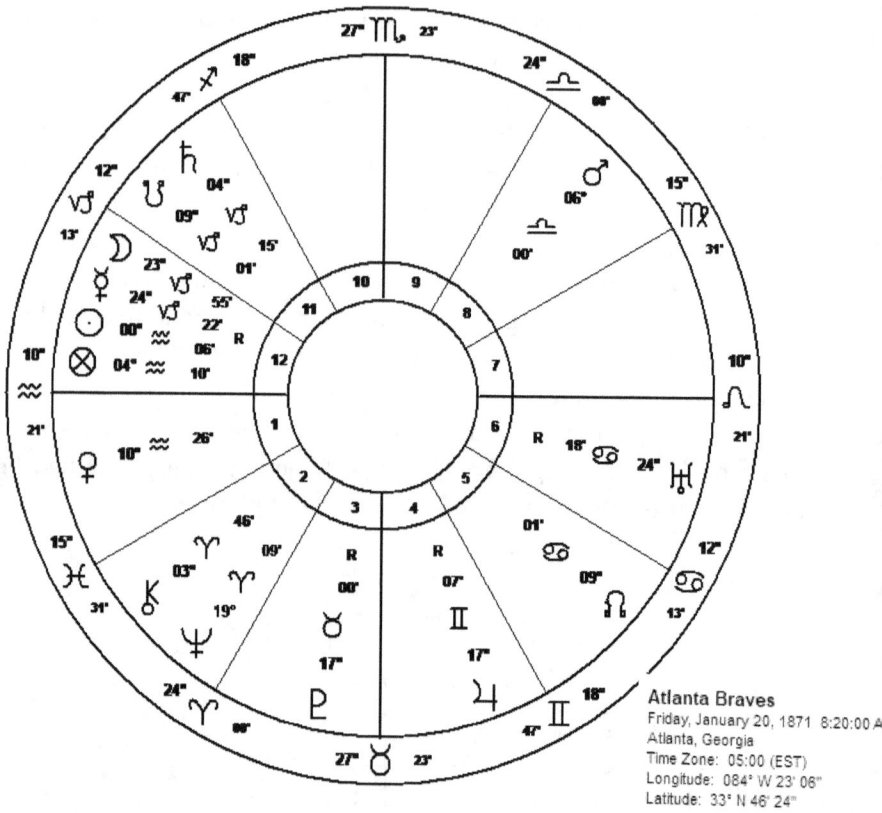

Atlanta Braves
Friday, January 20, 1871 8:20:00 A
Atlanta, Georgia
Time Zone: 05:00 (EST)
Longitude: 084° W 23' 06"
Latitude: 33° N 46' 24"

The franchise known as the Braves was born on January 20, 1871[96] at 8:20 EST[97] in Boston. They have lived in three cities: Boston, Milwaukee and Atlanta. Their birthchart[98] has the Sun and Venus conjunct in Aquarius. The Braves' Moon is in the sign of Capricorn and heavily afflicted. The Moon is conjunct to Mercury and in opposition to Uranus in Cancer. The Moon's position is very late within the lunar cycle, actually conjunct to

---

96. Onigman, Mark: *This Date in Braves History*, p. 71
97. I rectified the Boston birthchart using solar arc progressions. In 1894, the Third House Pluto progressed to a conjunction with the IC, which coincided with the fire at the South End Grounds. In 1915, the team moved into Braves Field, as the progressed IC became conjunct with their natal Uranus in Cancer, and the progressed MC became conjunct with the Braves natal Moon.
98. A different birthchart is cast for each of the three cities where the team has lived: Boston, Milwaukee and Atlanta. In the Milwaukee chart, the Braves' Aquarius Sun is conjunct to the Ascendant, while the Atlanta birthchart has Venus conjunct to the Ascendant.

the Sun. The Braves of the early 21st Century are a successful modern franchise that consistently contends. Their history includes the proud moment of Hank Aaron breaking Babe Ruth's career home run record, a manifestation of their Aquarian planets. However, much of their long history has been a struggle. This team won several pennants in the 19th Century, but generally experienced hardships in the 20th Century until the 1990s. The history of the Braves franchise has a theme of the Sun dominating the Moon, which has played out in owners exploiting players, ill-treatment of fans, and tragic events experienced by catchers.

Boston Braves
Friday, January 20, 1871 8:20:00 AM
Boston, Massachusetts
Time Zone: 05:00 (EST)
Longitude: 071° W 05' 42"
Latitude: 42° N 20' 48"

This team had a series of names before settling on the "Braves." Originally, they were called the Red Stockings, copying the name of the Cincinnati team. The team has also, over time, been called the Red Caps, the Beaneaters, the Rustlers, the Doves, and the Bees. The

Milwaukee Braves
Friday, January 20, 1871 7:20:00 AM
Milwaukee, Wisconsin
Time Zone: 06:00 (CST)
Longitude: 087° W 56' 42"
Latitude: 43° N 02' 48"

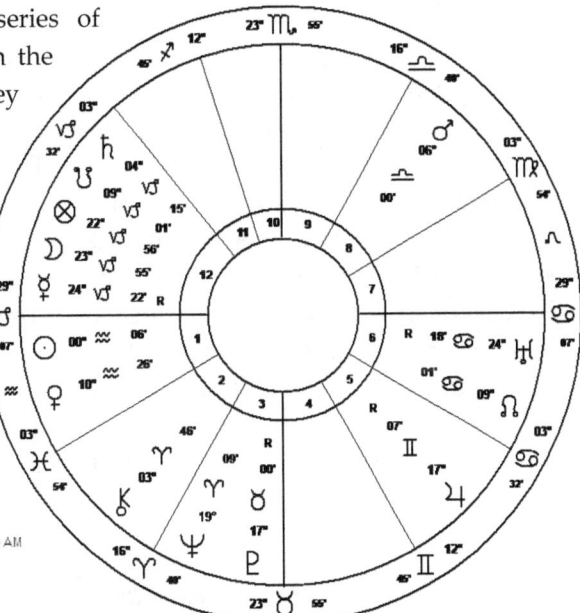

franchise resided in Boston for 81 years, from its birth through the 1952 season. The Braves would play in Milwaukee from 1953 through 1965. They have made Atlanta their home from 1966 to the present.

A balance usually exists between the Sun and Moon in a birthchart. The Sun establishes an identity and grows by asserting itself. The Moon counters the Sun's assertions with emotions and memory. An Aquarius Sun, like that of the Braves, is hyper-rational and future-oriented. It is busy planning new projects and exploring new markets. The Moon will seek to slow the Sun's ambitions and protect that which is organic and homegrown. A Moon normally counters such a Sun with emotional appeals, such as ties to family and heritage. But the Braves' Moon is so afflicted that it can offer little resistance. A Moon is naturally weak when in the sign of Capricorn, but the Braves' Moon is further debilitated by the conjunction of Saturn to the South Node. The Braves' Moon also suffers from an opposition with Uranus, the despositor of the Braves' Sun in Aquarius. All these afflictions form chains around the Moon. The Braves' Moon, for much of the team's history, has been enslaved by the Sun, Saturn, and Uranus. The Moon of a baseball team is manifest in its catcher, its fans, the home field, and the home city. In labor relations, the moon embodies the players as workers in their struggles against management. In the history of the Braves, all of these lunar manifestations have suffered.

Hank Aaron aside, most of the Braves contributions to the history of baseball have come from the owners, rather than the players. Their Sun in Aquarius has given ownership an innovative character. Owners such as Arthur Soden and Ted Turner have been groundbreakers. It was Arthur Soden who invented the reserve clause that bound players to one team. Then, almost 100 years later, it was Ted Turner who finished its dismantling when he signed the first free agents of the 1970s.

The Braves organization introduced the reserve clause to organized sports in 1879.[99] Owner Arthur Soden devised the system by which players were bound to one team for their careers and could not offer their services to other teams. In the early days of the reserve clause, only five players per team could be "reserved." But the number would gradually increase to include all the players of each team. Soden's invention was a response to the loss of important players, specifically George Wright and Jim O'Rourke, who left Boston after the 1878 season to play for the Providence Grays. The reserve clause is an example of the domination of the Braves' Sun over the

---

99. Pietrusza, p. 43. Soden introduced the reserved list on Sept. 29, 1879 at a league meeting in Buffalo, New York, as the Sun at 6 degrees Libra was conjunct the Braves' Mars and square their Saturn.

Moon. In labor relations, the Sun represents ownership, whereas the Moon represents the players as employees. Baseball's reserve clause, which would endure until the 1970s, was an anomaly in the labor law of the United States. Its success in restricting basic rights enjoyed by workers in other professions mirrors the severe afflictions suffered by the Braves' Moon.

The next major innovation by the Braves also strengthened the Sun's subjugation of the Moon in the realm of labor relations. The Braves were the first franchise to buy a player. On February 14, 1887, the Boston franchise purchased the services of Mike "King" Kelly, the most popular player of the late Nineteenth Century. Previously, Kelly had played for the Chicago White Stockings. Fittingly, King Kelly played catcher, the position of the Moon.

The Braves' Moon is in Capricorn, the sign of structure and discipline. Lunar qualities, particularly the emotions—joy, sorrow and anger—desire to flow unfettered. Emotions prefer to follow their whims. Many fans attend games because ballparks are venues where their emotions are allowed freedom, where they can freely verbalize their joys and frustrations. But feelings are not easily expressed when the Moon is in the stodgy sign of Capricorn. This placement often results in emotional blockages and depression. The Braves' Capricorn Moon has often been manifest in frustrated fans, poor attendance, stadium problems, and tragedies involving their catchers.

Bad things would happen with the Braves' Moon in 1894, a year in which Pluto, by solar arc progression, formed a conjunction to the Braves IC. Neptune and Pluto were also conjunct the Braves' IC that year. On January 10, 1894, catcher Charlie Bennett slipped on ice while boarding a moving train. He was subsequently run over by the train, losing his legs. Transits of the day show trouble for the lunar points in the Boston birthchart. Not only were Pluto and Neptune conjunct to the Boston Braves IC of 10 degrees Gemini, but Mercury, in transit at 9 degrees Capricorn, was conjunct the Braves' South Node. Moreover, Saturn, in transit at 24 degrees Libra, was square to the Braves natal Uranus.

The Braves' Moon suffered another calamity on May 16[100] of that year when their home field, the South End Grounds, burned down. The fire began in the right field bleachers when a discarded cigarette ignited peanut shells. The fire was ignored because, at the time it started, a fight broke out on the field. The Boston team, then called the Beaneaters, was

---

100. *http://en.wikipedia.org/wiki/South_End_Grounds*

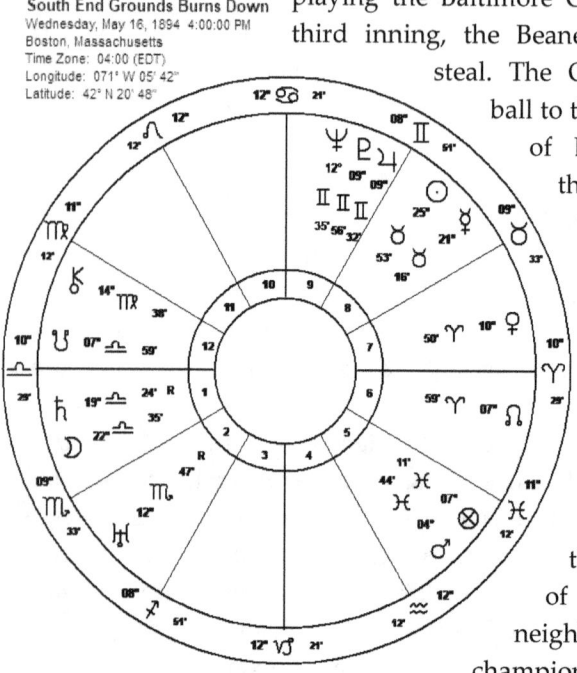

South End Grounds Burns Down
Wednesday, May 16, 1894 4:00:00 PM
Boston, Massachusetts
Time Zone: 04:00 (EDT)
Longitude: 071° W 05' 42"
Latitude: 42° N 20' 48"

playing the Baltimore Orioles. In the top of the third inning, the Beaneaters[101] began a double steal. The Oriole catcher threw the ball to third base. Tommy Tucker of Boston slid safely into third, only to be kicked in the face by Oriole third baseman John McGraw. Tucker, of course, retaliated. With all attention on the fight, the fire was soon out of control. When it was finally extinguished, the fire had destroyed the stadium, 12 acres of buildings in the neighborhood, and the 1893 championship pennant. Transits for the afternoon show Pluto, Neptune, and Jupiter conjunct the IC of the Boston Braves' chart. Mars, generally involved in fires, was positioned 4 degrees Pisces, inconjunct to the Braves' Saturn.

The worst tragedy to involve the franchise occurred on January 19, 1900, when Boston catcher, Marty Bergen, killed his wife, his two children, and himself.[102] The previous summer, a son of Bergen's had died.

Marty Bergen Trajedy
Friday, January 19, 1900 12:00:00 PM
Brookfield, Massachusetts
Time Zone: 05:00 (EST)
Longitude: 072° W 06'
Latitude: 42° N 13'

---

101. In this era, the home team could bat first.
102. Dewey and Acocella, p. 32

The catcher had behaved erratically during the 1899 season, even saying that the players of his team reminded him of his dead son. He often asked for permission to go home to Brookfield, Massachusetts.[103] If permission was denied, he would leave for home anyway. Transits for the day of the slaying include Pluto and the South Node conjunct to the Braves Jupiter in the Fourth House of catchers. Jupiter, usually a benefic, is often involved in excessive acts. Mars and the Sun, at 28 and 29 degrees Capricorn, were conjunct to the Braves' Sun of 0 degrees Aquarius during the slaying.

The Braves afflicted Moon has been felt by the fans. For most of their long history, the Braves were a difficult team to support. Braves' fans endured many second in division finishes in the first half of the 20th Century. The team suffered after the American League placed a team in Boston in 1901. The new AL club, which would eventually be called the Red Sox, soon became the more popular team. Attendance sank and profits lagged for the Braves. The team went into a long period of decline.

In the early part of the Twentieth Century, Braves ownership became notorious for penny pinching. They paid their players poorly, well below the major league average. In 1905, Soden told his new manager, Fred Tenney, "We don't care where you finish, so long as you don't lose money with the team."[104] As a result, Braves fans often witnessed the ignoble sight of Tenney entering the stands during games to retrieve foul balls. A Saturnian manager taking foul balls away from fans is a sad but fitting sight for a team with a Capricorn Moon.

Braves' fans have suffered the worst injury of all: to have their loyalty and affection spurned when the franchise moves. The moves to Milwaukee and to Atlanta are manifestations of the Braves' Moon in opposition to Uranus.[105] The Moon in such a challenging aspect to Uranus indicates a tendency toward moves that are uprooting. The Moon represents one's

---

103. Connie Mack was another catcher from the community of Brookfield. Interestingly, Mack also has a Capricorn Moon. (See Athletics section.)
104. Kaese, p. 111
105. The petition to move from Boston to Milwaukee was approved by the National League on March 13, 1952 with transiting Uranus conjunct the Braves North Node of 9 degrees Cancer and transiting Mercury square to the Nodes from 10 degrees Aries. The first Braves game in Milwaukee occurred April 14, 1953 at County Stadium as transiting Jupiter was conjunct the 24 Taurus IC of the new Milwaukee chart. The machinations of the Braves' move from Milwaukee to Atlanta occurred between 1964 and 1966. The absentee ownership, headed by William Bartholomay, was not committed to the city of Milwaukee (Eckhouse, pp. 49-50). When the Braves played their first exhibition game in Atlanta on April 9, 1965, transiting Jupiter would be conjunct the IC of the Atlanta birthchart. A year later, when they played their first official game on April 12, 1966, the transiting North Node would be conjunct the IC of the new Atlanta birthchart.

home environment, and Uranus brings radical and uprooting dislocation.

The Braves Moon is conjunct to Mercury. At its earliest, this aspect was embodied by George and Harry Wright, the brothers who played on the 1869 and 1870 Cincinnati teams. Mercury rules siblings. Harry Wright had managed the Cincinnati Red Stockings teams of 1869 and 1870. His brother George Wright, a shortstop, was considered the best player of the era. The brothers joined the newly formed Boston Red Stockings in 1871. Harry Wright became the manager, the position represented by the Moon's sign of Capricorn. Mercury also rules pitching. More than 100 years later, the Braves Moon-Mercury conjunction became manifest in a team based upon solid starting pitchers. In the 1990s, the arms of Greg Maddox, John Smoltz and Tom Glavine anchored the Braves pitching, providing a staff with the Capricorn qualities of consistency and dependability.

Aquarius is a sign with a great social conscience. Although the early years of the Braves show an absence on such fronts, the Braves were the first professional team in Boston with an African American player.[106] The Braves broke ground for civil rights in Boston, a city with a history of difficult race relations. Sam "Jet" Jethro made his debut as Boston's first African-American professional athlete on April 21, 1950. Jethro batted one-for-three in a game that would be halted in the eighth inning because of rain. Thunder and lightning, which are Aquarian and Uranian manifestations, also occurred during the game.[107] Uranus manifests in both electricity and the homerun.[108] The game

Jet Jethro's Debut
Friday, April 21, 1950 2:00:00 PM
Boston, Massachusetts
Time Zone: 05:00 (EST)
Longitude: 071° W 05' 42"
Latitude: 42° N 20' 48"

---

106 Chuck Cooper would be the first African-American player for the Celtics, later, in 1950.
107 Nowlin, Bill: sabr.org "April 21, 1950: A barrier partially falls: Sam Jethroe's first game in Boston" (*https://sabr.org/gamesproj/game/april-21-1950-barrier-partially-falls-sam-jethroes-first-game-boston*)
108 See Section I: Chapter 5.

occurred under transits that emphasized this energy. Uranus at 1 degrees Cancer, the Sun at 1 degree Taurus and Jupiter at 1 degree Pisces, all made aspects to the Braves natal Sun in Aquarius. Interestingly, Sam Jethro has the same birthday as the Braves, January 20, which makes their natal Suns conjunct to each other and suggests a shared destiny. On the day of his first game, both he and the Braves would undergo the same Uranian transit to their natal Suns.

Twenty-four years later, Hank Aaron hit his 715th homerun, breaking Babe Ruth's career homerun record. The record was broken at 9:07 EDT[109] on the night of April 8, 1974. The Sun, in transit at 19 degrees Aries, was exactly conjunct to the Braves' natal Neptune and square to the Braves natal Uranus in Cancer. This transit directed the Sun's energy to Aaron, who played left field, the Uranus position. Aaron, a black man who was subjected to racial death threats, broke the most cherished record in baseball. The birthchart of Hank Aaron, like that of Babe Ruth, has the Aquarius emphasis of a homerun hitter. His chart has the Sun, Mercury, Venus, Saturn and the North Node in the sign of Aquarius. However, to break Babe Ruth's record involved more than the Aquarian manifestation of the homerun. It was also a milestone for the advancement of racial equality, an Aquarian cause. The Braves, with their Sun and Venus in Aquarius, were a suitable vehicle for this historic event.

Hank Aaron 715
Monday, April 8, 1974 9:07:00 PM
Atlanta, Georgia
Time Zone: 04:00 (EDT)
Longitude: 084° W 23' 06"
Latitude: 33° N 46' 24"

Aaron was not a showboat Leo-type player who drew attention to himself. Instead, he was a consistent player who amassed solid statistics over a long career. His consistency was an embodiment of the Sun conjunct to Saturn in his birthchart. Aaron nobly withstood the pressure and the racial death threats that came with his pursuit of Ruth's record. Aaron's highly evolved Saturn gave him his strength. Hank Aaron also spoke out on

---

109 Eckhouse, p. 55

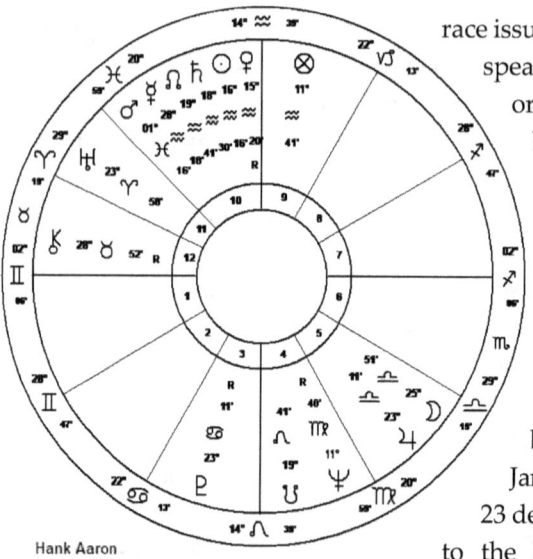

Hank Aaron
Monday, February 5, 1934 12:00:00 PM
Mobile, Alabama
Time Zone: 06:00 (CST)
Longitude: 088° W 04' 36"
Latitude: 30° N 41' 36"

race issues,[110] as an Aquarius will likely speak his mind. Aaron criticized organized baseball and the Braves franchise in particular for not hiring African-Americans as managers and front office personnel.

Ted Turner purchased the Braves from William Bartholomay in January of 1976. The sale was approved by the Major Leagues on January 14, 1976[111], as the Sun, at 23 degrees Capricorn, was conjunct to the Braves Moon and Mercury. Instead of repeating the Braves' usual patterns of exploiting players and neglecting fans, the sale of the Braves to Turner would be a windfall for the Braves' Moon, proving favorable to both fans and players. Turner soon angered other baseball owners by signing free-agent players. He signed pitcher Andy Messersmith, a free agent player, on April 10, 1976[112]. Messersmith had been blackballed by the owners for spearheading the challenge for free agency. When Turner signed Messersmith to a multi-year deal, Pluto was in transit at 10 degrees Libra and square to the Braves Lunar Nodes. Mars, in transit at 11 degrees Cancer, was conjunct to the Braves North Node.

When Turner signed Messersmith, he defied not only the baseball establishment but the Braves' history of shackling players. The signing of Messersmith was a redemptive moment for the Braves' Sun, a deed by a Braves owner that restored balance between the owners and players. The North Node of the Moon[113] contains possibilities for growth and rewards. Nevertheless, for generations, the Braves South Node in Capricorn, with its conjunction to Saturn, kept the lunar energy mired in the past and blocked the flow of energy in the direction of their Cancer North Node. When the

---

110 Dewey and Acocella, p. 3
111 Eckhouse, p. 56
112 Eckhouse, p. 56
113. A polarity exists between the North and South Nodes of the Moon. The South Node represents the past, while the North Node represents the future and opportunities for growth. Planets conjunct the South Node can bring blocks toward such opportunities.

Braves signed the first free-agent players, they opened the floodgates of their North Node. Today, the Braves routinely sign free agents to highly paid contracts. They are among the teams with the highest salaries in professional sports, a trend that is the opposite of their early days. Far away from the poverty they endured in Boston, they reap the rewards of their North Node as a thriving franchise that regularly contends.

Teams such as the Braves, with a Saturn and Capricorn emphasis, excel in extra-inning games and comebacks. The longest baseball game on record locked the Braves against the Brooklyn Dodgers for 26 innings. The game occurred May 1, 1920, with Saturn in transit at 4 degrees Virgo and trine to the Braves natal Saturn. Venus, in transit at 24 degrees Aries, was in square to the Braves' natal Moon and Mercury in Capricorn. When it became too dark to play, the game ended in a 1-1 tie. Joe Oeschger pitched the entire game for Boston. Leon Cadore of Brooklyn matched him for all 26 innings.

When they appear hopelessly out of it, the Braves have the Saturnian ability to come from behind and win. The 1914 "Miracle Braves" pulled off arguably the most stunning comeback ever by a pennant winner. Their story lacks the dramatic homerun ending of Bobby Thomson and the 1951 Giants, but the Braves' 1914 comeback, in terms of movement in the standings, is more of an accomplishment. The 1914 season began poorly for the Braves. In mid-July, they sat in the National League cellar, and yet their record from July 4th onward was an astounding 68-19. Down the stretch, the Miracle Braves beat out the powerhouse New York Giants for the pennant. In the World Series, they quickly swept the Philadelphia Athletics. A more recent example of a Braves' Capricorn comeback occurred in the 1996 League Championship Series against St Louis. The Braves were down three games to zero before winning the next four games and the National League pennant.

The Braves have four astrological bodies in the sign of Capricorn: Saturn, the South Node, the Moon and Mercury. They have an equal number in Aquarius: the Sun, Venus, Ascendant, and Venus. Although the Braves' Capricorn Moon has suffered, the team's Capricorn energy has also supplied the ballast necessary for the team's Aquarian projects to become institutionalized. The history of the Braves demonstrates how the conservative force of Capricorn and the radical force of Aquarius are both present when enduring social change occurs.

THE DODGERS

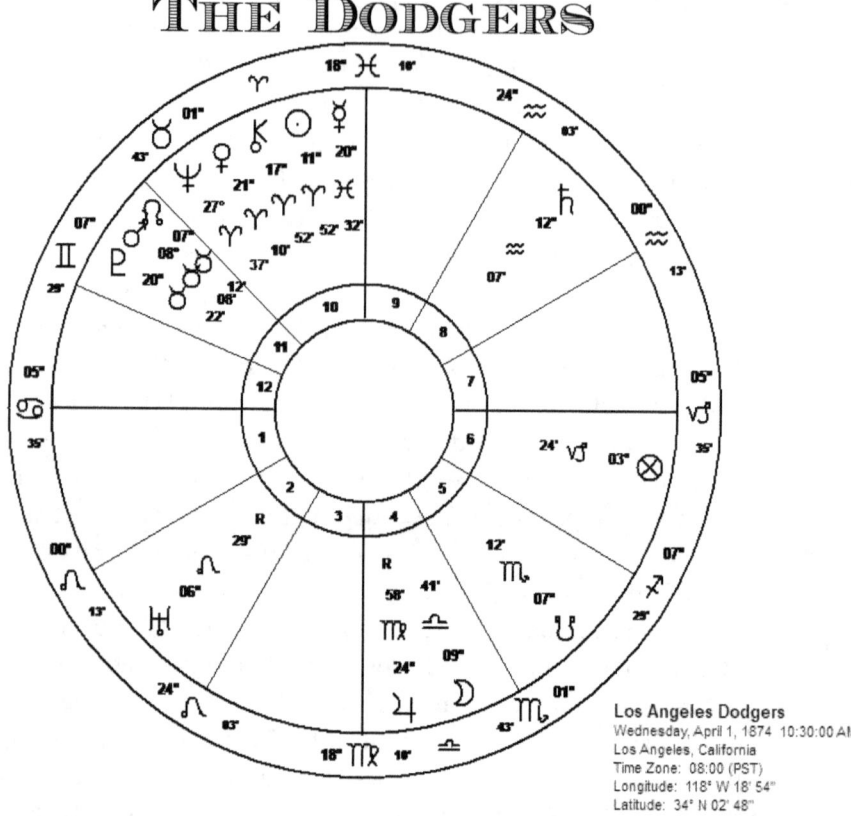

Los Angeles Dodgers
Wednesday, April 1, 1874 10:30:00 AM
Los Angeles, California
Time Zone: 08:00 (PST)
Longitude: 118° W 18' 54"
Latitude: 34° N 02' 48"

The Dodgers were born April 1, 1874[114] at 1:30 pm[115] EDT. They lived in Brooklyn until 1958 when they moved across the country to Los Angeles. They were born on a spring full moon with the Sun in Aries opposite the Moon in Libra, an aspect that manifested in the passion of Brooklyn fans. The birthchart also has Saturn in Aquarius in opposition to Uranus in Leo, which gave Dodgers' ownership the forward-thinking ability to have Jackie Robinson integrate the game.

The love affair between the Dodgers and the community of Brooklyn

---

114. I came across this date somewhere in the San Francisco Public Library during the early days of my research. When I wrote the date in my notebook, I did not consider it a serious possibility for the Dodgers' birthday, since it seemed too early a year. April 1, 1874 has proven to be the correct date, but I have been frustrated in my attempts to relocate the source of this date.

115. Rectification Note: In 1898, a progressed Moon by solar arc would be conjunct an IC of 6 degrees Scorpio, the year the team moved into Washington Park. In 1913, their natal Jupiter, progressed by solar arc, would be conjunct an IC of 6 Scorpio, the year the team moved into Ebbetts Field. In 1958, their natal Saturn, progressed by solar arc, would be opposite an IC of 5 degrees Scorpio, the year the team moved to Los Angeles.

has been called the most passionate love affair ever between fans and a team.[116] Their intensity was so great that, in 1938, a Dodger fan actually murdered two people who had been needling him about his team's poor showing.[117] The emotion between the Dodgers and their Brooklyn fans was an incarnation of the Libra Full Moon within the Dodgers' birthchart. The Dodgers' chart holds an intense opposition between the Sun in Aries and the Moon in Libra. The masculine Sun is in the masculine sign of Aries, while the feminine Moon is located in the feminine sign of Libra. The Dodgers' birthchart is both very male and very female. The natural attraction between the Sun and Moon is intensified when these planets are placed in the opposite signs of Aries and Libra. In this opposition, the Moon is represented in the fans, while the Sun represents the team in its relationship to its fans.

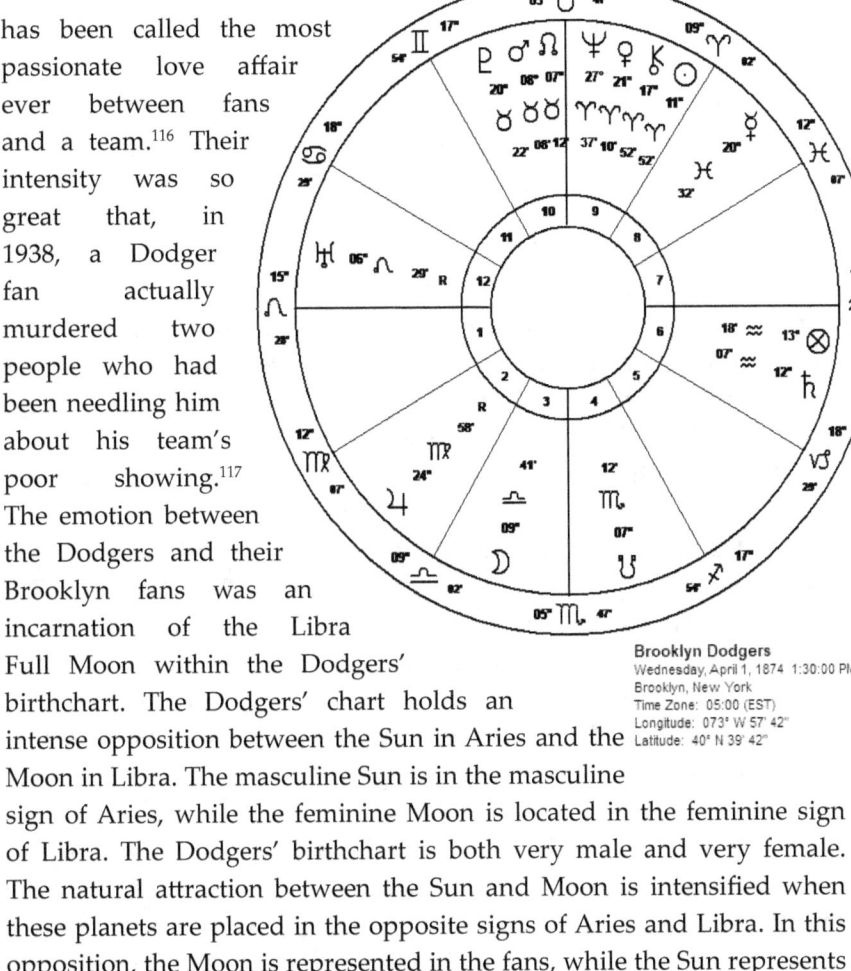

Brooklyn Dodgers
Wednesday, April 1, 1874 1:30:00 PM
Brooklyn, New York
Time Zone: 05:00 (EST)
Longitude: 073° W 57' 42"
Latitude: 40° N 39' 42"

In their Brooklyn chart, the Dodgers' Moon is located in the Third House of communication. As the Moon is the vessel for emotions, a Third House lunar placement lets those emotions be expressed rather openly. Brooklyn fans were famous for their verbosity. Libra is usually a civil sign, known for fairness and politeness. But the Moon in the Brooklyn Dodgers' chart is accented by a Fourth House Scorpio cusp. Likewise, Mercury, the ruling planet of the 3rd House, was located in the Eighth House. These aspects gave the Brooklyn Moon a thick Scorpio accent. This Moon had a very sharp tongue. Brooklyn fans were notorious for the heaps of abuse they dumped onto opposing teams and umpires. But more significant was

---

116. Bjarkman, p. 74
117. Dodgers fan Robert Joyce murdered two people in a Brooklyn cafe on July 12, 1938. (Cliff Gewecke, *Day by Day in Dodgers History*, p. 46)

the abuse that Dodgers' fans poured onto their own team. Much like a wife who never stops insulting her husband, they routinely referred to their own team as "Dem Bums."

It is interesting to explore the abuse from the husband's perspective. The Ninth House Aries Sun identified as a warrior who traveled to distant lands to do battle. He usually returned victorious, but he often lost the final battle. He just couldn't beat the barbarians from across the town, the hated Yankees. At the end of a season, he just couldn't please his wife who always grumbled he had let her down again. She would throw harsher insults with every lost World Series. After many years of abuse, the insults took their toll on the relationship. Perhaps they made him question his Aries masculinity. He was wrong to leave her, but in the end, he did.

The name "Dodgers" is a shortening of "Trolley Dodgers," an early name for the team. At the turn of the Twentieth Century, a maze of trolley cars and tracks operated near Ebbetts Field. A Brooklyn pedestrian needed to be skilled at dodging trolleys. At first observation, the act of dodging is antithetical to the basic Aries act of charging. To dodge is to bounce away, to elude. An Aries charges into battle. It is the pacifist who avoids battle, who avoids war and dodges the draft. A dodger avoids confrontation, whether from war or from a streetcar barreling in one's direction. Another paradox of the word "dodge" and the sign of Aries exists within an image of Dodge automobiles. The Dodge auto company uses a ram, the Aries animal, as its emblem. Their commercials advertise that "Dodge trucks are ram tough," and use an image of two rams butting horns.[118] Dodge manufactured a car called the "Dodge Charger," which also appears as an oxymoron since one cannot both dodge and charge. But the paradox is solved when one considers that both acts, to dodge and to charge, require quick bursts of energy. Aries energy is employed in such spurts. In both of these actions, to confront head on and to deftly step aside, one moves quickly from a state of repose into a state of action. One who dodges does not necessarily flee. A dodger can cleverly step aside, not from fear, but to cause his opponent to use his own force against himself. This is the strategy behind the martial art of aikido. By skillfully dodging, one can defeat a larger opponent. Indeed, the Brooklyn Dodgers generally identified as the underdogs against larger and more powerful opponents, notably the Giants and Yankees.

---

118. Such Aries images are more common to the game of football than baseball. The Rams football team, which plays in Los Angeles like the Dodgers, has a ram horn as their insignia. In football, the offensive and defensive lines charge into each other much like Rams butting horns.

The Dodgers

The Dodgers have had other names, including the Superbas, the Bridegrooms and the Robins. "Bridegrooms" was a suitable mascot. In 1890, six players on the team were newlywed, prompting Brooklyn sports writers to christen them the Bridegrooms.[119] The name did not stick, but Bridegrooms was a well-tailored name for a team with the passion of an Aries Sun and a Libra Moon.

In a comic touch, the Dodgers were born on April Fools' Day. There is a goofy quality to the Dodgers. In the 1920s and 30s, they were known as "the Daffiness Boys" for their absent-minded bonehead plays. A famous goofball play occurred on August 15, 1926. Babe Herman hit a sure double, but, instead of stopping at second base, he ran all the way to third. When he made it to third, he found two other Dodger runners, Dazzy Vance and Chick Fewster, already there.[120] In 1983, second baseman Steve Sax mysteriously lost his ability to throw to first base. His fellow infielder third baseman Pedro Guerrero also lacked consistency, but he made up for it with his wit. Manager Tommy Lasorda quizzed Guerrero on a hypothetical throwing situation:

Three Dodgers On a Base
Sunday, August 15, 1926 3:00:00 PM
Brooklyn, New York
Time Zone: 04:00 (EDT)
Longitude: 073° W 57' 42"
Latitude: 40° N 39' 42"

Lasorda: The tying run's on, one out in the ninth. What are you thinking?
Guerrero: I'm thinking, don't hit the ball to me!
Lasorda: C'mon Pedro. What else are you thinking?
Guerrero: You really want to know?
Lasorda: Yes.

---

119. Dewey and Acocella, p. 77
120. This play occurred on Aug 15, 1926 (Gewecke, p. 59)—oddly during a Mars return that also included an opposition from the Moon in Scorpio and a square from Mercury in Leo. The Dodgers' natal Pluto of 20 degrees Taurus, the planet of third base, was also heavily aspected, receiving an opposition from Saturn in Scorpio, squares from the Sun and Neptune conjunct in Leo, and Jupiter in Aquarius.

Guerrero: I'm thinking, don't hit the ball to Sax![121]

This goofiness is an embodiment of the Dodgers' Mercury in Pisces in opposition to Jupiter in Virgo. Mercury, which rules common sense reasoning, becomes afflicted when placed in the murky sign of Pisces. Similarly, a Jupiter opposition to Mercury throws off sense perceptions. Judgments of distance and proportion become difficult to make accurately. The perceptions needed by a fielder to judge the trajectory of a moving ball are distorted by expansive Jupiter.

There is a less conspicuous manifestation of the Dodgers' Mercury, one suitably hidden and watery, like the sign of Pisces. As Mercury rules the pitcher, one manifestation of Mercury in the watery sign of Pisces is the spitball. The Dodgers have had spitball pitchers[122] on their staff that included Burleigh Grimes, who threw the spitter in the 1920s. Grimes won 271 games in his career, and he was inducted into the Hall of Fame. In the 1950s, Preacher Roe also mastered the spitball.

Jackie Robinson wore Dodger blue when he broke the color line. The Brooklyn Dodgers' were a team well suited to orchestrate such an important moment in history. The Dodgers' birthchart does not have an obvious Aquarian and Uranus emphasis, but it does have Uranus in opposition to Saturn, as well as a Uranus in square to the MC of the Brooklyn chart. These aspects brought a social consciousness to the front office. Branch Rickey, the Dodgers' general manager and the architect of Robinson's integration of Major League baseball, made use of the Uranus aspect for a social cause. Jackie Robinson, like Hank Aaron, had multiple planets in the sign of Aquarius. Robinson's birthchart has the Sun, Moon, Venus,, and Uranus in Aquarius. Robinson's Uranus and Venus are in opposition to his Saturn in Leo. An aspect between Uranus and Saturn can indicate an historical figure, one who employs

Jackie Robinson
Friday, January 31, 1919 12:00:00 PM
Cairo, Georgia
Time Zone: 05:00 (EST)
Longitude: 084° W 13'
Latitude: 30° N 53'

---

121. http://www.futilityinfielder.com

122. The spitball was banned in 1920 with Saturn in transit in Virgo, the sign opposite Pisces.

the energy of Saturn to manifest a Uranian cause.

Jackie Robinson made his major league debut on April 15, 1947, with the Moon poetically in Aquarius. That afternoon, Robinson would play first base,[123] the Neptune position. As all eyes were on Robinson, the stars were aligned to showcase his position. Neptune, the planet of first base, was in transit at 9 degrees Libra and conjunct to the Dodgers' Moon. Saturn in transit at 2 degrees Leo was conjunct to Pluto in transit at 11 degrees Leo. Their midpoint of 6 Leo was exactly conjunct to the Dodgers' Uranus of 6 degrees Leo. In the Brooklyn chart, their natal Uranus resided in the 12th House, another correspondence with first base.[124]

Jackie Robinson Debut
Tuesday, April 15, 1947 2:00:00 PM
Brooklyn, New York
Time Zone: 04:00 (EDT)
Longitude: 073° W 57' 42"
Latitude: 40° N 39' 42"

The Dodgers left Brooklyn after the 1957 season. Two key aspects within the Dodgers' birthchart set up the heartbreak of Brooklyn. In the Brooklyn Dodgers' chart, Uranus was square to the IC and to the lunar nodes. Hard aspects from Uranus to the Moon, the IC—or, the lunar nodes—frequently manifest in uprooting moves. The Brooklyn Dodgers had as loyal a fan base as any team, yet Walter O'Malley saw more money to be made in Los Angeles and moved the team. Negotiations for the move to Los Angeles occurred in 1957, while the birthchart of the Dodgers underwent a Uranus return. Uranus, in transit through Leo, formed a conjunction to its natal position in the Dodger chart. There, Uranus also repeated its square to the Brooklyn Dodger's IC and lunar nodes, thus uprooting the team.

The other aspect that set the stage for the move from Brooklyn is that the Dodgers' Moon is conjunct to the fixed star of Vindemiatrix. Aspects with certain stars are considered to bring major misfortune. Vindemiatrix has been called the "Widow Maker."[125] Although the community of Brooklyn

---

123. In seasons to follow, Robinson would play second base, third base and left field.
124. On April 15, 1947, Jackie Robinson's natal Uranus underwent a sextile from the Sun in Aries and a square from Jupiter in Scorpio.
125. Robson, Vivian E., *Fixed Stars and Constellations in Astrology* (1923), pp. 214-216.

was not literally widowed, it was devastated. Another calamity involving the Dodgers Moon and Vindemiatrix was suffered by the community of Chavez Ravine, a Mexican-American neighborhood in Los Angeles that was entirely demolished for the construction of Dodger Stadium. Both the abandonment of Brooklyn and the destruction of Chavez Ravine reflect the ruthless energy of Vindemiatrix.

In the winter between the Dodgers' last fall in Brooklyn and their first spring in Los Angeles, catcher Roy Campanella suffered an automobile accident that left him paralyzed. It was cruelly poetic that the catcher, who shares the Moon with the fans and the home city, would never play in Los Angeles. Campanella's accident was another blow in the terrible drama of the Dodgers' betrayal of Brooklyn.

Roy Campanella Accident
Monday, January 27, 1958 3:34:00 AM
Glen Cove, NY
Time Zone: 05:00 (EST)
Longitude: 073° W 38'
Latitude: 40° N 52'

Another manifestation of the Dodgers' Moon in Brooklyn became devastated. Tragedy befell, not only the fans and the community of Brooklyn, but the catcher, as well. The accident occurred on the evening of January 26, 1958[126] while the lunar nodes were reversed from their original north and south positions. The North Node was exactly conjunct to the Brooklyn IC of 6 degrees Scorpio. The Sun, in transit at 6 degrees

Roy Campanella
Saturday, November 19, 1921 12:00:00 PM
Philadelphia, Pennsylvania
Time Zone: 05:00 (EST)
Longitude: 075° W 09' 48"
Latitude: 39° N 59' 18"

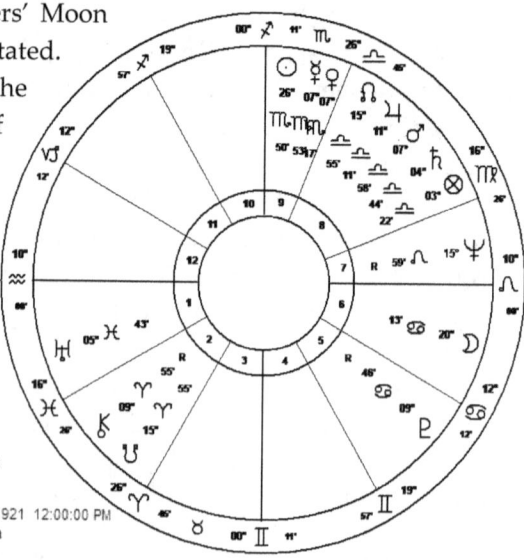

---

126. *Boys of Summer*, p. 329.

Aquarius, was not only square to the lunar nodes, but conjunct to the Dodgers' Saturn and opposite to the Dodgers' Uranus. Uranus is often present in accidents. Campanella's own birthchart also received difficult transits on the night of his accident. His Mercury and Venus were conjunct at 7 degrees Scorpio, which suffered squares from the Sun in Aquarius the night of the accident. Campanella's Mercury and Venus were conjunct to the Dodgers' Brooklyn IC, an aspect that demonstrates how deeply his fate was tied in with the Brooklyn team. Campanella also had four planets in Libra—Saturn, Mars, Jupiter and the North Node—all conjunct to the Dodgers' Moon.

The death of Roy Campanella also occurred under highly relevant transits. When the Dodgers moved to Los Angeles, their Rising Sign shifted from Leo to Cancer. With a Cancer Ascendant, catchers became a more visible part of the Dodgers organization. When Roy Campanella died on June 26, 1993, the Sun, in transit at 5 degrees Cancer, was exactly conjunct to the Los Angeles Dodgers' Ascendant. Also, Jupiter and the Moon, both in transit at 5 degrees Libra, were conjunct to each other and square to the Sun and the Dodgers' Ascendant. Venus, in transit at 20 degrees Taurus, was conjunct the Dodgers' Pluto, the planet of death. The news of Campanella's death was announced during the 8th inning of a Dodgers game against the Cubs. The Dodgers, playing at home, were rallying from a 4-1 deficit. As the news was announced, Mike Piazza, then a rookie catcher, hit a single to right field. Piazza would soon score what became the winning run.[127] Even on the day of his death, Roy Campanella was an inspirational figure. It is poetic that Mike Piazza, a rookie on his way to establishing himself in the line of great Dodger catchers, would score a winning run soon after Campanella's death was announced. Mike Piazza would also become elected to the Hall of Fame.

Upon moving to Los Angeles, the Dodgers' birthchart underwent

---

127. *Los Angeles Times*, July 27, 1993, p. C1

a more radical change than the birthchart of the Braves had in either of their moves. While the Braves maintained an Aquarius Ascendant in each of their three home cities, the Dodgers' Ascendant would shift from Leo to Cancer upon moving to the West Coast. Mercury would shift from its Eighth House placement in the Brooklyn birthchart into a conjunction with the MC. Saturn, in the Sixth House in Brooklyn's chart, swung into the Eighth House within the Los Angeles chart.

As Cancer is the sign of families, the Cancer Ascendant became reflected in an image of the Dodgers family[128] that embraced all of its employees. Until the sale to News Corp in 1998, the Los Angeles Dodgers ownership would remain in the hands of the O'Malley family for forty years. The franchise also enjoyed stability within its management. Walter O'Malley handed down control to his son Peter in 1970. On the field, Walter Alston managed the team for 18 years, to be followed by Tommy Lasorda, who managed for 20 years.

The Cancer Ascendant is also embodied in Dodger Stadium, a ballpark with an unusually large foul territory. The catcher has a rare advantage in Dodger Stadium where he has lots of room to catch foul pop flies. Although Roy Campanella would never play at Dodger Stadium, catchers have excelled in Los Angeles. The Dodgers have enjoyed a succession of outstanding catchers since they came to Los Angeles that include Johnny Roseboro, Steve Yeager, Mike Scocia and Mike Piazza.

An odd manifestation of the Cancer Ascendant was the phenomenon of Wally Moon. Before the opening of Dodger Stadium, the team played in the Los Angeles Coliseum from 1958 through 1961. The baseball dimensions in the Coliseum included a right field fence that was a far 440 feet from home plate. The left field fence, however, was only 251 away. To prevent average pop flies from floating for home runs, a 42-foot fence was raised. As a left handed batter, Wally Moon was at a disadvantage attempting to pull a home run to the far away right field fence, but he figured out how to hit high fly balls that would drop over the left field screen a short distance away. These high but short fly balls that dropped for home runs became known as "Moon Shots." The apparition of the Moon Shot, in a home ballpark, from a player named Moon, is a bizarre but profound manifestation of a Cancer Ascendant.

The move to Los Angeles would improve the aspects to the Dodgers' Mercury. As Mercury became conjunct the MC and Saturn left the Sixth House, the Dodgers pitching blossomed. In Brooklyn, a lumbering Sixth

---

128. Dewey and Acocella, p. 284

House Saturn hampered the pitching staff, but in Los Angeles, the Dodgers have had great success with pitchers. The birthchart of the Los Angeles Dodgers has Mercury in an elevated position, in the Tenth House and conjunct to the MC. Moreover, Saturn is no longer in the Sixth House but, rather, in the Eighth House. The fruits of their elevated Mercury include not only their pennants and World Series wins, but Hall-of-Fame pitchers Sandy Koufax, Don Drysdale and Don Sutton. There have been other great pitchers that have played for the Los Angeles Dodgers who are not in the Hall of Fame. These include Claude Osteen, Fernando Valenzuela, Orel Hershiser, and Hideo Nomo.

The Dodgers are one of baseball's most storied franchises. Their birthchart mirrors their roles as underdogs, revolutionaries, goofballs, and champions.

THE DETROIT TIGERS

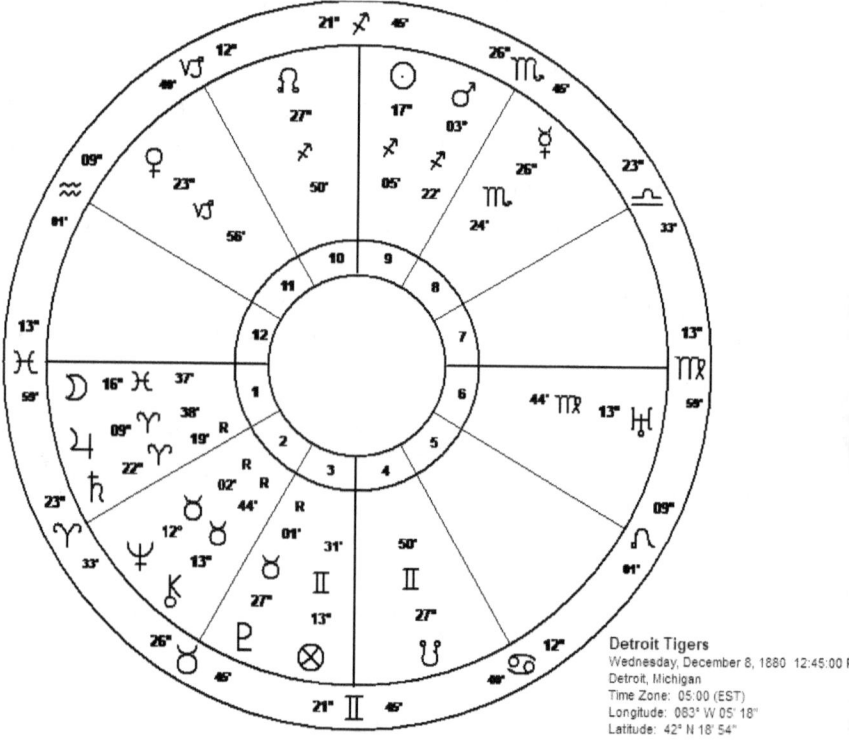

Detroit Tigers
Wednesday, December 8, 1880 12:45:00
Detroit, Michigan
Time Zone: 05:00 (EST)
Longitude: 083° W 05' 18"
Latitude: 42° N 18' 54"

The Tigers franchise was born on December 8, 1880,[129] at 12:46 pm EST.[130] Before the transfers of the Brewers to the National League and the Astros to the American League, the Tigers were the only team to have been a member of both the National and American Leagues. The birthchart of the Tigers has a first quarter square between the Sun in Sagittarius and the Moon in Pisces. Three planets in the First House — the Moon, Jupiter and Saturn — reflect the fierceness of the franchise. The team's fervor is embodied in its mascot, its fans, its managers, and its most famous player, Ty Cobb. The excellence of Detroit's hitting is an

---

129. *Spaulding's Baseball Guide*, 1881, pp. 89-90.
130. This author's rectified chart of the franchise has a birth time of 12:46 pm EST, giving the chart an Ascendant of 14 Pisces and an IC in the 21st degree of Gemini. The 14 degrees Pisces Ascendant, when progressed by solar arc, enters the sign of Aries in 1896, the year the team received the name of Tigers and went into the sign of Aries. A 14-degree Pisces Ascendant, when progressed to 1905, the year Ty Cobb joined the team, becomes conjunct the Tigers First House Jupiter. When Tiger Stadium opened in 1912, the progressed IC of 21 Gemini became opposed to the Tigers' Venus. When Comerica Park opened in 2000, the progressed IC was opposite the Tigers' natal Saturn.

embodiment of the Tigers' Sun and Mars in Sagittarius, the sign of the batter. The Tigers' Pisces Moon has given the Tigers a series of outstanding first basemen in their long history.

On the same day that the Detroit franchise was born and admitted to the National League, the Cincinnati team was booted from the National League. The Reds were kicked out for serving liquor at their ballpark and for playing games on Sunday, and the city of Detroit was chosen to replace Cincinnati in the National League.[131] The birthcharts of the Tigers and Reds have an interesting tension between them. The Tigers' Sun and Moon are positioned at 17 degrees Sagittarius and nearly 17 degrees Pisces. These planets form oppositions and squares with the Sun and Moon of the Reds, which are located at 17 degrees Virgo and 16 degrees Gemini. The challenging aspects between the luminaries of these teams are an interesting reminder that Detroit once replaced Cincinnati in the National League.

The early Detroit team of the National League was called "the Wolverines." They would win the National League pennant in 1887 and defeat St Louis in that year's World Series. However, after their fifth place finish in 1888, financial difficulties hit the franchise. Many of the Detroit players were sold to other teams. The Wolverines then withdrew from the National League. A Detroit team played the following two years in the International Association, a minor league. This Detroit team won the 1889 and 1890 International Association championships, but, after 1890, the Detroit team drops out of history for three years.[132] Perhaps the team either played in semi-pro leagues or did not take the field at all.

On November 20, 1893, the Western League was organized in Sioux City, Iowa. The Western League[133] was a minor league that had a business relationship with the major leagues to develop their players. A team representing Detroit joined the Western League that day.[134] This Detroit team would maintain the same astrological chart as the original National League Wolverines. On the date of the Western League's birth, the Sun, positioned at 28 degrees Scorpio, formed an opposition to the Detroit Pluto of 27 degrees Taurus. Quite possibly, the Detroit franchise had been dormant for the three years missing from the history books, and their resurrection occurred on the day the Western League was born. Pluto is the planet of death and regeneration. Eight years later, in 1901, the Western League shed its minor league status and metamorphosed into

---

131. Dewey and Acocella, p. 230.
132. Lieb, Frederick, *The Detroit Tigers*, pp. 18-19
133. See Western League chapter.
134. Lindberg, Richard, "Chicago White Sox: Second Class in the Second City," p. 55.

the American League. Detroit, which had played its first eight seasons in the National League, would become an original member of the American League.

There is a fierce and aggressive quality to the Detroit team that is embodied not only in its mascot the Tiger, but also in its most famous player, Ty Cobb. This fierceness is a reflection of various aspects in the team's birthchart. Mars and Mercury are conjunct and opposite to Pluto. The team also has three planets in the First House: the Moon, Jupiter and Saturn. First House planets bring an assertive energy. Although the Tigers have Pisces Rising, an aspect that often results in a passive personality, any weak appearance is negated by the Tigers' Pisces Moon just two degrees from the Ascendant. The Tigers also have Jupiter and Saturn in the First House. Both these planets are in the aggressive sign of Aries.

Ty Cobb
Saturday, December 18, 1886 1:20:00 PM
The Narrows, Georgia
Time Zone: 05:00 (EST)
Longitude: 085° W 38'
Latitude: 34° N 26'

The Detroit team became christened the Tigers in 1896, when its Ascendant of 14 Pisces progressed by solar arc entered the sign of Aries, the fiercest sign of the zodiac. That year, the team received new uniforms with black and yellow-brown stripes on their socks. Fans and reporters soon began calling them "the Tigers" in reference to their socks.[135] The mascot of a large, pouncing feline is a well-chosen one for a team with three First House planets. The earlier mascot of Wolverines also suited Detroit's muscular First House. A wolverine is an aggressive animal known to be stronger and fiercer than one would expect from its size.

Saturn is one of the planets in the Tigers' First House. This Saturn is also in the sign of Aries. As Saturn is embodied in a team's manager, this First House Aries Saturn has given the Tigers a series of brawling aggressive managers. Jim Leyland and Sparky Anderson, who managed

---

135. Leib, p. 22

the Tigers from 1980 through 1995, do not fit the mold of the typical Tigers manager. Detroit teams have historically had Billy Martin-type managers, aggressive boisterous skippers who berate umpires and opposing teams. Hughie Jennings managed the Tigers from 1907 to 1920. Earlier, Jennings had played with John McGraw on the rowdy Baltimore Orioles of the 1890s. Jennings managed the Tigers not from the bench, but from the third base coach's box, where he regularly displayed his bile by yelling and blowing a whistle.[136]

George Stallings is another example of a Tigers manager in the Saturn in Aries mold. Stallings, who would later lead the "Miracle Braves" of 1914, managed the Tigers in the Western League and in their first AL season of 1901. Fred Lieb described Stallings not only as "The Dr. Jekyll and Mr. Hyde of baseball," but as profane and crazy. "He probably was the most handsome manager ever to get into evening clothes. In that attire, he was a suave, cultured Southern gentleman. However, in his baseball clothes, whether he wore a uniform, as he did in Detroit, or civilian bench attire, as he did later in Boston, he was often a raving maniac."[137] Ty Cobb, who also personified the Saturn-in- Aries style, managed the Tigers from 1921 to 1926, and Billy Martin himself held the Tigers' reigns from 1971 through 1973.

The Tigers were the first baseball team to be born with a Sun in Sagittarius,[138] the sign of the batter. With not only the Sun in Sagittarius, but also Mars and the North Node in the sign of the batter, the Tigers have excelled at hitting. The Tigers also have Jupiter, the dispositor of Sagittarius, in the First House, a placement that further strengthens their Sagittarian emphasis. The Tigers are a team of consistently good hitters. More batting titles have been won by Detroit hitters than by any other American League team.[139] The birthchart of Ty Cobb, arguably the best hitter in the history of the game, has the Sun in Sagittarius conjunct to the Tigers' North Node. Ty Cobb won nine consecutive batting titles from 1907 to 1915 and retired with a record career batting average of .367.

Although Ty Cobb is the most famous of the Detroit hitters, there have been other great Detroit hitters in addition to Cobb. Sam Thompson, who batted .372 in 1887, was the first batter to have 200 hits in a single season. Sam Crawford, an outfielder elected to the Hall of Fame, played largely in

---

136. Dewey and Acocella, p. 236
137. Lieb, *The Detroit Tigers*, p. 21
138. Other teams with the Sun in Sagittarius would follow: the Giants, the Phillies, and the Brewers.
139. Eckhouse, Morris, p. 144

Ty Cobb's shadow. Crawford batted .378 in 1911, a year in which Ty Cobb hit .420. Harry Heilman won four batting titles in the 1920s. Al Kaline would have over 3000 hits in his 22-year career, all in a Tigers uniform. In 1955, Kaline, then 20-years-old, became the youngest player to win a batting title. Interestingly, the previous player to hold that distinction had been Ty Cobb in 1907. Kaline would break Cobb's record by one day.[140]

Ty Cobb's rectified birthchart[141] has a Sagittarius Sun in the Ninth House, a placement that made Cobb a natural hitter. His birthchart also has the Ascendant in Aries, the sign of the warrior. This persona was embodied in Cobb's tough personality and his "baseball is war" attitude. Mercury in opposition to Pluto added to his fierceness and gave Cobb his base-stealing ability. Mars in Capricorn and the Tenth House is opposed by Saturn in Cancer and the Fourth House. By itself, Mars in Capricorn is very competitive. The added aspects of the Tenth House and the opposition from Saturn further forged Cobb's dogged determination to win every battle. Saturn in his Fourth House also reflects his difficult early home life, particularly his overbearing and stern father. The opposition between the planets in his Fourth and Tenth Houses also manifested in the fatal conflict between his mother and father. Cobb's mother fatally shot his father. She would be acquitted of having acted in self-defense by believing his silhouette was of an intruder and not recognizing that he was her husband.

Jupiter is the planet of gamblers, while Sagittarius is the sign of the

---

Al Kaline
Wednesday, December 19, 1934 12:00:00 PM
Baltimore, Maryland
Time Zone: 05:00 (EST)
Longitude: 076° W 37' 12"
Latitude: 39° N 18' 48"

---

140. Al Kaline was born on Dec. 19, 1934, while Cobb was born on Dec 18, 1886, making Kaline in 1955 one day younger than Ty Cobb in 1907.

141. Rectification Note: I have rectified his time of birth to 1:20 pm EST in The Narrows, Ga. In 1905, the year his mother killed his father, an IC of 6 degrees Cancer progressed by solar arc would be opposite his 10th House Mars in Capricorn. Cobb also made his major league debut in 1905.

gamblers. The Tigers' Jupiter and Sagittarian emphasis has brought them scandals involving gamblers. Interestingly, the earliest scandal involved an umpire. In 1882, umpire Dick Higham was accused of fixing games for gamblers. Team owner W. G. Thompson presented evidence at a league meeting that forced the umpire to resign.[142] Then in 1885, a Detroit umpire named Herman Doescher was also forced to step down after fixing games.[143] The Tigers' Jupiter is loosely conjunct to Saturn, with a wide orb of 11 degrees. In these incidents, Saturn was represented in the umpires, while Jupiter became manifest in gamblers. The Jupiter-Saturn conjunction became manifest in the Saturnian authority of the umpire under the sway of Jupiterian gamblers. Twenty-one years later, Jupiter's influence over Saturn would bring down not an umpire but a manager. On January 12, 1903, Tigers manager Win Mercer committed suicide. Although his suicide note said he was driven to take his life by problems with women, Mercer was known to be a heavy gambler. He was also on a losing streak when he took his life.[144]

In 1926, Ty Cobb, then Detroit's player-manager, and Cleveland manager Tris Speaker were accused of having fixed a game on Sept. 24, 1919. The transits for the game support the charges. The Moon at 7 degrees Libra formed a square to Pluto in transit at 7 degrees Cancer. Both planets formed hard aspects to the Tigers' natal Jupiter of 7 degrees Aries. Both Cobb and Speaker were eventually exonerated but not before they were made to resign.[145] Many years later, Denny McLain, who won 31 games in 1968, was suspended for his associations with gamblers. After he had left baseball, McLain's links to underworld figures led him to prison.

Frank Navin owned the Tigers from the early 1900s until his death in 1935. Navin not only gambled but owned race horses. Sagittarius is the sign of horses. Frank Navin would actually die on his horse. Soon after the Tigers won the 1935 World Series, Navin suffered a heart attack while horseback riding. Years later, echoes of Navin's horse's hoof beats were heard in the words of manager Mayo Smith. When the Tigers lost the 1967 pennant, Smith was accused of overusing a relief pitcher. Smith defended his decision with Sagittarian language: "I'm a gambler, and I ride a hot horse!"[146]

---

142. Dewey and Acocella, p. 230; Lieb, p. 6
143. Lieb, p. 7
144. Lieb, p. 52
145. Alexander, p. 185
146. Green, Jerry, *Year of the Tiger*, p. 141.

The Tigers' Moon is in the sign of Pisces. The Moon in a birthchart represents one's past, heritage, and family. The sign of Pisces is associated with things hidden away, and the Tigers' past is very well hidden. Even knowledgeable baseball fans do not know Tigers history earlier than Ty Cobb. Historians do not connect the Wolverines of the 1880s with the current Tigers. Fred Lieb wrote a thorough account of 19th Century baseball in Detroit, but even his history has gaps, missing the hidden years of 1891 to 1893.

As the sign of Pisces rules First Base, the Tigers' Pisces Moon has given the team a tradition of great first basemen. Tigers first baseman Hank Greenberg hit 58 homeruns in 1958 and was the first Jewish-American sports star. First baseman Norm Cash hit .361 in 1961, the highest average of any player in the 1960s. In 1961, Cash was also the first player to hit a home run out of Tiger Stadium.[147] The Tigers have also had a father-and-son duo of Cecil and Prince Fielder at the first base bag.

The team played in Tiger Stadium from 1912 through 1999. Before settling on the name of Tiger Stadium, the park had been called Briggs Stadium, Navin Field, and Bennett Park. The names of Briggs Stadium and Navin Field were given for the owners Walter O. Briggs and Frank Navin, but the name Bennett Park honored Charley Bennett, the catcher who lost his legs in a train accident while playing for the Boston Braves.[148] The name of Bennett on the stadium honored a catcher from the Tigers' earliest roots, as Charley Bennett had played for the Detroit Wolverines of the

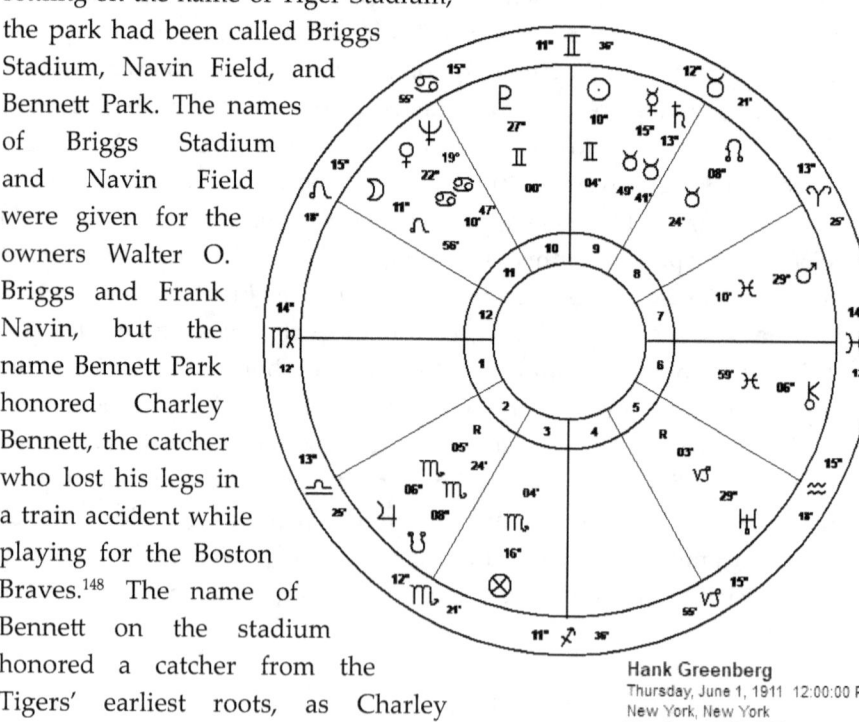

Hank Greenberg
Thursday, June 1, 1911 12:00:00 PM
New York, New York
Time Zone: 05:00 (EST)
Longitude: 073° W 59' 30"
Latitude: 40° N 45' 00"

---

147. http://en.wikipedia.org/wiki/Norm_Cash
148. See Braves chapter.

1880s. Since the Moon rules both catchers and stadiums, it is fitting that the stadium was named for a catcher.

The Tigers' Moon is in the First House, within two degrees of the Ascendant. This Moon also receives an opposition from Uranus in Virgo. Such a Uranus aspect can bring licentious behavior, as Uranus relishes challenging authority. Planets in the First House have a Mars-like aggression. Since the Moon rules the fans, the lunar placement so close to the Ascendant, combined with a Uranus opposition, have made Tiger fans a visible and aggressive bunch. Tiger fans have rioted. During a game on June 13, 1924, a brawl erupted between the Tigers and the Yankees. Ty Cobb and Babe Ruth wrestled near home plate. Tiger fans were not content to watch. Many ran onto the field and joined the fight. The umpires were unable to restore order and declared the game forfeited by Detroit.[149] That afternoon, Uranus, in transit at 21 degrees Pisces, was square to the Tigers IC. The Sun, in transit at 22 degrees Gemini, was square to Uranus and conjunct to the Tigers natal IC, a dispositor of the Moon. These transits triggered both the lawless impulses of Uranus and the aggressiveness of the Tiger Moon.

Ten years later, Tiger fans nearly caused a World Series game to be forfeited. In Game Seven of the 1934 World Series against the Cardinals, Detroit was behind 8-0 and likely to lose the Series. Tiger fans began pelting Cardinal left fielder Joe Medwick with garbage. Earlier in the game, Medwick had earned the fans' ire when he'd fought with Tigers' third baseman Marv Owen. The barrage of fruit and debris from the fans was so disruptive that Commissioner Landis, who was present for the World Series, ordered Medwick removed from the game to prevent a riot or forfeit.

Another riot occurred after the last game of the 1967 season. On October 1, 1967, the Tigers lost the pennant by one game to the Boston Red Sox. When the game ended, the fans' frustration boiled over. They attacked the field, throwing metal box seats onto the field. They attacked the dugouts, destroying bench pads, water coolers and pipes. Fans who brought weapons to the game stabbed at the pitcher's mound with their knives, digging out the pitching rubber.[150]

A more civil expression of the Moon in opposition to Uranus was the Tigers' early labor consciousness. The Tigers were the first baseball team to go on strike. On May 18, 1912, Tiger players walked off their jobs for

---

149. Dewey and Acocella, p. 236.
150. For a description of the riot, see Green, Jerry, *Year of the Tiger*, pp. 13-14. The transits included an opposition from the Sun at 8 degrees Libra to Saturn at 9 degrees Aries. The Sun was also semi-square to Neptune, in transit at 22 degrees Scorpio and inconjunct to the Tigers' natal IC.

one game. The strike was triggered by Ty Cobb's suspension. Cobb had been suspended after the incident in which he'd entered the stands and attacked a heckling fan. The players struck to have Cobb's suspension lifted. Detroit's "replacement players" lost the game 24-2 to the Athletics. Transits for the strike show a lunar and Eleventh House emphasis. The Moon, in transit through Gemini, was conjunct to the Tigers' IC.[151] Mars, in transit at 24 degrees Cancer, formed an opposition to the Tigers' Eleventh House Venus. Planets in the Eleventh House have an affinity for social causes and labor issues.

The 1984 Tigers, who would beat San Diego in that year's World Series, had perhaps the most impressive start ever to a baseball season. They began the season with a 9-game winning streak, but much more extraordinary was their 35 and 5 record by early May. The Tigers were able to take advantage of beneficial transits during the beginning of the 1984 season. Jupiter at 12 degrees Capricorn was trine to both the Tigers' natal Neptune of 12 degrees Taurus and natal Uranus of near 14 degrees Virgo, while Uranus, in transit near 13 degrees Sagittarius, was square to the Tigers' natal Uranus.

---

151. The Tigers' replacement catcher, Ed Irwin, responded to the transit of the Moon conjunct the IC by hitting two triples. (Dewey & Acocella, p. 237)

The Pirates

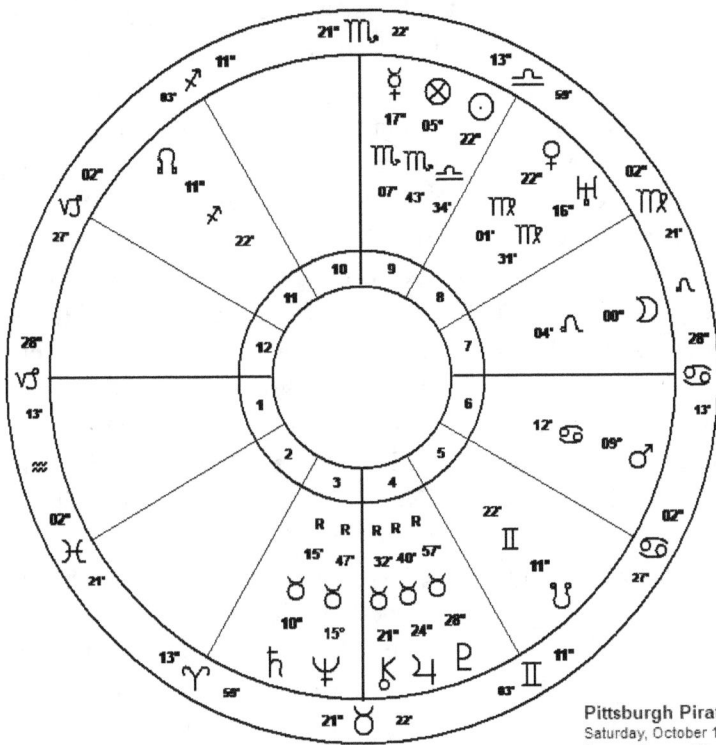

Pittsburgh Pirates
Saturday, October 15, 1881 1:58:00 PM
Current Day and Time
Pittsburgh, Pennsylvania
Time Zone: 05:00 (EST)
Longitude: 080° W 00' 06"
Latitude: 40° N 26' 06"

The Pittsburgh Pirates were born on October 15, 1881[152] at 1:58 pm EST.[153] Their birthchart has the Sun in Libra, a placement that has manifest in the Pirates' tradition of great second basemen. The Pirates' Mercury is opposed by both Neptune and Saturn. Odd happenings with Pirate pitchers, such as Steve Blass' mysterious loss of effectiveness and Doc Ellis's no-hitter on LSD, are manifestations of these heavy aspects to Mercury.

With the Sun in Libra, the Pirates have excelled at the position of second base. Bill Mazeroski, perhaps Pittsburgh's greatest hero, played second base. Danny Murtaugh, who managed the Pirates for parts of three decades, was also a Libra and a second baseman. Murtaugh, who managed the Bucs in the

---

152. Pietrusza, David, *Major Leagues: The Formation, Sometimes Absorption and Mostly Inevitable Demise of 18 Professional Baseball Organizations, 1871 to Present*, p. 63.
153. Rectification Note: An MC of 21 Scorpio, progressed by solar arc to 1889, the year the team merged with Louisville and was purchased by Barney Dreyfuss, becomes conjunct to the North Node of 10 degrees Sagittarius. An IC of 21 Taurus, when progressed to 2001, the year PNC Park opened, becomes conjunct to the teams natal Venus of 22 degrees Virgo.

1950s, '60s and '70s, was known for his evenhanded Libra demeanor. Lou Bierbauer, the player whose acquisition gave this club the name of "Pirates," was also a second baseman. When the Players League folded in 1891, major league players who had joined the insurgent league were forced to return to their former teams in the National League and American Association, which had previously bound them by contract. But the names of two players were accidentally removed from list of reserved players: outfielder Harry Stovey and second baseman Lou Bierbauer. Bierbauer signed with Pittsburgh rather than return to his former team in Philadelphia.[154] The American Association protested the signing of Bierbauer, calling it a "piratical act." [155] Out of this accusation, the name "Pirates" would emerge. The new name replaced the earlier names of "Alleghenys" and "Innocents." Lou Bierbauer would play second base for the Pirates from 1891 through 1896. His birthchart, with the Sun, Mars, Saturn and the North Node in Libra, shows he was a natural second baseman. Bierbauer's birthchart also displays his affinity with the Pirates franchise, as his North Node of 22 degrees Libra is conjunct to the Pirates' Sun.

Bill Mazeroski's home run that won the 1960 World Series was hit on October 13, 1960, at 3:36 pm.[156] Mazeroski's home run is sometimes called the greatest home run in baseball history. For many years, it stood as the only time a World Series had ended with a walk-off home run.[157] That day, Venus, in transit at 20 degrees Scorpio, was conjunct to the Pirates' MC. The MC represents the position of highest achievement within a birthchart. The transit from Venus, the planetary ruler of second base, would lift a second baseman, Mazeroski, to a place of highest honor. The Libra Sun of the Pirates is also embodied

Bill Mazeroski
Saturday, September 5, 1936 12:00:00 PM
Wheeling, West Virginia
Time Zone: 00:00 (UT)
Longitude: 080° W 43'
Latitude: 40° N 04'

---

154. Bierbauer (born Sept. 28, 1865 in Erie, Penn) played for the Philadelphia Athletics of the American Association from 1886-1889.
155. Dewey and Acocella, pp. 448-9.
156. http://en.wikipedia.org/wiki/Bill_Mazeroski
157. Joe Carter's home run, 34 years later, ended the 1994 World Series between the Blue Jays and Phillies. See Blue Jays chapter.

Pittsburgh Pirates

in a peacemaking ability. The sign of Libra brings a balanced perspective and negotiating skills. At the turn of the Twentieth Century, the National League and the newer American League were engaged in a bitter conflict, competing for players, fans and revenue. It was the Pirates franchise who made the peace overtures that helped bring a treaty between the leagues.[158] The Pirates would help to legitimize the new American League when they played in the first World Series of 1903. The next year, however, John McGraw and the New York Giants, who had won the National League pennant, refused to play Boston in the World Series. The Pirates would finish in fourth place in 1904, but Barney Dreyfuss, the Pirates owner, cleverly had his fourth-place Pirates play the Cleveland Indians, the American League's fourth-place finisher, in that year's World Series.

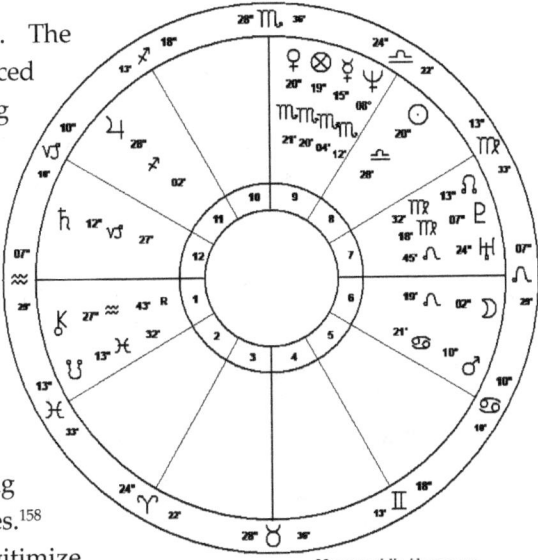

Mazeroski's Homerun
Thursday, October 13, 1960 3:36:00 PM
Pittsburgh, Pennsylvania
Time Zone: 04:00 (EDT)
Longitude: 080° W 00' 06"
Latitude: 40° N 26' 06"

Earlier, the Pittsburgh club had helped to bring peace between the National League and the American Association. Owner Denny McKnight represented the American Association in the "Harmony Conference" of 1883. This meeting resulted in the Tripartide Agreement, which brought cooperation between the American Association, the National League and the Northwestern League. The Tripartide Agreement, which authorized territorial exclusivity and the validity of player contracts, would later be called the National Agreement.[159] The agreement brought peace between teams within the three leagues, which had been raiding each other for players and threatening each others' territories and markets.

A Libra often becomes involved in business mergers.[160] A merger,

---

158. When peace was restored between the two leagues, Dreyfuss secured the condition that no American League team could move into Pittsburgh and compete for the Pirates' fan base. Earlier, a possibility had existed that the Detroit Tigers would move to Pittsburgh. A Libra often receives something for his peacemaking efforts.
159. Dewey and Acocella, p. 445.
160. The Dodgers, a team with the Moon in Libra, also have significant mergers in their history.

in which two business entities or teams join resources, is much like a marriage—another realm of Libra. The Pirates merged with the Louisville Colonels after the 1899 season. From the Louisville club, the Pirates received four future Hall of Fame players: Honus Wagner, Fred Clarke, Tommy Leach, and Rube Waddell. Before the merger with Louisville, Pittsburgh had not been a strong contender, whether in the American Association or the National League. However, one year later, the Pirates leaped to second place. In 1901, they won the NL pennant by 27 games and a gaudy winning percentage of .741. Furthermore, the Pirates repeated as National League champs in 1902 and 1903.

The Pirates' first star was Honus Wagner, who would win eight batting titles and become one of the first players elected to the Hall of Fame. The birthchart of Wagner shows his versatility. Wagner may have excelled at any position. With a strong Mars in its own sign of Aries, Wagner played most of his career at shortstop. His Sun in Pisces allowed him to play first base, the position he had played early in his career. His conjunction of the Sun and Venus brought Wagner to play also second base and center field. Wagner's birthchart also has the Moon in Gemini in square to Mercury, aspects that gave him the speed to excel as a baserunner. Wagner would lead the National League in five different seasons and finish his career with 703 stolen bases.

Honus Wagner
Tuesday, February 24, 1874 12:00:00 PM
Current Day and Time
Carnegie, Pennsylvania
Time Zone: 05:00 (EST)
Longitude: 080° W 05'
Latitude: 40° N 24'

The Pirates' Moon is located at 0 degrees Leo. A Moon in Leo suggests a showboat quality to the catcher and to the team in general. But the Pirates are not known as a flamboyant team. The Pirates' Moon resides in the evenhanded Seventh House, conjunct the Descendant, which tempers the desire of egotistical Leo-like displays. The team's birthchart also has a Capricorn ascendant, which prefers a more staid appearance. In the early 1920s, however, the Pirates did have a showboat clique of players known as the "Banjo Players." First baseman Charlie Grimm was the Pirate who actually played the banjo. Rabbit Maranville,

George Whitehead, Jim Tierney, and Chief Yellowhorse were his partners in song and mischief. The Pirates of the 1970s had a flashy appearance, but much of their flamboyance had to do with the bright colors and fabrics of the decade. In general, Pirate fans disapprove of showboats, even booing hometown hotdogs Dave Parker and Barry Bonds.

One of the most cherished players in Pirates history is Roberto Clemente. His relationship to the Pittsburgh fans is mirrored in an aspect between his birthchart and that of the Pirates. Clemente's birthchart has a Venus of 1 degree Leo, which is conjunct to the Pirates' Moon. Moreover, Clemente's Jupiter of 20 degrees Libra is conjunct to the Pirates' Sun, the planet of right field. Clemente's own Sun in the sign Leo made him a natural right fielder. His Sun was also opposed by Saturn in Aquarius, an aspect that brought his leadership ability. The opposition from Saturn may have also brought his early death.

The death of Roberto Clemente occurred on December 31, 1972. Clemente died in an airplane accident while participating in relief efforts following the Managua earthquake. That day, Saturn, in transit at 15 degrees Gemini, was square to the Pirates' natal Uranus. Venus, in transit at 16 degrees Sagittarius, was also square to the Pirates Uranus. In addition, Uranus, in transit at 23 degrees Libra, was conjunct to the Pirates' Sun, the planet of the right field: Clemente's position. Uranus rules air travel, and such difficult aspects from Uranus are associated with airplane accidents.

Roberto Clemente
Saturday, August 18, 1934 12:00:00 PM
Carolina, Puerto Rico
Time Zone: 04:00 (AST)
Longitude: 066° W 04'
Latitude: 18° N 27'

In the season following Clemente's death, Manny Sanguillen, the Pirates catcher, was given the difficult assignment of filling Clemente's shoes in right field. It was a strange change of position for the catcher, since Sanguillen was not an outfielder. He had been, however, Clemente's best friend. When manager Bill Virden directed Sanguillen to step into his friend's old position, the move made little sense other than as an appeal to some sentimentality.¹⁶¹ There was, however, astrological logic behind the move. Since the Pirates' Moon is in the right fielder's sign of Leo, the catcher, ruled by the Moon, has a close link to right field.

The Pirates' Mercury in Scorpio is overloaded with challenging aspects. Mercury is in the Ninth House, which is a difficult placement in an individual's chart. Mercury concentrates on particulars and details, but has difficulty when facing the abstract mental processes of the Ninth House and Sagittarian realms. For a baseball team, the Ninth House corresponds with batters, making it an afflicted placement for Mercury, the pitcher's planet. The Pirates' Mercury is also opposed by Neptune and Saturn. Both these planets are placed in the Third House, a house of the pitcher. The Pirates' pitchers, however, do benefit from the South Node in Gemini, a pitcher's sign.¹⁶²

The opposition of Neptune and Saturn to the Bucs' Mercury has had a variety of odd manifestations for Pirates pitchers. Neptune in the pitcher's Third House would indicate spitball pitchers.¹⁶³ Burleigh Grimes, a Hall of Fame spitball artist, made his debut with the Pirates in 1916. A Neptune opposition can also bring mental afflictions, as it distorts perceptions of reality. Pitcher Rube Waddell joined the Pirates after the merger with Louisville in 1899. Waddell was well-known for erratic behavior, such as chasing fire engines. There is also the strange case of the Pirate pitcher who went insane during the World Series. During the 1903 World Series against Boston, pitcher Ed Doheny

Steve Blass
Saturday, April 18, 1942 12:00:00 PM
Canaan, Connecticut
Time Zone: 05:00 (EST)
Longitude: 073° W 19'
Latitude: 41° N 58'

---

161. Admoites, p. 469-70.
162. The Pirates South Node of 10 degrees Gemini actively responds to transits. Between June 2 and June 9, 1903, Pirate pitchers hurled 6 consecutive shutouts. During the streak, Mercury, in a retrograde transit, made a slow passing conjunction to the South Node. The Sun, also in transit through Gemini, formed a conjunction to the Pirates South Node during the streak. (Lieb, *The Pittsburgh Pirates* p. 97)
163. See Dodgers' chapter for a discussion of spitball pitchers.

was committed. While in an asylum, the pitcher attacked a medical aide, hitting him with a cast iron footrest. Doheny never recovered his sanity and lived the rest of his life locked away.[164] Neptune can bring mental illnesses in which the boundaries between imagination and reality are dissolved. A mental affliction also doomed Steve Blass. In the early 1970s, Blass had been an elite pitcher, even winning Game Seven of the 1971 World Series. However, in 1973, he mysteriously lost his ability to pitch effectively. Nothing was wrong with him physically, yet neither psychotherapy nor transcendental meditation was able to help him. Blass never regained his effectiveness and was released by the Pirates in 1975.[165]

As Neptune rules drugs, the Pittsburgh Drug Trials of 1985 were another manifestation of the afflictions of Neptune and Saturn to the Pirates' Mercury. Pirate pitcher Rod Scurry would eventually die of a cocaine-related heart attack.[166] However, drug use was reported to involve most of the team, including Dave Parker and Dale Berra. The trials and investigation would expose rampant cocaine use among MLB players. It also divulged how the person serving as the Pirates' parrot mascot had been enlisted by players to bring them drugs.[167] The FBI investigation of drug use in the Pirates clubhouse began in 1984, as Saturn transiting through Scorpio formed a conjunction to the Pirates Mercury and oppositions to the Pirates' natal Saturn and Neptune. Saturn assumed the role of the authority figure who brought the necessary bust that ended the party.

One legendary manifestation of the Pirates' opposition between Mercury and Neptune is the no-hitter thrown by Doc Ellis. According

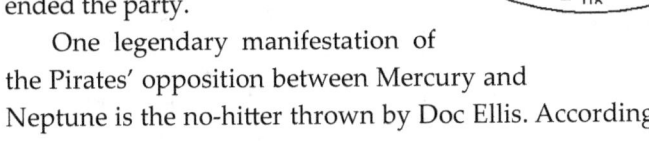
Rod Scurry
Saturday, March 17, 1956 12:00:00 PM
Current Day and Time
Sacramento, California
Time Zone: 08:00 (PST)
Longitude: 121° W 27' 00"
Latitude: 38° N 35' 48"

---

164. Admites, pp. 460-461.
165. Hurte, Bob, *Sabre Baseball Biography Project: Steve Blass*
166. Scurry would die in 1992 when he was no longer with the team.
167. HBO Real Sports with Bryant Gumbel. 2006. http://www.hbo.com/real-sports-with-bryant-gumbel/episodes/0/114-september-19-2006/synopsis.html

to his own admission, on June 12, 1970, Doc Ellis pitched a no-hitter against San Diego while tripping on LSD. [168] Reporters who were at the game deny that Ellis could have been on LSD,[169] but transits for the game support his claim. That evening, Mercury, the planet of pitchers, was stationed at 29 degrees Taurus and in opposition to Neptune, the planet of drugs, at 29 degrees Scorpio. Mercury was also conjunct to the Pirates natal Pluto. Doc Ellis' birthchart, like that of the Pirates, also has an opposition between Mercury and Neptune. Ellis' Sun is in the sign of Pisces, which gave him an affinity with Neptune energy. Ellis abused drugs during his baseball career, but he would become sober and even work as a drug counselor upon retiring from baseball.

The 1979 Pirates, who won the World Series, held the persona of a large and supportive family. Willie, Stargell, who led this team, has the North Node conjunct to the Pirates' Sun. The "We are Family" team was a manifestation of two aspects in the Pirates' birthchart. The Bucs have Mars in Cancer, the sign of families, an aspect that strengthens family bonds. The Bucs also have Jupiter in the Fourth House of family, an aspect that can make families large and generous.

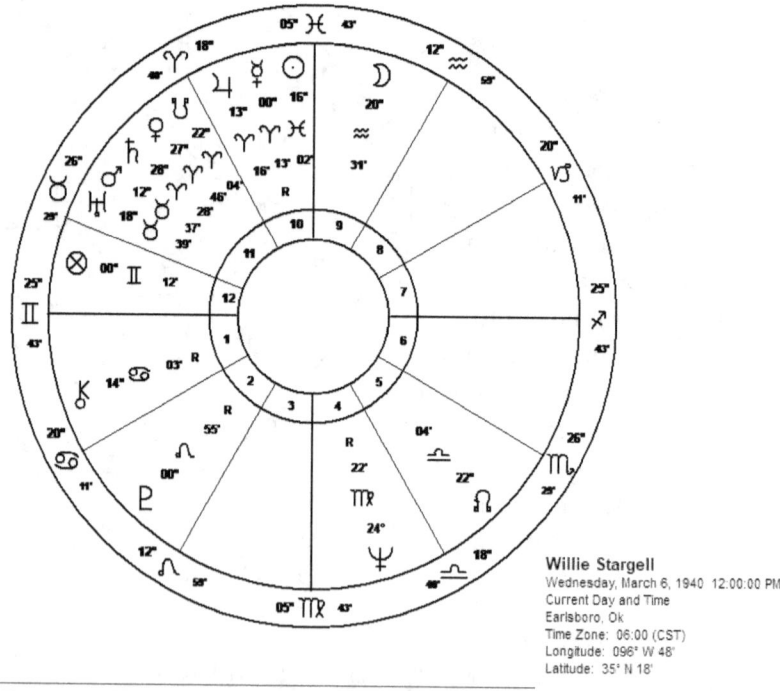

Willie Stargell
Wednesday, March 6, 1940 12:00:00 PM
Current Day and Time
Earlsboro, Ok
Time Zone: 06:00 (CST)
Longitude: 096° W 48'
Latitude: 35° N 18'

---

168. Hall, Donald, with Ellis: *Dock Ellis in the Country of Baseball*, 1989, pp. 162-163, 316-317
169. https://en.wikipedia.org/wiki/DockEllis

St. Louis Cardinals

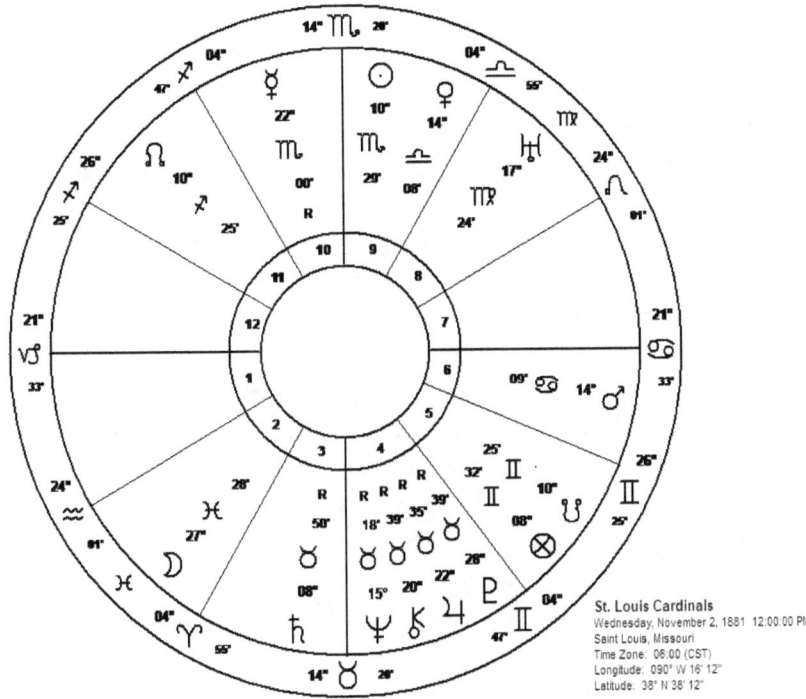

St. Louis Cardinals
Wednesday, November 2, 1881 12:00:00 PM
Saint Louis, Missouri
Time Zone: 06:00 (CST)
Longitude: 090° W 16' 12"
Latitude: 38° N 38' 12"

The St. Louis Cardinals were born on November 11, 1881[170] at 12:00 pm CST.[171] Before taking the name of "Cardinals," the team had been variously called the Brown Stockings, the Browns, and the Perfectoes. The Cardinals' Moon is in the sign of Pisces. Their Sun in Scorpio is opposed by Saturn and Neptune. The Cardinals' Mercury is retrograde in the sign of Scorpio and opposed by Neptune, Jupiter, and Pluto. Both of these challenging oppositions have proven bountiful for the St. Louis franchise.

The Cardinals' Mercury is channeling a vast amount of power from the three planets opposing it. Jupiter, Neptune, and Pluto are all retrograde

---

170. Golenbach, Peter, *Spirit of St. Louis: A History of the Cardinals and Browns*, p. 16. This date may also serve as the founding of the American Association, also known as the "Beer and Whisky League."
171. Rectification Note: The Sun of 10 Scorpio progressed by solar arc becomes conjunct an MC of 14 Scorpio in 1885, the year of the St. Louis team's first pennant. Venus of 14 Libra progressed by solar arc becomes conjunct an MC of 14 Scorpio in 1911, the year the team was inherited by Helen Britton, Major League Baseball's first female owner.

and in fixed signs, indicating a high concentration of energy. Mercury, itself, is also retrograde. Ordinarily, such a heavily aspected Mercury would manifest in frequent accidents and severe health problems.[172] However, the Cardinals' Mercury is buttressed by its placement in the fixed sign of Scorpio. The Cardinals' Mercury also occupies the Tenth House of achievement, while the three opposing planets are assembled in the Fourth House of emotions, fans, and ancestors. The Cardinals' Fourth House is bursting with strong passion. The team has generally been successful in channeling its Fourth House passions into its Tenth House Mercury. The Fourth House is also the house of heritage. The Cardinals' heritage is very rich, not only for the many World Series victories but for their contributions to the game of baseball and to American culture.

The Cardinals' Neptune in Taurus is very favorably aspected. It forms a grand trine with Uranus in Virgo and the Capricorn Ascendant. This outer planet is also conjunct to the Cardinals' IC, a dispositor of the Moon. This aspect reinforces the team's Moon in Pisces, as Neptune is the despositor of the sign Pisces. With Neptune conjunct the MC, one can almost say the Cardinals have a double Moon in Pisces. An obvious manifestation of the Cardinals' Pisces and Neptune emphasis is the team's association with the Neptune product of beer. Long before the team was purchased by the Busch family, the franchise was founded by Chris Von der Ahe, a German immigrant. Von der Ahe was less a baseball man than he was a brewer. Von der Ahe's intention was to make money by selling beer to baseball fans. In the 1880s, the Cardinals' home stadium was part of Von der Ahe's amusement park complex, which included horse racing, log rides, and a beer garden. His

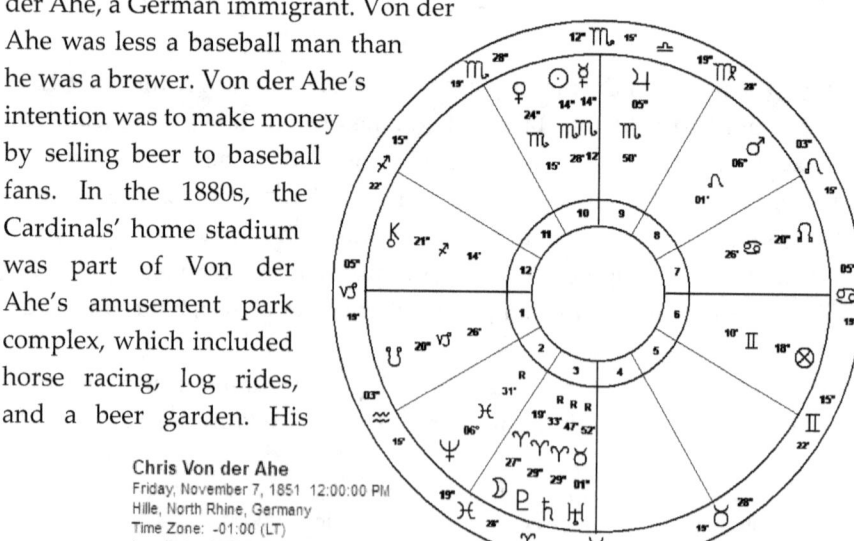

Chris Von der Ahe
Friday, November 7, 1851 12:00:00 PM
Hille, North Rhine, Germany
Time Zone: -01:00 (LT)
Longitude: 008° E 45'
Latitude: 52° N 20'

---

172. The Pirates' franchise has a similar aspect of Mercury in Scorpio opposed to Neptune and Saturn in Taurus, which has manifest in mental illness and drug abuse. (See Pirates chapter.)

team proved itself a winner, not only for the beer business, but also on the field. The early Cardinals, then called the Brown Stockings, would win four consecutive pennants from 1885 to 1888.

In 1953, the Cardinals were purchased by Anheiser-Busch. August "Gussie" Busch Jr., the man whose marketing ability made Budweiser the most popular beer in the United States, became the Cardinals' high profile owner. On opening days, Gussie Busch would ride around the diamond in the Budweiser beer wagon pulled by Clydesdale horses. Soon after getting his hands on the franchise, Gussie Busch planned to change the name of Sportman's Park to Budweiser Park, but he was talked out of it. Nevertheless, in 1966, the Cardinals' new park would be named Busch Stadium. Gussie Busch would have a stadium named not only after his beer, but after himself and his family. Since the Moon rules stadiums, a ballpark with the same name as a beer label is a suitable fit for a team with a Pisces Moon. In the 1980s, the national mood became critical of drunk drivers. Beer drinking lost its cool, and some teams removed beer advertisements from their stadiums. While the Cardinals' close relationship with beer embarrassed the rest of the league, their ownership was unapologetic.[173]

The genius of the St Louis Cardinals has been to generate a synergy between the planets Neptune and Mercury, planets whose energies are often at cross purposes. In the game of baseball, Neptune rules first base, while Mercury rules the pitcher. With a strong Mercury, the Cardinal franchise has excelled at pitching. Cardinal pitchers in the Baseball Hall of Fame include Jesse Haines, Grover Cleveland Alexander, Dizzy Dean, and Bob Gibson. With their Moon in Pisces and a strong Neptune, the Cardinals also have many stellar first basemen in their history. The lineage of great Cardinal first basemen includes Jim Bottomley, Johnny Mize, Bill White, Keith Hernandez, Mark McGwire, and Albert Pujols. The Cardinals' Neptune is very strong, not only because of its alignment with the Moon but from its conjunction with Jupiter.[174]

An early St. Louis first baseman brought together the Mercurial energy of the pitcher and Neptunian energy of the first baseman. The manager for St. Louis's championship teams of the 1880s was a young first baseman named Charles Comiskey. His birthchart has Neptune in Pisces conjunct the Cardinals' Moon and Jupiter in Cancer conjunct to the St. Louis Mars. Comiskey would later own the Chicago White Sox and have their stadium named after him, but when he was with St. Louis, the

---

173. Dewey & Acocella, p. 499.
174. Prior to the discovery of Neptune in the Nineteenth Century, Jupiter had been considered the despositor of Pisces.

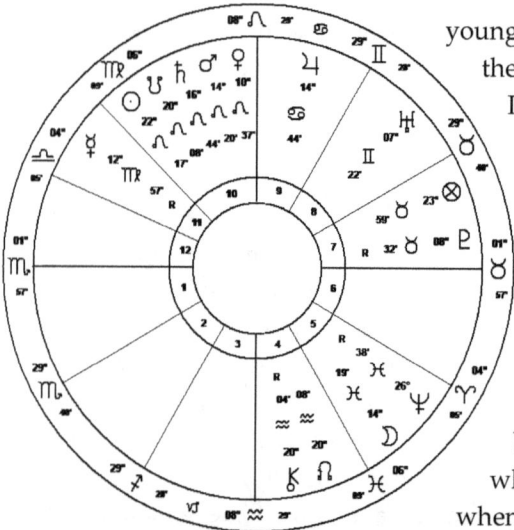

Charles Comiskey
Monday, August 15, 1859 12:00:00 PM
Chicago, Illinois
Time Zone: 05:00 (CDT)
Longitude: 087° W 39' 42"
Latitude: 41° N 51' 54"

young Comiskey revolutionized how the first base position was played.[175] Previously, first basemen played with one foot on the first base bag regardless of whether a runner needed to be held. The Cardinal first baseman considered playing away from the bag and deeper towards right field. This positioning allows the first baseman a greater range within which to field batted balls. But when positioned this way, the first baseman may have to field a ball so far away from the bag that he cannot beat the runner in a footrace to first base. It was Comiskey who devised the technique that, in such plays, the pitcher would run to the first base bag and receive the throw from the first baseman. This defensive innovation by Comiskey came from a creative synergy between the Cardinals' Mercury and Neptune.

An often-told tale from the lore of the St. Louis Cardinals is that of Grover Cleveland Alexander (born Feb. 26, 1887) in the 1926 World Series. The story also demonstrates cooperation between the energies of Mercury and Neptune, particularly Mercury's job of pitching and Neptune's condition of the hangover. Alexander's alcoholism is mirrored in his birthchart, which has the Sun, Mercury, Venus, and Mars in Pisces. In Game Seven of the 1926 World Series, a hung-over Grover Cleveland Alexander steps onto the pitching mound with the game and the Series on the line. The day before, Alexander had won Game Six for the Cardinals. Afterwards, Alexander had celebrated his victory by getting quite drunk. Unfortunately, it would seem, now it was the seventh inning of the Seventh Game. The Yankees have loaded the bases. Alexander is brought from the bullpen to pitch to the dangerous Tony Lazzeri. On the first pitch, Lazzeri hits the ball deep, yet foul, just missing a grand slam by a few feet, but then the hung-over pitcher proceeds to strike out Lazzeri, ending the inning and the threat. Alexander holds the Yankees hitless for the rest of the game. The Cardinals win Game Seven and the World Series. This is

---

175. Golenbock, p. 23.

an often told baseball tale, but it is also a quintessential Cardinals event in that it involves a blending of the seemingly antithetical energies of Mercury and Neptune.

The Cardinals of the 1930s were called "the Gas House Gang." The team included rowdies Leo Durocher, Pepper Martin, and Dizzy Dean. They became famous for their drunken escapades and their unkempt, shabby appearance.[176] Interestingly, their image was promoted by the Cardinals' general manager Branch Rickey,[177] who publicized exaggerated tales of their off-field antics to the press. Rickey promoted a Neptunian image even though his own lifestyle was quite the opposite.[178] Branch Rickey did not smoke or drink and led a clean Virgo lifestyle. Here, not only did the values of Virgo and Neptune co-exist, but a Virgo actually abated a Neptune lifestyle.

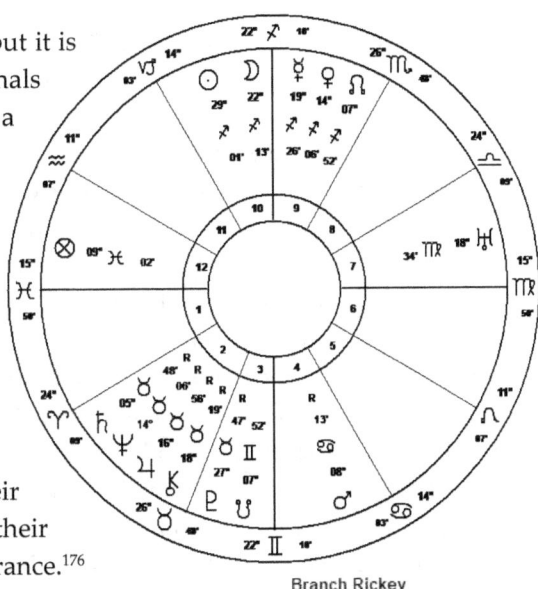

Branch Rickey
Tuesday, December 20, 1881 12:00:00 PM
Portsmouth, Ohio
Time Zone: 05:00 (EST)
Longitude: 082° W 57'
Latitude: 38° N 44'

The modern baseball farm system, in which a major league team owns a number of minor league teams to develop players, was created within the Cardinals organization. Branch Rickey realized the Cardinals could not compete with wealthier clubs who could offer large bonuses to unsigned players. In 1919, Rickey began signing a great number of prospects at low salaries. Only a small percentage of these minor league players would ever reach the big leagues. But the great volume of players under contract would maintain a steady stream of quality players for the Cardinals. Rickey's invention was a manifestation of the Cardinals' Moon in Pisces. The Cardinals' Moon is in the Second House, while its depositor, Neptune, is in the sign of Taurus. The Second House and Taurus rule agriculture and farms. In a baseball farm system, young

---

176. http://en.wikipedia.org/wiki/Gashouse_Gang
177. Branch Rickey was born in 1881, the same year as was the Cardinals team. The outer planets of his birthchart are conjunct those of the Cardinals. He would also become the general manager of the Pirates, another team born in 1881.
178. Dewey & Acocella, p. 494.

players are cultivated much as livestock and agriculture are produced on a conventional farm. The Moon, meanwhile, provides the nurturing that young men need to develop and mature.

Although the Cardinal farm system produced great players such as Stan Musial, the system had a sinister side. The Moon has a regressive pull, much like a mother who does not want her sons to grow up and leave home. Many players became mired within the Cardinal farm system, unable to advance. With countless players on many teams, the Cardinals' farm system was vast, much like the oceanic waters of Pisces. At times, the Cardinals controlled entire leagues. It was easy for a player to become overlooked or forgotten. Pisces, the last sign of the zodiac, is associated with things lost and hidden. On March 23, 1938, as Mars and Uranus were conjunct the Cardinals' Saturn in Taurus, Commissioner Landis granted free agency to 74 players within the Cardinals' farm system. He declared that Branch Rickey and the Cardinals had engaged in monopolistic practices and had violated the rules of competitive opportunity.[179]

Neptune shenanigans have landed Cardinal owners in jail. The planet Neptune brings more than beer and spirituality. It also brings deceit and jail time. Jail has a correspondence with Pisces, Neptune and the 12th House. It is a place of solitude and lost volition. In 1952, Cardinals owner Fred Saigh was found guilty of tax evasion and sentenced to 15 months in federal prison. He was sentenced on Jan. 28, 1953,[180] while Neptune in Libra was square to the Cardinals' Capricorn Ascendant and the Sun in Aquarius was square to the Cardinals' Saturn. Earlier in 1898, Chris Von der Ahe was kidnapped by private detectives who jailed him in Pennsylvania, a state where he had previously jumped bail. The kidnappers were employed by Pittsburgh Pirates owner William Nimick. Von der Ahe had owed money to Nimick for years. The Cardinals' owner was soon forced by the courts and the National League to sell his club.

1898 was a particularly bad year for the St. Louis franchise, as their Moon, progressed by solar arc, became square to Mars and opposite Venus. Not only was the owner kidnapped, but the team lost 111 games. Perhaps worse, a fire broke out while a game was in progress. The fire occurred on April 18, as Mercury and Venus were conjunct the Cardinals' IC, an indicator of stadiums. The fire destroyed the stadium and the club offices, including trophies and Von der Ahe's fancy clothes. Sadly, the owner's dog died in the fire. Many fans became injured, and Von der Ahe was soon besieged

---

179 Dewey and Acocella, p. 496.

180. *The New London Conn*: "Fred Saighn, Cardinal Owner, gets 15 Months in Jail for Tax Evasion," Jan. 29, 1953, p. 12.

with lawsuits. Von der Ahe was forced to sell the team in bankruptcy court. The sale took place on March 14, 1899[181] under a t-square between Neptune at 22 degrees Gemini, Saturn at 23 degrees Sagittarius, and the Sun at 23 degrees Pisces. These planets were all in aspect to the Browns' Capricorn Ascendant and to their 10th House Mercury, points in the Cardinals' chart that correspond with ownership. Another difficult transit for that day was Mars at 21 degrees Cancer conjunct to the Browns' Descendant.

In the following year of 1899, the new owners made an effort to clean up the image of the Browns. The events of 1898 had badly sullied the organization, but the franchise would channel its Virgo energy and give itself a thorough wash. The name "Browns" was dumped, along with the brown uniforms. The new uniforms were a bright red color. To match these red uniforms, the name "Cardinals" emerged.[182] But the "birds on a bat" logo would have to wait for several more years, not making its appearance until 1922.[183]

The Cardinals have the Sun, their Mercury, and the MC in Scorpio, the sign of the third baseman. An early third baseman for this franchise was Arlie Latham, who played on the championship teams of the 1880s. Latham is little remembered today, but his contribution to culture is lasting. Peter Golenbock describes him as the original trash-talker,[184] a designation in keeping with verbal Mercury in the coarse sign of Scorpio. Golenbock states that bench-jockeying to irritate the opposition began with this St. Louis third baseman.[185] Latham's birthchart has Venus and Pluto in Taurus conjunct to the Cardinals' Third House Saturn. Latham also has the Sun and Neptune conjunct the Cardinals'

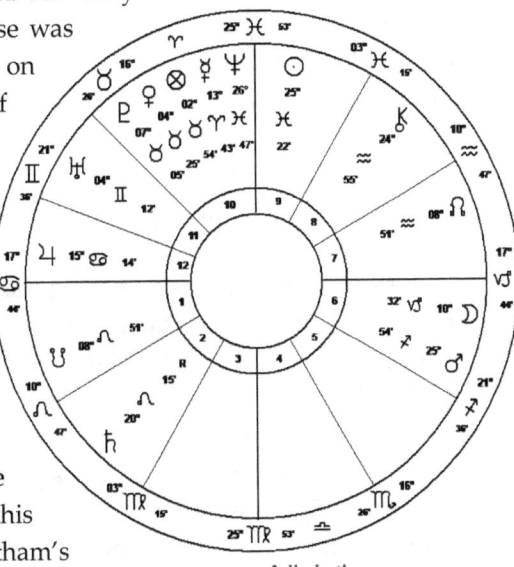

Arlie Latham
Thursday, March 15, 1860 12:00:00 PM
West Lebanon, New Hampshire
Time Zone: 05:00 (EST)
Longitude: 072° W 18'
Latitude: 43° N 39'

---

181. Hetrick, Thomas *Chris Von Der Ahe and the St. Louis Browns*, p. 224.
182. Carlson, p. 532; Golenbock, p. 55.
183. Okkonen, Mark, *Baseball Uniforms of the Twentieth Century*, p. 80.
184. Golenbock.p. 20
185. Golenbock.p. 20

Moon in Pisces.

The Cardinals have a rich history at third base. In the 1930s, Pepper Martin (born Feb. 29, 1904) manned the hot corner. Martin had previously played the Sun position of right field. To transfer from right field to third base was an easy transition for a team with the Sun in Scorpio. A leader of the Gas House Gang, Martin's South Node and Jupiter in Pisces are conjunct the Cardinals' Moon. Third baseman Ken Boyer became the Cardinals' captain in 1959. He would win the National League MVP in 1964 and then have his number 14 retired by the Cardinals in 1984. Mike Shannon, like Pepper Martin, made the transition from right field to third base. Eventually, Shannon would also represent the Cardinals' Mercury in Scorpio as the team's broadcaster. In the 2011 post-season, third baseman David Freese won the NLCS MVP and the World Series MVP. His clutch hitting in Game Six[186] of the World Series kept the Cardinals from being eliminated and allowed them to win the Series in Game Seven.

The Cardinals' Mercury in the Tenth House is represented in their owners, executives, and managers. Cardinal managers and front office executives have displayed conspicuous Mercury traits of the Virgo sort. Branch Rickey never drank or smoked. While he was the Cardinals' field manager in the 1920s, Rickey refused to attend games on Sundays. On the Sabbath, one of his coaches would manage the team. Johnny Keane, who managed the Cardinals in the early 1960s, also had a clean, temperate persona. Before becoming a manager, Keane had attended a seminary. In his early years as a manger, Keane had a difficult time swearing.[187] The birthchart of Chris Von der Ahe has the Sun conjunct to Mercury. His Sun and Mercury are conjunct at 15 degrees Scorpio and conjunct the Cardinals' MC. However, Von der Ahe is not remembered for any Virgo qualities. Sources depict him as a flamboyant Leo personality, an image that mirrors his Mars in Leo square to his Jupiter in Scorpio.

The Cardinals' prominent Mercury has made them a team of daring base runners. Speed is an attribute of Mercury, the fastest planet orbiting the Sun. Daring base running won the 1948 World Series for the Cardinals. In the 8th inning of Game Seven, Enos Slaughter scored the Series-winning run when he came home all the way from first base on Harry Walker's single. Although Mark McGwire broke Roger Maris's single season home run record as a Cardinal, St. Louis does not traditionally

---

186. Game Six began on Oct. 27, 2011 as Mercury, Venus and the Moon were conjunct the Cardinals' Mercury in Scorpio. Additionally, Mars in Leo was square to the Cardinals' Mercury. For more on this game, see Rangers' chapter.

187. Halberstam, *October 1964*, pp. 105, 116.

rely on home runs and big innings. Instead, the Cardinals play a speed game.[188] Lou Brock's transition, when he came from the Cubs to St Louis, exemplifies the Cardinals use of speed. David Halberstam, author of *October 1964*, explained the contrasting offensive philosophies of the Cubs and Cardinals.[189] The Cubs played in a small windy park where many homeruns were hit. The Cubs organization, conscious of the high probability of homeruns, would wait for an inning in which the long ball would score them multiple runs. The Cubs, therefore, were cautious base runners. Once a runner was on base, the Cubs' strategy was to wait for him to be batted in by a home run. The Cardinals, in contrast, played in a home park with deep power alleys. Sportmans' Park had a less than average potential for home runs, while holding a greater than average potential for extra base hits. Aggressive base running would score more runs in such a park. When Lou Brock was traded from the Cubs to the Cardinals in 1964, he was given the green light to attempt to steal a base whenever he saw the opportunity. The Cardinals' philosophy of aggressive baserunning allowed Brock to blossom as a player when he came to St. Louis.[190] In 1974, Brock would steal 114 bases and break Maury Wills' single season record.

The Cardinals' opposition from the Sun to both Saturn and Neptune has manifested in owners both inebriated and controlling. With Capricorn Rising, the team was founded by a high-profile owner. Chris Von der Ahe was the obnoxious face of the franchise. Often he would walk through St. Louis with his hunting dogs. At the end of a game, he would place the day's cash earnings in a wheel barrow and cart them to the bank, accompanied by armed security guards. Von der Ahe even had a statue of himself cast and placed in front of Sportsman's Park. He knew little about the subtleties of baseball, and the local press enjoyed making fun of his ignorance by reporting statements of his such as "I have the biggest (baseball) diamond in the world."[191] Von der Ahe went far in attempting to control his team, even insisting that his players could only drink at his saloons and room in his boarding houses.[192] He also gave unwelcome and ignorant advice to his managers, many of whom grew tired of mediating between him and his players, whom he was often fining and berating.[193]

More than fifty years after Von der Ahe was forced to sell the team,

---

188. Halberstam, p. 134
189. Halberstam, p. 134 &140-141.
190. Halberstam, p. 141
191. Golenbock, p. 17
192. Golenbock, p. 18
193. Golenbock, p. 18

the Cardinals would be owned by another flamboyant beer baron, Gussie Busch, who threw the wildest and most extravagant parties in St. Louis.[194] Like Von der Ahe, he knew more about beer than he did about baseball. Busch also had the misfortune to preside over a major league team in the 1960s and '70s, as the players began asserting their labor rights. Their challenge to the owners' authority did not sit well with him. Early in the 1969 season, Busch lashed out at his players for wanting more money.[195] Soon, the great team that had won back-to-back pennants became demoralized. Busch was not changing with the times, and he began trading players over differences of values. He forced his general manager to trade Jerry Reuss because he refused to shave his beard. Similarly, future Hall of Famer Steve Carlton was traded over a $10,000 disagreement in contract negotiations and because Busch considered Carlton to be a "smart-aleck."[196]

Although the opposition from Saturn has brought overbearing owners, it has also provided stability and success to the Cardinals. Saturn rules championships. In their long history, the St Louis team has never moved. The Cardinals have also won more pennants and more World Series than any National League team. In spite of its conjunction with Neptune, the Cardinals' Saturn has provided an anchor of stability and a pattern of winning. The conjunction of Saturn and Neptune has also provided a vehicle for the dreams of Neptune to become manifest through the clay of Saturn. The team has allowed its fans to dream of championships and then fulfilled their dreams.

In the 1960s, the St. Louis Cardinals became a model of racial harmony. Two important events occurred in 1961 that led Cardinal players to look beyond their racial differences. During Spring Training of 1961, first baseman Bill White led a protest against the exclusion of African-Americans from a players' breakfast at the St. Petersburg Yacht Club.[197] The breakfast occurred on March 9[198], as Uranus at 22 degrees Leo and Mercury at 24 degrees Aquarius were in opposition to each other and square to the Cardinals' Mercury.[199] That same spring, the Cardinals team would also protest the segregated accommodations in the state of Florida. African-American players had been forced to stay in boarding

---

194. Golenbock, p. 399
195. Golenbock, p. 504
196. Golenbock, p. 519
197. Golenbock, p. 439.
198. *Jefferson City Post-Tribune*: "St. Petersburg Denies Snubbing Negro Players," March 9, 1961, p. 9.
199. The breakfast occurred on March 9, but the protest around it likely happened in the days prior, as the opposition between Mercury and Uranus was exact.

houses in non-Caucasian parts of town. However, in 1961, the Cardinals lodged together in a motel where players of all colors were welcome. In a display of solidarity with their African-American teammates, Stan Musial and Ken Boyer gave up their beachfront homes and brought their families to the integrated motel. This experience of living together within the same motel gave the Cardinals team a cohesion that would last through the turbulent decade of the 1960s.[200]

The protest led by Bill White[201] and the experience of the integrated hotel both occurred as Neptune, in transit at 10 degrees Scorpio, was exactly conjunct the Cardinals' Sun. Actions for civil rights are usually associated with the planet Uranus, and the Yacht Club protest was indeed triggered by a transit from Uranus square to the Cardinals' Mercury. However, the actions for Civil Rights taken by the Cardinals in the 1960s were also inspired by Neptune. A Uranian social act occurs on an intellectual plane as the Aquarius mentality discerns an injustice. Neptune, however, functions on a refined emotional plane, manifesting a universal love that dissolves differences between peoples. The

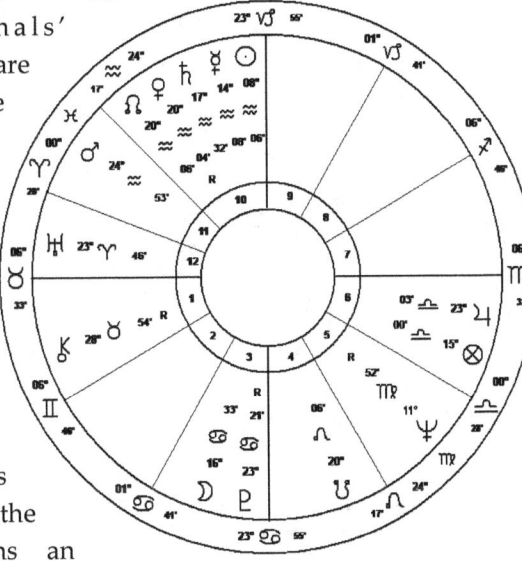

---

200. Dewey & Acocella, p. 500.
201. Bill White's birthchart has multiple planets in Aquarius.

Cardinals of the 1960s dissolved their racial differences in the waters of their Neptune and Pisces Moon. While staying at the same hotel, their families even swam together in the same swimming pool.[202]

Free agency is one of baseball's most enduring legacies from the social upheaval of the 1960s and '70s. The events that led to free agency for baseball players began in 1969 when the Cardinals traded center fielder Curt Flood to the Phillies. The trade between St. Louis and Philadelphia was executed on October 8, 1969[203] as the Cardinals were experiencing a Saturn return. But the key transits to the trade were the aspects of Sun and Jupiter conjunct to the Cardinals' Venus, the planet of center field. Additionally, Mars in Capricorn was forming a square to the Sun and Jupiter. Transiting Mars also formed an opposition to the Cardinals' natal Mars in Cancer and a square to the Cardinals' Venus. These transits unleashed a torrent of resentment within the Cardinals Mars and Venus. The Cardinals have a natal square between Venus and Mars. This aspect breeds jealousy and ill-will between partners. A person with this aspect commonly experiences bitter and near-violent breakups. The breakup between Curt Flood and the Cardinals led to events that nearly burned down baseball's existing order. After the trade, Curt Flood refused to report to Philadelphia. In court, he challenged a team's right to retain his services and the legality of the reserve clause. Although he lost his court challenge and was soon out of baseball, Flood's stance led to rulings that began free agency in the decade that followed. Interestingly, Flood was born in 1938, the year that Commissioner Landis granted free agency to many players in the Cardinals farm system. Landis's ruling and Curt Flood's birth occurred as Uranus was conjunct the Cardinal's Saturn in Taurus. With his

Curt Flood
Tuesday, January 18, 1938 12:00:00 PM
Houston, Texas
Time Zone: 06:00 (CST)
Longitude: 095° W 23' 24"
Latitude: 29° N 46' 06"

---

202. Golenbock, p. 441; Halberstam *October 1964*, p. 59.
203. Golenbock, p. 507.

Uranus of 10 degrees Taurus conjunct the Cardinals' Saturn, Curt Flood would grow up to embody the Uranian challenge to Saturn's authority. Flood's Uranus was also conjunct to the National League[204] Moon, the planet of workers in labor disputes. Flood's birthchart would cast him in the role of Uranian liberator.

The Cardinals have made enormous contributions to baseball. Their history demonstrates how the love and dreams of Neptune become manifest in the victories and institutions of Saturn.

---

204. The National League was organized on February 2, 1876. My rectified birthchart for the NL has a Moon of 9 degrees, 48 minutes Taurus.

The Giants

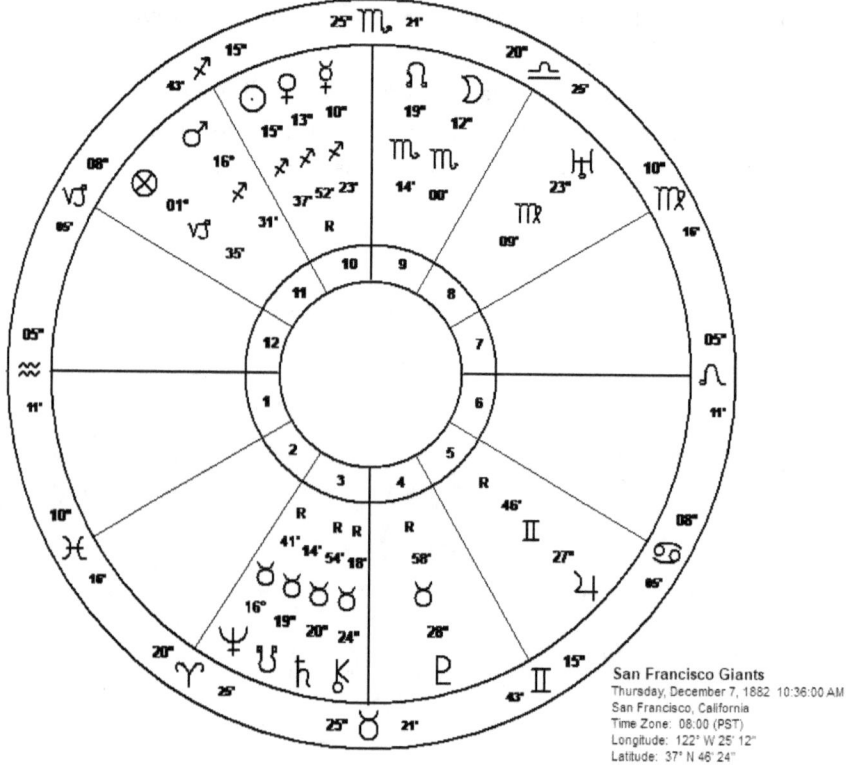

San Francisco Giants
Thursday, December 7, 1882 10:36:00 AM
San Francisco, California
Time Zone: 08:00 (PST)
Longitude: 122° W 25' 12"
Latitude: 37° N 46' 24"

The Giants, along with their twin franchise, the Phillies, were born on December 7, 1882[205] at 1:36 pm EST.[206] The Giants lived in New York until 1958, when they moved west to San Francisco. The move to San Francisco changed the Giants' Ascendant from Aries to Aquarius. The birthchart of the Giants has four inner planets—the Sun, Mercury, Venus, and Mars—in Sagittarius. The Moon and North Node are in the sign of Scorpio and in opposition to Neptune and Saturn, which are conjunct in Taurus. This opposition has brought the transformative nature of Scorpio to the Giants. The team also has Jupiter in square to Uranus, the aspect which has brought both home run hitters and steroid abuse to the franchise.

With so many planets in Sagittarius, the Giants have been a team of

---

205. Stein & Peters, *Giants Diary*, p. 1.
206. An MC of 10 Capricorn, when progressed by solar arc to 1902, the year John McGraw became manager, advances to 0 degrees Aquarius. McGraw remained the manager of the Giants for 30 years, while the MC was progressing through the sign of Aquarius.

The Giants

strong hitters. Barry Bonds holds the current record for home runs, with 762. Willie Mays competed with Hank Aaron to break Babe Ruth's home run record and finished with 660 career home runs. Mel Ott, for many years, held the record of most National League home runs, with 511. Willie McCovey holds the National League record of 18 career grand slams. Bill Terry, who batted .401 in 1930, was the last National League player to hit over 400. There are feats of lesser known Giant hitters worth noting. Giants' first baseman Roger Conner was one of the few power hitters of the Dead Ball Era. Conner hit 136 home runs in the 1880s, the most by any player in the decade.

In New York, the Giants' home field was called "the Polo Grounds." In their many years in New York, the Giants played in three different stadiums with this name.[207] A baseball team usually changes the name of a single stadium during the decades it plays there. The Giants, however, kept the name while changing stadiums. The name Polo Grounds was kept because it was liked and because of its astrological correspondence with the team. Polo is a game played on horses, a Sagittarian game, and interestingly, the game of polo was actually played at the first Polo Grounds.

New York Giants
Thursday, December 7, 1882 1:36:00 PM
New York, New York
Time Zone: 05:00 (EST)
Longitude: 073° W 59' 30"
Latitude: 40° N 45'

Saturn is conjunct to the Giants' South Node. The South Node and planets conjunct a South Node represent points of ease in a birthchart, skills quickly mastered and strengths that easily bear fruit. In contrast, the North Node represents challenges to be met. The fruits of the North Node are ultimately greater than those of the South Node, as the North Node represents callings and life challenges. However, a tendency exists, especially when a planet is conjunct to the South Node, to rely upon the easier means of success. For many years, The Giants had a tendency to rest on their South Node accomplishments. Saturn conjunct to the South Node brought the Giants early success with managing. Yet, in time, strong

---

207. https://en.wikipedia.org/wik/Polo_Grounds

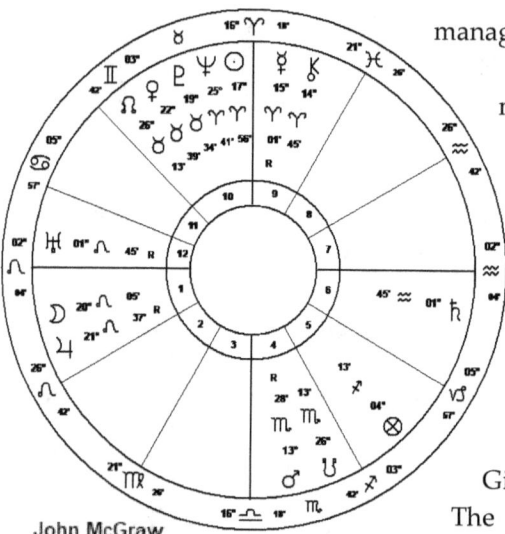

John McGraw
Monday, April 7, 1873 12:00:00 PM
Truxton, New York
Time Zone: 05:00 (EST)
Longitude: 076° W 01'
Latitude: 42° N 42'

management became a liability.

John McGraw was the Giants' manager for 30 years. With Saturn in the Giants' First House, McGraw became the face of the Giants franchise. When one thought of the Giants, one thought of McGraw. The birthchart of John McGraw has Pluto and Venus conjunct in the sign of Taurus. Both these planets are conjunct the Giants' Saturn and South Node. The Giants would excel soon after McGraw became their manager in 1902. The Giants' greatest success occurred during his reign. With McGraw in charge, the Giants won ten pennants and three World Series. McGraw was the first manager to try to control every facet of the game,[208] sometimes going so far as to call the pitches. He managed aggressively, often calling for the hit and run. McGraw instituted the platoon system and the use of late-inning defensive replacements. These methods would be copied by other managers to a point where they are now standard practices.

McGraw's sense of control extended beyond his players to the fans. When umpire calls went against his team, McGraw often made a grandstand display against the umpire. Such theatrics were purposely designed to excite the crowd. McGraw knew that emotional fans could both inspire his players and intimidate the umpires. McGraw's birthchart has the Moon conjunct Jupiter in the sign of Leo. This aspect made him a natural at playing to crowds. The Giants' birthchart also has an opposition aspect between Saturn and the Moon, which invited the Saturnian manager to influence the lunar fans.

The weakness of the Giants South Node-Saturn aspect became exposed in the 1910s. The Giants would lose three consecutive World Series from 1911 to 1913. Afterwards, Giants pitcher Christy Mathewson wrote an article stating that the Giants had lost the three World Series because their players were unable to take initiative as individuals. Instead, the Giants were, he claimed, "a team of puppets worked from the bench by a string."

---

208. Alexander, Charles: *John McGraw*, p. 322.

THE GIANTS

They habitually always looked to McGraw for instructions. By contrast, Connie Mack's Athletics, who beat the Giants in the 1911 and 1913 World Series, were trained to take initiative and think for themselves, and the A's, unlike the Giants, played steadily under the pressure of the World Series.[209] Decades later, similar South Node-Saturn tendencies surfaced in the 1980s under manager Roger Craig. He continuously tinkered with the lineup, often calling for pinch hitters, squeeze plays, and the hit and run. Craig would even call pitches from the bench. When he would call his favorite pitch, the split finger fastball, the result was sometimes a wild pitch.

The Giants' Saturn is also conjunct to Neptune. Aspects between Saturn and Neptune are common in sports franchises. Much of the experience of following a sports team involves the dreaming of a championship followed by the disillusionment of losing or the fulfillment of winning. These emotions are functions of Neptune. Together Neptune and Saturn can manifest in the realization of dreams, as the inspiration of Neptune becomes embodied through the earth energy of Saturn. On the other hand, the two planets can bring disillusion as the dreams of Neptune are interrupted by the hard reality of Saturn.

Neptune is inspirational and religious, but it can also be alcoholic and lethargic. Together, Neptune and Saturn suggest both inspirational leadership or owners and managers who abuse alcohol. Owner Horace Stoneham was a convivial drinker. He liked to stay up until the early morning, drinking and talking about baseball. McGraw had well-publicized occasions on which he drank excessively, but, by the standards of the day and the industry, his drinking was not unusual. More striking are the stories of McGraw attempting to help alcoholic players such as Bugs Raymond and Henry Zimmerman.[210] Here, the Saturnian manager imposed discipline on Neptunian alcoholics.

Among Giants fans, Willie Mays has a magical aura unlike any other baseball player. Willie Mays is likely the most beloved Giant to play in San Francisco. Fittingly, Mays' Sun in Taurus is conjunct the Giants' Neptune. Willie Mays evokes a Neptunian love from Giants fans that is not explained by his greatness as a player. It is his Neptune resonance with the Giants' birthchart that gives Mays his elevated place within the pantheon of Giants. Willie Mays' Sun, Venus and North Node are conjunct in Taurus, the aspect that made him a natural center fielder. His great fielding ability is captured in film of his famous catch during the 1954 World Series. Willie

---

209. Alexander, p. 191.
210. Alexander, Charles, pp. 143, 192

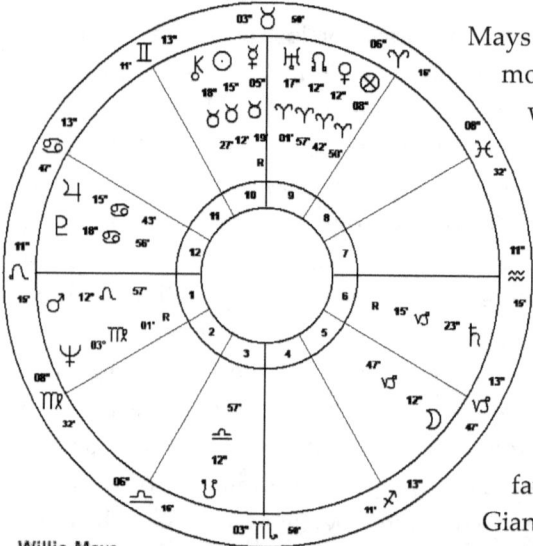

Willie Mays
Wednesday, May 6, 1931 12:00:00 PM
Westfield, Alabama
Time Zone: 05:00 (EST)
Longitude: 087° W 00'
Latitude: 33° N 48'

Mays also holds the record for most putouts by an outfielder, with 7,095.[211]

The Giants' Moon and North Node are conjunct in the sign of Scorpio. The Scorpionic nature of the Giants is reinforced by a strong Pluto in Taurus. When John McGraw died in 1934, columnist Heywood Broun wrote a famous description of the Giants: "An important part of McGraw's capacity for leadership," Broun wrote, "was that he could take kids out of coal mines and wheat fields and make them walk and talk and chatter and play ball with the look of eagles."[212] McGraw's discipline was often brutal. He could berate players unmercifully. Off the field, McGraw had his players spied on to keep them under his control. Yet, within the crucible of McGraw's leadership, crude boys metamorphosed into men. McGraw also took in players given up on by other teams as discipline problems: players such as Mike Donlin and Henry Zimmerman.[213] He regenerated their careers and redeemed them as men. Although McGraw was a very tough boss, the Giants were paid better than the players of all other teams. They always had first-class accommodations, rare treatment for baseball players of that era.

In astrological symbolism, the eagle is an exaltation of Scorpio. The scorpion is related to the eagle, the way coal is related to the diamond. A scorpion is an arachnid, a creature low on the scale of evolution. It crawls under rocks and dwells in dark places such as caves and mines. The sign of Scorpio is the most feared sign of the zodiac because, like the scorpion, its energy is often threatening and destructive. However, once a Scorpio gains discipline, once those powers are harnessed, a transformative process begins. Through discipline and introspection, a Scorpio is refined. The lowly scorpion, like McGraw's boys who once slaved in mines,

---

211. http://www.baseball-almanac.com/rb_ofpu.shtml
212. Alexander, Charles, p. 5
213. Alexander, Charles p. 107, 192.

becomes an eagle—a poised, intelligent and magnificent animal with the power of flight. The Giants of the 1920s possessed a mystique similar to that of the Yankees of the 1950s. They walked with a poise and bearing beyond professionalism. A sharpness and professional bearing emanated from their appearance. This was the look of eagles.

The birthchart of the New York Giants had Pluto, the despositor of Scorpio, in the Second House. The Second House rules property and wealth. The planet Pluto in the New York Giants' Second House manifested in a series of plutocratic owners. Andrew Freedman, John Brush, and Charles Stoneham all fit the profile of rich, powerful, and corrupt men. Andrew Freedman held strong connections with Tammany Hall, the patronage machine of New York politics. John Brush gave the name to "Brushism," the monopolistic practice whereby major league owners held stock in more than one team, thereby enabling themselves to shift players and resources between teams. Lopsided trades were purposely made to assist the chosen team. While Brush controlled the Reds, he traded away budding star Christy Matthewson to the Giants, a team in which he had a greater interest. In exchange, the Reds received Amos Rusie, whose best years were obviously behind him. Charles Stoneham operated a Casino-style brokerage that dealt in stock hypotheticals. A partner of Stoneham's was Arnold Rothstein, the man who supplied the money to fix the 1919 World Series. In the 1920s, Stoneham would be indicted for illegal finance activities,[214] but he was never convicted.

In 1958, Horace Stoneham, Charles Stoneham's son, moved the Giants to San Francisco in search of a more lucrative market, one he would not have to share with the Yankees.[215] Although the San Francisco Giants have been frequent contenders and have won championships, the Giants have not enjoyed the level of success in San Francisco that they had in New York, neither on the field nor financially. The Giants' birthchart, since they relocated to San Francisco, no longer has the powerful Second House Pluto. The Second House of finance is now empty, with unreliable Pisces on the house cusp. Financial problems, on two occasions, brought the San Francisco Giants to the brink of moving. In 1976, the Giants almost relocated to Toronto, and, in 1992, the team nearly moved to St Petersburg.

In San Francisco, the Giants' Pluto is located in the Fourth House. The Giants organization does not have the political clout that the Second House Pluto allowed them in New York. The ownership in San Francisco has

---

214. Dewey & Acocella, p. 348.
215. The Giants' plutocrats were ultimately defeated by the Yankees' plutocrats. (See Yankees Chapter).

not been plutocratic, as were its New York predecessors. But the building of Candlestick Park, which opened in 1960, did involve questionable patronage. The stadium was built on land sold to the city by a friend of Mayor George Christopher. This suspicious deal resulted in the ballpark built in an inconvenient and uncomfortable location. Strong winds from San Francisco Bay made Candlestick Park an uncomfortable stadium for both fans and players. The cold weather marred the fan experience, which hurt attendance and reduced revenue. In 2000, the Giants moved to Pacific Bell Park. Interestingly, the building and financing of the new ballpark was relatively free of political peddling, something unheard of in the Second House Pluto days of New York.

To understand the pitching of the New York Giants, we need to observe not only Mercury, which is part of the stellium in Sagittarius, but the Third House Jupiter in Gemini and the Sixth House Uranus in Virgo. Jupiter and Uranus are planets associated with batters, but within the Giants' birthchart, their sign and house placements make them representative of the team's pitching. Both planets are in pitchers' signs and pitchers' houses. Their placement in the pitchers' houses made Giants' pitching generally strong in New York. Pitcher Christy Matthewson won 373 games for the New York Giants. His clean-cut Virgo demeanor made him one of America's first sports role models.[216] Matthewson's nickname "Big Six" was the perfect name for a Virgo athlete, as the number six corresponds with the sign of Virgo, the sixth sign of the zodiac. Amos Rusie, an overpowering fastballer, pitched for the Giants in the 1890s. It was Rusie who caused the mound to be moved to its current 60 feet 6 inches distance from the plate. The speed of Rusie's pitches had put the batters at such a disadvantage that the mound needed to be moved.[217] Joe "Iron Man" McGinnity, another New York Giants pitcher in the Hall of Fame, pitched both games of double headers on five occasions. Carl Hubbel is best remembered for his performance in the 1934 All-Star game in which he struck out five future Hall of Famers in a row: Babe Ruth, Lou Gehrig, Jimmy Fox, Al Simmons, and Joe Cronin.

The Giants' birthchart, when relocated to San Francisco, removed Jupiter and Uranus from its Third and Sixth Houses. Nevertheless, transits to these planets still affect the pitching, since Jupiter and Uranus remain in the pitcher's signs of Gemini and Virgo. In San Francisco, the Giants' Third House now has Neptune and Saturn. San Francisco Giants pitching,

---

216. Stein, p. 307; Dewey & Acocella, p. 343.

217. The distance from the mound to homeplate was changed in 1893. (Dewey and Acocella, p. 339)

as a result of Saturn and Neptune in the Third House, has tended to be inconsistent and injury prone. As of this writing, San Francisco has had only one pitcher who played consistently for a great number of years, Juan Marichal. The energy of Neptune is often an affliction for pitchers, as it tends to blur a pitcher's focus and control. Neptune also brings walks. Saturn, meanwhile, brings limitations, including injuries. The tragedy of Dave Dravecky, in which he came back from cancer in his pitching arm and then became reinjured, occurred against the backdrop of the Giants' Third House Saturn. Dravecky broke his arm on Aug. 15, 1989, as the Sun, in transit at 23 Leo, made a square to the Giants' Saturn.

The Aries Rising of the New York Giants was strengthened by the conjunction of Mars and the Sun, with both planets trine to the Ascendant. This trine channeled a free flow of Mars energy through the Ascendant. Indeed, the Giants' Ascendant mirrored the rougher side of Aries. They inherited the "Old Oriole" style of play brought to them by their manager. John McGraw had played both shortstop and third base for the National League Baltimore Orioles of the 1890s. The "Old Orioles" are considered one of the rowdiest group of players ever assembled. They often provoked brawls and they continuously abused umpires. The New York Giants inherited their style. Shortstop Bill Dahlen, known as "Bad Bill," often started fights with the slightest provocation.[218] Pitcher Iron Man McGinnity holds the peculiar record of having hit by a pitch the highest percentage of batters. In his career, McGinnity hit one of every nineteen batters he faced.[219] The New York chart also has Saturn in the First House. The ringleader and the role model of their behavior was obviously the manager, McGraw.

"Giants" is an Aquarian name. The name Giants was first heard spoken regarding baseball in 1885[220] by manager Jim Moultrie. Moultrie is quoted as having exclaimed "My big fellows! My Giants! We are the people!"[221] The 1885 team had players who were physically large. A giant, however, is more than a large human being. A giant is symbolic of an example of humanity's potential, of the great possibilities inherent in the human species. A giant represents the values of humanism, brotherly love, and the dignity and worth of individuals. These values and qualities are representations of the sign of Aquarius. The city of San Francisco is a suitable place for the Giants, since San Francisco is very much an Aquarian

---

218. Dewey & Acocella, p. 344.
219. Dewey & Acocella, p. 344
220. The earlier New York mascot was "the Gothams."
221. Stein, p. 304

city. It is not only a place of intellectual and technological leadership, but also a city known for tolerance and humanistic values. San Francisco was the birthplace of the United Nations, and it is known for its acceptance of ethnic and sexual diversity.

The Giants in San Francisco display an Aquarian personality not only by hitting home runs but through their international quality. The San Francisco Giants have had an international cast from early on. The Giants were the first team to scout the Dominican Republic. Juan Marichal, the Alou brothers, and Manny Mota were among the first Dominicans signed by the Giants.[222] In the late innings of a game on Sept. 15, 1963, the three Alou brothers, Felipe, Matty and Jesus, played the three outfield positions. During that game, the Sun at 23 degrees Virgo was conjunct to the Giants' Uranus, while Venus at 27 degrees Virgo was square the Giants' Jupiter in Gemini, the sign of brothers. For many years, the Giants were also the only team to have had a Japanese player. Masanori Murakami pitched well for the Giants in 1964 and 1965, but contractual problems forced him to return to Japan. No other Japanese player would play in the major leagues until 1995, when Hideo Nomo made his debut with the Dodgers.

In 1964, manager Alvin Dark was quoted as saying that African-American and Latino players lacked both hustle and intelligence.[223] Alvin Dark denied making the remarks but was fired at the end of the season. Dark had played shortstop for the New York Giants in the 1950s. Interestingly, Dark had played the position of the Giants' Rising Sign back when they had had an Aries Ascendant. When the Giants moved to San Francisco, Dark would find himself in conflict with the values and personality of the new Aquarius Ascendant. Times had changed. It was now the 1960s in San Francisco. The Aquarius values of equality and diversity would bring down Alvin Dark of the old paradigm.

The Giants' Jupiter is in square to Uranus, a hybrid aspect that produces power hitters. The 1947 Giants set the record of most home runs by a team in a season, with 221. Neither Mays, Ott, nor Bonds played on this team. The Giants' Uranus-Jupiter square also brought steroid abuse and the rise and fall of Barry Bonds. Uranus rules technological advancements such as performance-enhancing drugs. The square from Jupiter created an excessive ability to hit the ball over the fence. It also brought a distortion to the meaning of the word "giant," as players on steroids increased their size and muscle mass.

---

222. Mandel, p. 56.
223. Dewey and Acocella, p. 530.

The narrative of Barry Bonds and his steroid use occurred under various aspects. In 1995, Uranus entered the sign of Aquarius. As it had done previously in 1911, Uranus in its own sign of Aquarius greatly increased the homerun totals. Roger Maris' record of 61 homeruns in a season, which was set in 1961, would be broken by Mark McGwire, who hit 70 home runs in 1998. McGwire's record would subsequently be topped by Bonds, who clubbed 73 home runs in 2001. At the time, baseball pundits explained the increased number of homeruns as a result of smaller ball parks and a "juiced ball." Later, it would be revealed that many sluggers had turned to steroids and other performance-enhancing drugs. All of this occurred while Uranus was in its own sign of Aquarius, as the influence of a planet is greatly increased when in its own sign. Uranus rules homeruns and steroids. The Giants' birthchart has a strong Uranus, which is enhanced both by the square from Jupiter and the Rising Sign of Aquarius. These aspects in the Giants' birthchart set the stage for San Francisco to become ground zero for baseball's steroid scandal. A square from Jupiter can enlarge something beyond normal limits. Here, the square from Jupiter took the Uranian quest for homerun power and literally put it on steroids.

The birthchart of Barry Bonds shows his own resonance with the Giants franchise. His father, Bobby Bonds, had been an important player and coach for the team. His godfather, Willie Mays, is a spiritual cornerstone of the franchise. Barry Bonds' birthchart has Venus and Mars conjunct in Gemini, planets that are square to the Giants' Uranus and conjunct to its Jupiter. His Moon in Aquarius made him a natural left fielder and homerun hitter. His Moon is also conjunct to the Giants' Ascendant, the aspect under which he bec

Barry Bonds
Friday, July 24, 1964 12:00:00 PM
Riverside, California
Time Zone: 07:00 (PDT)
Longitude: 117° W 22' 48"
Latitude: 33° N 57' 36"

franchise from 1993 to 2007.

On Sept. 5, 2003, federal investigators raided the home of Bonds' friend, Greg Anderson. The raid occurred as Mercury retrograde at 23 Virgo was exactly conjunct the Giants' Uranus. As the 2004 baseball season began, Pluto in transit at 22 Sagittarius was exactly opposite the Giants' Uranus and square to their Jupiter. The energy of Pluto exposes and purges that which is hidden. The bit-by-bit exposure of Bonds' steroid use would continue through the following years as he pursued and broke Hank Aaron's hallowed record of 755 home runs. The drama unfolded as the opposition and the square from slow-moving Pluto continued. Barry Bonds would break Hank Aaron's record on Aug. 7, 2007, while Venus at 24 degrees Virgo was exactly conjunct the Giants' Uranus and square to Bonds' Venus and Mars in Gemini.[224] However, with his legal case pending and the bad publicity generated by the steroid controversy, Bonds had become a liability to the Giants. On the night of Sept 20, with the Sun at 28 Virgo square to Mars at 27 Gemini, and both these planets in square and conjunction to the Giants' natal Jupiter and Uranus, Bonds was told he would not be signed for the following year.[225]

The Giants often play poorly in the month of June. Giant fans call this malaise "the June Swoon." It is a mystery why the Giants, in some seasons, after playing well and contending in April and May, suddenly collapse when June arrives. The mystery is solved upon considering the Giants' stellium in Sagittarius. The first planet of the stellium, Mercury, is located at 10 degrees Sagittarius. The last planet, Mars, is close to 17 degrees Sagittarius. On the first day of June, the Sun is in transit near 10 degrees Gemini, the degree exactly opposite the Giants Mercury. Since Sagittarius is a mutable sign, it has difficulty absorbing transits from challenging aspects such as the opposition and the square. In the first week of June, the Sun forms a series of oppositions with the Giants' planets in Sagittarius: Mercury, Venus, the Sun, and Mars. Additionally, Mercury is always within 28 degrees of the Sun, and Venus is always within 47 degrees of the Sun. This often places them in Gemini and opposite the Giants' Sagittarius planets during the month of June. Oppositions from Mercury and Venus can also contribute to a June Swoon.

The 1989 World Series between the Giants and the Athletics is

---

224. Bonds also experienced Saturn transits as he broke the record. Saturn at 27 degrees Leo was conjunct his Mercury, the despositor of his Gemini planets. When he broke the record at 8:51 pm PDT in San Francisco, the Ascendant was 1 degree Pisces, conjunct his natal Saturn of 4 degrees Pisces.

225. Espn.com news services, "Barry Bonds Steroids Timeline" http://www.sports.espn.go.com

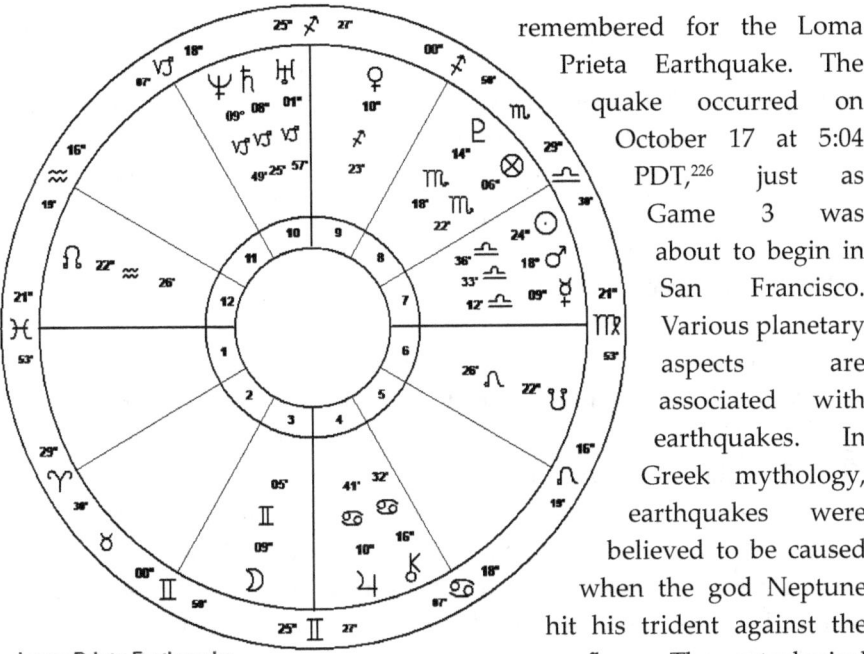

Loma Prieta Earthquake
Tuesday, October 17, 1989 5:04:00 PM
San Francisco, California
Time Zone: 07:00 (PDT)
Longitude: 122° W 25' 12"
Latitude: 37° N 46' 24"

remembered for the Loma Prieta Earthquake. The quake occurred on October 17 at 5:04 PDT,[226] just as Game 3 was about to begin in San Francisco. Various planetary aspects are associated with earthquakes. In Greek mythology, earthquakes were believed to be caused when the god Neptune hit his trident against the ocean floor. The astrological chart for the 1989 earthquake shows Neptune to have been the dominant astrological energy. When the quake struck, five planets and the Part of Fortune were in aspect to Neptune. Both Neptune and Saturn, conjunct near 9 degrees Capricorn, formed semi-squares to the S.F. Giants' MC.[227] Mercury in transit at 9 Libra was square to Neptune and Saturn, while Jupiter at 10 degrees Cancer formed an opposition to Neptune and Saturn. In addition, the Moon at 9 Gemini was quincunx to Neptune, and Venus formed a semisextile to Neptune from 10 degrees Sagittarius. It would have been interesting to observe what would have occurred on the field if Game Three had been played under such extreme transits.

Before the Giants won the 2010 World Series, 56 years had passed since their last World Series victory in 1954. The Giants were experiencing the third longest draught since a Series win, following the Cubs and Indians. Giants' pundits had begun speaking of a curse. The 2010 Giants would defeat the Rangers in the World Series as Uranus and Jupiter were conjunct in Pisces and opposite and square their natal Uranus and Jupiter. Perhaps more importantly, from late in the season, Mars was in transit through the sign of Scorpio. Mars formed conjunctions to the Giants'

---

226. http://en.wikipedia.org/wiki/1989_Loma_Prieta_earthquake
227. Interestingly, both planets were actually conjunct the MC of the New York Giants' birthchart.

Scorpio planets and oppositions to their Taurus planets. Shortstop Edgar Renteria, who won the World Series MVP, embodied the transit with clutch hitting. The highly pressurized potency of Mars in Scorpio held the energy for the Giants' late season surge and post-season victories. The Giants played several tense games with close scores that were decided in late innings. Followers of the team described these games as "torture." Indeed, an excess of Mars and Pluto energy can lead to genuine torture, the deliberate and cruel infliction of pain. However, in 2010, the concentration of energy involving Mars, Pluto, the Moon and Saturn brought the Giants a World Series trophy after a 56-year wait.

A cherished moment in the history of the Giants is the homerun hit by Bobby Thomson to win the National League pennant of 1951. Bobby Thomson hit the home run at 3:58 pm on October 3, 1951, a day on which he was playing third base. Transits were set for a third baseman to be a hero, as they featured Pluto and the sign of Scorpio. Pluto at 20 degrees Leo had been in square to the Giants' Saturn since August, the aspect that had enabled them to win 50 of their last 62 games and end the season in a tie with the Dodgers. On the day Thompson hit his walk-off homerun, the Moon was in Scorpio, the third baseman's sign, while Mars, in transit at 29 degrees Leo, was square to the Giants' Pluto. At 3:58, the precise moment of the "Miracle of Coogan's Bluff," Mars was setting, exactly conjunct the Descendant.[228]

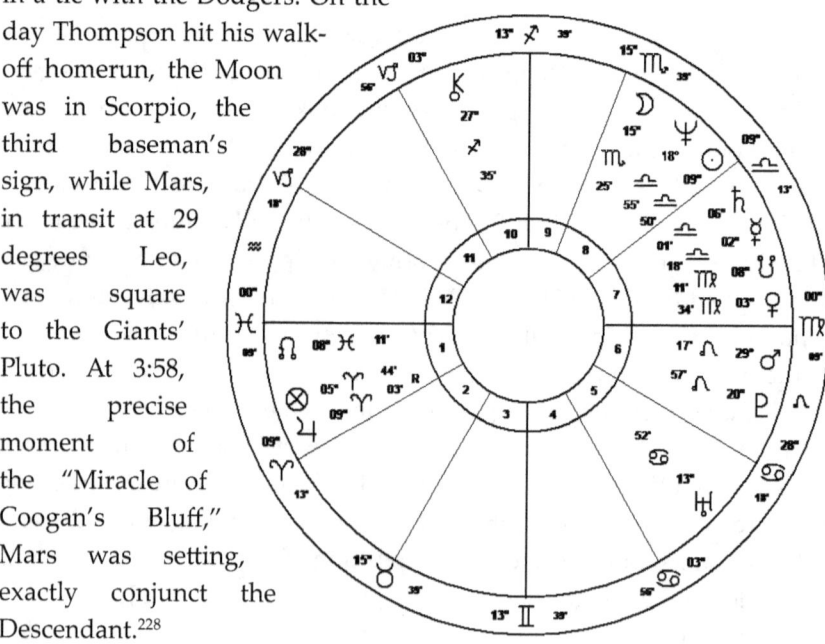

Bobby Thomson Home Run
Wednesday, October 3, 1951 3:58:00 PM
New York, New York
Time Zone: 05:00 (EST)
Longitude: 073° W 59' 30"
Latitude: 40° N 45'

---

228. Stein, p. 319.

The Phillies

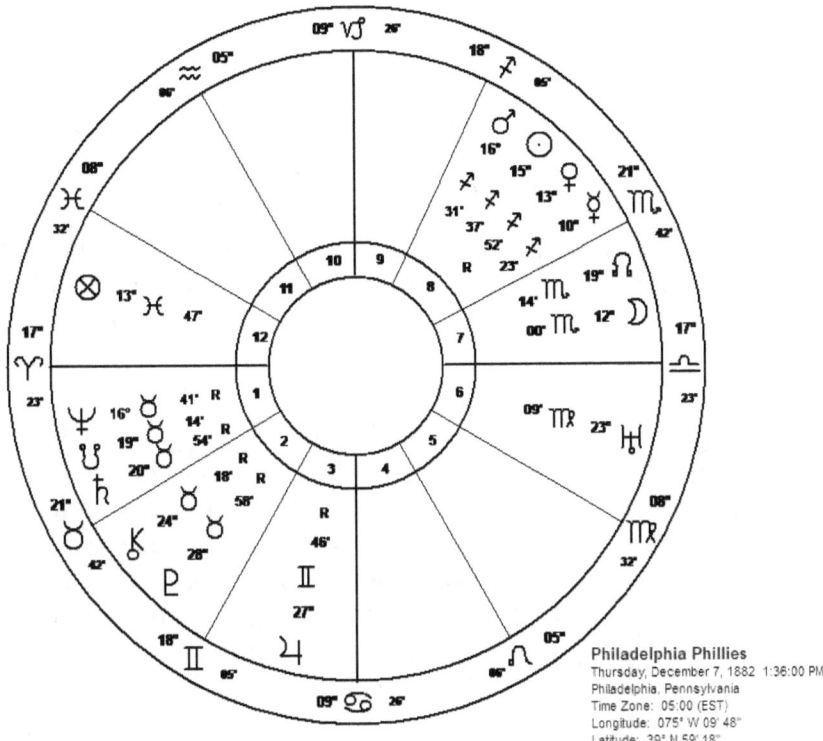

Philadelphia Phillies
Thursday, December 7, 1882 1:36:00 PM
Philadelphia, Pennsylvania
Time Zone: 05:00 (EST)
Longitude: 075° W 09' 48"
Latitude: 39° N 59' 18"

The Phillies, and their twin franchise, the Giants, were born on December 7, 1882[229] at 1:36 pm EST.[230] Their birthchart has four inner planets in the sign of Sagittarius, which gives the Phillies their strong offense. The Moon and North Node are conjunct in the sign of Scorpio and in opposition to Neptune and Saturn, which are conjunct in Taurus, aspects that have resulted in stingy owners, and passionate fans.

With four planets in Sagittarius—Sun, Mercury, Venus and Mars, the Phillies are a team of big bats and heavy hitters. Mike Schmidt hit 548 home runs in the 1970s and '80s, but Phillies history includes outstanding hitters from their beginning. Sam Thompson, who played for the Phillies in the 1880s, twice hit over 160 RBIs in a season. Lefty O'Doul batted .398 in 1929. Chuck Klein, among the most powerful sluggers of the 1930s,

---

229. Stein & Peters, *Giants Diary*, p. 1.
230. This chart is rectified for the opening of Citizen's Bank Park in 2004. Using solar arc progressions, the Phillies' IC of 9 Cancer became conjunct to the Phillies' Moon that year.

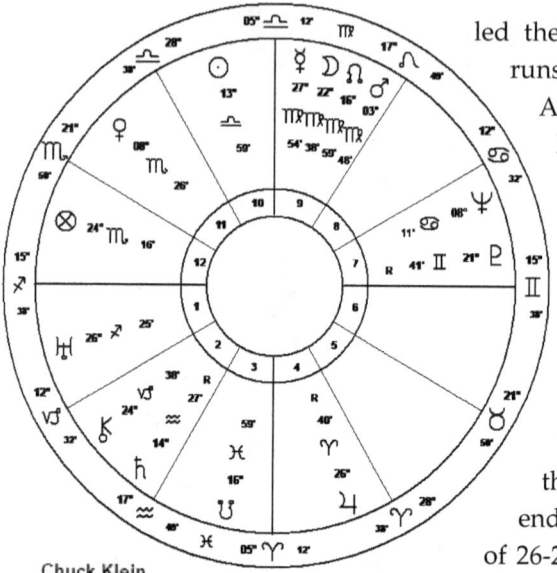

Chuck Klein
Friday, October 7, 1904 12:00:00 PM
Indianapolis, Indiana
Time Zone: 05:00 (EST)
Longitude: 086° W 08' 24"
Latitude: 39° N 48' 12"

led the National League in home runs in four different seasons. As a team, the Phillies offense has done amazing things. Their collective average for 1894 was .349, the record for the highest average by a team.[231] On August 25, 1922, the Phillies participated in the highest scoring game on record. That day, the Phillies played the Cubs in a game which ended with the whopping score of 26-23.[232] In 1932, a year of high batting statistics, the Phillies led the National League with a team average of 292. Even more amazing is the fact that, in that year, the National League's top three RBI leaders were all Phillies: Don Hurst 143, Chuck Klein 137, and Pinky Whitney 127.

The pitching of the Phillies is an embodiment not of only Mercury in Sagittarius, but also of Jupiter in Gemini and Uranus in Virgo, which are square to each other in pitchers' signs. Each of these three planets is in a problematic placement astrologically. Traditional astrology states that Mercury is afflicted when in the sign of Sagittarius. Likewise, Jupiter is afflicted when in the sign of Gemini.[233] In baseball astrology, one can explain the affliction this way: Mercury, the planet of the pitcher, is in Sagittarius, the sign of the batter. The planet of the pitcher is in the sign of its natural opponent. Jupiter, the planet of the batter, occupies not only a sign of the pitcher, Gemini, but one of the pitcher's houses, the Third. Uranus, the planet of the home run, rests in the pitcher's other house, the Sixth. Uranus in the Sixth House suggests pitchers who are prone to giving up home runs. Altogether, the placements of Mercury, Jupiter and Uranus create challenges for Phillies pitching.

Pitching was an issue for large parts of Philadelphia history. In 1932, when the Phillies led the National League with a .292 average, Phillies

---

231. Dewey & Acocella, p. 415.
232. This game is analyzed in Section III.
233. A planet is considered to be afflicted when placed in a sign that is opposite to its own sign.

pitchers answered with a 4.47 ERA, the worst in the league. Nonetheless, the Phillies have had great pitchers who rose beyond the debilities of the Phillies' birthchart. Grover Cleveland Alexander won over thirty games in 1915, 1916, and 1917. Before his trade to the Cubs in 1918, Alexander often led the league in wins, strike outs, and innings pitched. Robin Roberts pitched solidly for the Phillies from 1948 to 1961. Roberts, who led the league in innings pitched from 1951 to 1955, was an efficient Virgo-style pitcher who got batters out with only a few pitches thrown. Steve Carlton won 27 games in the strike-shortened season of 1972, a year the Phillies finished 59-87 and in last place.

The South Node of a birthchart indicates an area of ease. When Saturn is conjunct the South Node, stubborn blocks and resistance to change often develop. The Phillies' conjunction of Saturn and the South Node has manifested differently in the history of the Phillies than in the history of the Giants. Whereas the Giants' South Node-Saturn revealed itself in managers who overmanaged, for the Phillies, the aspect became manifest in a constraint over money. Saturn and the South Node are both in the sign of Taurus, the sign of wealth and property. Saturn causes blockages, impediments to normal flows. Saturn in Taurus often brings financial hardships. Nevertheless, even in times of prosperity, Saturn in Taurus can manifest in parsimonious behaviors such as an impulse to hoard and an unwillingness to spend or invest.

For many years, Saturn conjunct the South Node manifested in Phillies owners with parsimonious ways. A line of notoriously stingy owners paid their players poorly and were unwilling to invest in the team. These owners would claim financial hardship and that their thrift was the result of tough times, but real greed was involved. Pluto in the Second House of finances corresponds to an intense desire for money. Unfortunately for the Phillies and their fans, it took many years for the owners to learn the value of investing for greater profit.

When the American League was launched in 1901, the unwillingness of the Phillies' ownership to compete with the higher salaries of the American League cost them their star players. Napoleon Lajoie and Ed Delehanty, both future Hall of Famers, defected to the new league. In 1900, the Phillies had been respectable contenders, but, by 1902, the Phillies sank to seventh place. In 1914, another upstart organization, the Federal League, competed for players against the established teams. Again the Phillies' cheap ways ruined a respectable team. The 1913 Phillies had placed second. That year, Tom Seaton led the National League in wins, with 27. Seaton expected a sizable raise after such a season, but Phillies owner William Baker offered him little, causing the star pitcher to jump to the Federal League. Soon the Phillies would lose shortstop Mickey Doolan, second baseman Otto Knabe, and pitchers Ad Brennan and Runt Walsh to the Federal League. The Phillies ended 1914 in seventh place.

It was the 1917 trade of Grover Cleveland Alexander and catcher Bill Killefer to the Cubs that historians claim instituted a lack of competitiveness for 30 years. Frederick Lieb wrote,

> *It was the start of a vicious circle which continued for years. Sell stars and meet the bills. With rundown teams, the patronage fell and fell. The remedy, of course: sell more desirable players. If you developed any players, sell them to the highest bidder. For some thirty years there was no thought of winning, but of keeping one's head above water and staying one jump ahead of the sheriff.*[234]

William Baker would die in 1930, but the next Phillies owner, Gerald Nugent, would maintain the same business philosophy, continuing the sales of homegrown talent. Casey Stengel and Dave Bancroft were sold to the Giants. Dolf Camili was dealt to the Dodgers in 1938. Three years later, Camili would win the National League MVP. In 1938 Bucky Walters was dealt to Cincinnati, where he won the MVP award in a Reds uniform.

There are other notorious examples of the cheapness of Phillies ownership. Pat Moran, who managed the Phillies from 1915 to 1918, was not allowed a coach.[235] In 1929, Chuck Klein led the league in home runs and was on his way to hitting over 50 home runs for the season. William Baker had the right field fence raised 15 feet. Baker did this to the disadvantage of Chuck Klein, his own player. It was said Baker did not want Klein's home run totals to reach "Ruthian dimensions," because then he would ask for a "Ruthian salary."[236]

Saturn conjunct to the South Node also brought the pattern of losing seasons to Philadelphia. Saturn, the planet of limitations and obstacles, brings losses. The Phillies have distinguished themselves with some inglorious records: the most consecutive games lost (23), from July 23 to Aug 20, 1961, and the most 100-loss seasons (14). Generations of Phillies fans came and went without a World Series trophy. Before 1980, the Phillies had won only two pennants in their history going back to 1883.

---

234. Lieb & Baumgartner, *The Phillies*, p. 142.
235. Dewey and Acocella, p. 419.
236. Lieb & Baumgartner, p. 167.

The Phillies won their first World Series in 1980, their 97th season. Just before that championship, the Phillies had begun to rise out of their South Node rut. On December 5, 1978, the franchised signed free agent Pete Rose to a four-year contract for $3.225 million. At the time, it was the highest salary of any professional athlete, as well as a signing unimaginable during the reigns of previous owners. On the day of the signing, the Sun and Mercury were conjunct in Sagittarius, and also conjunct to the Phillies' natal Venus, the planet of money and a dispositor of the Phillies' Saturn in Taurus. Uranus, in transit through Scorpio, was conjunct to the Phillies North Node. This transit from Uranus freed them from the regressive pull of the South Node that had held them back for so many years.

The Phillies' Moon is in the sign of Scorpio, the most passionate sign of the zodiac. This Scorpio Moon is embodied in the Phillie fans, who are both extreme and abusive. Scorpios can be self-destructive, directing their venom inwardly. Indeed, a scorpion will even commit suicide by stinging itself. Understandably, the Phillies have fielded teams that could send some fans towards thoughts of suicide. The venom of the Phillies' fans has indeed been directed inwardly, onto their own team. Fans in Philadelphia are notorious for booing their own players. Interestingly, the objects of their harshest abuse have been third basemen, the Scorpio position. Self-destructive Scorpio fans boo the position of their sign. In the 1960s, third baseman Dick Allen was booed by the Phillie fans.

Mike Schmidt
Tuesday, September 27, 1949 12:00:00 PM
Dayton, Ohio
Time Zone: 04:00 (EDT)
Longitude: 084° W 12' 12"
Latitude: 39° N 45' 30"

Allen had clashed with teammates and management. He was also outspoken on race issues. In the 1970s, Phillie fans abused mild-mannered Mike Schmidt, also a third baseman. Schmidt was a solid slugger, on his way to the Hall of Fame. Yet the fans abused him for his weak hitting in post-season play. In 1993, closer Mitch Williams received death threats from fans irate over the lost World Series. Williams had been unable to hold leads in the last two games of the Series. In the following off-season, the front office was justifiably worried about how the fans would respond to Williams the next season. They traded Williams before the next Opening Day.

Early in the Twentieth Century, an ugly incident occurred in which the Phillie fans turned on their twin franchise, the Giants. One day in April of 1906[237] with Mars at 20 degrees Taurus and conjunct the Phillies Saturn and South Node, a series of events occurred that culminated in an attack by a mob of Phillie fans against the Giants players. During a game, a verbal exchange between John McGraw, who had been coaching in the third base box, and Phillie third baseman Paul Sentelle, led to a fight between them on the field. Both benches cleared and a brawl followed. McGraw and Sentelle were both ejected. The two would, however, continue their fight, taking it underneath the grandstand. The fans were in a foul mood. Meanwhile, the Giants proceeded to win the ballgame.

The Giants were unpopular in Philadelphia that year. They were the strutting World Champions who had beaten the AL Philadelphia team, the Athletics, in the previous World Series. After the game, the Giants left the stadium in their fancy open carriages pulled by black horses wearing yellow blankets with letters bragging, "New York Giants, World's Champions." Phillie fans outside the park attempted to grab these blankets off the horses. Consequently, a Giant player took the carriage driver's whip and began swinging it at the crowd. The crowd then began pelting the Giants with lemons and ice available from nearby lemonade vendors. In the last carriage, Giant Catcher Roger Bresnehan was standing and kicking at the fans. He soon lost his balance and fell from his carriage. The catcher was alone on the street facing an ugly mob, while the other Giants carriages continued on, unaware of his plight.

Bresnehan was reportedly alone against 1000 angry Phillie fans. Bresnehan, the Giants catcher, was an embodiment of that team's 12 degree Scorpio Moon. The resentful Phillies Moon of the same degree, represented in their fans, attacked the Giants' catcher, the lunar embodiment of their much more successful twin. Roger Bresnahan held

---

237. Dewey & Acocella, p. 417. Author's note: I have not found a primary source that documents the date of this riot. But it likely occurred in the late afternoon of April, 14, 1906, after the Phillies lost an extra-inning game to NY. That afternoon, Mars was conjunct the Phil and NY South Node and Saturn. Uranus and Neptune were opposed to each other and conjunct both teams' MC and IC axes. Mercury at 9 degrees Aries completed a t-square to both planets.

his own, swinging his fists and kicking with his spikes. He then made it into a grocery store, where he barricaded the door. Half an hour later, he was finally "rescued." When the Philadelphia police arrived, they were also hostile to Bresnahan. Instead of arresting the rioters, the police cited the Giants' catcher for disturbing the peace and fined him $10.[238]

There is a gentler story between the two teams that shows brotherly love by the Phillies for their twin, the Giants. This was a moment when the Phillies Moon was quite generous towards the Moon of its New York sibling. In 1890, Phillies catcher Harry Decker designed the first modern catcher's mitt. The glove would become named the "Decker Safety Catching Mitt." But the first player to use the new mitt in an actual game would not be Harry Decker, but Buck Ewing, the catcher for the Giants.[239] Harry Decker generously allowed his lunar counterpart on the Giants to use his mitt before he had done so himself.

A Moon is also embodied in a team's stadium. As Scorpio is the sign of death, a horrible accident happened at the Baker Bowl that resulted in the death of 12 fans. On August 6, 1903, with the Sun in Leo square to the Phillies' Scorpio Moon,[240] the left field bleachers of the Phillies ballpark, the Baker Bowl, collapsed. The tragedy began when a building across the street from the left field stands caught fire. Fans in the stands took more interest in the fire than the game. Soon spectators from other parts of the stadium joined those in left field. The Baker Bowl had been in disrepair for years. Its metal grandstands were rusty and unable to bear the weight of the extra fans. When the foundation gave way, 12 fans were killed and about 200 were injured.[241]

A more unusual manifestation of the sign Scorpio was built into Veteran's Stadium, where the Phillies played from 1971 to 2003. The number 8 is associated with the sign Scorpio, as Scorpio is the eighth sign of the zodiac. The number eight was embodied in the perimeter of Veterans Stadium. The ballpark appeared to be another cookie-cutter circular-shaped stadium, but it was not really the shape of a circle. Instead, eight lines formed the perimeter of the stadium, which made it an octagon.

1950 is remembered fondly by Phillie fans as the year of the "Whiz Kids," the team that won the Phillies' second pennant. Phillies pitching was outstanding in 1950, leading both leagues with a 3.50 team ERA.

---

238. Lieb & Baumgartner, pp. 74-75.
239. Dewey & Acocella, p. 415.
240. Other transits include Pluto, Jupiter and Uranus in hard aspects to the Phillies' Uranus. Uranus rules left field.
241. Lewis, Allen & Schenk, Larry: *This Date in Philadelphia Phillies History*, p. 118.

Robin Roberts won 20 games, and reliever Jim Konstancy won the National League MVP. Their pitching was backed by a transit from Mars. Early in the season, Mars, in transit through Virgo, formed a conjunction to the Phillies Uranus and a square to the Phillies Jupiter. However, come September, Saturn, the malefic, which had also been in transit through Virgo, would conjunct the Phillies' natal Uranus. The Phillies' pitching would falter. Curt Simmons was drafted into the military, and the rest of the staff showed fatigue as the regular season came to a close. The Phillies led the NL for most of 1950, then nearly lost the pennant to the Dodgers.[242]

A season earlier, Phillie First Baseman Eddie Waitkus was shot by a female fan in a Chicago hotel room. The shooting of Waitkus took place on June 14, 1949.[243] The first baseman nearly died. Elements of Waitkus's life would echo into Bernard Malamud's 1952 novel, *The Natural,* and the character of Roy Hobbs. In 1950, the Year of the Whiz Kids, Waitkus came back and even batted leadoff for the Phillies. He played all 154 games and batted .284. That year, Pluto was in transit near 16 degrees Leo and square to the Phillies' natal Neptune. As Neptune corresponds with Waitkus's position of first base, the transit from Pluto brought regeneration to the Phillies first baseman.

1964 is a bad memory for Phillies fans. The Phillies had a seemingly comfortable 6 1/2 game lead on Sept 21. However, their pitching became erratic as Uranus, in transit at 10 degrees Virgo, formed a square to their natal Mercury. Ray Culp and Dennis Bennett became injured. Jim Bunning and Chris Short were overused and tired.[244] Also that September, Saturn, in a retrograde transit through Aquarius, formed a square with the Phillies' Pluto. These aspects brought about the horrible end to the season, as the Phillies finished 1964 one game behind the Cardinals. The Phillies went down in agonizing defeat. A Scorpionic loss is the most painful of all.

The Phillies finally won a World Series in 1980. Since their birth in 1882, the Phillies had never before won a Series. It is interesting to observe under which transits such a long-sought goal is finally reached. In September and October of 1980, Neptune was in transit near 20 degrees Sagittarius, and Pluto was in transit near 20 degrees Libra. Together, Neptune and Pluto formed a yod to the Phillies Saturn of 20 degrees Taurus. It was these powerful transits to Saturn that delivered the trophy. Saturn becomes a benefic in time. The transit from Pluto would be harnessed by third

---

242. The dramatic last game of the 1950 season is examined in Section III of this book.
243. http://en.wikipedia.org/wiki/Eddie Waitkus
244. Halberstam, David. *October 1964,* p. 303.

baseman Mike Schmidt. This third baseman, who would win the World Series MVP, had an unusually good post-season. The transit from Neptune was harnessed by first baseman Pete Rose,[245] whose veteran leadership provided stability for the 1980 team.

The Phillies would win the pennant in 1993 as the Uranus-Neptune conjunction of that year formed a trine to their natal Saturn. In addition, Saturn in Aquarius was square to Pluto in Scorpio during the 1993 seasons. These planets would square and oppose the Phillies' Taurus and Scorpio planets. In 1964, a transit from Saturn in Aquarius had helped to ruin them, but in 1993, Saturn in Aquarius provided stability.

A fascinating figure from the 1993 season is their closer, Mitch Williams. Williams' birthchart has the Sun at 25 degrees Scorpio in square to Saturn[246] at 29 degrees Aquarius. This aspect creates a person meant to carry an extreme amount of pressure. In 1993, Williams was holding not only the energy of his natal Sun square to Saturn, but the energy of the Saturn-Pluto square. Pluto in transit was conjunct to his Sun, while Saturn in transit was conjunct to his natal Saturn. Mitch Williams underwent an unfortunate Saturn return in 1993.

Mitch Williams
Tuesday, November 17, 1964   12:00:00 PM
Santa Ana, California
Time Zone: 08:00 (PST)
Longitude: 117° W 51' 24"
Latitude: 33° N 44'

Interestingly, Williams had been born in 1964, that horrible year for the Phillies, two months after their September collapse. Fittingly, Saturn, in the birthchart of Williams, is located uncomfortably near to the position it held during the 1964 collapse, square to the Phillies' Pluto. The Scorpio Phillies fans had an unfortunate date with Mitch Williams' bad luck Saturn return. Attempting to close Game 6 against Toronto, he gave up the home

---

245. See Reds' chapter for more about Pete Rose.
246. Saturn rules the late innings. The birthcharts of successful closers will have strong Saturn aspects. The sign of Scorpio also corresponds to the role of the closer. Scorpio is the sign of death. See Chapter One for the symbolic element of death in the game of baseball.

run to Joe Carter, which lost the series for Philadelphia. Williams' Saturn aspects saddled him with the role of the goat.

The Phillies' next appearance in the World Series took place in 2008. The deciding Game 5 proved riveting for the rain delay that lasted almost two days. On October 27, at 10:40 EDT, Game 5 was suspended after 5 ½ innings of play, soon after the Rays tied the game 2-2 in the top of the sixth inning.[247] Phillies fans complained the game should have been suspended sooner instead of after the game had become tied. The Phillies were holding a 3-1 lead in the World Series and were poised to win their first Series since 1980, but their fans feared the trophy would be swept away in the rain delay, as momentum could easily swing towards Tampa Bay. Transits for the game supported their concerns. The Phillies' Neptune was undergoing heavy aspects, and Neptune brings both rain and disillusionment. The Phllies' natal Neptune of 16 Taurus had been enjoying a trine from Jupiter at 16 degrees Capricorn, but it was also suffering an opposition from Mars at 16 Scorpio. The Phillies' natal Neptune is also conjunct to their natal Saturn of 20 Taurus. If the Series had proceeded to seven games, the transits could have brought them Saturnian hard luck, as Mars was soon to form an opposition to natal Saturn. Fortunately, the rains stopped in time. Two nights later, on Oct 29, the Phillies won Game 5 and the 2008 World Series. The final out was recorded at 9:58 EDT while the Moon at 19 degrees of Scorpio formed a conjunction with the team's North Node and a benevolent opposition to their natal Saturn.

The history of the Phillies demonstrates how Saturn aspects mature in time. An opposition transit from the Moon to natal Saturn, which in previous decades would likely have doomed them, in 2008 crowned them as champions.

---

247. Hoch, Bryan, "In a First, World Series Game Suspended," MLB.com, Oct. 28, 2008.

The Western League

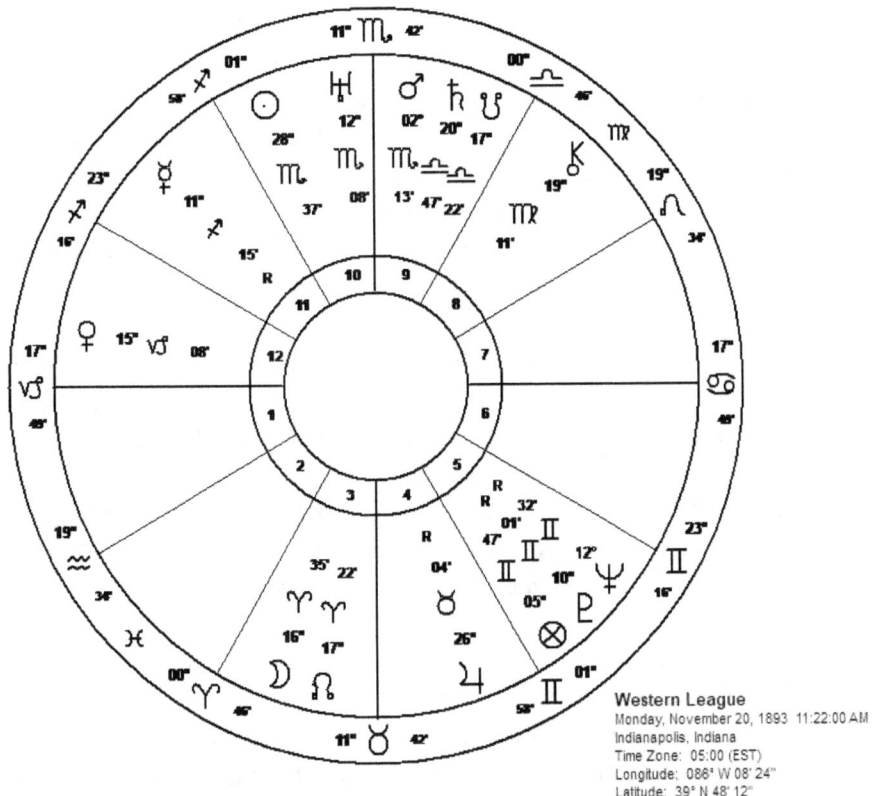

Western League
Monday, November 20, 1893 11:22:00 AM
Indianapolis, Indiana
Time Zone: 05:00 (EST)
Longitude: 086° W 08' 24"
Latitude: 39° N 48' 12"

On November 20, 1893[248], the Western League[249] was born in Indianapolis. The Western League was a minor league that would eventually metamorphose into what is now called the American League. The league included eight teams in the Midwest region of the United States. The eight cities with teams in the league were Indianapolis, Sioux City, Grand Rapids, Toledo, Kansas City, Milwaukee, Minneapolis, and Detroit. Of these eight teams, seven were born with the inception of the league. An eighth team, Detroit, had played its earliest seasons in the National League.

Of the seven teams born with the league, four would survive to 1901, the first season of the American League as a major league. These four

---

248. *Reach's Official Base Ball Guide*, 1894 edition. p. 33
249. Three different leagues have been called the called the "Western League." A Western League existed prior to the one outlined here. A different Western League would exist after this one.

teams are thriving to this day as the Cleveland Indians, Chicago White Sox, Minnesota Twins, and Baltimore Orioles. None of these four teams would remain in the city of their birth. The Kansas City team would move east in 1901 and become the Washington Senators. In 1961, this same team would move to Minneapolis and be renamed the Minnesota Twins. The Grand Rapids team would move to Cleveland in 1900, where it eventually took the name "Indians." The Milwaukee team moved to St Louis in 1902, where it was called "the Browns." In 1954, the Browns moved to Baltimore and became the current Orioles. The Sioux City team would move to St. Paul in 1895, and then to Chicago in 1900, where they are now known as the White Sox. The Western League teams born to Indianapolis, Minneapolis and Toledo would fall from the history books. Perhaps they continued in other minor leagues.

My rectifications show that the four surviving teams were all born at 11:22 AM EST.[250] There is a strong Scorpio emphasis to these birthcharts. The Sun, Mars, Uranus, and MC are all in the sign of Scorpio. These birthcharts also have a strong opposition between the Sun in Scorpio and Jupiter in Taurus. Pluto and Neptune are conjunct in the sign of Gemini and opposite to Mercury retrograde in Sagittarius. The Moon and North Node are conjunct in Aries and in opposition to Saturn and the South Node in Libra.

The various longitudes and latitudes of the home cities give these birthcharts their differences and the teams their distinctions. All four birthcharts have a Scorpio MC and a Capricorn Ascendant, but the degrees of their axes differ. The MCs and ICs form differing aspects with the planets. The White Sox have their Ascendant in conjunction with Venus. The Indians have an Ascendant in square to Saturn. The Orioles have their Ascendant in sextile to the Sun. The Twins have Mars in close conjunction with the MC. While the teams share similar tendencies, they have distinct differences in their histories, which reflect the different aspects of their axes.

The metamorphosis of the Western League into the American League occurred in 1900 and 1901. The Western League was a minor league until 1901. As a minor league, it maintained an agreement to develop players for the major league teams. Those players' services would be purchased by the major league teams when the players became ready. Ban Johnson, backed by the finances of Charley Somers, masterminded a challenge to the entrenched National League, which was undergoing player discontent.

---

250. At that moment in Indianapolis, Uranus was conjunct to the MC within one degree, an aspect that reflects the challenging nature of the new league.

The Western League

On October 14, 1900, The Western League announced that it had become a new major league and would henceforth be called the American League. It drew players away from the NL by offering higher pay and better working conditions. The new league also added three new teams in the fall and winter of 1900-01: Philadelphia, Boston, and Baltimore. The Baltimore team would move to New York in 1902 and become known as the Yankees.

The launch of the Western League and its subsequent metamorphosis into a major league was a very bold venture, which is reflected in the aspect of Sun opposite Jupiter in its birthchart. When the will of the Sun joins forces with the expansiveness of Jupiter, such ventures are possible. Also, the metamorphosis of a minor league into a major league is indicative of the Scorpio planets in the Western League's birthchart. Scorpios have the capacity to radically transform themselves.

Ban Johnson is the central figure in the birth of the Western League and the rise of the American League. In 1900, he was the league president at the young age of 26. He would remain in office until he was ousted in 1927. Ban Johnson's birthchart shows his strong synastry with the league. Johnson's natal Sun of 15 degrees Capricorn is conjunct to the Western League's Venus. Johnson's Moon, North Node, Venus, and Jupiter are all conjunct the Western League Sun in Scorpio. His Saturn of 18 degrees Libra is conjunct to the Western League Saturn of 20 Libra, the aspect which shows his capacity to be American League president. Ban Johnson's Sun in Capricorn displays his natural executive ability.

Another man deeply involved with the history of the American League is Bill Veeck. At different times, Bill Veeck would own three of the four Western League teams. In the late 1940s, he owned the Cleveland Indians. He next owned the Browns in the early 1950s. Veeck owned the White Sox in the 1950s, only to sell the team and buy it back again in the 1970s. Bill Veeck's birthchart shows his strong synastry with the American League. His Sun and Venus are conjunct at 20 degrees Aquarius and trine to the Western

Ban Johnson
Tuesday, January 5, 1864 12:00:00 PM
Norwalk, Ohio
Time Zone: 05:00 (EST)
Longitude: 082° W 35'
Latitude: 41° N 14'

League Saturn. Veeck's natal Saturn of 11 degrees Gemini is conjunct to the Western League's Neptune and Pluto conjunction. Bill Veeck had four planets in Aquarius: the Sun, Venus, Jupiter and Uranus. He was very much an Aquarius, preferring to sit in the bleachers among working class fans rather than lounge in the luxury suites with the One Percent. His zany stunts and promotions were also manifestations of his Aquarius personality.

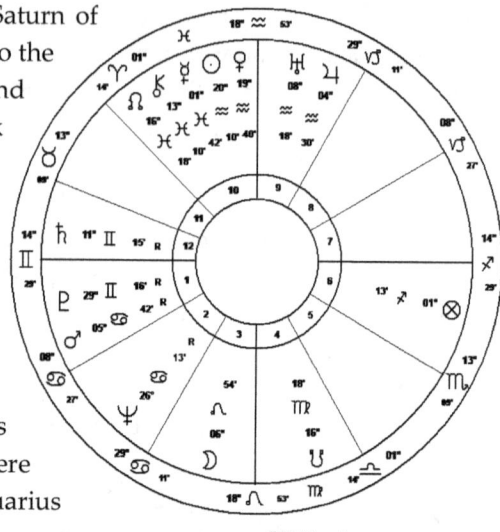

Bill Veeck
Monday, February 9, 1914   12:00:00 PM
Chicago, Illinois
Time Zone: 06:00 (CST)
Longitude: 087° W 39' 42"
Latitude: 41° N 51' 54"

These four teams have a conjunction between Neptune and Pluto, the most infrequent conjunction between the known planets. Occurring approximately every 500 years, this aspect is credited with the major cultural changes of civilization. Richard Tarnas, author of *Cosmos and Psyche*, credits the 1893 aspect with the end of the old order based on conventional Christian tradition and the emergence of long-suppressed unconscious Dionysian impulses.[251] Since the Neptune-Pluto cycle is such a long one, it is difficult to assess how the Western League teams have been or will become agents of such a major cultural shift. Nevertheless, I will speculate that these teams are playing a role in the return of earth-centered values. As spiritual energies from the Earth become more valued in the emerging cultural paradigm, a recognition of baseball's origin as a fertility ritual may play a part in the Dionysian awakening.

---

251. Tarnas, Richard, *Cosmos and Psyche*, p. 418. Tarnus gives the Neptune-Pluto conjunction a 15-degree orb, which allows the conjunction to also exist in the birthcharts of the Tigers, Pirates, Cardinals, Phillies, Giants, A's, Yankees, and Red Sox.

The Chicago White Sox

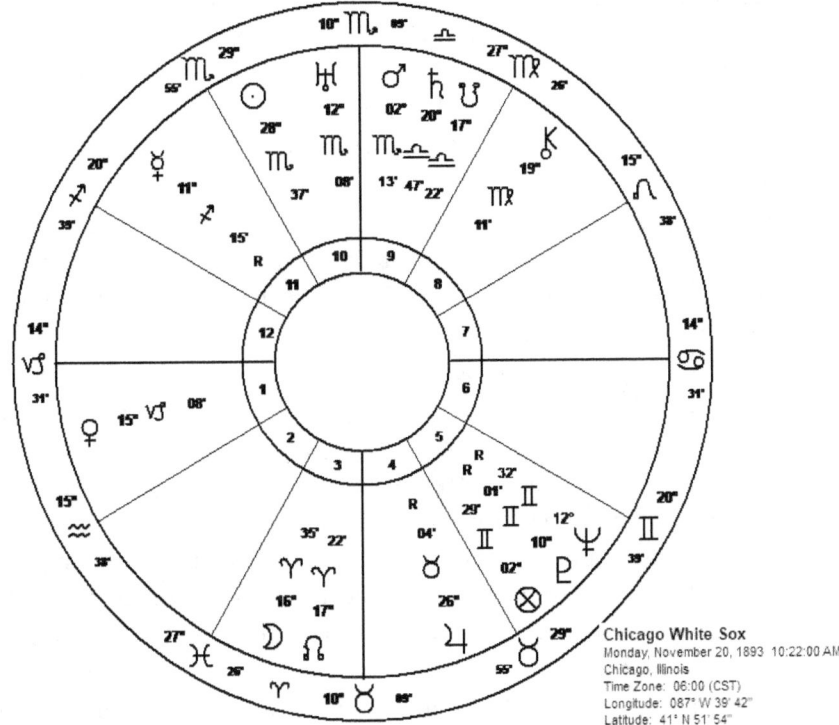

Chicago White Sox
Monday, November 20, 1893 10:22:00 AM
Chicago, Illinois
Time Zone: 06:00 (CST)
Longitude: 087° W 39' 42"
Latitude: 41° N 51' 54"

The American League White Sox franchise was born with the other Western League clubs on November 21, 1893[252] at 10:22 am CST.[253] This team played its first season in Sioux City, Iowa. Although they would win the first Western League pennant of 1894, poor attendance forced them to move. The following year, the team played in St. Paul, Minnesota. In 1900, the franchise moved to the South Side of Chicago, where they have played ever since. In Chicago, the team would take the name "White Stockings," a name previously used by the Cubs. The name was soon shortened to "White Sox." The White Sox share the same planetary positions as are active in the other Western League teams. Like their siblings, the Sox have a Scorpio and Aries emphasis. The aspects that distinguish the White Sox from the other Western League clubs involve their Ascendant-Descendant axis and their MC-IC axis. The White Sox Ascendant of 15 degrees Capricorn is exactly

---

252. *Reach's Official Base Ball Guide*, 1894 edition. p. 33.
253. Rectification Note: In the Chicago chart, an IC of 10 Taurus progressed by solar arc becomes conjunct the team's Fourth House Jupiter in 1910, the year the team moved to Comiskey Park.

conjunct to Venus and square to Saturn and the Moon. The White Sox' MC of 10 degrees Scorpio is not only conjunct to both Mars and Uranus, it is also inconjunct to Pluto at 10 degrees Gemini. These aspects to their MC have given the Sox their fierceness and their coarseness.

There is a crude quality to the White Sox that is not apparent in the other Western League teams. Unrefined attributes of Aries and Scorpio exhibit themselves in the White Sox. The history of the White Sox exposes both the ruthlessness of Scorpio and the aggression of Aries. The other Western League clubs have kept these darker aspects of Scorpio and Aries largely in check, as their strongly positioned Saturn inhibits much of the aggression. The White Sox, however, have a more difficult time sublimating their Mars and Pluto intensity. Even a routine trip to the White Sox ballpark can become an uncouth experience. For many years, Comiskey Park was in olfactory distance of the Chicago stockyards. At the ballpark, one was forced to smell cow manure.[254] The nearby stockyards were a manifestation of the team's Fourth House Jupiter in Taurus, the sign of cattle, opposed by the Sun in Scorpio, the sign of butchers.

There are several instances in history that demonstrate the coarseness of the White Sox. The Sox participated in the fixing of the 1919 World Series. In 1979, Sox fans rioted at Disco Demolition Night. The White Sox have a harder time than the other Western League clubs containing the antisocial urges of their Mars and Pluto because of the difficult aspects from their birthchart's axes. The Sox' Ascendant forms a tight square to their Aries Moon, allowing the angry emotions of the Aries Moon to be easily triggered. Also, the Sox' Pluto receives a challenging quincunx from the MC and a semi-sextile from the IC.

A contrast exists within the White Sox between the image and the substance, between the intended genial impression of the Rising Sign and the dark substance behind it. The White Sox have a veneer of goodness. Venus, the planet of justice and fairness, is conjunct to the Ascendant. When playing in St Paul, they actually called themselves the "Saints" and the "Apostles." However, in St. Paul, they were unable to sustain a holy facade. The Saints ignored the sabbath and played games on Sunday. The Saints were then actually kicked out of St. Paul for disobeying the city's blue laws, but this proved only a small problem for their crafty owner Charles Comiskey. He built a grandstand just outside the city limits where his team could play and he could sell all the booze he wanted.[255] The names "White

---

254. Nack, William: "Hey, Hey, Hey, Good Bye!" *Sports Illustrated*, Aug. 20, 1990.
255. Lindberg, Charles, *Who's on 3rd?* p. 21

Stockings" and "White Sox," like the color white, connote virtue, innocence, and high moral character. The name makes them sound baptized and cleansed, but after the 1919 World Series, this facade cracked and revealed pollution underneath. The team became slapped with the label "Black Sox."

The ownership of Riensdorf and Einhorn attempted to refine the image of the Sox. After they purchased the team in the early 1980s, they changed the ambiance at Old Comiskey Park. Security was increased. Harry Carey, the announcer who had encouraged beer drinking, was fired. The "Golden Boxes" were installed. These were expensive and exclusive seats intended to separate rich customers from the common rabble.[256] In spite of the efforts to improve their image, the Sox' uniforms are an unsubtle reminder of their past. The current uniforms are a solid black. Since 1991, the White Sox have worn black uniforms that make them look like the Raiders of the NFL, another team with a coarse reputation.

The most famous event in White Sox history is the fixing of the 1919 World Series. Astrologically, it almost appears as if the drama of 1919 Series could have occurred with any of the four Western League teams. In 1919, Mars, progressed by solar arc,[257] was conjunct to the Sun in the birthcharts of all these teams.[258] However, it was the White Sox who took the stage in this tragedy. It happened to the White Sox because of the specific degree of their MC, which caught a fateful transit in the fall of 1919. The transit that triggered the Black Sox scandal was the conjunction between Jupiter and Neptune near 10 degrees Leo in September and October of 1919. Jupiter and Neptune would form a square to the White Sox' MC of 10 degrees Scorpio. Gambling scandals happen when the excesses of Jupiter meet the deception of Neptune. Jupiter and Neptune were also in aspect when Hal Chase of the Cincinnati Reds threw games for gamblers.[259]

The idea to throw the World Series originated with Chick Gandil, the Sox first baseman. The narrative would naturally begin with a first baseman, the Neptune position, as Neptune is usually present in moments of scandal and deceit. Sport Sullivan was the liaison between the players and Arnold Rothstein, who supplied the money for the fix.[260] The initial meeting between Chick Gandil and Sport Sullivan occurred on September

---

256. Eskenazi, Gerald, *Bill Veeck: A Baseball Legend*, pp. 176-177.
257. See chapter 2 for an explanation of progressions.
258. In 1919, the Western League teams were 26 years old, the approximate age of many of the players involved. The birthcharts of many of the players involved have the same Neptune-Pluto conjunction as the Western League teams.
259. See Reds Chapter.
260. Asimov, Eliot, *Eight Men Out*, p. 6.

10, 1919. On that day, Mars, Jupiter, and Neptune were conjunct near 10 degrees Leo, and all three of them were square to the White Sox' MC of 10 degrees Scorpio.

The White Sox, like the other Western League clubs, have an opposition between their Moon in Aries and Saturn in Libra. A peculiar manifestation of this opposition occurred during the Black Sox days. A class conflict existed between groups of players within the team.²⁶¹ The 1919 White Sox were divided into two cliques, one a manifestation of the Libra Saturn, the other an embodiment of the Aries Moon. The players of the Libra Saturn faction were well-educated and from the upper classes. The players in the Aries Moon faction were from lower socio-economic backgrounds. In mundane astrology, the Moon represents the masses of people, while Saturn represents those in authority. The Moon's opposition to Saturn manifested itself in class resentment. The epitome of the Sox Saturn clique was the rich and well-educated Eddie Collins. Second baseman Collins was also the team captain. The title of captain corresponded with Saturn, while second base is the position of Libra. Collins was paid twice the salary of any other Sox player. Collins was also an Ivy League graduate of Columbia. Ray Schalk, the catcher, was a companion of Collins. Ostensibly, Schalk appears as if he belonged with the Aries Moon clique, as he was a catcher with an Aries Moon in his own birthchart, but Schalk was an authority figure with a bossy commanding presence, which brought him into the Saturn faction. Pitchers Red Fabar and Dickey Kerr were the other members of the Saturn in Libra clique. Red Faber had studied at a college prep academy and his father was also a rich hotel owner.²⁶²

Ray Schalk's birthchart has an Aries Moon and Leo Sun. His Aries

---

261. Asimof, pp. 18-19.
262. https://en.wikipedia.org/wiki/Red_Faber

Moon is conjunct to the White Sox Aries Moon, the aspect that made him a natural catcher for the White Sox. With red hair and a quick-tempered personality, Schalk was very much an Aries. He was only five feet, eight inches tall, but a very aggressive player. On the field, he constantly yelled at his pitchers. His nickname was "Cracker" for his whip-like attitude. When he didn't like a pitch, he threw the ball back very hard to the pitcher. Lefty Williams started Game Two of the 1919 World Series and pitched shoddily, according to the plan. Ray Schalk suspected the fix. After the game, he sought out Lefty Williams and actually beat him up.[263]

The opposing Aries Moon clique consisted of the players who took part in the fix: Chick Gandil, Eddie Cicotti, Lefty Williams, Swede Risberg, Joe Jackson, Buck Weaver, Happy Flesch, and Fred McMillen. These men were a resentful and underpaid class within the team. They hated Eddie Collins, resented his high salary and cultivated background. In practices, they often refused to throw the ball to Collins. Together they had an unrefined manner, as Aries, the youngest sign of the zodiac, often lacks the social graces. Joe Jackson was an unsophisticated country boy. His nickname "Shoeless" gives the impression he was a barefoot hillbilly. Lefty Williams, like Joe Jackson, was a Southerner. Chick Gandil and Swede Risberg were tough guys. Gandil had been a professional boxer. Happy Felsch was uneducated and raucous. Together, these players embodied the Aries Moon: its rough style and its angry resentments.

The problems of the Sox' Saturn-Moon opposition did not end after 1919. On May 15, 1929, first baseman Art Shires got into a fist fight with manager Lena Blackburne. The trouble started when Art Shires wished to wear a bright red hat while taking batting practice. Red is the color of Aries, the sign of the Sox' Moon. The manager objected to the red hat. After harsh words from Shires, Blackburne suspended and fined the first baseman. Eventually the two men came to blows.[264] More Moon-Saturn fisticuffs occurred after a double header in St. Louis on May 1, 1949, when White Sox catcher Joe Tipton exchanged punches with manager Jack Onslow.[265]

During Spring Training of 1940, the White Sox' second baseman, Jackie Hayes, was stung by a bee in his right eye. The bee is a Mars and Aries organism. A second baseman stung by a Mars creature is another unfortunate manifestation of the Sox' Saturn Moon opposition in the signs of Aries and Libra. By August of that year, the bee sting brought blindness

---

263. Asimov, Eliot, p. 90.
264. Lindberg, *Who's on 3rd?* p. 51 Lynch, Mike, "Art Shires" SABR bio project
265. Lindberg, *Who's on 3rd?* p. 66.

to Jackie Hayes' right eye. The second baseman would eventually also lose the sight in his left eye as well. [266]

The White Sox' Scorpio Sun has brought ruthless owners so intent on getting what they want that they ignore collateral damage. History judges Charles Comiskey for setting the stage for the Black Sox scandal by paying his players pitiful wages.[267] The White Sox of the late 1910s were one of the greatest baseball teams ever assembled, yet the players were among the poorest paid in the majors. Comiskey's greed tempted the players to sell the World Series to gamblers. Jerry Riensdorf, the current owner, is another ruthless Scorpionic character. Riensdorf plotted the ousting of Commissioner Fay Vincent in 1992.[268] Reinsdorf was also a hawk during the strike of 1994-95. His hard, uncompromising stance against the Players Association contributed to the cancelation of the 1994 World Series.

Before their victory in the 2005 World Series, the White Sox were considered cursed by their followers. Fans of the team referred to the "Black Sox Curse," the "Comiskey Curse," and the "Cissel Curse."[269] Others noted that Comiskey Park had opened on a Friday, the traditional day of bad luck for the Irish.[270] Like the birthchart of the Indians, another hard luck team, the birthchart of the White Sox also has Saturn in square to the Ascendant. Saturn is the planet of hard knocks. In such a difficult angle to the Ascendant, it brings obstacles and stumbling blocks.

Richard Lindberg's book about the White Sox is titled *Who's on Third?* Lindberg points out that the White Sox have been unable to maintain consistency at the third base position. Lindberg lists over forty men[271] who played third base for the Sox between 1901 and the year of his book's publication in 1983. In the next decade of the 1990s, Robin Ventura would anchor third base, and even becomes the Sox manager in 2012. Still, it is surprising that a team with a Scorpio Sun lacked stability at third base, the Scorpio position. Stability at the Sun and Moon positions are keys to fielding a winning team. Problems at third base reoccur because the White Sox' Pluto, the planet of third base, maintains an afflicted quincunx angle to the Sox MC.

---

266. Lindberg, *Who's on 3rd?* p. 61
267. It is forgotten that Charles Comiskey had been an influential player with the St. Louis Browns of the 1880s. See Cardinals chapter.
268. Dewey & Acocella, p. 166.
269. Dewey & Acocella, p. 147.
270. Lindberg, Richard, *Who's on Third?* p. 33
271. Lindberg, *Who's on 3rd?* p. 9

Buck Weaver is arguably the best third baseman to ever play for the White Sox. Weaver played all of his eight-year, major league career with the White Sox. He began as a shortstop in 1912 but was converted to a third baseman in 1916. By 1919, Weaver was a .300 hitter and outstanding fielder. Even Ty Cobb respected his fielding skills, as Weaver was the only third baseman whom Ty Cobb would not bunt against.[272] However, Buck Weaver would be banned from baseball for his involvement in the 1919 fix. Although he was one of the original conspirators, Weaver had changed his mind about it once the World Series began. He played his hardest and batted .324 for the Series. He received no money from the gamblers, yet he was grouped with the other Black Sox and received the lifetime ban. His crime was that he did not turn in the others, but Weaver could never have snitched. It is against the nature of a Scorpionic third baseman to tell a secret. A portion of the sympathy given to Joe Jackson should be given to Buck Weaver, as the ban of him was the most unjust. Perhaps his ghost was exacting revenge on the White Sox by cursing his former position and that the White Sox' inability to maintain a steady third baseman should be called "the Curse of Buck Weaver."

Unlike the instability at third base, the White Sox have been solid at shortstop, the position of their Aries Moon. The Aries Moon has blessed the Sox at the shortstop position. Hall of Famer Luke Appling anchored the Sox at shortstop for 20 years. Luis Aparicio held the position in the 1950s and would also enter the Hall of Fame. Ozzie Guillen won the Rookie of the Year award in 1985 as the Sox shortstop and remained at the position through 1997. Guillen returned to the Sox as a manager in 2004. He was at the helm when they won the World Series in 2005.

Disco Demolition Night was not an anomaly, as there are many

---

272. Asimov, Eliot, pp. 19-20

incidents involving rowdy fans in the history of the White Sox. White Sox fans have a reputation as an unruly lot. These fans are an embodiment of the Aries Moon. Aries, the sign of warriors and pugilists, often lacks cultivation. A team of the Great Unwashed, the White Sox have long had a blue-collar appeal. From early on, the Sox fanbase has been wage earners and beer drinkers.[273] The other Western League teams also have an Aries Moon, but the White Sox fans are distinguished by the harsh square of their Ascendant to the Moon. In 1906, Comiskey had to stop the sale of pop bottles at games, as fans along the first base line were throwing the bottles at players and umpires. Such behavior gave the Sox an early reputation for abusive fans.[274] In 1968, the Democratic Party held its convention in Chicago. The convention brought delegates from states outside of Illinois to a White Sox game. On August 25, supporters of George Wallace and Eugene McCarthey clashed inside the ballpark. Once inside Comiskey Park, the delegates forgot the rules of parliamentary debate and began taunting each other. Security guards stepped in to prevent another Chicago riot.[275] In 1974, streaking was a popular fad. That year's Opening Day festivities were highlighted by streakers in the upper deck and on the field. Even the 35-degree temperature did not prevent the streakers from removing their clothes.[276]

Disco Demolition Night occurred on July 12, 1979 at Comiskey Park. That evening, a doubleheader was scheduled against the Detroit Tigers. The promotion was the idea of Mike Veeck, the son of White Sox owner Bill Veeck. A reduced-price ticket was available to anyone who turned in a disco record. The records were to be blown up between the games of the double header. The event was hosted by

Disco Demolition Night
Thursday, July 12, 1979 8:00:00 PM
Chicago, Illinois
Time Zone: 05:00 (CDT)
Longitude: 087° W 39' 42"
Latitude: 41° N 51' 54"

---

273. Lindberg, *Who's on 3rd?* p. 4.
274. Lindberg, *Who's on 3rd?* p. 4.
275. Lindberg, *Who's on 3rd?* p. 130.
276. Lindberg, *Who's on 3rd?* pp. 152-153.

Steve Dahl, a disc jockey at radio station WLUP-FM and a proponent of the "Disco Sucks" craze. Comiskey Park was sold out, as many of Dahl's listeners came to the ballpark that night. The gates were closed, but many rockers climbed the fences to get inside. Since many of the records were not turned in upon entering, they were thrown around like Frisbees during the first game of the doubleheader. When the first game ended, the records were ceremoniously blown up, as scheduled, but, afterwards, thousands of rockers swarmed the field. They tore up the playing area and refused to go back into the stands. In desperation, Bill Veeck and Harry Carey descended to the field, pleading with the rioters to go back into the stands. But the two men were ignored. Police in riot gear finally restored order, but the second game had to be forfeited. [277] It was a shocking night for Bill Veeck. The Aquarian Veeck had always liked to think the best of people, but he had never had to confront this side of humanity: a lunar mob out of control. [278]

That night, the transits were ripe for a riot. The Sun was not only in Cancer, the sign of fans, mobs, and riots, but it was also exactly square to the White Sox Saturn of 20 degrees Libra. Authority would be defied as Saturn received a square from the Sun in Cancer. Pluto, in transit at 16 degrees Libra, had been conjunct the White Sox' South Node and opposite their Moon. Mars, in transit at 11 degrees Gemini, was square to Saturn at 10 degrees Virgo, setting up a confrontation between youth and authority. Mars was also conjunct to the White Sox natal Pluto and Neptune, triggering the dark energy within the psyche of the organization.

For most of their history, the Sox played in a pitcher-friendly park, as the White Sox Moon is in the Third House, a house of the pitcher. Also, the IC within the Sox birthchart, another indicator of the home ballpark, receives a quincunx from Mercury. These aspects brought the influence of Mercury, the planet of pitchers, to the White Sox home field, making Old Comiskey Park a stadium that favored pitchers. The stadium was planned with the assistance of Ed Walsh, the White Sox star pitcher of the 1900s. Comiskey Park, with its deep outfield walls, originally 362 feet to the foul poles and 420 feet to center field, was designed for low-scoring games. The White Sox' best days were in the Dead Ball Era, a time of low scores. Their birthchart, with its pitching emphasis, gave them an advantage in an era when high scoring games were rare. In 1900, the Sox actually won the pennant with the worst hitting in the league. [279] Similarly, the 1906 White Sox were known as

---

277. Eskenazi, p. 166; Lindberg *Who's on 3rd?* p. 175.
278. Eskenazi, p. 175.
279. Lindberg, "Second Class in the Second City," p. 57.

"the Hitless Wonders" for their ability to win a pennant and World Series due to weak hitting. The Sox of the early Twentieth Century won pennants with a combination of pitching, defense and speed. Runners who reached first base were advanced by sacrifices, stolen bases, and hit-and-runs. Games in the Dead Ball Era were often decided by one run. Teams could not wait for the three-run homer, so they played for one run at a time. The Go-Go Sox of the 1950s won with a similar style. "Go-Go" was a chant from the crowd for a runner to steal a base. The 2005 Sox, although they played in a stadium of average dimensions,[280] also won with speed and defense. That year, left fielder Scott Podsednik stole 59 bases.

In 2005, the White Sox found redemption and shed their curse by winning the World Series against Houston in four games. The transits for 2005 included a Lunar Node return. For much of the season, the North Node of the Moon was conjunct the Sox' natal North Node and Moon in Aries. This transit brings a reorientation in which past patterns are discarded. Here, the aspect allowed the club to exorcise the curses and demons of its past. The North Node return also brought A. J. Pierzynski to the catcher position. Before joining the White Sox, Pierzynski had been a divisive figure on other teams for his obnoxious clubhouse behavior and his taunts towards opposing players. Nevertheless. his style would blend with the coarse ways of the Sox, and he steadied the team.

A degree of the zodiac that had brought them grief in 1919 would help the Sox in 2005, as Saturn, the planet of post-season victory, was square to the Sox MC from 10 degrees Leo. When the Sox threw the 1919 World Series, Jupiter and Neptune were conjunct at 10 degrees Leo. But 86 years later, that degree of the zodiac had been washed clean for the Sox. The tenth degree of Leo held Saturn as it brought the championship ring to Chicago.

Saturn and the Moon, which had manifest so many conflicts in Sox history, were both present and cooperative in 2005, the White Sox' year of redemption.

---

280. In 2005, US Cellular Field had fouls lines of 330 and 335 feet and a center field 400 feet from homeplate. *wikipedia.org*

THE BROWNS/ORIOLES

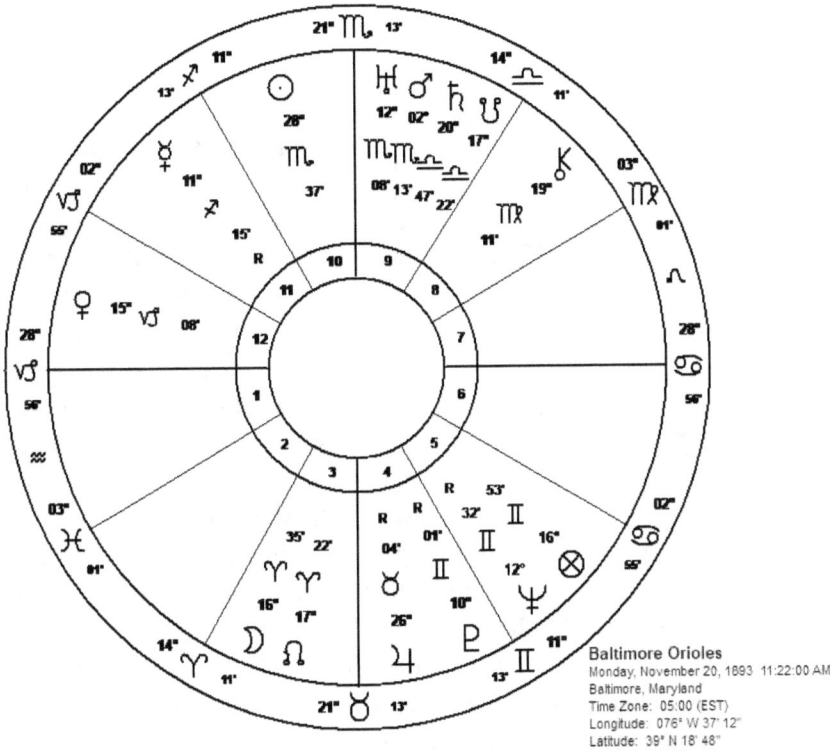

Baltimore Orioles
Monday, November 20, 1893 11:22:00 AM
Baltimore, Maryland
Time Zone: 05:00 (EST)
Longitude: 076° W 37' 12"
Latitude: 39° N 18' 48"

The team now known as the Baltimore Orioles was born simultaneously with the other Western League clubs on November 20, 1893.[281] The team made Milwaukee its home from its birth through 1901. In Milwaukee, this team was called the "Brewers." In 1902, the franchise moved to St Louis, where it took the name "Browns," a name used in the 1800s by the team currently known as the St Louis Cardinals. The American League Browns played 52 baseball seasons in St. Louis. In 1954, the team moved to Baltimore, where it took the name "Orioles." This team shares the same planetary positions as its Western League siblings. When the team moved to Baltimore, their new birthchart received favorable angles from the axes, allowing them success they had rarely achieved in St. Louis.

The history of the Browns lacks such narratives as the tragedies

---

281. *Reach's Official Base Ball Guide* 1894 edition. p. 33

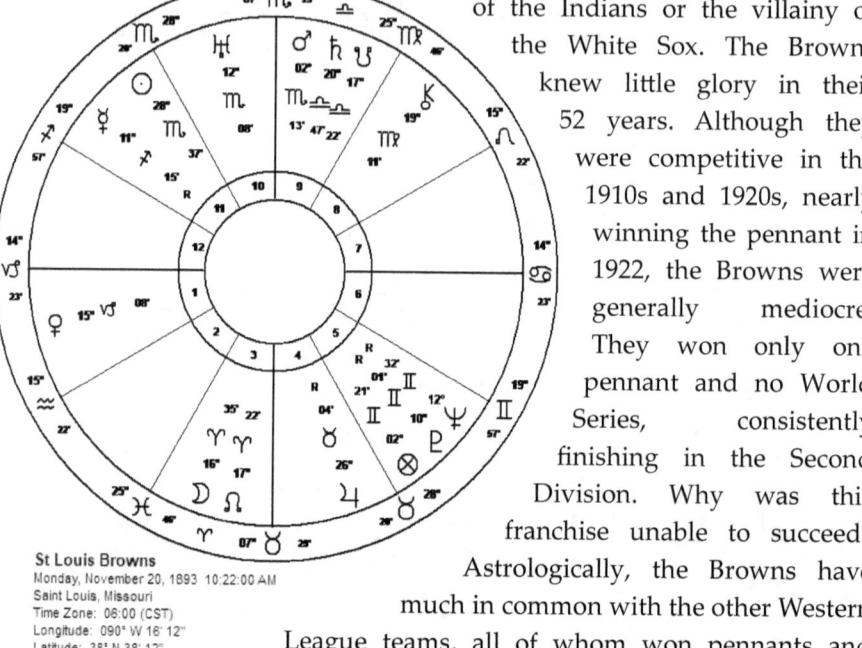

St Louis Browns
Monday, November 20, 1893 10:22:00 AM
Saint Louis, Missouri
Time Zone: 06:00 (CST)
Longitude: 090° W 16' 12"
Latitude: 38° N 38' 12"

of the Indians or the villainy of the White Sox. The Browns knew little glory in their 52 years. Although they were competitive in the 1910s and 1920s, nearly winning the pennant in 1922, the Browns were generally mediocre. They won only one pennant and no World Series, consistently finishing in the Second Division. Why was this franchise unable to succeed? Astrologically, the Browns have much in common with the other Western League teams, all of whom won pennants and World Series competitions within the first fifty years of the American League. The birthchart of the Browns also has the same malefic aspects that plagued the others, including Saturn square to the Ascendant and Pluto quincunx to the MC, as did the White Sox and Indians. In fact, these harsh aspects from the axes were actually softer for the Browns than they have been for the Chicago and Cleveland teams. The square from Saturn to the Ascendant for the Indians has a less than 1-degree orb, whereas the Browns' square had an orb of about 5 degrees. The quincunx from Pluto to the White Sox IC is within 1 degree, and yet, for the Browns it is more than 2 degrees. It was the severity of the tighter orbs experienced by the Indians and White Sox that created tensions that forced them to adapt and improve. The looser orbs within the Browns' birthchart did not force such crises, and the team was allowed to remain mediocre. Still, within their third-rate performances, the Browns were glorious. One remarkable distinction they earned is that the children's book *Strange but True Baseball Stories*[282] dedicates three chapters to doings by the Browns.

The Browns' square of Saturn to the Ascendant and Venus manifested in players with disabilities and other physical limitations. Saturn, the planet of accidents and limitations, rules disabilities. When the Browns

---

282. Bisher, Furman, *Strange but True Baseball Stories* (1972).

won the pennant in 1944, they fielded a team composed of 4-F players. During World War II, most of the regular players were drafted into the service. Major League baseball continued with players who did not pass the physical exams for combat duty. Such men, who were classified as 4-F, were excluded from military service because of conditions such as flat feet and diabetes. The 1944 Browns' Opening Day roster included 18 players with 4-F classifications. Indeed, the entire Browns infield was 4-F, including shortstop Vern Stephens, who had been disqualified from combat due to a knee injury. That year, Stephens would lead the American League in RBIs. The roster also included nine players who were too old to be drafted.[283] With these players, the Browns began the 1944 season with nine straight wins. On the last day of the season, they won the pennant with a victory against the Yankees.[284]

In the following year of 1945, the Browns' Saturn square to Venus and the Ascendant manifested in the arrival of Pete Gray. It was Pete Gray who played center field for the Browns with one arm. Saturn rules disabilities, and Venus is the planet of center field. Pete Gray would catch balls with his gloved left hand. To make a throw, he would tuck both the ball and glove into his right armpit. Then with his gloveless left hand, he took the ball from his armpit and flung it. On offense, opposing pitchers could not throw a fastball past his one-armed swing. Even Bob Feller admitted he could not get his fastball past Pete Gray. But pitchers eventually discovered they could get him out with a change-up. Gray's birthchart has a conjunction of Mercury, Mars and the North Node in Aquarius, which mirrors his independent courage. But his Aquarian conjunction is also square to the Browns' Jupiter in Taurus and Sun in Scorpio. His

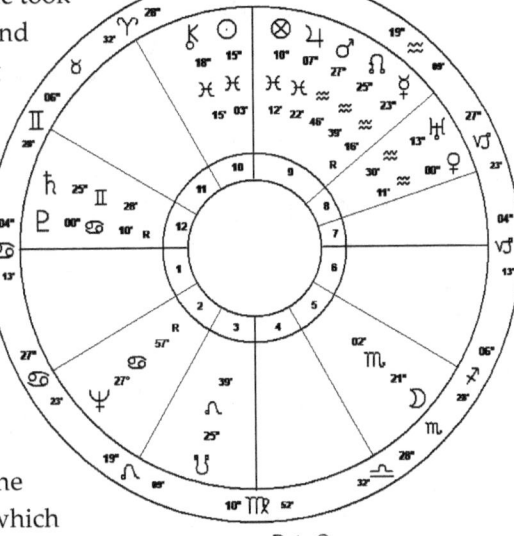

Pete Gray
Saturday, March 6, 1915 12:00:00 PM
Nanticoke, Pa
Time Zone: 05:00 (EST)
Longitude: 076° W 00'
Latitude: 41° N 12'

---

283. http://en.wikipedia.org/wiki/1944_St._Louis_Browns_season
284. The game took place on Oct. 1, 1944 at Sportsman's Park and featured two homeruns by left fielder Chet Laabs.

Aquarian individuality may have chafed against the Jupiterian largess of the team. Sadly, Pete Gray did not get along with his teammates, who found him surly and may have been jealous of the attention he was given.[285]

The most famous event in the history of the Browns was also a manifestation of Saturn square their Ascendant. On Aug. 19, 1951, Eddie Gaedel, a 3-foot, 7-inch dwarf, led off the first inning of a game for the Browns. Detroit's Bob Cain walked Gaedel on four pitches. Once on first base, Gaedel was replaced by a pinch runner. Unfortunately, the Browns lost the game 6-2. The next day American League President William Harridge banned dwarves from baseball.

The limited size of dwarves is a manifestation of Saturn's affliction to the Browns' Ascendant. In the birthchart of Eddie Gaedel, the Moon and Jupiter are conjunct in Capricorn, a sign of limitations. As Jupiter is associated with largeness, the issue of size was likely an intense one for Gaedel. It is striking that both his Moon and Jupiter are conjunct to the Browns' Ascendant, the aspect which has kept Gaedel as the face of the Browns' franchise long after the team's demise. The birthchart of Gaedel also has

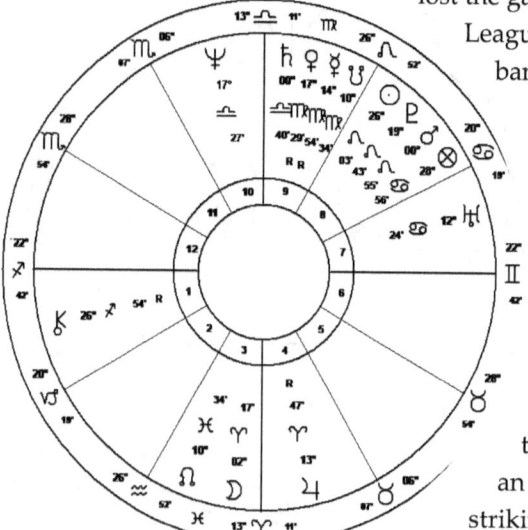

Eddie Gaedel Plays
Sunday, August 19, 1951 4:00:00 PM
Saint Louis, Missouri
Time Zone: 05:00 (CDT)
Longitude: 090° W 16' 12"
Latitude: 38° N 38' 12"

---

285. Dewey & Acocella, p. 514; Mead, William, *Even the Browns*, pp. 207-211.

Saturn at 8 degrees Scorpio, which is conjunct to the Browns' MC. On the day he played, the Sun, in transit at 26 degrees Leo, was square to the Browns Jupiter of 26 degrees Taurus. The Sun in the theatrical sign of Leo engendered the sheer spectacle of Gaedel's at bat. In addition, the square to the Browns' Jupiter was a provocative challenge against the dominion of the biggest planet, defying the practice of the large lording over the small. The walk by Eddie Gaedel subverted this dominant assumption.

The Browns' Saturn-Moon opposition became embodied in conflicts between fans and owners, as Saturn represents the owner and the Moon represents the fans. Until the final move to Baltimore, the owners usually lost those battles. The St. Louis Browns had decent owners who willingly invested in the team and made improvements to their stadium. But often the players whom they paid well did not live up to expectations, and the fans did not do their part by coming to the ballpark and paying for tickets.

Philip Ball, who owned the Browns from 1915 until his death in 1933, was in many ways a model owner. Ball did indulge in tantrums, and he feuded with Commissioner Landiss and some of his own players. But Ball, a millionaire who bought the team as a hobby, was unconcerned whether the team lost money. He also was not meddlesome, allowing most of the running of his team to the General Manager Bob Quinn.[286] After the Browns nearly won the pennant in 1922, attendance was good. Ball paid to extend the second deck of Sportsman's Park. Then in 1926, Ball added bleachers, expanding the stadium in anticipation of hosting a World Series. But it would be the other residents of Sportsman's Park who hosted the 1926 World Series. That other St. Louis team also played in Sportsman's Park, renting from Ball.

In the 1930s, with the country mired in the Great Depression, baseball attendance sank, as the masses had little money to buy tickets. The Browns suffered severely as attendance dropped below 100,000 in three different years. In 1935, the Browns drew only 80,922 for the entire season.[287] By the end of the 1930s, the Browns were in difficult financial straits. They probably would have moved to Los Angeles before the 1942 season, but the start of World War II derailed the plan. New capital came from Richard Muckerman, who stepped in and invested $300,000 to keep the Browns afloat. With the infusion of new money, the Browns improved in the early 1940s, winning the pennant in 1944. In 1947, Muckerman invested $500,000 to refurbish Sportsman's Park. Unfortunately, the team played poorly in the

---

286. Lieb, Frederick, *The Baltimore Orioles*, p. 190.
287. Dewey & Acocella, p. 513.

post-war years and attendance dwindled. Soon the team was on hard times again, which led Muckerman to sell off veteran players to meet expenses.

The greatest affront against the Browns' Saturn occurred on August 24, 1951. Bill Veeck, who would also mastermind Eddie Gaedel's at bat, had recently purchased the Browns. That afternoon, Veeck staged "Grandstand Managers' Day." A Brown official would hold up cards with proposed moves such as: warm up a relief pitcher, sacrifice, or send the runner. The 4,000 fans in attendance voted on the proposed managerial moves by showing a green placard for "yes," and a red one for "no." Votes were then counted and relayed to the players. Meanwhile, the real manager, Zack Taylor, was placed in a rocking chair atop the dugout wearing slippers and smoking a pipe. Taylor sat there until the umpire objected, after which Taylor was placed in a box seat. The Browns actually won that day, beating the Athletics, 5-3.[288] The promotion showed a lack of respect for Saturn by allowing lunar fans to play the role of the Saturnian manager. That day, Neptune, in transit at 18 degrees Libra, was opposite to the Browns' Moon and conjunct to the Browns' South Node and Saturn. A Neptune aspect to Saturn often brings a melting of authority.

Another manifestation of Saturn bowing to appease the lunar masses of St. Louis occurred when Bill Veeck had an apartment built inside Sportsman's Park in which he lived with his wife. It was a loss of personal boundaries for the owner to live in the building of the fans. Few things went well for Veeck in St. Louis, and he ended up alienating the fans. Attendance dwindled as fans did not want to give money to an owner whom they distrusted and believed had designs to sell the team. Even a no-hitter by a Browns rookie turned unlucky for Bill Veeck. May 6, 1953 was a cold, drizzly night at Sportsman's Park. Before the game started, Veeck announced that the game would be on him, and fans would get a rain check for braving the foul weather. The game proceeded, and the Browns' Bobo Holloman threw a no-hitter against the Athletics. Soon Veeck picked up the pitcher's option for $25,000. Bobo, however, could only finish the 1953 season with a 3-7 record and a 5.23 ERA. He would never pitch another season in the major leagues. Worse, the $25,000 spent on Holloman deprived Veeck of money with which he could have purchased the contract of Ernie Banks from the Negro Leagues.[289]

In 1953, the franchise's last season in St. Louis, the fans hung Bill Veeck in effigy. On September 27, a dummy whose clothing mimicked

---

288. Dewey & Acocella, p. 516.
289. Dewey & Acocella, p. 517.

Veeck's open-necked sports shirt hung from the upper deck of the right field grandstand of Sportsman's Park. One side was labeled "Bill Wreck," and the back side read "Traitor's End."[290] The incident is especially charged because Bill Veeck, an Aquarius, had styled himself as a populist, a man of the people, but in the people's eye, Veeck had done the cruelest, most unforgivable deed an owner could do to the fans when he moved the team. That night, Mercury, in transit at 19 degrees Libra, was conjunct to the Browns' South Node and Saturn and opposite the Browns' Moon. The Moon in Taurus was near the Browns IC.

The Browns' best player was George Sisler, who played for them from 1915 through 1927. Originally a pitcher, Sisler was converted to a position player for his good hitting. His primary position became first base. Sisler batted .407 in 1920, the year he set the record for most hits in a season, with 257. In 1922, Sisler would bat .420. George Sisler was born March 24, 1893, the same year that the Western League was born, making many of the outer planets in his birthchart conjunct to those of the Browns and the other Western League teams. Nevertheless, Sisler's inner planets also show a resonance with the Browns. His Mercury of 16 Aries is conjunct to the Browns' Moon, and his Mars of 27 Taurus is conjunct the Browns' Jupiter.

George Sisler
Friday, March 24, 1893 12:00:00 PM
Akron, Ohio
Time Zone: 05:00 (EST)
Longitude: 081° W 31' 24"
Latitude: 41° N 03' 48"

Once in Baltimore, the franchise took the name of "Orioles," a name previously used by various teams.[291] The transformation from the St. Louis Browns into the Baltimore Orioles was a Scopionic metamorphosis of the first order. An ugly duckling became a

---

290. Lieb, p. 220.
291. The National League Orioles team, which played in the 1890s, made significant contributions to the history of baseball. Ned Hanlon, John McGraw, and Wilbert Robinson, players who had great influences on the game, were members of this team.

beautiful swan. The franchise has played much better in Baltimore than it ever could in St. Louis. The team's birthchart, relocated to Baltimore, has an Ascendant of 29 degrees Capricorn and an MC of 21 degrees Scorpio. Rather than suffering with Saturn square the Ascendant, as they did in St. Louis, they play under the Baltimore chart that has a sextile aspect from the Sun to the Ascendant and a trine from the Sun to the Descendant. The MC is now semi-sextile to Saturn, while the IC is inconjunct to Saturn. These new aspects allow the franchise to blossom in their current longitude and latitude of Baltimore. The Baltimore Orioles' most famous players have been Brooks Robinson and Cal Ripken, Jr. The Orioles, with a well-aspected Sun in Scorpio, would naturally manifest a star third baseman such as Robinson. Ripken, who played most of his seasons as a shortstop, was an incarnation of the Orioles' Moon in Aries.

Brooks Robinson became the Orioles' starting third baseman in 1958. Soon he emerged as a cornerstone of the franchise. Robinson's birthchart shows he was born to be an Oriole. His Sun of 27 degrees Taurus is conjunct to the Orioles' Jupiter, and his Mars of 28 degrees Scorpio is exactly conjunct to the Orioles' Sun. Robinson's Jupiter of 27 Capricorn is conjunct the Orioles' Ascendant, the aspect that made Robinson an enduring face of the franchise. He played his entire 23-year major league career in Baltimore and will be forever identified with the Orioles. A first-ballot member of the Hall of Fame, Robinson is considered one of the best third basemen ever to play, a designation that reflects his Mars in Scorpio.

The franchise won its first championship in 1966. That year, the Orioles would win the American League pennant by 9 games and then sweep the Dodgers in the World Series. In 1966, Neptune in Scorpio was conjunct to the Orioles' MC, allowing the energy of Neptune to be channeled by first baseman Boog Powell, who had 109 RBIs in 1966. Saturn, in transit through Pisces, was trine to the Orioles Sun much of this year. Right Fielder Frank Robinson responded to this Saturn aspect by winning the Triple Crown. The

Brooks Robinson
Tuesday, May 18, 1937 12:00:00 PM
Little Rock, Arkansas
Time Zone: 05:00 (CDT)
Longitude: 092° W 19' 36"
Latitude: 34° N 44' 12"

World Series included a pitching performance for the ages by the Orioles staff. The Dodgers, who were the defending World Series champs, could score only two runs in four games. Jim Palmer, Wally Bunker, and Dave McNally each threw complete game shut-outs.

The city of Baltimore is a short distance from Washington D.C. making the birthchart of the Baltimore Orioles nearly identical to the birthchart of the original American League Washington Senators.[292] Only the MC and IC differ by a degree. Both teams' ascendants of 29 degrees Capricorn are conjunct to Pluto in the United States birthchart.[293] The Senators, who played in the nation's capitol and seat of power, would naturally have an aspect with the U.S. Pluto to reflect their connection with the nation's plutocrats. But the Orioles' tie with the nation's Pluto is not as thick as the one held by the Senators. Eli Jacobs, who owned the Orioles from 1989 to 1993, enjoyed powerful connections with New York and Washington politicians, including Presidents Gerald Ford and Ronald Reagan.[294] However, current owner Peter Angelos has demonstrated more Uranian politics than plutocratic ones. Angelos made his fortune litigating class action suits against asbestos manufacturers and tobacco companies.[295] Angelos also worked as a labor attorney.

During the strike of 1994 and 1995, the eyes of the baseball universe were on Baltimore. The owners had planned to field "replacement players" for the 1995 season. If Baltimore's replacement players played one game, Cal Ripken Jr.'s pursuit of Lou Gehrig's consecutive game streak would be lost. In February and March of 1995, with Opening Day looming, Uranus was in transit through late Capricorn and exactly conjunct to the Orioles' Ascendant. The planet Uranus will side with striking labor, and the Orioles' Capricorn Ascendant corresponds with their owner. Peter Angelos stood by his Uranian principles and refused to follow the owners' plan. On March 20, with the Moon in Scorpio conjunct the Orioles MC, he cancelled the rest of his team's Spring Training. Finally, On March 31, 1995, with the Moon in Aries conjunct the Orioles' North Node and natal Moon, the strike was settled in favor of the players.[296] The strike of 1994-95 was a manifestation of the opposition between the Western League's Moon and Saturn. The

---

292. The original American League Washington Senators moved to Minnesota in 1960 and became the Twins.
293. Pluto, in the July 4, 1776 U.S. chart, is located at 27 degrees, 26 minutes Capricorn.
294. *New York Times*, Aug. 3, 1993, p. B9:5
295. http://en.wikipedia.org/wiki/PeterAngelos
296. The injunction by Judge Sonia Sotomayor was issued in the late afternoon with the Moon near 19 degrees Aries.

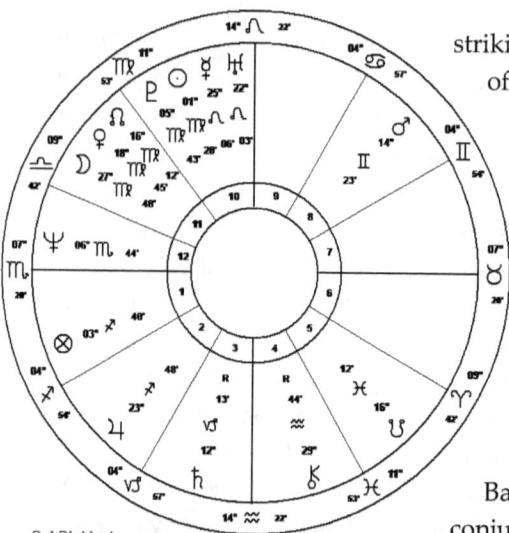

Cal Ripkin Jr.
Wednesday, August 24, 1960 12:00:00 PM
Havre de Grace, Maryland
Time Zone: 04:00 (EDT)
Longitude: 076° W 06'
Latitude: 39° N 33'

striking players were embodiments of the Aries Moon, which had a long history of conflicts against management, embodiments of Saturn.[297] On this day, the Moon triumphed.

Cal Ripken Jr. broke Lou Gehrig's record of 2130 consecutive games on September 6, 1995. When the new record became official at 9:30 pm EDT, the Descendant in Baltimore was 1 degree Scorpio, conjunct to the Orioles Mars, the planet of Ripken's shortstop position. That day Ripken experienced a Venus return, and the Sun was conjunct his North Node in Virgo.

Ripken's birthchart shows his durability and work ethic. He has the Sun, Moon, Mercury, Pluto, and the North Node in Virgo, the sign of the worker. Virgo is also the sign of health. Ripken remained amazingly free from injuries when in pursuit of Gehrig's record. His unrectified noon chart[298] does not show him to be a natural shortstop, the position he played most of his career. Rather, the Sun conjunct Pluto in his birthchart suggests he was a natural third baseman, the position he played both early and late in his career.

Together the history of the Browns and Orioles demonstrate how a Scorpio team can undergo a radical transformation when relocated to a new longitude and latitude.

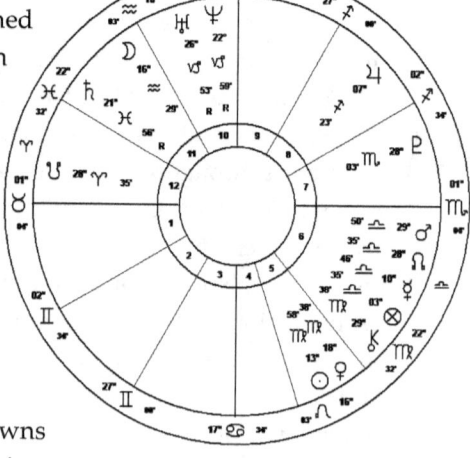

Cal Ripken Breaks streak
Wednesday, September 6, 1995 9:20:00 PM
Baltimore, Maryland
Time Zone: 04:00 (EDT)
Longitude: 076° W 37' 12"
Latitude: 39° N 18' 48"

---

297. See Indians and White Sox chapters.
298. On the night Ripken broke Gehrig's record, the planets in transit likely formed aspects to his MC. The birthchart for Ripken in this book does not have a time of birth, nor is it rectified. The degree of his MC is not known by this author.

The Senators / Twins

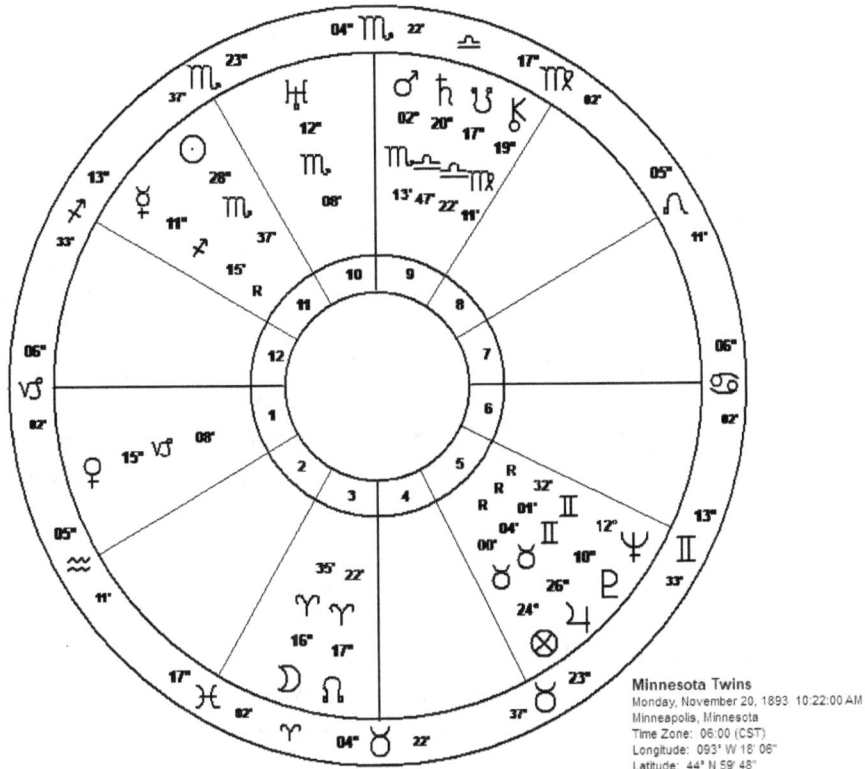

Minnesota Twins
Monday, November 20, 1893 10:22:00 AM
Minneapolis, Minnesota
Time Zone: 06:00 (CST)
Longitude: 093° W 18' 06"
Latitude: 44° N 59' 48"

One of the original Western League clubs, this team's first home was Kansas City, where it played from 1894 until 1900. When the Western League metamorphosed into the American League in 1901, this franchise moved to Washington. In the nation's capital, the team was called both "the Senators" and "the Nationals." In 1961, the franchise moved to Minnesota and changed its name to "the Twins." That same year, an expansion team would replace the Senators in Washington. The "New Senators" resided in Washington through the 1971 season. In 1972, the New Senators moved to Arlington, Texas and became the Rangers. The current Washington Nationals began playing in the nation's capital in 2005. Previously, they had played in Montreal and had been called the Expos. The aspects that distinguished the Senators' birthhchart from the other Western League clubs were the Sun in sextile to the Ascendant and

Saturn semi-sextile to the MC and inconjunct the IC. The Twins' birthchart is distinguished by Mars conjunct to the MC. [299]

The Senators are remembered as a losing team. A vaudeville joke was often told that Washington was first in war, first in peace, and last in the American League.[300] The movie and play *Damn Yankees* tells the story of a Senators fan who makes a deal with the Devil so his team can win a pennant. These comic portrayals of the Washington Senators are misleading. The Senators had some great seasons. They also made key contributions to baseball history and to American culture.

An American tradition began with the Washington Senators on April 14, 1910. That day, President William Howard Taft threw out the first ball on Opening Day. Almost every United States president since Taft has taken part in an Opening Day first ball ceremony.[301] The ceremony of a president throwing the first ball has a significance similar to that of the umpire yelling, "Play ball!"

Washington Senators
Monday, November 20, 1893 11:22:00 AM
Washington, Dist of Columbia
Time Zone: 05:00 (EST)
Longitude: 077° W 01' 42"
Latitude: 38° N 53' 48"

President Taft Throws out 1st Ball
Thursday, April 14, 1910 1:00:00 PM
Washington, Dist of Columbia
Time Zone: 05:00 (EST)
Longitude: 077° W 01' 42"
Latitude: 38° N 53' 48"

---

299. Rectification Note: In the Washington birthchart, Mars progressed by solar arc becomes conjunct the MC of 21 degree Scorpio in 1901, the year the franchise moved to DC and became a major league team.
300. Dewey and Acocella, p. 568.
301. Povich, Shirley *The Washington Senators* p 56-57. As of this writing, Jimmy Carter was the only president after Taft who did not participate in the tradition.

discussed in Chapter Six, but, instead of signaling the commencement of a particular game, the president's throw inaugurates the baseball season. By throwing out the first ball, he indicates that spring has arrived, and it is now time for baseball. The president symbolically plays both a solar and a Saturnian role. The president embodies Saturn as the Lord of Time. His throw indicates that baseball time has begun. The president simultaneously plays a solar role as the head of state. As a representative of the Sun, a head of state also acts as a fertility agent. His throw to the catcher is a symbolic act of fertility. The masculine Sun in communion with the feminine Moon germinates the nation.[302]

Transits for the Opening Day throw of William Howard Taft bring light to how a tradition is founded. The Sun, in transit at 24 degrees Aries, was conjunct to Saturn at 26 degrees Aries. Both the Sun and Saturn were square to Uranus, in transit at 25 degrees Cancer. Saturn is present at every successful founding. For a tradition to be set in stone, Saturn, which brings solidification, will need to be in attendance. Uranus, meanwhile, brings newness. Today, an Opening Day throw is now no longer novel, but on the afternoon of April 14, 1910, the throw from a president was original and Uranian.

A similar but odder event occurred on August 21, 1908, when Senators catcher Gabby Street caught a ball thrown from the Washington Monument. Unlike the throw from the President Taft, his catch did not become a tradition. The feat had been previously attempted by various catchers but never successfully. Whether anyone could catch a ball from the 550-foot monument had been a topic of

Gabby Street At Washington Mnt
Friday, August 21, 1908 11:00:00 AM
Washington, Dist of Columbia
Time Zone: 04:00 (EDT)
Longitude: 077° W 01' 42"
Latitude: 38° N 53' 48"

---

302. In sports astrology, the Sun is embodied in the offense, while the Moon is represented by the defense. It might seem more poetic for the president to bat out the first ball, since batting is an act of offense more in line with a solar figure such as a president. In throwing, the president plays a role from the defense. One does so because the United States is a nation with the Sun in Cancer, the sign of the Moon and the defense.

debate in Washington. After several attempts, Gabby Street caught a ball with his hands over his head as if awaiting a routine pop foul. The catcher staggered to the ground under the estimated 300 pounds of gravitational force, but he was uninjured and hung onto the ball.[303]

That morning, the Sun, Mars, and Mercury were all conjunct at 28 degrees Leo. The event was a Leo spectacle with fans and photographers present. These planets in Leo formed a t-square to the Senators' Sun and Jupiter. The show began at 11:00 am EDT.[304] The Moon, at that precise moment, was at 29 degrees, 47 minutes Gemini. Gaby Street missed twelve throws[305] before the ball was finally was thrown near enough for him to catch it. The Moon likely entered Cancer, the catcher's sign, close to the moment he made the catch. Another notable transit was the moment's conjunction between Venus and Neptune at 15 and 16 degrees Cancer, the sign of catchers. Neptune is often present in extraordinary feats. A conjunction with Neptune in the sign Cancer made the Senators' catcher into a superman.

The catch from the Washington Monument has symbolic content similar to that of the throwing of the first ball in a Presidential Opener. The Washington Monument is a Saturnian edifice, tall and phallic, representing the first president, the Father of our Country.[306] Like a ball thrown from a president, a ball thrown from a Saturnian edifice functioned as a fertility ritual. Catcher Gabby Street symbolized the mother becoming germinated.

The close relationship between the Senators and America's plutocrats is evident in the aspects between their chart and the chart of the United States. The Senators' Ascendant of 29 degrees Capricorn was conjunct to the U.S. Pluto of 27 degrees Capricorn, while the Senators' Sun of 28 Scorpio was sextile to the U.S. Pluto. It is fitting that a team with such aspects to the U.S. Pluto would play in the nation's capital. Washington is the country's seat of power, the place where Pluto's influence is most evident. At Senators games, the powerful ones were always nearby.

The Senators were under the control of Clark Griffith from 1912 until his death in 1955. Although his team was not a powerhouse, Clark Griffith was a powerful man. Living in Washington, he was well-connected with presidents and other policy makers. History shows that Griffith used his

---

303. Povich pp. 53-55.
304. Garnet, Vance, "The Washington Monument and Baseball: Related Icons" *The Washington Times Communities*. Oct. 10, 2011 http://communities.washingtontimes.com
305. http://en.wikipedia.org/wiki/Gabby_Street
306. Both Venus and Neptune were in square to the United States Saturn of 14 degrees Libra when the catch was made.

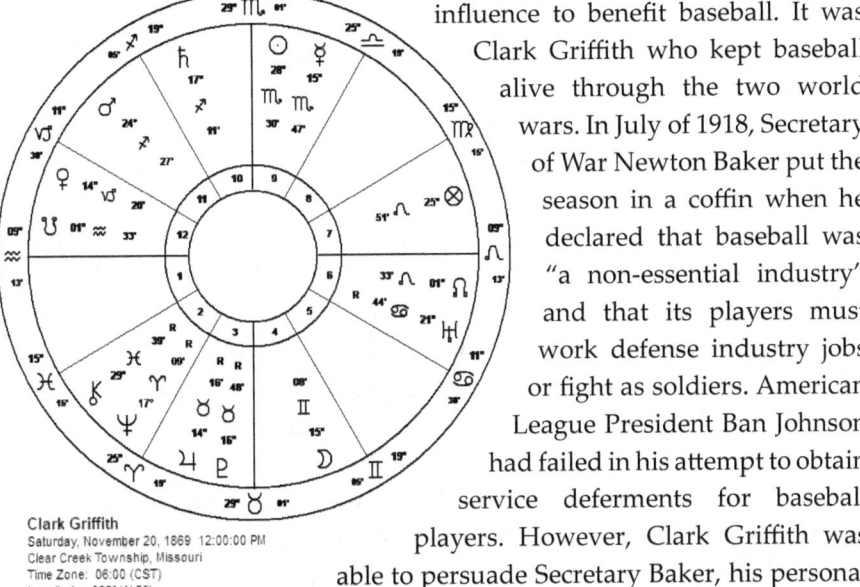

Clark Griffith
Saturday, November 20, 1869 12:00:00 PM
Clear Creek Township, Missouri
Time Zone: 06:00 (CST)
Longitude: 092° W 59'
Latitude: 38° N 52'

influence to benefit baseball. It was Clark Griffith who kept baseball alive through the two world wars. In July of 1918, Secretary of War Newton Baker put the season in a coffin when he declared that baseball was "a non-essential industry" and that its players must work defense industry jobs or fight as soldiers. American League President Ban Johnson had failed in his attempt to obtain service deferments for baseball players. However, Clark Griffith was able to persuade Secretary Baker, his personal friend, to allow the baseball season to continue through Labor Day. Players were granted draft deferments, but each team was assigned a drill sergeant who led the players in pre-game drills. In lieu of rifles, the players marched with bats over their shoulders.[307] When the next world war began, Clark Griffith again saved baseball. In 1942, he visited FDR at the White House and persuaded him to allow baseball to continue. Griffith also dined regularly with draft board officials. Through his contacts with the draft board, Griffith gained draft deferrals for many of the Senator players.[308]

Clark Griffith was very much a man of the American League. He and the Western League shared the birthday of November 20, although Griffith, born in 1869, was 14 years older than the league. Naturally, his Scorpio Sun is conjunct the Sun of the Western League. But further synastry existed, as Griffith's Venus of 14 degrees Capricorn is conjunct to the Western League Venus of 15 degrees Capricorn. At the turn of the Twentieth Century, Griffith was a pitcher for the Chicago Cubs. He was also the vice president of the Players Protective Association, an early labor organization for baseball players. It was Griffith, in his role as a labor advocate, who convinced players to leave the National League for the better pay and conditions of the new American League. Griffith had a list of 40 players whom he sought to enlist in the new league. Of these

---

307. Povich, p. 96.
308. Dewey & Acocella, pp. 572, 576

40 players, Griffith was able to persuade 39[309] to join him. Much of the senior circuit's best talent would join him—players such as John McGraw, Napoleon LaJoie and Ed Delahanty.

Like the other Western League teams, the Senators had the difficult aspect of Saturn in Libra opposite to the Moon in Aries. In Washington, this aspect played out in a gentler fashion than with the other teams. The lunar fans did boo manager Bucky Harris in the late 1920s, but Washington was not the graveyard of managers that Cleveland became, nor did the fans ever hang the owner in effigy as had the fans of St Louis. Instead, the Moon-Saturn opposition became manifest in a family business. The Moon rules families, while Saturn represents the owner of the team. In Washington, these two bodies were successfully integrated. Clark Griffith became a benevolent patriarch who steered the organization for 43 years. Griffith treated his team like a family. He only hired managers who were former Senator players.[310] Griffith managed the team himself from 1912 to 1920. Following him, all the Senator managers would be former Senator players including Bucky Harris, Walter Johnson, and Ossie Bluege.

The harmonious relationship between the Senators' Saturn and Moon allowed for the Moon to influence the manager's role. Indeed, the Senators' Aries Moon brought youth to the manager's chair. Aries is the youngest sign of the zodiac. In 1924, Bucky Harris managed the Senators while only 27 years old. Despite his youth, the rookie manager led the Senators to their first pennant and only World Series win in 1924. The next year, the Senators would repeat as pennant winners but lose the World Series to the Pirates. In 1933, Joe Cronin, only 26 years old, managed the Senators to their third pennant. Cronin also played shortstop, the Aries position. The Senators won three pennants in their history, and all three were won with boy-managers at the helm. A similar young manager, Lou Boudreau, managed the winning of the World Series for the Indians in 1948. Boudreau, like Cronin, was a shortstop, the position of the Aries Moon.

When the Senators lost the 1925 World Series to the Pirates, Bucky Harris was criticized by Ban Johnson for overusing Walter Johnson for a "sentimental" reason. "Sentiment has no place in the World Series," Ban Johnson wrote Harris in a telegram. In truth, the Senators' pitching staff was depleted with injuries, and Bucky Harris had no choice but to go

---

309. Griffith was unable to get Honus Wagner to join the American League (Povich pp. 76-77).

310. When Charlie Dressen was named manager in 1955, he became the first outsider to manage the team since the arrival of Griffith. Dressen was not hired by Clark Griffith, but by his nephew Calvin Griffith.

with Johnson.[311] The charge of allowing sentiment to cloud judgment was not valid in the 1925 World Series, but it would prove quite true in later years for the Senators. Sentiment, as in many family-run organizations, became a strong motive. Clark Griffith traded players from motivations of sentiment and family loyalty. Players traded away would often return to the team. Pitcher Bobo Newsom had five separate tours with the Senators. Griffith would trade him away and then trade for him back. One player actually married his way into the family. In 1934, Joe Cronin married Clark Griffith's niece, Mildred Robertson, who had been employed as Griffith's secretary.[312] In 1940, the Senators promoted Sherry Robertson, a nephew of Griffith, to play for the Senators. Robertson had been billed as a solid hitter and base stealer, but the nephew would only bat a lifetime .230 and never steal more than 10 bases in a season. Sherry Robertson would play ten years in the majors, all but his last season with his uncle's club.[313]

A trade in 1949 raised the most eyebrows. That year, Griffith traded for Joe Haynes, the husband of his niece and adopted daughter Thelma. In exchange for Haynes, an average relief pitcher with a history of arm troubles, Griffith traded Early Wynn, a future Hall of Famer. Other players were involved in the deal, and Wynn was not yet a star, but the trade became criticized and ridiculed as "Thelma's deal." Thelma had expressed a desire to live in Washington. It was assumed that Uncle Clark had created a job for Thelma's husband, so she could live in the city of her wish.[314]

One of the biggest mysteries in the history of baseball is the death of Ed Delahanty. One of the best hitters at the turn of the Twentieth Century, Delahanty batted over .400 in three separate

Death of Ed Delahanty
Thursday, July 2, 1903 12:00:00 PM
Niagra Falls, Ontario
Time Zone: 05:00 (EST)
Longitude: 079° W 04'
Latitude: 43° N 06'

---
311. Povich, p. 147.
312. Povich, p. 189.
313. Povich, p. 226, Acocella pp. 577-578.
314. Povich, p. 228, Acocella pp. 577-578.

years: 1894, 1895 and 1899. In 1902, he joined the Washington Senators. That year he batted .376, barely losing the batting title by .002 to Napoleon Lajoie. The next year, Delahanty was hitting .333 in mid-season when he died mysteriously on July 2, 1903. The Senators were in Detroit when Delahanty disappeared. Delahanty reportedly boarded a train while intoxicated. On the train, he got into a fight with the conductor. Near the Ontario border, he was forced to leave the train. There he wandered onto the International Bridge, from which he jumped, fell, or was pushed into the Niagara River. A few days later his body washed ashore.[315] The transits of July 2, 1903, suggest violence and foul play. Mercury, in transit at 18 degrees Gemini, was conjunct to Pluto at 20 degrees Gemini. This aspect also suggests a bad day to travel. Mars, in transit at 11 degrees Libra was conjunct the North Node, also at 11 degrees Libra. Both Mars and the North Node were in a semi-square aspect to Delahanty's Mars-Saturn conjunction of 24 degrees Scorpio. Mars in such a difficult transit to one's natal Mars or Saturn can easily trigger a fight.

Walter Johnson was the best player in the history of the Senators and the Twins. One of history's greatest pitchers, Johnson holds the record for most career shut-outs, with 110. For many years, he held the record for most career strike-outs, with 3508. Johnson struck out batters in an era in which strike-outs were less frequent than they are today. In his day, batters rarely swung from their heels, aiming for homeruns. Nolan Ryan broke Johnson's record in an era when batters regularly swung hard for home runs, often striking themselves out. Johnson played his entire 21-year career in Washington. Later he would return to the team as a manager. Johnson's Sun and Jupiter are both conjunct to the Senators' Uranus and MC.

Walter Johnson
Sunday, November 6, 1887 12:00:00 PM
Humbolt, Kansas
Time Zone: 06:00 (CST)
Longitude: 095° W 26'
Latitude: 37° N 49'

---

315. Dewey & Acocella, p. 569; Povich, p. 39

Johnson's Mercury is in Sagittarius, usually an affliction and an unfavorable placement for a pitcher, but, in his case, his Mercury was opposed by Pluto in Gemini. This opposition allowed much of his Scorpionic power to be channeled through his Mercury. Even with an unusual sidearm delivery, Johnson was a power pitcher who threw at a very high velocity. A highly refined Scorpio, he claimed to have only once thrown at a batter, the Athletics' Frank Baker,[316] and that was only to keep him from crowding the plate. Johnson proved that a Scorpio can be free of malice.

The Senators, with the Sun in Scorpio, were solid at the third base position, even in bad times. Ossie Bluege played his entire 18-year major league career, 1922 to 1939, as a Washington Senator, most of those years as the starting third baseman. Bluege would return to the Senators as their manager from 1943 to 1947. Eddie Yost was the Senators starting third baseman from 1947 to 1958. He maintained a consecutive games streak of 829 from 1949 to 1955, ninth on the all-time list. A leadoff batter who drew a high percentage of walks, Yost led the American League in walks four times.

Clark Griffith died on October 27, 1955, under a combination of transits, each of which by itself could have brought down a patriarch. Saturn in Scorpio was conjunct the Senators MC, Pluto was square to the Senators Sun, and the Sun was conjunct the Senators' Mars. The franchise would undergo a radical change after his death. Calvin Griffith, a nephew of Clark Griffith, inherited control of the team. After the 1960 season, the team left Washington and moved to Minnesota. Once in Minnesota, the team changed its name and its colors. This was a Scorpionic transformation, a metamorphosis. A Scorpio can change radically and reinvent itself. One needs to look hard to see a trace of the former Senators in the current Twins. The birthchart of the Twins has an MC of 4 degrees Scorpio conjunct to Mars of 2 degrees Scorpio. With Mars conjunct the MC, the Minnesota Twins have a stronger emphasis at the shortstop position than did the Washington Senators. An early Twins star was shortstop Zoilo Versalles, who won the MVP in 1965 and led them to a pennant.

On the field, the team has performed better than its days in Washington. Even without strong financial support from ownership, the Twins have often fielded competitive teams. The Twins won pennants in 1965, 1987 and 1991. The 1965 team featured future Hall-of-Famers Rod Carew and Harmon Killebrew. The pitching staff included Mudcat Grant, the first

---

316. Thomas, Henry W: *Walter Johnson: Baseball's Big Train*, p. 125.

African American pitcher in the American League to win 20 games. In both 1987 and 1991, the Twins won the World Series under Neptune transits. Neptune, in transit through Capricorn, was conjunct to the Twins Ascendant in 1987. First baseman Kent Hrbek responded to the transit by hitting 37 home runs. The 1991 champions followed a 1990 last-place finish. In 1990, Saturn in Capricorn was square the Twins natal Saturn in Libra, bringing bad fortune to a quality team. But in 1991, Neptune in Capricorn was conjunct to the Twins' Venus, which was channeled through the play of center fielder Kirby Puckett, who batted .319.

Mars conjunct the MC in the Minnesota chart has brought unsympathetic owners to the franchise. Calvin Griffith did not follow his uncle's pattern as a benevolent patriarch of a family business. Instead, the nephew publicly criticized his players and even made racist remarks. In Minnesota, the franchise reverted to the characteristic Western League drama of fans against owners. In 1969, Twins fans sided with manager Billy Martin in his dispute with Calvin Griffith.[317] In his most notorious incident, the nephew put himself figuratively in boiling water at a Lion's Club social. While drunk, he told the gathering that he moved to Minnesota because there were only 15,000 African-Americans in the Twin Cities region. Griffith's remarks were made on Sept. 27, 1978, as Mars in transit at 5 degrees Scorpio was conjunct the Twins MC.[318] In the early 1980s, Twins fans would wear "Trade Calvin" buttons. Such conflicts did not occur with the Washington Senators of Clark Griffith, but the relocation to Minnesota brought the aspect of Mars conjunct to the MC, which has manifested in a selfish management with an unrefined Mars edge.

In 1984, Carl Pohlad gained control of the team, ending the legacy of Griffith family ownership. Pohlad bought the controlling share of the team on June 22, 1984, as Mars and Saturn were both at 11 degrees Scorpio and conjunct to the Twins' Tenth House Uranus. Although Pohlad was one of the richest men in baseball, he was unwilling to adequately finance his own team.[319] Pohlad frequently threatened to move the team if he did not get a new publicly funded stadium. In 2002, he actually agreed with the commissioner on a plan to eliminate the franchise. The threat of "contraction" began in the fall of 2001. The economy had sunk in the

---

317. Dewey & Acocella, pp. 317-318.
318. Earlier in 1962, the franchise was investigated by the Minnesota State Commission on Discrimination for segregating their Spring Training facilities. Guntze, Jeff Severns, *Minnesota Post*: "Racial Justice for the Minnesota Twins: the Forgotten Battle" Sept. 8, 2010.
319. Caple, Jim: *Pohlad was Good, Bad for Twins*, ESPN.com Jan. 6, 2009.

wake of the September 11 attacks, and attendance was on hard times all around the league. Saturn, near 12 degrees Gemini, was conjunct to the Twins' natal Pluto and Neptune. Pluto, in transit through Sagittarius, was opposite these planets and conjunct the Twins' Mercury. Saturn was in Gemini, the sign of twins. It was this aspect, and the opposition from Pluto, that had brought down the Twin Towers of the World Trade Center. Now it was threatening the very existence of the Twins. But the Twins proved more resilient than the towers, surviving the threat and even winning the 2002 American League Central Division.

THE CLEVELAND INDIANS

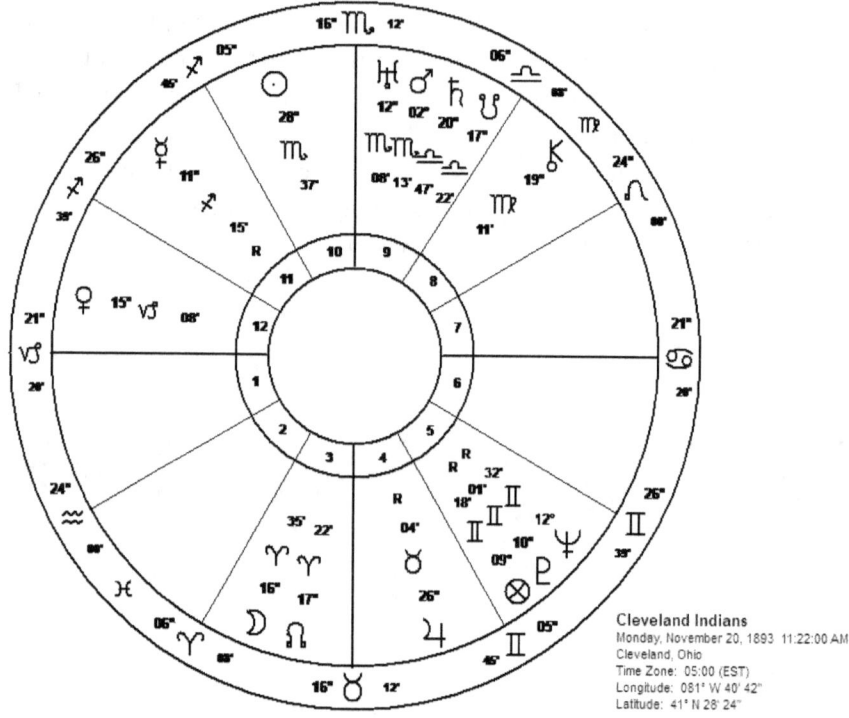

Cleveland Indians
Monday, November 20, 1893 11:22:00 AM
Cleveland, Ohio
Time Zone: 05:00 (EST)
Longitude: 081° W 40' 42"
Latitude: 41° N 28' 24"

The Cleveland Indians were born alongside the other Western League clubs on November 21, 1893 at 11:22 am EST. [320] The first home of this franchise was Grand Rapids, Michigan, where the team played in the early years of the Western League. In 1900, the team moved to Cleveland, Ohio. When the Western League became the American League in 1901, the team remained in Cleveland. The Indians' birthchart is distinguished from its Western League siblings by the square of Saturn to the Ascendant, the difficult aspect that has made Cleveland a hard-luck franchise.

Like that of its Western League siblings, the birthchart of the Indians has a heavy Scorpio emphasis. The Sun, Mars, Uranus and the MC are all in the sign of Scorpio. An early owner of the team was Charles Somers, a coal baron. Coal mining is a Scorpionic industry, as mines are dark hidden places, and coal is an energy source that has undergone a pressurized

---

320. Rectification note: When the Indians moved into Cleveland Municipal Stadium in 1932, their natal Pluto, progressed by solar arc, became conjunct to their Descendant of 21 degrees Cancer. An axis with a degree in Cancer is an indicator of the home ballpark.

transformation. Charles Somers's coal money would finance not only the Indians, but much of the embryonic American League. Charles Somers is credited with providing the financial assistance without which the American League could never have battled the established National League. Somers would fund not only his team in Cleveland but the Red Sox franchise. Somers financed the Boston team for its first two years, before a permanent owner could be found. In addition, Somers loaned money to Connie Mack to keep the Athletics franchise afloat, and he loaned the money to Charles Comiskey that built Chicago's Comiskey Park.[321]

Cleveland fans explain the sad luck of their team as "the Curse of Rocky Calovito." Indeed, the square of Saturn to the Ascendant in the Indians' birthchart is consistent with hard luck. The Ascendant represents one's contact and interactions with the external world. A square from Saturn, the planet of limitations, often brings hardship and adversity. On April 17, 1960, general manager Frank Lane traded popular right fielder Rocky Calovito to Detroit for Harvey Kuen. Transits for the trade do suggest ill fortune by emphasizing Saturn and Capricorn. That day, the Moon and Saturn were conjunct in Capricorn. They were also square to the Indians' natal Saturn and conjunct their natal Venus and Ascendant. However, long before the trade of Calovito, tragedy and ill-fortune had reoccurred in Cleveland history. Cleveland has had great teams, but pennants and World Series wins have been elusive. The Indians, in their long history, have claimed only five pennants and two World Series championships. The 1908 Cleveland team lost the pennant by 1/2 game. A rained out game accounted for the difference. Now a rule exists that states that any game missed that affects the final outcome of the standing must be replayed. But the rule was not instituted until after 1908, when the bad luck of the Indians proved it necessary. In the 1950s, the Indians had outstanding teams, but they were consistent also-rans to the Yankees, winning a pennant only in 1954. That year, the Indians had one of the best pitching staffs ever assembled, with Bob Feller, Early Wynn, Bob Lemon, and Mike Garcia. Cleveland set a record with 111 wins, but they would be swept in the World Series by the New York Giants. The 1990s also brought outstanding teams to Cleveland, but the team would lose the World Series in 1995 and 1997.

Horrible tragedies have struck the Indians. Eddie Joss, a Hall of Fame pitcher, died of spinal meningitis before the 1911 season. Shortstop Ray Chapman may be the only baseball player to have died as the result of an

---

321. Lewis, *The Cleveland Indians* pp. 32-34.

on-field injury.[322] Chapman died after being hit by a pitch from Carl Mays of the Yankees on August 16, 1920.[323] The birthchart of Ray Chapman has Mercury retrograde at 21 degrees Capricorn, aptly conjunct to the Indians' Ascendant, which is square to Saturn. Lefthander Herb Score had been an overpowering pitcher on his way to glory. He had earned the Rookie of the Year award in 1955, and he would win twenty games and post a 2.53 ERA in 1956. Then Herb Score was struck in the face by a line drive from the bat of Yankee Gil McDougold on May 7, 1957. Score survived the injury and remained an active player, but he would never again play a season in which he won more games than he lost.

The worst tragedy in Cleveland Indians history was the 1993 boating accident that killed pitchers Tim Crews and Steve Olin and injured pitcher Bob Ojeda. The accident occurred in Florida at Little Lake Nellie during Spring Training. The players' boat was circling the lake after sunset when it crashed into an unlit peer. Tim Crews, who was driving the boat, had an alcohol level above the legal limit. Transits for the day involved multiple planets. In the spring of 1993, Uranus and Neptune were conjunct at 21 degrees Capricorn, exactly conjunct the Indians' Ascendant. A transit from Uranus to an Ascendant brings a surge of new energy. Such an aspect can also bring accidents, as the energy of Uranus is quick and unpredictable. It often leaves one

Indians Boating Accident
Tuesday, March 23, 1993 7:52:00 PM
Little Lake Nellie, Fla
Time Zone: 05:00 (EST)
Longitude: 081° W 46'
Latitude: 29° N 29'

---

322. The death of the Athletics' Doc Powers may also have been the result of an on-field injury. See Athletics Section.

323. On August 16, 1920, the day Ben Chapman was beaned, Uranus, in transit at 4 degrees Pisces, formed a semi-square to the Indians' Ascendant. There were major aspects to the Yankees Mercury of 5 degrees Sagittarius. Venus at 6 degrees Virgo was opposed to Uranus, and both planets were square to the Yankees' Mercury. Carl Mays' natal Venus of 4 degrees Sagittarius is conjunct the Yankees Mercury. Carl Mays and Ben Chapman were both born in 1891 in Kentucky, but their unrectified birthcharts do not suggest an obvious karmic connection between them.

unprepared, as if one has stepped on an accelerator and found more power than expected. A transit from Neptune can bring alcohol and obscured perceptions. In the boating accident, Neptune supplied the water, the boat, the alcohol, and the unlit dock. The accident occurred on the evening of March 23, 1993, near 7:52 pm[324] as Neptune and Uranus were conjunct the IC. On the day of the accident, Uranus and Neptune were part of a grand cross that included Jupiter in Libra, Mars in Cancer,[325] and Venus and the Moon in Aries. Mercury was retrograde at 10 degrees Pisces and square to both the Indians' Mercury and the Pluto-Neptune conjunction. Mercury retrograde is also often present in accidents. Mercury, in the birthchart of a baseball team, represents the pitching staff: Tim Crews, Steve Olin, and Bob Ojeda were all pitchers.

The Indians, like all four Western League teams, have the Moon in Aries in opposition to Saturn. The Indians' Moon of 16 degrees Aries is conjunct to the North Node of 19 degrees Aries. The Indians share a warrior Moon with the other Western League teams. The launching of the American League was an embodiment of this assertive Moon and its opposition to Saturn. In a mundane chart, the Moon represents the workers in opposition to capital and management. The birth of the American League was helped by the mass of players who, in a labor conflict with the Saturnian owners, angrily left the National League because of the low pay and poor working conditions.

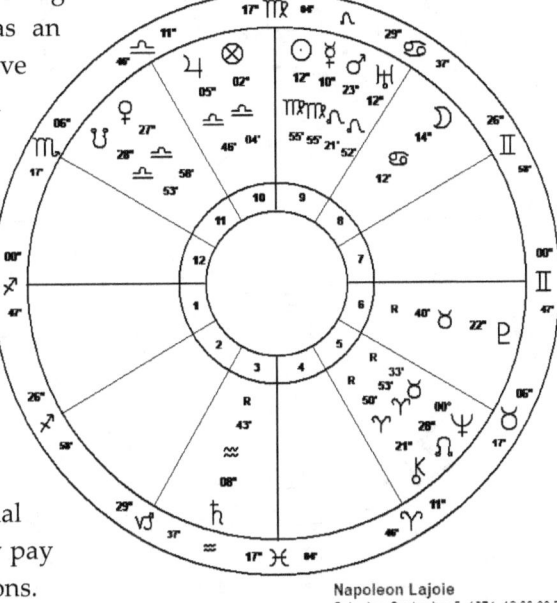

Napoleon Lajoie
Saturday, September 5, 1874 12:00:00 PM
Woonsocket, Rhode Island
Time Zone: 05:00 (EST)
Longitude: 071° W 31'
Latitude: 42° N 00'

The Indians' Saturn is in the sign of Libra. Napoleon Lajoie, an early player-manager of the Indians, embodied this Saturn in Libra placement.

---

324. The 911 call was placed at 7:52 pm. *LA Times* "Boat Crash Kills Olin of Indians: Baseball: Former Dodgers Crews, Ojeda injured in high-speed wreck on lake in central Florida, near Cleveland's spring training base." March 23, 1993.
325. Tim Crews (born April 3, 1961) experienced a Mars return that day.

Lajoie was the Cleveland manager, and he played the second base position. Lajoie as a combined manager and second baseman would embody Saturn, the planet of the manager, in Libra, the sign of second base. The most memorable Indian managers, however, have been shortstops. The tight square of Saturn to the Ascendant links the position of shortstop, a manifestation of the Ascendant, with the manager. Roger Peckinpaugh played shortstop for Cleveland in the 1910s. He returned to manage the team from 1928 to 1932 and then again in 1941. Lou Boudreau managed and played shortstop for the Indians from 1942 through 1950.

Lou Boudreau would first manage the Indians when he was only 26 years old. Aries, the first sign, is represented in youth. Boudreau was a favorite of the fans. In 1947, owner Bill Veeck planned to trade Boudreau to the St. Louis Browns, but the Moon guards not only home plate but the player embodied in its sign. The fans, representatives of the Indians' Moon in Aries, defended their shortstop. When Veeck's plan became public, the fans rose in defense of Boudreau.[326] Cleveland fans signed petitions and protested to keep Boudreau. Fans demanded that Veeck should leave town instead of the shortstop. Under pressure, Veeck changed his mind and made public appearances, admitting his plan was a mistake. Boudreau was soon given a two-year contract. The next year, Boudreau won the MVP award, and the Indians won the World Series.

Lou Boudreau
Tuesday, July 17, 1917 12:00:00 PM
Harvey, Ill
Time Zone: 05:00 (CDT)
Longitude: 087° W 39'
Latitude: 41° N 36'

The opposition from the Moon places excessive pressure on Saturn. The fans, the players, and the press make things difficult for Saturn's representatives. Cleveland has proven a tough place for managers, general

---

326. Dewey & Acocella, p. 218.

managers, and owners. The difficult opposition between the Moon and Saturn has especially taken its toll on managers. Author Franklin Lewis called Cleveland "the Graveyard of Managers."[327] Many managers have suffered bitter failure in Cleveland. Bobby Bragan, who managed part of the 1958 season, was one of many fired after short stints at managing the Indians. Upon being fired, Bragan allegedly took his revenge by hexing the team.[328]

The opposition from the Moon to Saturn has brought bitter conflicts between the players and managers. The Moon becomes embodied in the players, forming a mass body asserting themselves against management. In the history of the Cleveland team, there have been reoccurring player rebellions against managers. Addie Joost died just before the 1911 opener, and his funeral became scheduled for the same date as Opening Day. The opener was to take place in Detroit. Neither Detroit nor Cleveland management were willing to postpone the game. The Cleveland players all signed a petition, stating their intention to attend the funeral. Then they left for the funeral without waiting for a response.[329]

On June 9, 1933, Walter Johnson became the manager of the Indians. Johnson had been one of the best pitchers in the history of the game, yet he proved an unpopular manager. Neither the players nor the fans liked him. On May 23, 1935, Johnson released catcher Glen Myatt and third baseman Willie Kamm with the accusation that they were leading a plot to get rid of him. Johnson also accused Myatt and Kamm of undermining his credibility and authority with the younger players. Soon Johnson was so unpopular with the lunar masses that extra security guards were hired at home games to protect him from the fans. Walter Johnson was soon fired, losing the helm on July 28, 1935, with Mars in Libra conjunct the Indians' Saturn and the Moon in the people's sign of Cancer.

A few years later, the Indians were playing well, contending for the pennant. Manager Ossie Vitt, however, would habitually criticize his players to the press, instead of privately. In June of 1940, Mel Harder and Hal Trosky organized a group of veteran players who met with the owner, Alva Bradley. The players sought to persuade the owner to fire Vitt. The meeting occurred on June 13, 1940. That day, Mercury, Venus, and Mars were conjunct in Cancer, the sign of people's revolts. But the Sun in transit at 21 degrees Gemini was trine to the Indians' Saturn. This

---

327. Lewis, Franklin, *The Cleveland Indians*, p. 174.
328. Dewey & Acocella, p. 221.
329. Lewis, p. 69.

favorable trine allowed Vitt to survive. Owner Bradley denied the players' request. The press soon found out about the meeting and sided with the manager. Newspapers branded the players as "crybabies," a tag which followed them wherever they traveled that year. They gave up trying to influence the owner, but the players found subtler ways to rebel. They would employ the hit-and-run without the manager's consent.[330] The 1940 season ended bitterly for Cleveland, as the Indians lost the pennant to the Tigers by one game. In the final series against Detroit, Ossie Vitt was criticized for overusing a tired Bob Feller. Naturally, Vitt was fired in the coming off-season.

Hank Greenberg was another Saturnian representative who faced difficulty in Cleveland. In the 1950s, Greenberg was employed as the Indians' general manager. When he left Cleveland in 1957, Greenberg blasted the fans and the press, charging that they were unable to support a big-league team. Frank Robinson made dramatic history in Cleveland as the first African-American to manage a major league team. Robinson, employed in a player-manager role, hit a home run in his first at-bat. This event occurred April 8, 1975, during a 5-3 win. Nevertheless, even Frank Robinson left the Graveyard of Managers without success. He frequently clashed with players, especially those who disliked his sharp tongue and his opinion that those not as good as he were simply not trying.[331]

The Indians' Saturn contends not only with the difficult aspects from the Moon and the Ascendant, but those from Venus, as well. Venus, in the Twelfth House and at 15 degrees Capricorn, is square to the Indians' Saturn. The Twelfth House represents things hidden. In 1919, a curious relationship developed between Manager Lee Fohl and center fielder Tris Speaker, an embodiment of Venus. Lee Fohl would consult Tris Speaker on all his pitching moves. On the afternoon of July 18, 1919, the Indians were playing the Boston Red Sox.[332] The Indians were ahead by three runs late in the game. However, the Red Sox had loaded the bases with Babe Ruth coming to the plate. The manager looked towards center field for Tris Speaker to signal which pitcher should face Ruth. Speaker signaled for the right-hander. Fohl, however, either misunderstood his signal or overrode it and brought in the left-hander, Fritz Coumbe, to face the lefty

---

330. Dewey & Acocella, p. 216.
331. Dewey & Acocella, p. 223.
332. This incident occurred on a heavily aspected day. Venus, in transit at 10 degrees Virgo, was square to the Indians' Pluto. Mars and Pluto, both in transit at 6 degrees Cancer, were conjunct each other and semi-square to Mercury, in transit at 21 degrees Leo. All three planets formed aspects to the Indians' Saturn and MC-IC axis.

Cleveland Indians

Ruth. Tris Speaker shouted "No! No, not Combe," which caused the infielders to look back at him. Speaker then turned his back to the plate and drooped his shoulders, a gesture that the fans noticed. A few pitches later, Babe Ruth hit a grand slam, and the game was lost. After the game, it was obvious that Lee Fohl was not the real authority. The center fielder, an embodiment of the hidden influence of Venus in the Twelfth House, was the real power. Soon Fohl resigned in disgrace. Tris Speaker, of course, would replace him.[333] The next year, Speaker led the Indians to their first pennant and a World Series victory.

A team's name, uniforms, colors and mascot are embodiments of the Ascendant. The Indians' square from Saturn to the Ascendant is embodied in the various names which this team has taken. In their earliest years in Cleveland, this team was called "the Blues" for their blue uniforms.[334] For short periods, the team was called the Bluebirds and the Broncos. In 1903, they took the name "Naps" or "Napoleons," for their manager Napoleon Lajoie. The Saturn square, combined with the Capricorn Ascendant, gave the name of the manager to the team as a whole. Nap Lajoie resigned as the manager in August of 1909, but he remained as the team's second baseman until the end of the 1914 season. Even without Lajoie as manager, Cleveland kept the name of the Naps until he left the team.

The name "Indians" was chosen in 1915 by a newspaper poll. Previously, the Cleveland Spiders, who played in the National League in the 1890s, had also been called the "Indians" for their right fielder Louis Sockalexis, a Pebnobscot Indian.[335] Sockalexis would die on Dec. 24, 1913.

Louis Sockalexis
Tuesday, October 24, 1871 12:00:00 PM
Current Day and Time
Penobscot Indian Island Rsrvtn, Maine
Time Zone: 05:00 (EST)
Longitude: 068° W 31'
Latitude: 45° N 22'

---

333. Lewis, pp. 100-102.
334. Okkonen, Marc: *Baseball Uniforms of the 20th Century*, p. 35.
335. Lewis, p. 75; Fleitz, David, "Louis Sockalexis." *Society for American Baseball Research* https://sabr.org/bioproj/person/2b1aea0a

When the poll was conducted to choose a new mascot, the memory of the Native American right fielder was fresh with Cleveland fans. The name "Indians" has remained for many decades, in spite of the controversy it generates. Native American groups have petitioned the team to change it, contending that the name and the Big Chief Wahoo logo are derogatory towards them. Although Cleveland owners have refused to change the name, they did remove the the Big Chief Wahoo logo from their caps in 2019, a year when Pluto, in transit at 21 degrees Capricorn, was exactly conjunct the Indians' Ascendant. Perhaps the hard luck that Saturn has brought to the franchise involves a curse from Native Americans for the disrespect they feel. It would be interesting to find out if a change in name would bring a change in fortune.

The Athletics

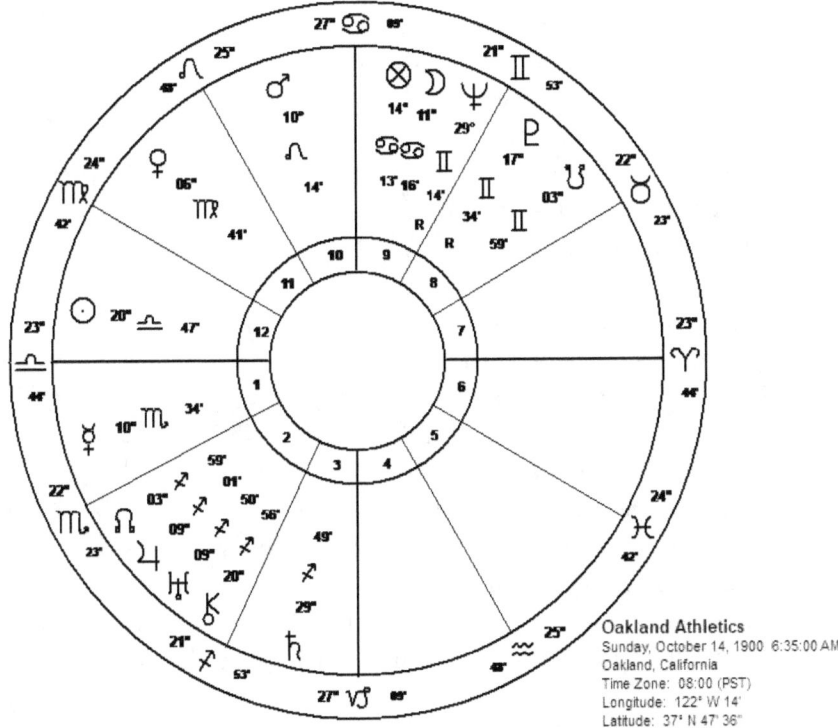

Oakland Athletics
Sunday, October 14, 1900 6:35:00 AM
Oakland, California
Time Zone: 08:00 (PST)
Longitude: 122° W 14'
Latitude: 37° N 47' 36"

The Athletics franchise was born on October 14, 1900[336], at 9:35 am EST.[337] The Athletics lived in Philadelphia from their birth until 1954. In 1955, the team moved to Kansas City, where they would reside through the 1967 season. Since 1968, the Athletics have made Oakland their home. The Athletics' birthchart has the Sun in the sign of Libra in square to the Moon in the sign of Cancer. The Sun in Libra has brought them both greatness and weakness at the second base position. The Moon in Cancer has manifested in outstanding catchers and it is reflected in the franchise as a family business.

The Athletics are the only major league baseball team with a Moon

---

336. On the same day the Athletics franchise was born, the Western League shed its minor league status and became a major league. It renamed itself the American League (Lieb, Frederick *Connie Mack: Grand Old Man of Baseball*, pp. 61-62). The Athletics' Sun of 20 degrees Libra is conjunct to the Western League Saturn.
337. Rectification Note: In 1909, when the team moved into Shibe Park, an IC of 15 Pisces progressed by solar arc became opposite the A's natal Venus. In 1954, when the team was sold and moved to Kansas City, the progressed IC became opposite the A's natal Mercury.

in Cancer, the Moon's own sign. The A's have an especially strong Moon, which has given them many of the positive and negative features of the sign Cancer. A Cancer organization stresses family ties. The Athletics have been a family-run business for most of their years. Connie Mack ran the Athletics from its founding in 1900 until soon before their sale and move to Kansas City in 1954. Mack, like Clark Griffith of the Senators, ran the A's as a family. His sons, Earle, Roy and Connie Jr., worked within the organization. Earle Mack even had a few at-bats as an A's player, but his father was wise enough to recognize his lack of major league talent. In Connie Mack's later frail years, Earle Mack occasionally managed in his father's place. Many former Athletic players have returned to the organization as coaches or managers, including Al Simmons, Mickey Cochran, Eddie Collins, and Tony LaRussa. In family organizations, the offspring often return to their original nest.

Philadelphia Athletics
Sunday, October 14, 1900 9:35:00 AM
Philadelphia, Pennsylvania
Time Zone: 05:00 (EST)
Longitude: 075° W 09' 48"
Latitude: 39° N 59' 18"

The birthchart of Connie Mack contains a Capricorn-Cancer polarity. His birthchart has the Sun, Mercury, and Venus conjunct in the early degrees of Capricorn. Mack's Moon is positioned in the late degrees of Capricorn. My rectified birthchart places his Sun, Mercury and

Connie Mack
Monday, December 22, 1862 10:28:00 PM
East Brookfield, Mass
Time Zone: 05:00 (EST)
Longitude: 072° W 01'
Latitude: 42° N 14'

Venus in the lunar Fourth House and his Moon in the Fifth House of sports. His rectified birthchart also has an Ascendant of 15 degrees Virgo, conjunct to the MC of the Philadelphia Athletics' team birthchart.[338] In his playing days, Connie Mack played the Cancer position of catcher. Many catchers have the Moon in Capricorn or aspects between their Moon and Saturn. A Capricorn Moon forces one to deal with lunar issues. Cancer issues such as nurturing are often addressed in their career paths by individuals with such lunar placements. Individuals with Capricorn Moons often become employed as caregivers. Similarly, a baseball player with a Capricorn Moon is likely to become a catcher.

Connie Mack remained as the Athletics' field manager through the 1950 season. Mack should have retired earlier, but lunar people can become mired in the past and have a difficult time moving on. Mack's final years as a manager were not his most capable ones. Nearly deaf and often falling asleep during games, he would call for sluggers to pinch hit who had long since left the team.[339] When Mack retired in 1950, the next generation of his family feuded over the control and direction of the franchise, a typical pattern for a family-run business. Similar drama played out with the Senators' franchise upon Clark Griffith's death.

Charlie Finley would become the next prominent owner of the Athletics. When relocated to Oakland, The Athletics' birthchart has an MC of 27 degrees Cancer, which is conjunct to Finley's Cancer Moon.[340]

Charlie Finley
Friday, February 22, 1918 12:00:00 PM
Birmingham, Alabama
Time Zone: 06:00 (CST)
Longitude: 086° W 48' 06"
Latitude: 33° N 31'

---

338. Rectification Note: An Ascendant of 15 Virgo progressed by solar arc becomes opposite Mack's natal Neptune at age 16, a year he became employed in a shoe factory. The same ascendant becomes conjunct Saturn at age 20, the year he chose a baseball career. In 1900, the year he founded the A's franchise, his progressed ascendant becomes conjunct his Jupiter of 23 Libra.
339. Dewey & Acocella, p. 441.
340. An unrectified noon chart for Finley has a Moon of 28 degrees Cancer. Interestingly, Finley's Moon and Mack's Moon are opposite to each other.

Finley, in true Cancer fashion, often made decisions from a place of emotions rather than from reason or wisdom. Mack, with his Capricorn planets, maintained a staid Saturnian persona. On the field, he wore a formal suit rather than a uniform. In contrast, Finley's persona was of a Leo showman, which reflected the Neptune and Saturn conjunction in Leo of his birthchart. His Cancer Moon was released in unpredictable emotions towards his players. He often lashed out at his players. Additionally, his players' requests for raises were usually denied, but Finley would give them bonuses when the mood struck him.[341]

Finley would move the franchise to Oakland and build the dynasty that won three consecutive World Series from 1972 to 1974. The genius of Charley Finley came from the conjunction between his Sun and Uranus. He also had Venus, Mercury and Uranus in the sign of Aquarius. Finley had many Uranian ideas for the game of baseball, most of them intended to increase the offense. Finley's ideas included the designated hitter, the designated runner, the three-ball walk and an orange baseball for night games. He also brought to baseball bright-colored uniforms, which were a mirror of his Leo planets.

The Athletics have sustained excellence at the Cancer position of catcher. Mickey Cochrane, a Hall of Famer who consistently batted over .300, is considered one of the best catchers to play the game. Outstanding catchers for the Oakland A's include Dave Duncan, Gene Tenace, Ray Fosse and Terry Stienbach. Gene Tenace, who was the star of the 1972 World Series, was one of the few players who four home runs in a World Series and the only player to hit home runs in his first and second World Series at-bats. Dave Duncan would return to the team as a pitching coach, and Ray Fosse would return as a broadcaster.

As Cancer rules stadiums, the Athletics were the first team to build a modern concrete and steel stadium when they opened Shibe Park in 1909. The other baseball teams would soon follow the Athletics and build their own modern ballparks. A strange death occurred with the opening of Shibe Park. On April 12, 1909, the day of its first official game, Athletics catcher Mike "Doc" Powers crashed into a wall while pursuing a pop foul.[342] Late in the game, Doc Powers would suffer sharp abdominal pains and would

---

341. Macht, p. 334.
342. Dewey & Acocella, p. 436.

collapse.[343] Powers would die on April 26,[344] two weeks after sustaining the injury. There is dispute about the cause of his death. Some reports say he died from gangrene of the bowels or of an intestinal lock.[345] Others claim his death was related to food poisoning. Regardless of the cause, Powers underwent three operations on his intestines before dying. He had been popular with the Philadelphia fans, having played with the team since their first game in 1901. The death of Mike Powers is eerily similar to the accident that ended the career of Roy Campanella. Between the Dodgers' last season in Brooklyn and their first season in Los Angeles, the Dodgers' catcher became paralyzed in an automobile accident. It is the catchers who are most intimately linked with home stadiums, since catchers and stadiums are both ruled by the Moon. When the Athletics moved from the old wooden grandstand of Columbia Park to the modern steel and concrete Shibe Park, Dock Powers died with the old Nineteenth Century ballpark. Campanella's career was ended when the Dodgers left Brooklyn and Ebbets Field. Catchers, like Cancers, do not adapt well to moves.

"The Wave," in which sections of fans within a stadium alternately stand and sit to produce an effect of waves, was first performed at an A's game. Krazy George Henderson, a cheerleader for the Athletics in the 1980s, is credited with its invention. Oakland, with its Cancer Moon, is the perfect place for The Wave to be born. Cancer and the Moon rule the fans, and thousands of fans cooperating in such an enthusiastic spectacle correspond with a Cancer Moon. The Wave's debut occurred during a playoff game on the evening of October 15, 1981. That night, multiple planets were in aspect to the A's Cancer MC, including a conjunction from the North Node, a trine from inventive Uranus at 28 Scorpio, and a square from Mercury at 28 Libra. Also in the sky, the Moon at 28 degrees Taurus formed a t-square with Uranus and Mars at 27 degrees Leo.

The Athletics' Sun in Libra has been embodied in both greatness and controversy at the second base position. In their first season of 1901, the Athletics' second baseman Napoleon Lajoie would bat .422, which remains the American League record. Lajoie had been a star with the Philadelphia Phillies, when he jumped to the Philadelphia team of the new American

---

343. On the day of the injury and of the opening of Shibe Park, Mercury at 12 degrees Aries was square to the A's Moon, and the Moon in Capricorn was opposite the A's Moon.
344. On the day of Powers' death, the A's natal square of Mars in Leo to Mercury in Scorpio was opposed by a transiting square of Mars in Aquarius square to Mercury in Taurus. Challenging aspects involving Mars or planets in Scorpio can bring death.
345. Macht cites that Powers died from gangrene of the bowels (p. 302). Lieb claims it was an intestinal lock.

League. In the following year of 1902, the Pennsylvania Supreme Court ruled that Lajoie's contract with the Phillies bound him to play with the Senior Circuit club. But the American League cleverly side-stepped the ruling by trading Lajoie to Cleveland, keeping him out of the court's Pennsylvania jurisdiction.

The Athletics would replace Lajoie with Danny Murphy. The A's new second baseman made a spectacular debut on July 8, 1902, by batting 6 for 6. Danny Murphy played 11 years with the Athletics. In 1909, he shifted from second base to right field, an easy transition on a team with the Sun in Libra. Hall-of-Famer Eddie Collins made his debut with the Philadelphia Athletics in 1906. When Danny Murphy moved to right field in 1909, Collins became the A's starting second baseman. In his career, Collins would bat .333 and steal 745 bases. Twice he stole six bases in one game.[346] Collins was a member of the Athletics' "$100,000 Infield,"[347] a team that won many games with their defense. Philadelphia fans would arrive early to Shibe Park to watch the infield practice of Eddie Collins and shortstop Jack Barry,[348] in a striking contrast from today's fans, who arrive early to watch batting practice.

When the A's moved to Oakland, the Sun in their relocated birthchart moved into the Twelfth House. This Twelfth House Sun in Libra has manifested as an affliction for Oakland's second basemen. The affliction is intensified by the squares of Uranus and Jupiter to Venus. The Oakland A's have lacked stability at second base. During the Finley era, notorious incidents took place at this position. In 1972, the A's lacked a strong bat at second base. The team kept extra infielders on the roster in order to pinch hit for the second baseman, whoever he was, at his every at-bat. Dick Green would usually start the game, only to be pinch hit for in his first at-bat. Dal Maxvill or Ted Kubiak would succeed him.[349] By the late innings, with most of the bench infielders already in and out of the game, non-infielders would sometimes be playing second base.

The A's 1972 pennant was almost lost when a catcher, Dave Duncan, manned the base in the 10th inning of Game 4 of the LCS. Duncan dropped a throw for an error, which was soon followed by Detroit's scoring the winning run. This game occurred on Oct 11, 1972, as Venus

---

346. http://en.wikipedia.org/wiki/List_of_Major_League_Baseball_stolen_base_records
347. In addition to Collins, the 100,000 Infield consisted of first baseman Stuffy McInnis, shortstop Jack Barry and third baseman Frank "Homerun" Baker. Bill James rated them the best infield ever. http://en.wikipedia.org/wiki/$100,000_infield
348. Macht, p. 302
349. Libby, Bill, *Charlie O. and the Angry A's*, p. 207

in transit through Virgo was conjunct to the A's natal Venus. The Moon, the catcher's planet, in transit at 7 degrees Sagittarius, was square to both the A's natal Venus and to Venus in transit. These difficult transits placed a large weight on the second base position and set the stage for Duncan, normally a catcher, to make the error.

The 1973 World Series brought intense hardship to the second-base position. On October 14, 1973, second baseman Mike Andrews made two errors on consecutive plays within the 12th inning. Andrew's errors lost Game 2 of the World Series against the Mets. Given that day's transits, even the most reliable of fielders would have been challenged in playing second base for the A's. Venus, in transit at 6 degrees Sagittarius, was conjunct to Neptune, in transit at 5 degrees Sagittarius. Both Venus and Neptune were in square to the A's natal Venus of 6 degrees Virgo. The Sun, in transit at 21 degrees Libra, was conjunct to the A's natal Sun. Uranus, in transit at 23 Libra, was conjunct to the Athletics Libra Ascendant. That day was also the Athletics' solar return and 73rd birthday.

After the game, A's owner Charlie Finley forced Mike Andrews to sign a statement that he was too injured to continue the World Series. With a newly injured player, Finley intended to petition the Commissioner's Office to allow the A's another player onto their roster. However, the news soon broke of how Finley had strong-armed Mike Andrews. With Uranus—the planet of labor actions—conjunct the A's Ascendant, the team considered striking in solidarity with Andrews. Commissioner Bowie Kuhn soon ordered that Andrews be reinstated. [350]

The Athletics have Mars in the sign of Leo, which is usually considered a strong placement. Unfortunately, the A's Mars has had its shortcomings. In the game of baseball, Mars is oftentimes a malefic. Baseball requires a degree of patience, as one must wait for the game to unfold. A baseball player generally must wait for the ball to come to him or her. Mars in Leo easily becomes impatient and aggressive. Mars in Leo can also be arrogant. When they are good, the A's become cocky and overconfident. The Athletics were heavy favorites to win the 1988 World Series against the Dodgers. However, the 1988 Series is best remembered for Kirk Gibson's ninth-inning home run off Dennis Eckersley, as the A's went down to defeat in five games. In 1990, the heavily favored A's again lost the World Series, when they were swept in four games by the underdog Reds. In earlier eras, the hubris of Mars in Leo would also lead the A's to collapses. The A's received a comeuppance when they were swept

---

350. Dewey & Acocella, p. 403

by the Boston Braves in the 1914 World Series. That year, the Athletics had been so confident they had not even bothered to scout the Braves. Furthermore, on the eve of the Series, several A's players were out all night, partying.[351] In 1912, the Athletics also suffered from overconfidence. Since they had won back-to-back world championships in 1910 and 1911, the baseball world considered the A's to be on their way to a third straight championship. The Athletics left the gate slowly in 1912, but they were not concerned. Not until August did they realize that they were in danger of losing the pennant.[352] When the season ended, the Athletics had finished in third place, 15 games behind the pennant-wining Red Sox.

The Athletics' Mars in Leo became more conspicuous when the team moved to Oakland. In the Philadelphia and Kansas City charts, Mars was positioned in the Ninth House. When the birthchart became relocated to its West Coast longitude, the A's Mars shifted to the Tenth House. A person with a Tenth House Leo Mars is often obnoxious or overbearing. Such Leos crave attention and resort to extremes of behavior and attire to receive it. The Oakland Athletics have a *showboat, hotdog* quality. Beginning in the 1960s, the A's responded to the innovation of color television by wearing bright-colored uniforms.[353] In the 1960s, most baseball teams wore white or gray uniforms with red and blue trim. The A's defied the convention by dressing up in gaudy green and gold uniforms. By the 1970s, A's players were well-known for their mustaches and long hair. In the 1972 World Series, their flamboyant look stood in colorful contrast to that of the conservative Reds,

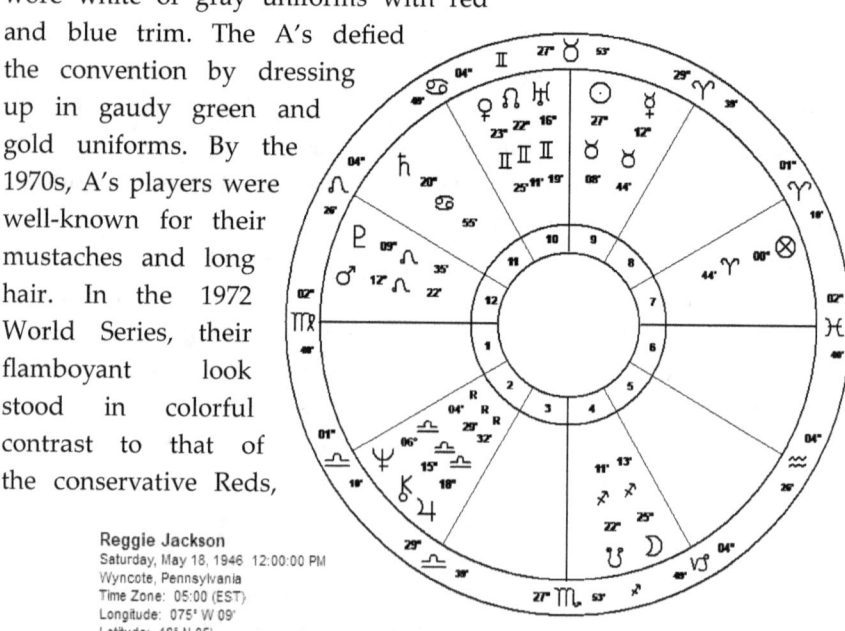

Reggie Jackson
Saturday, May 18, 1946 12:00:00 PM
Wyncote, Pennsylvania
Time Zone: 05:00 (EST)
Longitude: 075° W 09'
Latitude: 40° N 05'

---

351. Lieb, pp. 176-177
352. Lieb, p. 162
353. Okkonen, Marc: *Baseball Uniforms of the 20th Century*, p. 59

who have a Capricorn Ascendant.[354] Well into the 21st Century, many A's players still wear moustaches and have their hair long.

The A's biggest hotdogs have resonance with the A's Tenth House Mars. Reggie Jackson has Mars and Pluto conjunct in Leo. Both planets are conjunct the A's Mars. Charlie Finley, the owner who unbridled much of the team's Leo flamboyance, had Saturn and Neptune in Leo, both conjunct to the A's Mars. Jose Canseco's Mars in Gemini is only sextile to the A's Mars, and yet, while playing right field for the Athletics, Canseco was adversely affected by the A's Leo energy. Canseco had been a balanced player, stealing bases while hitting for both power and average. However, after several seasons in Oakland's right field, Canseco appeared to care only about hitting home runs. Ruben Sierra, who succeeded Canseco in right field, came to the Athletics as a .300 hitter in 1992. After a spell as the A's right fielder, Sierra's approach also changed. He became accused of being a selfish player who was unwilling to take walks.

Jupiter and Uranus are conjunct at 9 degrees Sagittarius in the Athletics' birthchart. This aspect has given innovation and versatility to the Athletics' offense. The A's were successful in the Dead Ball Era, when stolen bases and defense were important to winning low-scoring games. The great A's teams of the 1910s won with this small-ball style of play. In the early 1980s, while Billy Martin managed the era of "Billyball," the Athletics employed a similar speed-and-defense type of play. During this decade, Rickey Henderson mastered the art of manufacturing runs. Henderson would regularly carve out a walk, steal a base to get into scoring position, then get batted in. In the 1920s, the game of baseball changed to emphasize the home run. The A's, with their Jupiter Uranus conjunction, easily adapted to the new longball game. The second great era of the Athletics, in which they won three consecutive pennants from 1929 to 1931, had a Uranian offense. That A's lineup included sluggers Mickey Cochrane, Al Simmons, and Jimmy Foxx. In 1932, Jimmy Foxx hit 58 home runs, which nearly broke Babe Ruth's single-season home run record. In recent decades, the A's won a World Series and three consecutive pennants from 1988 to 1990 with a home run offense that featured sluggers Jose Canseco and Mark McGwire.

Uranus conjunct Jupiter brings innovation to the offense, as the ingenuity of Uranus influences the bat of Jupiter. Charlie Finley was a longtime supporter of the designated hitter before it became adopted by the American League. Some pundits even credit Finley with the idea of the DH, although others credit Bill Veeck. One undisputed original idea

---

354. See Reds chapter

of Finley's is that of the designated runner. In 1974, Finley hired Herb Washington, a world class sprinter, to run the bases. Washington never batted or picked up a glove. He only ran in place of another Athletic when the situation called for a fast runner on the bases. Unfortunately, Washington's stolen base percentage would prove to be only average. In 1974, he stole 29 bases, but was also caught stealing 16 times. His lack of versatility eventually proved a liability in a limited 25-man roster. The Moneyball approach of the 2002 season, in which on-base percentages were emphasized, is another example of an A's Uranus-Jupiter innovation.

The A's Uranus-Jupiter conjunction also brought steroids[355] to Oakland. Jose Canseco claimed that, when he had played for Oakland in the late-1980s, he had started the widespread use of steroids among baseball players. In his book *Juiced*, Canseco calls himself "the Godfather of Steroids." The Athletics' birthchart and the transits for the period support his claims. In 1988, when Canseco allegedly taught McGwire about steroids and injected him in the gluteus muscle,[356] Uranus, the planet of steroids, was in transit near 29 degrees Sagittarius and opposite the A's Neptune, the planet of McGwire's position: first base. The A's Uranus-Jupiter conjunction is trine to their Mars in Leo. The easy flow of this trine generates a lot of fire energy. As a showboat and a right-fielder, Canseco embodied the A's Mars in Leo. The trine from Uranus and Jupiter allowed him to tap the innovative energy of the Athletics. In his book, Canseco narrates how he learned all about steroids by experimenting on himself. Although questionable, his method was very Uranian and in keeping with the A's history of innovations.

Jose Canseco
Thursday, July 2, 1964 12:00:00 PM
Havana, Cuba
Time Zone: 04:00 (EDT)
Longitude: 082° W 23'
Latitude: 23° N 08'

---

355. See Giants chapter for a further discussion on steroids.
356. Canseco, Jose: *Juiced*, p. 74.

The Athletics

The Athletics' Oakland chart includes the placement of Saturn in the Third House. Unlike the San Francisco Giants, whose Third House Saturn has hindered their pitching, this placement has enhanced the pitching of the Athletics. The Oakland Athletics have excelled at relief pitching. As Saturn rules the late innings, Saturn in the Third House corresponds to relief pitchers. Rollie Fingers was the star reliever for the A's of the 1970s. Dennis Eckersley had a similar role in the late 1980s and early 1990s. More importantly, it was the Athletics who changed the nature of relief pitching. Tony LaRussa, who managed the A's from 1986 through 1995, set the standard for calls to the bullpen. He frequently brought pitchers into a game to only face one batter. Nowadays this is the accepted strategy for managers, but it had taken Tony LaRussa and a team with a Saturn in the Third House to make this a regular practice.

The Athletics made Kansas City their home from 1955 to 1967, an era considered an ignoble one in baseball history, as the Kansas City Athletics were accused of being a farm team for the Yankees. The first Kansas City Athletics owner, Arnold Johnson, had financial ties to the Yankee organization. Johnson, who was the deed holder on Yankee Stadium,

Kansas City Athletics
Sunday, October 14, 1900 8:35:00 AM
Kansas City, Missouri
Time Zone: 06:00 (CST)
Longitude: 094° W 33' 48"
Latitude: 39° N 07' 30"

was believed to be operating the A's, not for their best benefit, but in the interest of the Yankees. The birthchart of the Kansas City A's supports this claim. When located in Kansas City, the A's MC was positioned at 25 degrees Leo, conjunct to the Yankees' Mars. Conspicuously lopsided trades were executed between the Kansas City A's and the Yankees. These trades generally favored the team from New York. Roger Maris had been an Athletic in 1959 before being traded to the Yankees. In 1960, the newly traded Athletic would win the American League MVP award as a Yankee. In 1961, Marris would break Babe Ruth's single-season home run record in a Yankee uniform. The birthchart of the Kansas City Athletics had Saturn in the Second House. Saturn in this House of money often brings the financial difficulties that this weak franchise experienced.

Rickey Henderson, the current leader in career steals, is one of the most recognized Oakland Athletics.[357] A native of Oakland and fan favorite, Henderson would have the field named after him in 2017. His birthchart shows his base-stealing ability and his resonance with the Athletics franchise. His Sun in Capricorn conjunct to Saturn in Sagittarius, mirrors his base-stealing ability. Author John B. Holway makes the connection between Capricorns and base-stealing ability. Like mountain goats, who are very adept at choosing when and where to step, base stealers are precise in their ability to take their leads and decide when to run. Interestingly, Henderson's aspect with the A's chart is a Saturnian one. Henderson's Saturn at 29 degrees Sagittarius is conjunct the A's Saturn. His Moon in the opposite degree of Gemini is conjunct the A's Neptune.

Rickey Henderson
Thursday, December 25, 1958 12:00:00 PM
Oakland, California
Time Zone: 08:00 (PST)
Longitude: 122° W 14'
Latitude: 37° N 47' 36"

The Athletics are known to have made use of astrology. The 1994 Ken Burns history of baseball notes that Finley consulted an astrologer, but Burns' mention is dismissive, placed in the context of Finley's eccentric tendencies and ideas. John B. Holway reported that, in the 1976 season, Finley had consulted an astrologer named Laurie Brady. Holway writes that Laurie Brady had predicted correctly that the A's would win the division in 1971 and then win three consecutive World Series. Holway also notes that, in 1976, Finley had Laurie Brady cast daily charts for every player. These charts were given to manager Chuck Tanner, who promptly threw them away.[358] The Athletics finished the 1976 season in second place. Perhaps, if the manager had taken the charts seriously, the team would have advanced to the post-season.

---

357. John B. Holway connects base-stealing ability and the sign of Capricorn in Henderson's chart. Holway, John B. *The Baseball Astrologer and Other Weird Tales* p.46
358. Holway, John B. *The Baseball Astrologer and Other Weird Tales* pp. 32-35.

THE YANKEES

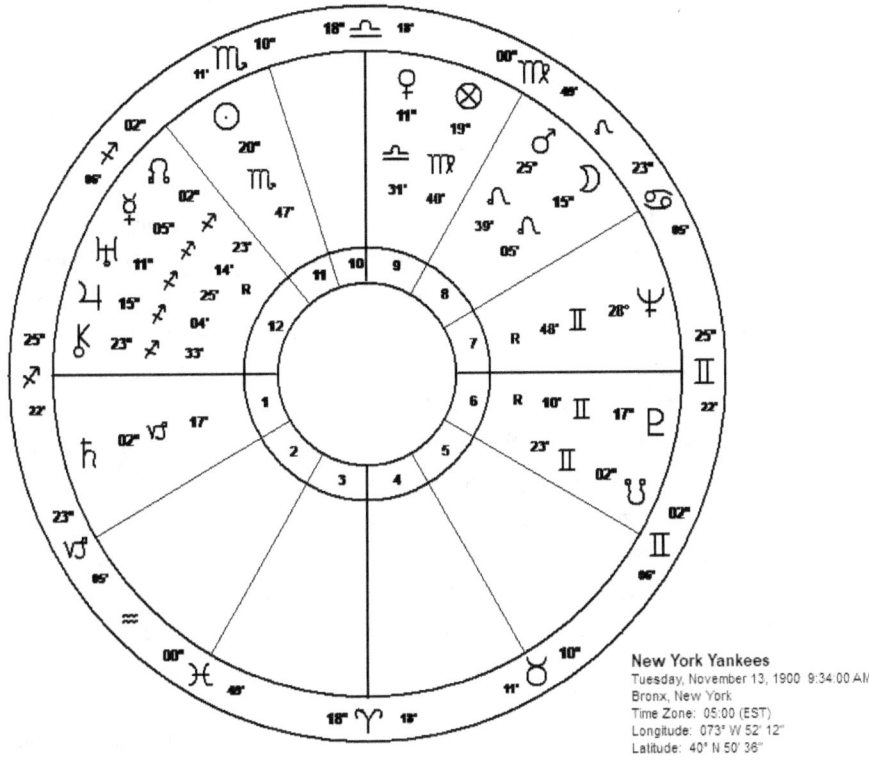

New York Yankees
Tuesday, November 13, 1900 9:34:00 AM
Bronx, New York
Time Zone: 05:00 (EST)
Longitude: 073° W 52' 12"
Latitude: 40° N 50' 36"

The Yankees franchise was born on November 13, 1900[359], at 9:34 am[360] EST in the city of Baltimore,[361] where they were one of a succession of teams to be called the "Orioles." In 1903, the team moved to New York. where they were first called the "Highlanders" for the location of their stadium in Hilltop Park, the highest elevation in Manhattan. By 1913, they

---

359. *New York Times* Nov. 14, 1900
360. Rectification Note: In 1923, the year Yankee Stadium opened, the North Node of 2 degrees Sagittarius became progressed to 25 degrees Sagittarius, conjunct the New York Ascendant. The Yankees' MC of 18 Libra has undergone striking transits during historical moments of the franchise. Mars was conjunct to the MC when Babe Ruth's contract was purchased on January 5, 1920. When George Steinbrenner purchased the team on June 3, 1973, Uranus was also conjunct the Yankees' MC.
361. This birthchart in this chapter is cast for the Bronx, New York, rather than Baltimore, the team's place of birth. The Baltimore birthchart has Chiron conjunct an Ascendant of 24 degrees Sagittarius. Chiron brings deep personal wounds. This conjunction involving the Ascendant brought the wound that nearly killed the franchise. Jupiter at 15 degrees Sagittarius is opposed Pluto of 17 degrees Gemini. This aspect became exact by solar arc progression in 1902, the year of the franchise's near death (Pluto).

were called the Yankees. The Yankees have Saturn is in the First House, an aspect that has given them their pinstripes and conservative style. They also have the Moon and Mars conjunct in the sign of Leo. Both these planets are square to the Sun in Scorpio. With the Sun in Scorpio square to Mars and the Moon conjunct in Leo, the Yankees' birthchart is very strong. A square this intense, involving personal planets in the powerful signs of Scorpio and Leo, establishes in a very formidable competitor.

Squares involving personal planets also indicate difficult early-life challenges in the realms they represent. Scorpio is the sign of death, and the Yankees franchise did suffer a near-death experience early in its history. The year the Yankees were born in Baltimore, the American League had hoped to place a team in New York but was prevented from doing so by the Giants. They were blocked by the National League team, which did not want competition for its attendance revenue. The Giants would use their Tammany Hall connections to protect their market. When the upstart American League launched in 1901, the two leagues were locked in a bitter war for fan attendance and for players, who had the opportunity to hop between the leagues for better salaries.

One particular battle in this war nearly killed off the Yankees at the hand of the Giants. John McGraw, the future Giants manager, played a key role in a plot to assassinate the Yankees franchise while it was still in its infancy. McGraw managed the Yankees for their first two years of life in Baltimore, but McGraw's rowdy style conflicted with the gentlemanly image that the new American League wanted to convey. The Baltimore manager was frequently suspended for his on-field antics and his disrespect of umpires. McGraw eventually became enmeshed in an acrimonious feud with American League President Ban Johnson. This grudge gave McGraw the impetus to

McGraw raids Orioles
Wednesday, July 16, 1902 12:00:00 PM
Baltimore, Maryland
Time Zone: 04:00 (EDT)
Longitude: 076° W 37' 12"
Latitude: 39° N 18' 48"

betray his own team. McGraw and Giants owner Andrew Freeman would mastermind a duplicitous plot. On June 18, 1902, McGraw secretly met with the Giants owner who offered him the job of managing the Giants. McGraw soon helped a front man for the rival National League named Joseph France buy a majority share of the Baltimore team. Then on July 16, 1902, while Mercury and Neptune were conjunct at 2 degrees Cancer and in exact opposition to the Yankees natal Saturn, the new owner released seven Baltimore players from their contracts.[362] The opposition aspect from Neptune to the Yankees' natal Saturn brought deceit and crossed-interests to the Saturnian figures of the owner and manager. The next day, only five Baltimore players arrived at the ballpark, and the game was forfeited. Meanwhile, five of the released players signed to play with the New York Giants, and two signed with the Cincinnati Reds. The turncoat McGraw soon joined the Giants and became their player-manager. After the Orioles' roster was gutted, the team finished the 1902 season in last place, thus dooming the franchise's future in Baltimore.

In Scorpionic fashion, however, the franchise would rise from the dead, transform, wait, and have its revenge. The next year, the remains of the franchise were moved to New York. The American League had found two men with the power to combat the political strength of the New York Giants, Frank Ferrell and William Devery. Ferrell had made his fortune operating gambling and prostitution establishments. Devery was a retired police chief who had become rich by accepting bribes not to close such establishments. The image-conscious American League had wanted to avoid associating with men who embodied the corrupt side of Scorpio. Nevertheless, since Ferrell and Devery had the necessary political clout, the American League allowed them to purchase the franchise with money earned through prostitution and bribery.

The New York Yankees were not winners in their earliest years. The team did not win a pennant until 1921. Of the original American League teams, the Yankees were, actually, the penultimate team to win a pennant.[363] The Yankees' early years in New York were characterized by frequent feuds between owners and managers. During games, Ferrell and Devery would sit near the dugout and yell unwelcome advice to manager Clark Griffith, who quit in 1908. In 1914, Frank Chance quit as manager after nearly punching Devery.[364] Their relationship was worsened by Devery's tolerance of first

---

362. Dewey & Acocella, p. 17
363. The St. Louis Browns were the last AL team to win a pennant in 1944.
364. Appel, p. 254

baseman Hal Chase,[365] who was known to throw games for gamblers.

If someone faces the hardships and resolves the struggles brought by a difficult square, that same aspect becomes a source of strength in later life. Through the 1900s and 1910s, the Yankees difficult square was becoming mature. It would eventually become a cornerstone of strength. In the 1920s, the Yankees evolved into the powerful franchise we now recognize. A balance needed to be established between the Scorpio Sun and the Moon and Mars in Leo. An equilibrium would emerge with the arrival of Babe Ruth. On January 5, 1920, while Jupiter in Leo was conjunct the Yankees' Leo Moon, the Yankees purchased the contract of Babe Ruth from the Boston Red Sox. With Ruth, the theatrical and flamboyant qualities of their Leo Moon burst upon the scene. Babe Ruth was the first Yankee to truly shine in the spotlights. Fans flocked to see the Bambino home run champ, and Babe Ruth became one of America's most popular stars of any era. A team with a Leo Moon, especially one located in New York City, the nation's media center, needs flashy characters such as Ruth, Mickey Mantle, and Reggie Jackson. Although most Yankee players go about their game in a business-like manner, this is a team of showmen who thrive on attention. Even George Steinbrenner enjoyed the Leo spotlight by appearing in TV commercials.

Babe Ruth[366] played both right field and left field for the Yankees. Ruth's birthchart shows his synastry with the Yankees. His natal Uranus of 20 degrees Scorpio is conjunct the Yankees' Sun. When his contract was

Babe Ruth
Wednesday, February 6, 1895 11:02:00 AM
Baltimore, Maryland
Time Zone: 05:00 (EST)
Longitude: 076° W 37' 12"
Latitude: 39° N 18' 48"

---

365. See Reds chapter for a discussion of Hal Chase.
366. Rectification Note: I have rectified the birthchart of Babe Ruth for 11:03 am EST in Baltimore. By solar arc progressions, an MC of 28 Capricorn becomes conjunct his Sun at age 19, the year he made his major league debut. He became married on Oct 17, 1914, when Mercury at 18 Scorpio was conjunct his Descendant.

purchased from the Red Sox on Jan. 5, 1920, Jupiter, in transit through Leo, was conjunct to the Yankees' Moon.[367] His aspects to the Yankees' Sun and Moon reflect how Ruth ignited the star element of the Yankees. Babe Ruth's own strength emerged from a t-square between his Sun in Aquarius, Mars in Taurus, and Uranus in Scorpio. The aspect between his Uranus and Aquarius Sun made him a natural home run hitter. The Uranus square also made him a libertine who often ignored rules.

The Yankees' pattern of winning was established in the 1920s. They have won many more World Series than any other baseball team. The Yankees win, not so much by employing high-priced talent, but by playing well under pressure. A team born under the sign of Scorpio, a highly pressurized water sign, will excel under tense conditions. There are several teams in the American League with Scorpio Suns, but the Yankees are distinguished by their Leo Moon, which is nourished by the energy of the public. The Leo Moon is fed by the big crowds and the media attention. The very conditions that might unnerve or freeze other teams bring out the best in the Yankees. Yankees are known to play well in important games, especially in the post-season. Additionally, it does not take a star to get the big hit. Many players in Yankee uniforms are capable of playing the hero, whether Bucky Dent in 1978 or Aaron Boone in 2003 — little-known players who had pennant-winning homeruns.

David Halberstam's book *Summer of '49* describes how many of the Yankees emotionally internalized the square of the Scorpio and Leo planets. They played hard because they were the Yankees. Expectations were enormous, as one strived to live up to the legends of the past. They performed and excelled under severe pressure to keep winning. However, the pressure took its toll, as many of them, including Joe DiMaggio, developed ulcers. DiMaggio nervously drank coffee and smoked cigarettes between innings.[368] Roger Maris lost his hair as he set the single-season home run record in 1961.

The winning ways of the Yankees are also a manifestation of Saturn in their First House. Saturn dwells a few degrees past the Sagittarius Ascendant in its own sign of Capricorn. Saturn in the Yankees' First House contributes to the Yankees' intimidating image as perpetual winners. Saturn is the planet of authority, and the Yankees are often the ones in charge. One expects to see them ahead in the standings or as the defending champions. The Yankees won five consecutive World Series from 1949 to 1953. The

---

367. Also in 1920, the Yankees' Sun progressed by solar arc become conjunct their natal Uranus, which brought the revolution of homeruns to the team.
368. Halberstam, *Summer of '49*, p. 118

Yankees of the 1950s appeared as a Saturnian castle that few teams could pass beyond. Saturn is also the planet that crowns the champions at the end of the season.[369] Those who persevere through baseball's marathon season until the last game of the World Series have the Saturnian qualities of tenacity and endurance needed to win championships.

Saturn in the First House often indicates a conservative appearance. Although the Yankees have a Sagittarius Ascendant, it is a First House Saturn in its own sign of Capricorn that has given the Yankees their distinguished look. The Yankees wear conservative pinstripe uniforms. They dismiss the bright colors worn by most teams. Conservative Saturn imparts on the Yankees their style of tradition which carries an aura of history. Pinstripes conjure memories from baseball's past and the many Yankee greats who wore their uniforms. Saturn is the ruler of time and institutions, and the Yankees appear as if they have existed from time immemorial. The oldest franchise in the major leagues is the Cincinnati Reds, but more baseball fans muse about the Yankees when they consider baseball's past.

The Yankees post-season fortunes are helped by a Tenth House with Libra on its cusp. Every October, as the shadows of the light towers lengthen over the field, one expects to see the Yankees in the playoffs. Come October, the Sun will transit through the Yankees 10th House. Also in October, Venus and Mercury, inner planets never far from the Sun, are in Yankees 10th House or close to it. Baseball's post-season usually begins near October 1 with the Sun around 8 degrees Libra. Around October 10, when the playoffs are in high gear, the Sun enters the Yankees 10th House. While the Sun is in their 10th House of highest achievement, the Yankees step up their game and rise to the challenge of post-season play. They may have an average regular season and barely get to the playoffs, but, when October arrives and planets transit through their 10th House, the Yankees play like champions. An example of how their birthchart has them ready for favorable October transits occurred on October 16, 2003. That evening, Mercury was in transit at 17 degrees Libra and conjunct the Yankees' MC. Aaron Boone responded by hitting an 11th-inning home run that beat the Red Sox for the pennant.

Along the way to becoming persistent winners, the Yankees had their revenge on the Giants, the team that had tried to kill them back in 1902. Since the Yankees of 1950s were consistent winners and had stars such as Whitey Ford and Mickey Mantle on their roster, New Yorkers preferred Yankees tickets to Giants tickets. With fewer fans paying to see them, the Giants left New York for San Francisco in 1958. The opposition between

---

369. See Section Three: Saturn in the Post-Season

the Giants' Saturn of 20 degrees Taurus and the Yankees' Sun of 20 Scorpio mirrors the tension between the teams.

Lou Gehrig's Gemini Sun was conjunct to the Yankees' Neptune, the planet of first base. This aspect is the perfect synastry for a Yankee first baseman. Gehrig's birthchart also has the Sun conjunct to Neptune, which made him a natural first baseman. His remarkable endurance emerged from a grand trine between Mercury in Gemini, Saturn in Aquarius, and Mars in Libra. Mercury is the planet of work and health. Since Mercury is mutable, one's health or attendance is easily upended by the energy of Mars or Saturn. Instead, Gehrig had these planets in a harmonious grand trine. Gehrig would play 2130 consecutive games, a record thought to be unbreakable before it was passed by Cal Ripken, Jr.

Gehrig's Moon in Aries is conjunct to his South Node. *Pride of the Yankees*, the movie about his life, includes an overbearing mother figure from whom Gehrig had to break away. His mother is portrayed as disapproving of his desire to play baseball. Instead, she wants him to become an engineer. Once he is married, his mother meddles in their relationship by choosing the furniture for him and his wife. The pull of a domineering mother is consistent with a conjunction between the South Node and a fire sign Moon.

Lou Gehrig died on June 2, 1941[370] from amyotrophic lateral sclerosis, two years after ending his consecutive games streak. His death also occurred exactly sixteen years from the day he replaced the slumping Wally Pipp at first base, the day that had begun his streak of consecutive games. When the Yankees retired Gehrig's number 4, they were the first team to pay homage this way. The Yankees, with such refined Saturn and Scorpio energy, knew how to honor a fallen hero.

Lou Gehrig
Friday, June 19, 1903 12:00:00 PM
Bronx, New York
Time Zone: 05:00 (EST)
Longitude: 073° W 52' 12"
Latitude: 40° N 50' 36"

---

370. On the day of Gehrig's death, the Sun at 12 degrees Gemini and Venus at 23 Gemini formed a midpoint of 17 Gemini, which is conjunct the Yankees' Pluto.

The Boston Red Sox

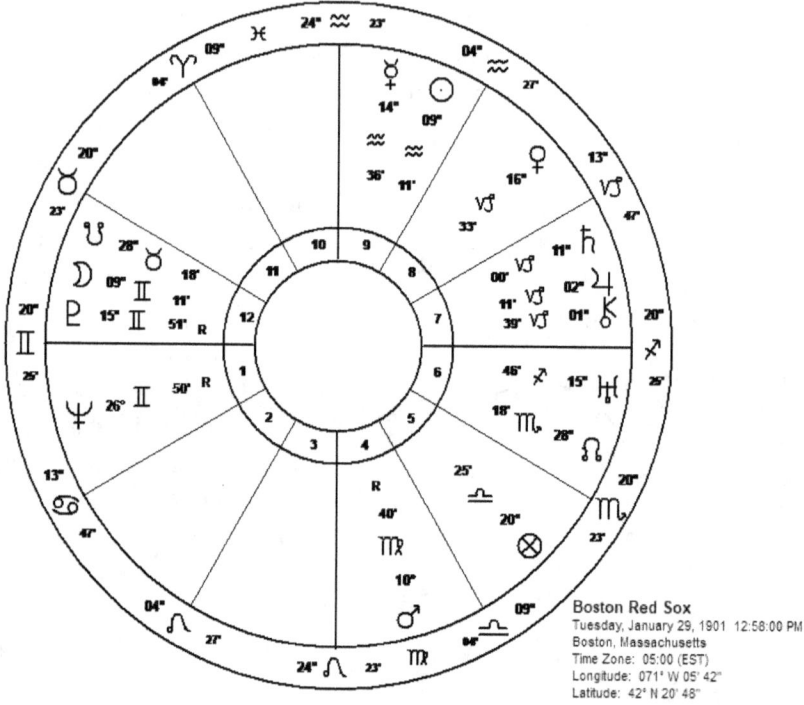

Boston Red Sox
Tuesday, January 29, 1901 12:58:00 PM
Boston, Massachusetts
Time Zone: 05:00 (EST)
Longitude: 071° W 05' 42"
Latitude: 42° N 20' 48"

The Red Sox were the last of the original 16 teams to be born. They were born on January 29, 1901[371] at 12:58 pm[372] EST. Neptune is in their First House, which is the aspect that has brought them so much hope and so much despair. The Red Sox' Moon is in Gemini, the aspect that attracts them to intellectuals. Their Sun and Mercury are conjunct in Aquarius, the sign of the human being. In many ways, the troubles and triumphs of the Red Sox are the troubles and triumphs of humanity.

Before their World Series win of 2004, there was a deep sense of doom associated with the Red Sox. The team's followers believed that the Red Sox were cursed to come inches from ultimate victory, only to fall a

---

371. Petrusza, David: *Major Leagues: The Formation, Sometimes Absorption and Mostly Inevitable Demise of 18 Professional Baseball Organizations, 1871 to Present*, p. 155

372. Rectification Notes: The Sun progressed by solar arc becomes conjunct an MC of 24 Aquarius in 1916, the year the team was purchased by Harry Frazee. An MC of 24 Aquarius progressed by solar arc becomes square to Neptune in 1933, the year the team was purchased by Tom Yawkey. An Ascendant of 20 Gemini progressed by solar arc becomes conjunct Neptune in 1907, the year the team is named the Red Sox. The Moon progressed by solar arc becomes conjunct an Ascendant of 20 Gemini in 1912, the year Fenway Park opens.

sliver short when the last out was recorded. The Red Sox often fielded competitive teams, yet they would suffer mysterious collapses and failures. This notion that the Red Sox were doomed to tragedy was known as "The Myth."[373] Later it became known as "The Curse of the Bambino."[374] The key to understanding the Red Sox' myth is the planet Neptune in the Red Sox First House. Neptune is the planet of hopes and dreams. It brings a belief that one can achieve the greatest of possibilities. However, when placed so prominently in the First House, Neptune brings daydreaming and an inability to concentrate on the task at hand. While dreaming of the Promised Land, concentration gets lost. Errors occur. Hopes and dreams slip through the webbings of gloves. Neptune is the planet of first basemen. A quintessential Red Sox image is that of the ball passing through the legs of first baseman Bill Buckner in the 1986 World Series. The dreams of Neptune are often followed by disillusionment. For the Red Sox and their followers, Neptune has brought much disillusionment, the evaporation of hopes and dreams.

The Red Sox Sun is in Aquarius, the sign of the most flawed creature, the human being. The Red Sox reside in New England, a region settled by the Puritans. Pundits speculated that the failures of the Red Sox were a legacy from New England's Puritan past. The Puritans were a people with a creed of intense cynicism towards the human condition. Humankind, the Puritans preached, is unworthy and destined to sin and failure. Only a chosen few are saved from Hell, and those few are still unworthy. Dan Shaughnessy, author of *Curse of the Bambino* and *Reversing the Curse*, likened the Puritan notion of unworthiness to the psychology of the Red Sox. Their sense of unworthiness does not allow them to win, since success leads to feelings of guilt. Once in first place, the Red Sox would await an inevitable fall.[375] The Puritans also believed in predestination, the idea that every event that has ever happened and will happen has been predetermined by God—that no individual has free will, and no one can do anything to affect one's fate. The Red Sox have perceptions of being fated. Players and fans claim to have felt premonitions before certain events happened. Various people claim to have anticipated Bob Stanley's

---

373. Ivor-Campbell, Frederick: "Boston Red Sox: Their Foot Shall Slide … Baseball's Most Potent Myth," p. 16
374. The sale of Babe Ruth from the Red Sox to the Yankees occurred on Jan 5, 1920. The transits for the sale were favorable for the Yankees (see Yankees chapter) but malefic for the Red Sox. Saturn at 11 degrees Virgo was conjunct the Red Sox Fourth House Mars and square their Moon. The Sun at 14 degrees Capricorn was conjunct the midpoint between their Venus and Saturn.
375. Shaughnessy, p. 17

wild pitch in the 1986 World Series.[376]

The Red Sox have a pantheon of fallen tragic heroes. Player-manager Chick Stahl committed suicide in 1906. Outfielder Tony Conigliaro had a promising career cut short when he was beaned in 1967. Conigliaro, who holds the record for most home runs hit by a teenager—with 24—would die young at age 45. In 1955, the Red Sox young first baseman Harry Agganis died in his second season. The death of a first baseman is noteworthy for a team with a Neptune-Pluto conjunction. The same Neptune-Pluto conjunction in the Yankees' birthchart became manifest in the death of their first baseman, Lou Gehrig. Agganis' birthchart[377] has Saturn in Capricorn, which is actually conjunct to the Red Sox' own Saturn in Capricorn. Agganis' Mars in Pisces, the sign of first basemen, is square to the Red Sox Neptune, while his Jupiter in Gemini is conjunct to the Red Sox Pluto, the planet of death. Agganis died on June 27, 1955 as Pluto at 24 degrees Leo was opposite the Red Sox' Sun, and Saturn at 14 degrees Scorpio was square the Red Sox' Mercury. Agganis died of a pulmonary embolism, a blockage to an artery in his lungs. As Mercury and Gemini rule the lungs, his illness and death were cruelly poetic for a team with the Moon conjunct Pluto in Gemini, which was experiencing a harsh transit to its Mercury.

The Red Sox also have their hall of goats. Shortstop Johnny Pesky is blamed for the loss of the 1946 World Series. His allegedly hesitant throw allowed Enos Slaughter of the Cardinals to score the Series winning run. Manager Charlie McCarthy's decisions on which pitchers would start the last games of 1948 and 1949 were thoroughly criticized.[378] In 1986, Bill Buckner let a ball go through his legs just as the Red Sox were poised to win the World Series. In Game Seven of the 2003 LCS against the Yankees, manager Grady Little did not take Pedro Martinez out of the game, while the Red Sox were ahead 5-2 in the eighth inning. The Yankees soon tied the game and won the pennant in extra innings. After the season, Little was let go. There is a sacrificial-lamb quality to these Red Sox who end up vilified. Neptune allows such individuals, who are deemed unworthy human beings, to absorb the dark energy for the Red Sox Nation.

The team came by the name of "Red Sox" in 1907, when the team currently known as the Braves discarded the same name. Previously, the team had been known as the Americans, the Pilgrims, the Puritans, and the Somersets. They were called the Puritans for American League

---

376. Shaughnessy, p. 168
377. Harry Agganis' date of birth is April 20, 1929
378. Halberstam, David: *Summer of '49*, pp. 6-9; p. 274.

President Ban Johnson's high moral tone. The name Somersets came from owner Charles Somers.[379] The name that finally stuck is the perfect one for a team with a First House Neptune. Names and team colors are functions of the First House. Socks are Neptunian garments, since they are worn on feet, which are ruled by Neptune. The color red is associated with the sign Aries, the planet Mars, and the First House. Hence, Neptune in the First House became manifest as red-colored socks.[380] Feet have proven to be uncommon objects of attention for the Olde Towne Team. In 1932, the Red Sox hired a specialist to attend to the players' feet.[381] Then, in 2004, almost 100 years after they were christened, the name of Red Sox took on new meaning when Kurt Schilling won an elimination game against the Yankees while pitching with a bleeding tendon in his foot.

The Red Sox Moon is conjunct to Pluto in the sign of Gemini. Pluto in conjunction to one's Moon brings deep emotions, hard-to-fill yearnings, and death. As the Moon rules the past, this aspect is embodied in the painful memories experienced by generations of Red Sox fans. There have been horrible losses for the Red Sox fans. There was an early tragedy in Red Sox history that has been overshadowed by more recent events. Early in the Twentieth Century, the Red Sox were managed by Chick Stahl and then by Jake Stahl. For years, the two were thought to have been family, as the *Baseball Encyclopedia* incorrectly identified them as brothers. Gemini, whose symbol is the twins, rules brothers. On March 28, 1907, while Pluto in Gemini was conjunct the Red Sox Ascendant, manager Chick Stahl committed suicide during Spring Training. He did so by drinking carbolic acid. Chick Stahl's final words reportedly were, "Boys, I couldn't help it. It made me do it."[382] But Chick Stahl did not explain what "it" was, and the motive for his suicide remains a mystery. The manager's poisoning by carbolic acid is a cruelly fitting method of death for a Moon-Pluto conjunction. Carbolic acid does damage to one's stomach, ruled by the Moon. It also damages the intestinal tract, ruled by Virgo, a disturbing fit for the Red Sox, who have Mars in Virgo in the Fourth House. Five years later, Jake Stahl would become the manager of the Red Sox. That same year of 1912, the believed-to-be younger brother guided the Sox to 105 wins and a victory in the World Series over the Giants.

Two men, thought to be brothers, hold the reigns as managers of the

---

379. Dewey & Acocella, p. 50
380. The Cubs, another team with a strong Neptune emphasis, were formerly called the "White Stockings."
381. Shaughnessy, p. 45
382. Dewey & Acocella, p. 52

Red Sox. One brother tastes the bitterest fate of suicide, under a mysterious motive. The other brother achieves the greatest victory of leading the Red Sox to a win of the World Series. For many years, the Stahls were believed to have been brothers until a SABR researcher[383] uncovered the facts. Even though the story of siblings was proven to lack basis in fact, it is still vital— perhaps even more so now. The truer more vital basis of the story is within the Gemini sign. The story of the Stahl brothers echoes the myth of Castor and Pollux, the twins of the Gemini constellation. Castor and Pollux were the twin sons of Leto the Swan. Although they were twins, they had different fathers. Pollux's father was the god Zeus, while Castor's father was a mere mortal. Together, the twins embarked on many adventures. They even ran with Jason and the Argonauts to go find the Golden Fleece. However, Castor would die in a cattle raid. His brother Pollux was so distraught over his brother's death that he asked Zeus to let him die in his place. Zeus agreed that Pollux could die, but the condition of his death would be that the twins would remain separate. Castor and Pollux would spend alternate periods between Hades and Mt. Olympus. One brother would stew in Hades, while the other

Jake Stahl
Sunday, April 13, 1879 12:00:00 PM
Chicago, Illinois
Time Zone: 06:00 (CST)
Longitude: 087° W 39' 42"
Latitude: 41° N 51' 54"

Chick Stahl
Friday, January 10, 1873 12:00:00 PM
Fort Wayne, Indiana
Time Zone: 05:00 (EST)
Longitude: 085° W 08' 24"
Latitude: 41° N 04' 18"

383. Thompson, Dick: "In Name Only." In *The National Pastime: A Review of Baseball History* (2000), No. 20, pp. 54-57

partied on Mt. Olympus. Then they would change places. Chick and Jake Stahl had alternate Heaven and Hell conditions while managing the Red Sox. Their story encompasses the emotional fate of the Red Sox fans, who also experience alternate states of Heaven and Hell.

The Red Sox' Moon in Gemini attracts the team to writers. Gemini is the sign of the scribe, and much is written about the Red Sox. The Red Sox have an intimate connection to writers and the press. Early in their history, the team was owned by the publisher of the *Boston Globe*. General Charles Taylor, publisher and editor of the *Globe*, bought the Red Sox to give his wastrel son John I. Taylor something to do.[384] Writers are intrigued by their tragic dramas. Many authors are Red Sox fans, including John Updike, Steven King, and Doris Kearns Goodwin.[385] Intellectuals, who normally thumb their noses at sports, find value in the Red Sox. The Red Sox also reside in Massachusetts, a state with many universities and a large intellectual community. The state has used much of its brain power in attempts to understand the Red Sox.

Literature about the Red Sox contains a level of analysis unmatched in the writings regarding other teams. *The Curse of the Bambino*, by Dan Shaunessy, includes detailed analyses seldom found in sports writing. His extensive second-guessing is representative of the critical Red Sox Virgo fan. Other writers approach the Red Sox as a text of classical literature or a tract of religious theology. John Updike described the three phases of Ted Williams' relationship to Boston as his embodiment of Jason, Achilles and Nestor.[386] A. Bartlett Giamatti wove theories that connected "the Myth" to original sin,[387] And Roger Engel pontificated that the Red Sox give New England authors a theme, once guilt and whaling became out of fashion.[388] Such cerebral discourse is rare to contemporary sports writing, but the Red Sox' Gemini Moon attracts an intellectual fan base that savors this kind of palaver.

A Gemini Moon can influence one to indulge in unwise verbal assaults. An incident of trash talk helped seal the Red Sox' fate in 1949. As the regular season was ending, the Red Sox and Yankees were locked in a tight pennant race. To reach the World Series, the Red Sox needed to win only one of two games in a final series against the Yankees. The first game of the series occurred on October 1 in New York. The Red Sox quickly had a 4-0 lead.

---

384. Dewey & Acocella, p. 51
385. Shaughnessy, p. 21
386. Updike, John: "Hub Fans Bid Kid Adieu," p. 2
387. Shaughnessy, p. 17
388. Shaughnessy, p. 21

Their lead seemed insurmountable, and the Red Sox became overconfident. Birdie Tebbetts, catcher for the Red Sox, would play the role of the indiscrete Gemini Moon. The name "Birdy" is Geminian, as small birds correspond with the air sign Gemini. In the bottom of the third inning, with Phil Rizzuto at bat, Birdy Tebbetts said to him, "Hey Rizzuto, tomorrow at this time we'll be drinking champagne, and we'll pitch the Yale kid against you guys. Think you can hit a kid from Yale, Rizzuto?" The Kid from Yale was rookie Frank Quinn, a bonus baby from Yale University who had not yet started a game. The usually mild-mannered Rizzuto was angered. After grounding out, he threw his bat and kicked the water cooler. He shared the insult with the rest of the Yankees. The entire Yankee team felt as if slapped in the face. New York had been demoralized by falling behind early in the game, but, when Tebbetts insulted them, the Yankees galvanized their energy.[389] The Yankees would win the game 5-4 and then beat the Red Sox for the pennant the following day.

The insult from Tebbetts is interesting for its reference to Yale, an Ivy League institution. Today, many baseball players attend college, but, in 1949, baseball players largely identified with the working class. A college-educated[390] player's abilities may or may not have been suspect, but an Ivy League player would have been resented for being of the upper class, much as was Eddie Collins, who attended Columbia, resented by his White Sox teammates.[391] Hence the insult was not only that Rizzuto wouldn't be able to hit the Kid from Yale, but that the Red Sox would further humiliate the Yankees by making them face an entitled Ivy Leaguer from the One Percent. This incident is also telling of the Scorpionic Yankees, who were quick to respond to such an insult. The angry Yankees regenerated and exacted their revenge.

The Red Sox are a high-strung team. The square from Mars in Virgo to the Moon and Pluto in Gemini has given them a nervous temperament. Mars in Virgo can manifest as critical and angry. The Red Sox' Mars is positioned in the Fourth House of home and mother. Mars is also in square to the Moon, the planet of home and mother. Such aspects involving the Moon and the Fourth House are generally manifest in an overly critical parent. For the Red Sox, this critical parental figure is embodied in the fans and the press. Ted Williams was one of the greatest of baseball players, yet

---

389. Halberstam, David: *Summer of '49*, pp. 257-258
390. Birdie Tebbetts, born Nov. 10, 1912, earned a degree in philosophy from Providence College. Like the Red Sox, his birthchart has the Moon conjunct to Mercury, but in the sign of Sagittarius.
391. See White Sox chapter.

he was never fully accepted or appreciated by the Red Sox fans.³⁹² The Boston press continuously criticized him. Williams' difficult relationship with the Boston fans mirrors the conjunction of the Red Sox' critical Mars to Williams' natal Sun and Mercury in Virgo. Ted Williams had an arrogant personality that served to shield himself against the press and the fans. However, other Boston players are prone to internalize the criticism. They suffer like a child who is constantly told he or she is not living up to expectations. When these players believe what is written about them, they cannot relax. In turn, they place too much pressure on themselves. The team plays stressed, attempting to do too much, especially trying to live up the expectations of the critical parent.

Ted Williams
Friday, August 30, 1918 12:00:00 PM
San Diego, California
Time Zone: 07:00 (PDT)
Longitude: 117° W 07' 48"
Latitude: 32° N 44' 54"

The square between Mars and the Moon exists in the pitcher's signs of Gemini and Virgo. Pitchers can be volatile on this team. There is a legacy of Boston pitchers becoming highly emotional while on the mound. In a game in 1917, Babe Ruth walked the first batter. He argued against the umpire's call and was subsequently ejected. Ruth's response was to punch the umpire.³⁹³ In 1919, Carl Mays stomped off the mound, accusing his team of trying to sabotage him with poor defense.³⁹⁴ Roger Clemens was ejected in Game 4 of the 1990 LCS versus Oakland and had to be restrained from assaulting the umpire.³⁹⁵ Red Sox players at other positions have also displayed emotional distress. Jimmy Piersall suffered a nervous breakdown in September of 1952. The movie *Fear Strikes Out*

---

392. Updike, John: "Hub Fans Bid Kid Adieu," p. 4
393. This game is analyzed in Section III of this book. The game is famous for the no-hitter by Ernie Shore that followed.
394. A brouhaha followed when Mays was subsequently traded to the Yankees, while American League President Ban Johnson intended to have him suspended.
395. Shaughnessy, pp. 216-217

depicts Piersall climbing up the backstop in the middle of a game. The film also paints the classic narrative of a father placing excessive pressure on his son to succeed. In 1958, Jackie Jenson, a power-hitting right fielder with the Red Sox, won the MVP award. However, after the 1959 season, Jenson retired because of a fear of flying.[396]

The Red Sox' Sun in Aquarius is embodied in outstanding left fielders, home run hitters, and the conspicuous left field wall at Fenway Park known as "the Green Monster." Although the wall is high, it is a relatively short distance from homeplate. The Green Monster is eccentrically Aquarian with its unusual dimensions and quirky bounces. Balls take odd bounces in left field of Fenway Park. Many balls hit off the wall result in singles, as a skilled left fielder can catch the ball as it bounces off the wall, then throw it to second base to limit the runner to a single. Ted Williams and Carl Yastrzemski are Red Sox left fielders in the Hall of Fame. Less well known is George Whiteman, the left fielder who made a homerun saving catch that won a game in the 1918 World Series.[397] It is also little remembered that Babe Ruth played left field for the Red Sox. Babe Ruth began his career as a pitcher for the Boston Red Sox. Once his hitting ability was recognized, he would play left field on the days he was not scheduled to pitch. Manny Ramirez played left field when the Red Sox won the World Series in 2004, a year he also won the World Series MVP.

A team is usually built to fit its home ballpark, and the Aquarian Red Sox, with their short left-field wall, emphasize right-handed home run hitters. Since the 1930s, when Tom Yawkey purchased the team, the Red Sox have styled their team to hit homeruns. The pattern was established when Yawkey purchased slugger

Karl Yastremski
Tuesday, August 22, 1939 12:00:00 PM
Southhampton, New York
Time Zone: 05:00 (EST)
Longitude: 072° W 24'
Latitude: 40° N 53'

---

396. Dewey & Acocella, p. 61
397. Ivor-Campbell, p. 23

Jimmy Foxx from the Philadelphia Athletics in 1936.[398] Shaunessey states that it was the purchase of Foxx that led the Red Sox to become a team of me-first individuals who neglected the well-being of the team. A team that stresses the home run will be prone to Aquarian individualism. As George Will noted, the home run fits the do-it-yourself character of the American.[399] However, such individualism can undermine team cohesion. Until the decade of the 2000s, Red Sox players tended to lack rapport with each other. Shaughnessy remarked that the Red Sox always needed 24 cabs for 24 players.[400]

There is a duality inherent in the sign of Aquarius in which the interest of the individual competes with that of the group. Aquarius is the sign of humanity, and humanity is defined through the individual, the strivings of one person to be free and to pursue one's self-identity. Nevertheless, humanity is also defined in a collective, the ability of people to identify with each other, to concern themselves with the good of the community. This dualism within the sign of Aquarius, when specific to a sports team, sets up the conflict of the player versus the team. Does a player concern himself more with his own salary and statistics or the good of his team? Does a player selflessly sacrifice a runner along or does he attempt to pad his own statistics?

Red Sox players have often sided with their individual interests rather than with the good of the team. In 1989, pitcher Dennis "Oil Can" Boyd lashed out, after having his start pushed back a day to accommodate Roger Clemens. Boyd was quoted as saying, "I'm not playing second fiddle to nobody. I ain't no fourth or fifth starter. I'm a bona fide major league pitcher. I'm not concerned about the ball club right now, I'm just worried about myself, and right now, I'm not happy at all." Shaughnessy commented, "Boyd's Me Manifesto exposed an attitude that has plagued the Red Sox for seventy years."[401] Later that season, another incident exposed the Red Sox' lack of team consciousness. In a June 29 game against the Rangers, pitcher Mike Smithson noticed that Ranger hitters were digging in against him. As pitchers often do in such situations, Smithson hit a batter. He hit Rafael Palmiero, who responded by charging the mound. Immediately the Texas bench emptied onto the field. Smithson looked around and noticed no one on his team coming to his defense.[402] In 1997, designated hitter Reggie

---

398. Shaughnessy, pp. 51-52
399. See positions chapter.
400. Shaughnessy, p. 195. Teams had 24-man rosters from 1986 to 1989.
401. Shaughnessy, p. 192-3
402. Shaughnessy, p. 197

Jefferson was batting well over .300, but did not have enough at bats to be listed in contention for the batting title. Manager Jimmy Williams would let Jefferson hit only when he could help the team. Jefferson commented, "I feel like I have a goal to do something, and they don't have the same goal for me, so they should trade me out of here."[403] A decade later, Manny Ramirez played the role of the self-centered player who took himself out of games for suspect injuries. In 2008, management traded Ramirez to the Dodgers. After he shoved the travel secretary, they decided that Ramirez was too destructive a presence in the clubhouse.

The Red Sox have shown themselves to be conservative on social matters, which is antithetical to the image of a radical Aquarius. The Aquarian Red Sox were the last baseball team to integrate. They passed on opportunities to sign both Jackie Robinson and Willie Mays.[404] Early in the Twentieth Century, they experienced another kind of intolerance, a split between Protestants and Catholics. In 1913, center fielder Tris Speaker and pitcher Joe Wood were pitted against second baseman Heinie Wagner and catcher Bill Carrigan. Newspapers' writers referred to the feud as a battle between the Masons and the Knights of Columbus.[405] In the previous year, the Sox had won 105 games and beaten the Giants in the World Series, but, in 1913, the Red Sox finished a distant fourth place, brought down by injuries, the firing of manager Jake Stahl, and their religious war. An Aquarius often goes out of one's way to embrace people of demographics different from one's own. The Red Sox, however, have a history of racial and religious intolerance.

The Red Sox birthchart has Saturn conjunct Venus. The lack of

Manny Ramirez
Tuesday, May 30, 1972 12:00:00 PM
Santo Domingo, Domenican Republic
Time Zone: 03:00 (BZT2)
Longitude: 069° W 57'
Latitude: 18° N 29'

---

403. *USA Today Baseball Weekly*, Aug 13-19, 1997
404. NPR.org, "The Boston Red Sox and Racism," Sept. 5, 2013. *http://www.npr.org/programs/morning/features/2002/oct/redsox/*
405. Dewey & Acocella, p. 53

fulfillment on the part of this team is one of the manifestations of Saturn bringing limitations onto Venus. While Saturn has hardened the expression of Venus, Venus has, in turn, softened the expression of Saturn. Tom Yawkey, who owned the team from 1933 until his death in 1976, paid his players generously, to the point of spoiling them.[406] Under Yawkey's reign, the Red Sox were described as overpaid underachievers. Dick Williams managed the Red Sox from 1967 through 1969. Williams was a tough manager who demanded a lot from his players, but he also received a lot from his players, including the 1967 pennant. Williams would berate his charges when they did not perform to his expectations. When he criticized Carl Yastrzemski, the owner came to his player's defense and sided against Williams, eventually firing him.[407] "Yawkey's millions produced a country-club atmosphere that catered to big-swing, one-dimensional ball players," Shaughnessy wrote.[408] The Red Sox' Saturn was made too soft by its conjunction with Venus. The result of an indulgent Saturn is an undisciplined team. A similar environment was created in the years that followed the Red Sox win of the 2004 World Series. The team no longer had the goal of ending the Curse. With a bloated payroll among the highest in the league, the Red Sox again were accused of being overpaid underachievers.[409]

There are sad and frustrating games in the memories of the Red Sox fans. Two of their most frustrating games have occurred under quincunx aspects from Mercury. Game Seven of the 1946 World Series occurred on October 15, 1946. That day, shortstop Johnny Pesky was blamed for making a hesitant throw that allowed the Cardinals' Enos Slaughter to score the winning run of the World Series. Transits for that afternoon show Mercury at 11 degrees Scorpio, forming a quincunx angle to the Red Sox Mars, the planet of the shortstop. A quincunx from Mercury also occurred on October 25, 1986, the night of "the Bill Buckner game." That night, Mercury at 26 degrees Scorpio formed a quincunx to the Red Sox Neptune, the planet of first base. Bill Buckner, of course, was playing first base when the ball went through his legs, just as the Red Sox were poised to win their first World Series in generations. The high-strung Red Sox respond adversely to difficult angles from Mercury. The "Bucky Dent Game," in which a weak-hitting Yankee hit a three-run homer to beat the Red Sox for the Eastern Division, occurred on October 2, 1978. Saturn was

---

406. Halberstam, p. 140
407. Dewey and Acocella, p. 62
408. Shaughnessy, p. 93
409. Macmullan, Jackie: "Unlikeable Red Sox flunked Chemistry," ESPNBoston.com Sept. 30, 2011

in transit at 8 degrees Saturn and square to the Red Sox Moon, in a perfect position to frustrate the Red Sox fans.

On the night the Red Sox won the 2004 World Series, Sox fans found significance in the lunar eclipse that painted the Moon their team color. Oddly, the eclipse of Oct 27, 2004, at 5 degrees Taurus, did not make a major aspect to the birthchart of the Red Sox, only a semi-square to their Ascendant. Far more significant was an aspect that occurred on the New Moon solar eclipse 14 days earlier. The solar eclipse of October 13, 2004, at 10:48 pm EDT, occurred at 20 degrees Libra, exactly conjunct the Red Sox Part of Fortune.[410] A New Moon plants its seeds in the degree of the zodiac where it lands. When a solar eclipse occurs on a New Moon, not only are new seeds planted but buried energy is also unearthed. The solar eclipse of October 13 exhumed the Red Sox good fortune that had been buried for so long. In the lunar cycle that followed, the Red Sox finally had the ball bounce their way. Two weeks later, the lunar cycle culminated in a World Series victory on the night of the Full Moon lunar eclipse. The night of the victory, Mars, in transit at 20 degrees Libra, would also be conjunct the Red Sox Part of Fortune.

2004 Solar Eclipse
Wednesday, October 13, 2004 10:48:00 PM
Boston, Massachusetts
Time Zone: 04:00 (EDT)
Longitude: 071° W 05' 42"
Latitude: 42° N 20' 48"

The other planets that came through for the Red Sox that October were Neptune—which was conjunct the midpoint of the Red Sox Sun and Mercury from 12 degrees Aquarius—and Saturn, in transit at 27 degrees Cancer and semi-sextile the Red Sox notorious First House Neptune.

The planet Neptune, which had led the Red Sox fans through so much heartbreak and disillusionment, had finally delivered.

---

410. The Part of Fortune is a degree within a birthchart upon which good luck manifests.

THE EXPANSION ERA

Fourteen Major League baseball teams were born between 1960 and 1995. In 1960, the National League gave birth to the Mets and the Astros. That same year, the American League delivered the Angels and the "New Senators." The "New Senators" would move to Arlington, Texas, in 1972 and become the Texas Rangers. In 1967 and 1968, four more teams were born: the Seattle Pilots, Kansas City Royals, San Diego Padres, and Montreal Expos. The Pilots played only one year in Seattle before they moved to Milwaukee. They remain in Milwaukee to this date, where they are called the Milwaukee Brewers. The Expos would move to Washington, DC in 2005 and become the Nationals. In 1974, the American League added the Seattle Mariners and Toronto Blue Jays. In 1991, the National League expanded to include the Florida Marlins and the Colorado Rockies. The Arizona Diamondbacks and Tampa Bay Devil Rays were born in 1995.

The teams from the expansion era lack the long history of the original sixteen teams. They also have less lore to draw upon. Many of these teams are still in the process of defining their identity. Consequently, the following chapters on the expansion era teams lack the depth of the chapters on the original 16 teams. In a few generations, however, these teams will have much more to contribute to this study.

The New York Mets

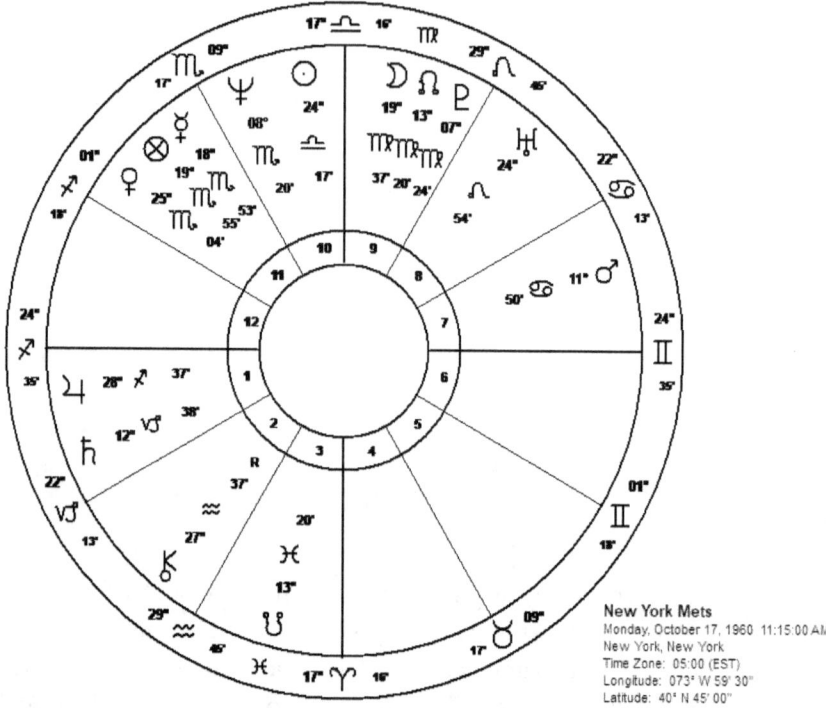

New York Mets
Monday, October 17, 1960 11:15:00 AM
New York, New York
Time Zone: 05:00 (EST)
Longitude: 073° W 59' 30"
Latitude: 40° N 45' 00"

The Mets franchise was born at 11:15 am EST[411] on October 17, 1960[412], a day with the Sun in the sign of Libra and Venus in square to Uranus. The circumstances surrounding the team's birth reflect the day's Libra and Venus emphasis, particularly the effort made for peace in the baseball world.

In 1960, there was pressure upon the Major Leagues to expand. Major League baseball had not added a new team since 1901, when Boston was added to the American League. Since then, the population and economy of the United States had greatly increased. By 1960, cities that had grown in size and political influence were close to demanding big league teams. The community of New York had recently lost its two National League teams when the Dodgers and Giants both moved to California in 1958.

---

411. The Mets were born simultaneously with the Astros. I have rectified the birth times of both teams to 11:15 am EST using events from the history of the Astros. (See footnote in the Astros Chapter.)

412. Cava, Pete: "New York Mets From Throneberry to Strawberry: Baseball's Most Successful Expansion Franchise," p. 343.

The mood in Congress was against the baseball establishment. Legislation had been proposed to rescind the anti-trust exemption enjoyed by Major League baseball. In addition, a rival baseball league, the Continental League, had formed and was poised to invade the market.

The Mets were born in a Libran peace gesture between the Major League establishment and the Continental League. The Major Leagues agreed to place four new franchises in cities that were members of the Continental League.[413] If the Major Leagues had not done so, the new league would have likely pulled star players from the existing teams by offering higher salaries, much as the American League had raided the National League at the turn of the Twentieth Century. A war between two rival leagues was prevented by the compromise. The agreement also mollified Congress, which soon forgot about the anti-trust legislation.

The choosing of the Mets colors, blue and orange, also reflects the Libran peace-making nature of the Mets. The colors blue and orange were taken from the two baseball teams that left the New York area after the 1957 season, the Dodgers and the Giants. The fans of the New York Giants and the Brooklyn Dodgers had been rabidly partisan. Neither of these teams' fans would have rooted for the colors of the rival team. Had the Mets chosen a color too close to Dodger blue or Giant orange, they would have alienated fans of the opposite stripe. The choice of a blue and orange combination was a brilliant Libran solution. By balancing blue and orange, the Mets brought together fans who had previously cheered both the Dodgers and the Giants.

Libra is a refined and feminine sign. The Sun within a team's birthchart is often represented in the owner, and the Mets' first owner was, appropriately, a woman, Joan Payson.[414] Pete Cava describes her as follows: "A true New York blueblood, she was the epitome of the gracious, well-bred sports magnates of a distant era. Many of today's owners should have taken lessons from this charming woman, who was as much at home in New York social circles as she was behind the home dugout, rooting for her team like any other rabid fan."[415] Mrs. Payson politely stayed in the background, allowing those she hired to run the team to do their jobs. Joan Payson's North Node and Mars in Libra are conjunct the Mets' MC. After her death in 1975, Joan Payson's daughter, Lorinda de Roulet, took over control of the Mets. De Roulet was assisted by her daughters, Whitney and

---

413. Cava, p. 343.
414 Joan Payson was born on Feb. 5, 1903.
415. Cava, p. 344.

Bebe.[416] Within the Mets organization, a baseball matriarchy was in the making. However, the blood line would be broken when the family sold the team to Fred Wilpon and Nelson Doubleday [417] in 1980.

The aspect of Neptune semi-square to the Ascendant shaped much of the early image of the Mets. In their early years, this aspect displayed itself in futility and error-prone play. The 1962 Mets lost 140 games, the modern record for most games lost in a season. The poster boy of the 1962 Mets was first baseman Marv Throneberry, who was famous for his poor base running and the many errors he committed at his position. Throneberry's birthchart has the Sun and Neptune conjunct in the sign of Virgo. Although the Sun conjunct to Neptune suggests a natural first baseman, Neptune is in its fall when in the sign of Virgo.[418] This placement made Throneberry a poor fielder. Despite their many lost games, the Mets and Marv Throneberry proved very popular with New York fans. Certain teams are loved precisely because they lose. The appeal of the early Mets emerged from a Neptunian pathos similar to the pathos that had endeared the Cubs for many years. The Mets' Neptune also brought the unlaudable qualities of inattentiveness and laziness. Casey Stengal, the Mets first manager, would fall asleep on the bench and sometimes not recognize his own players.[419] In the 1980s, both Darryl Strawberry and Kevin McReynolds were accused of lax play. [420]

Mars is opposite to Saturn in the birthchart of the Mets. This aspect often brings father-versus-son conflicts, in which the archetype of the father, Saturn, is pitted against that of the son, Mars. Age and wisdom are opposed by youth and idealism. In a sports team, this conflict typically manifests as a clash between players and their manager. Interestingly, the Mets most famous team came of age in the 1960s. The "Miracle Mets" who won the 1969 World Series were very much a manifestation of the 60s. They were part of the era in which sons protesting the war in Vietnam were divided from their fathers who had fought in World War Two. This "generation gap" of the 1960s was echoed in the opposition between Mars and Saturn in the Mets' birthchart. After the victory of the 1969 World Series, a telling incident occurred. At a Mets' victory banquet, Florida Governor Claude Kirk began speaking in support of the Vietnam War. As

---

416. Dewey & Acocella, p. 394.
417. Cava, pp. 371-2.
418. A planet is said to be "in its fall" when placed in the sign that is opposite to its natural sign.
419. Dewey & Acocella, p. 389.
420. Dewey & Acocella, p. 398.

the governor spoke, Tom Seaver and Tug McGraw led a group of players who walked out of the room in protest of the war and the governor's speech.[421] This protest was another manifestation of the Mets' Sun in Libra, the sign of peace movements. It also shows how the Mets were a child of the 60s.

Tom Seaver's politics were criticized by old school columnist Dick Young of the *New York Daily News*. Dick Young, a Saturnian and venerable sports writer, disliked Seaver's anti-war stance, his union activism, and his salary demands. Dick Young, who had personal ties to Mets executives, would even play a role in the events that led to the trade of Tom Seaver, when he criticized Seaver's wife in his column. On June 15, 1977, Young wrote that it was Nancy Seaver who was to blame for her husband's high salary demands, since she was jealous that Nolan Ryan was paid more money than her husband.[422] Afterwards, Tom Seaver demanded a trade. As the sign of Libra rules spouses, a wife would easily be pulled into the troubles of a Libra team.

The Miracle Mets would overtake the Cubs for the Eastern Division and beat the heavily favored Orioles in the World Series. They were assisted by a solar eclipse and by the planet Jupiter. A New Moon solar eclipse occurred on September 11, 1969 at 19 degrees Virgo, conjunct within a degree to the Mets' natal Moon. During the World Series, which culminated with their victory on October 16, 1969, Jupiter, the Great Benefic, was in transit at 17 degrees Libra, conjunct to the Mets' MC.

Gil Hodges, the Mets' manager, platooned aggressively in 1969. Hodges made thorough use of his bench in order to get favorable results from his hitters against opposing

Gil Hodges pulls Cleon Jones
Wednesday, July 30, 1969 3:00:00 PM
Flushing, New York
Time Zone: 04:00 (EDT)
Longitude: 073° W 50'
Latitude: 40° N 45' 12"

---

421. Dewey & Acocella, p. 392
422. Dewey & Acocella, pp. 392, 394

pitchers. Only two Mets players had more than 400 at-bats in 1969. A manager's strategy is a manifestation of Saturn. As the 1969 season turned to late summer and fall, the Mets were helped by Saturn stationary and retrograde between 8 and 6 degrees Taurus, sextile their natal Pluto and opposite their Neptune.[423] Indeed, Saturn was conspicuous in what pundits call the pivotal game of the 1969 season. On July 30, the Mets were having a bad day. Having already lost the first game of a double header 16-3, they were behind 7-0 in the second game. Left fielder Cleon Jones appeared to give a lax effort in retrieving a double hit to the warning track. Gil Hodges called time, took a slow walk to the outfield, and removed Cleon Jones from the game.[424] The Mets were not likely to mount a comeback, but the players were shocked into realizing that each of them had better play his best, no matter what the score. That day, the Sun at 7 degrees Leo was square to Saturn at 8 degrees Taurus. Together, these planets formed a tight opposition and square to the Mets' Neptune, challenging the team to overcome their tendency towards laziness. The Mets did indeed overcome this tendency and find the higher miraculous expression of Neptune.

---

423. With Saturn in opposition to the Mets' Neptune, Gil Hodges platooned his first basemen in 1969, alternating Ed Kranpool and Donn Clendenon.

424. Dewey & Acocella, pp. 391-2; *www.centerfieldmaz.com/2009/07/today-in-mets-history-1969-gil-hodges.html*

THE HOUSTON ASTROS

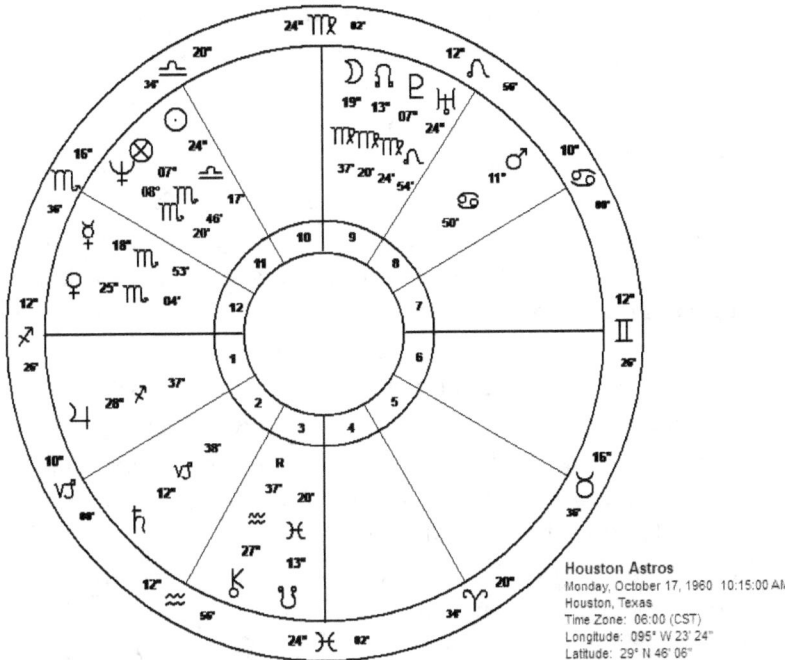

Houston Astros
Monday, October 17, 1960 10:15:00 AM
Houston, Texas
Time Zone: 06:00 (CST)
Longitude: 095° W 23' 24"
Latitude: 29° N 46' 06"

The Astros were born on October 17, 1960[425] at 10:15 am CST[426] simultaneously with the Mets. The historical circumstances surrounding the birth of the Astros are similar to those of the Mets. The city of Houston, like New York, was a member of the Continental League. Houston, like New York, was given a National League franchise as a Libran compromise with the Major Leagues. The Astros have the Sun in Libra and the Moon in Virgo, which has given them a tradition of outstanding second basemen and strong pitching. The Astros also have Mars in opposition to Saturn, an aspect that has given them a legacy of unusual extra-inning games.

The Astros' Ascendant is the sign of Sagittarius. In addition, their First House has Jupiter in its own sign of Sagittarius, further strengthening the team's Sagittarius persona. A team's Rising Sign is embodied in its name and its mascot. Until 1965, the Houston team was called the "Colt .45s," a

---

425. *New York Times: Encyclopedia of Sports*, Vol 2, p. 127.
426. Rectification Note: The Astros' Moon progressed by solar arc becomes conjunct an MC of 24 Virgo in 1965, the year the Astros moved into the Astrodome. In 1976, the year the team was sold to creditors of GE and Ford, the Astros' progressed Pluto also becomes conjunct an MC of 24 degrees Virgo. Pluto can bring bankruptcy.

name that drew on the region's Old West cowboy heritage. The name was also an embodiment of the Sagittarius Rising Sign. Astrologer Liz Greene associates the Sagittarius Ascendant of the United States birthchart with the American persona of the cowboy.[427] Greene connects the cowboy archetype with the outgoing vigorous impulses of Sagittarius. The cowboy rides a horse, the Sagittarian animal. The cowboy also lives on the frontier, ever exploring the wide outdoors to fulfill the Sagittarian aspirations of travel and exploration. The cowboy follows his Sagittarian instinct by venturing west. In 1975, ten years after shedding the Colt 45s mascot, the Houston team began wearing uniforms with the horizontal orange stripes of a sunset. A cowboy rides off toward the setting Sun, the Sun that sets on the western horizon.

In 1965, the team was renamed "the Astros," a name that is also an embodiment of the Sagittarius Ascendant. It was an easy leap for Houston to change its persona from that of the cowboy to that of an astronaut of the Space Age. Astronauts are also followers of the Sagittarian urge to venture and explore the frontier. The television show *Star Trek* was famously introduced with the line "Space, the final frontier." In 2013, the Astros moved to the American League, becoming one of the few teams to have played in both leagues. Although fans complained about leaving the National League, something in the Sagittarius nature of the team sought new territory to explore.

With a Sun in Libra, an anchor at second base is important. The Astros have maintained franchise players at the second base position. Joe Morgan is remembered for his years as the second baseman of the Big Red Machine, but, prior to his trade

Joe Morgan
Sunday, September 19, 1943 12:00:00 PM
Bonham, Texas
Time Zone: 06:00 (CST)
Longitude: 096° W 11'
Latitude: 33° N 02'

---

427. Greene, Liz: *The Outer Planets and their Cycles*, p. 113.

to Cincinnati, Morgan played seven years for the Astros. Joe Morgan's Sun of 25 degrees Virgo is conjunct to the Astros MC of 24 degrees Virgo. His Mars of 13 Gemini is also conjunct the Astros' Descendant, which corresponds to the second base position. The Astros lost a key part of their team when they traded him. Morgan did, however, return to the Astros late in his career and helped them win the Western Division in 1980. Upon rejoining the Astros, Morgan took his rightful role as the team's inspirational leader.[428]

Craig Biggio proved to be another franchise player at second base. In 1996, Biggio signed a four-year contract for less money than he could have received from Colorado or St. Louis.[429] Biggio displayed a loyalty to his city and his team that was rare for a player in the 1990s. The birthchart of Craig Biggio shows his synastry with the Astros organization. A noon birthchart for Biggio shows his Virgo Moon conjunct to the Astros North Node and Virgo Moon. Biggio's Uranus and Pluto, conjunct to each other at 18 and 19 degrees Virgo, are also conjunct the Astros Moon of 19 degrees Virgo.

Jose Altuve, who joined the team in 2011, would join the line of great Astro second basemen. Altuve won batting titles in 2014, 2016 and 2017. He would also win the MVP award in 2017, the year the Astros won their first World Series.

When the Astrodome opened in 1965, it was the first indoor stadium in the Major Leagues. Although the New York Cubans of the Negro Leagues had played in an indoor stadium in 1939,[430] it was the Astrodome that would lead other cities to build indoor stadiums for baseball and football. The IC corresponds to a team's home ballpark. The birthchart of

---

428. Carroll, p. 251.
429. *The Sporting News 1996 Baseball Yearbook*, p. 117.
430. Dewey & Acocella, p. 256.

the Astros has the planets Uranus and the Sun both inconjunct to the IC. The aspect of Uranus to the team's IC would bring a Uranian Space Age atmosphere to the Astrodome.

The installation of Astroturf was a manifestation of the square of Uranus to Venus within the Astros birthchart. Astroturf was originally called "ChemGrass," but it became renamed "Astroturf" upon its use in the Astrodome.[431] The new artificial grass was brought into the Astrodome when the natural grass within the domed stadium died. Soon into the 1965 season, fielders began having difficulty catching fly balls against the glare of the plexiglass roof. To assist the fielders, the ceiling glass had been painted. The weakened sunlight, however, caused the grass to die. The Astroturf carpet was installed during the course of the 1965 season.[432] Venus rules vegetation such as grass. Uranus gives birth to things manufactured and modern. The hard square from Uranus to Venus brought manufactured, modern grass to Houston. Soon many baseball teams followed the Astros by installing artificial grass in their own stadiums.

The Astros' Moon is in the pitcher's sign of Virgo. As the Moon rules the home ballpark, the Moon in Virgo made the Astrodome a pitcher's park. Batted balls did not carry well in the Astrodome. General Manager Tal Smith recognized this. Smith downplayed the power offense. He also traded and drafted to build a team strong in pitching and defense. Much of the success of the Astros teams of the late 1970s was due to this plan of Tal Smith.[433] The Astros left the Astrodome for Minute Maid Park in 2000. The new park was configured while Uranus was in Aquarius, an era that emphasized the home run. With a left field foul line of only 315 feet, Minute Maid Park is less favorable to pitchers than the old Astrodome.

The Astros' Mars in Cancer is tightly opposed by Saturn in Capricorn. Such a hard opposition causes efforts to collide against the boundaries and limitations of Saturn.[434] Whereas the Mets' Mars-Saturn opposition has manifest in conflicts between youth and authority, the Astros' Mars-Saturn opposition has been embodied in frustrations against the boundary of time. In baseball, time is structured into the procession of innings within a game. Time is also structured into the schedule of the season, which concludes with the post-season and championship games. The influence of Saturn is greatest in late innings and post-season games.[435] The Astros'

---

431. http://en.wikipedia.org/wiki/AstroTurf
432. Carroll, p. 244.
433. Carroll, p. 249.
434. See Chapter Six for the discussion on the boundaries and limitations of Saturn.
435. During the course of the regular season, a valuable indicator that a team will ad-

Mars-Saturn opposition has manifest in an unusual number of extra-inning games in the post-season. Long before their 2005 pennant run, the Astros played a number of extra-inning games in the post-season, losing almost all of them. Saturn would thwart them this way.

After the Astros won the Western Division in 1980, the League Championship Series matched them against the Phillies. Four of the five games in the Series lasted into extra inning, the Astros only winning one of them.[436] The Astros next played a League Championship Series in 1986, when they played their twin franchise, the Mets. Annoyingly, they would lose Game Five in 12 innings. Then on October 15, the season ended for the Astros when they lost Game Six in the 16th inning. Until their 2005 game against the Braves, this loss would stand as the longest post-season game on record. During the 1986 LCS, Saturn, in transit at 6 degrees Sagittarius, formed a square to both the Astros and Mets' Pluto. The day the pennant was lost, the Sun, in transit at 22 degrees Libra, formed a semi-square to Saturn in Sagittarius, a transit that proved malefic to the Astros but beneficial for the Mets.

In 1995, the Astros were battling the Rockies for the National League wild card. On September 26, they were just one game behind Colorado for the playoff slot. The Rockies would slump at the finish, losing six of their final ten games. The Astros efforts, however, would be stymied by Saturn, in transit at 20 degrees Pisces and opposed to their Moon. On Sept. 27, 28 and 29, they lost three consecutive extra-inning games to the Pirates and Cubs, which sunk them from the wild card.

The Astros won their first pennant in 2005. During their post-season run, they won a classic game against the Braves that lasted 18 innings. This October 9 game would set a record for longest post-season game.[437] Saturn had previously frustrated the Astros in such elongated games. In Game Four of the Division Series, however, Saturn proved benefic. That day, Saturn was in transit at 9 degrees Leo, square to the Astros' Neptune and in a semi-square to the Astros' MC. The game involved a relief appearance and win by Roger Clemens, a grand slam by Lance Berkman, and a walk-

---

vance to the post-season is its ability to win extra-inning games and to come from behind. A team that wins these kinds of games is operating under favorable influences of Saturn.

436. During the 1980 LCS, Saturn, in transit at 2 degrees Libra, did not make a significant aspect to a planet or axis within the Astros' birthchart. But Saturn did form significant aspects with the Phillies' Neptune, Ascendant and Descendant. In the 1980 regular season, Saturn, in transit through late Virgo, did form major aspects to the Astros birthchart. J. R. Richard experienced his stroke on the morning of July 30 while Saturn was conjunct to the Astros' MC.

437. This record has since been tied twice.

off homerun by Chris Burke. The homeruns hit by both Berkman and Burke were caught by the same fan, Shaun Dean. The game clinched the Division Series for the Astros, who soon beat St. Louis for the pennant.[438]

Weirdly, soon after winning the longest post-season game in history, the Astros lost the longest World Series game in history. Game Three of the World Series occurred on October 25 against the White Sox. The game ended after 14 innings, tying what was then[439] the record for longest World Series game in innings with Game Two of the 1916 World Series. The game went on to last 5 hours 41 minutes, which broke the record for length of a World Series game in chronological time.

Astros win 18 inning LCS game
Sunday, October 9, 2005 5:50:00 PM
Houston, Texas
Time Zone: 05:00 (CDT)
Longitude: 095° W 23' 24"
Latitude: 29° N 46' 06"

Then, in 2017, the Astros would play in the second-longest World Series game measured in conventional time. The game lasted only 10 innings of baseball time, but it would continue through 5 hours and 17 minutes of clock time. The game ended in a 13-12 walk-off win against the Dodgers. This game showed that the Astros' relationship with the Lord of Time had changed. Their record in previous seasons had not been good in such games, but this long game was won, and the Astros would continue to win the 2017 World Series in seven games. Houston had endured a 57-year wait for their first World Series win. When the Series was won, Saturn was positioned at 24 degrees Sagittarius, square to the Astros' MC and IC axis. This is generally considered a malefic aspect, but the seasons had given the Astros the ability to channel a challenging transit from Saturn into a World Series win.

---

438. Author's note: I calculated the time at the end of the game to have been 5:50 or 5:55 CDT by adding the time of game to the start time. Different start times are listed: 12:00 and 12:05 CDT. With either start time, the game would have ended with the Descendant on or near 24 degrees Virgo, conjunct the Astros' MC.

439. The current record for longest World Series game in both innings and time was set on Oct. 26, 2018 when the Dodgers beat the Red Sox in 18 innings. The game took 7 hours 20 minutes.

The Washington Senators/ Texas Rangers

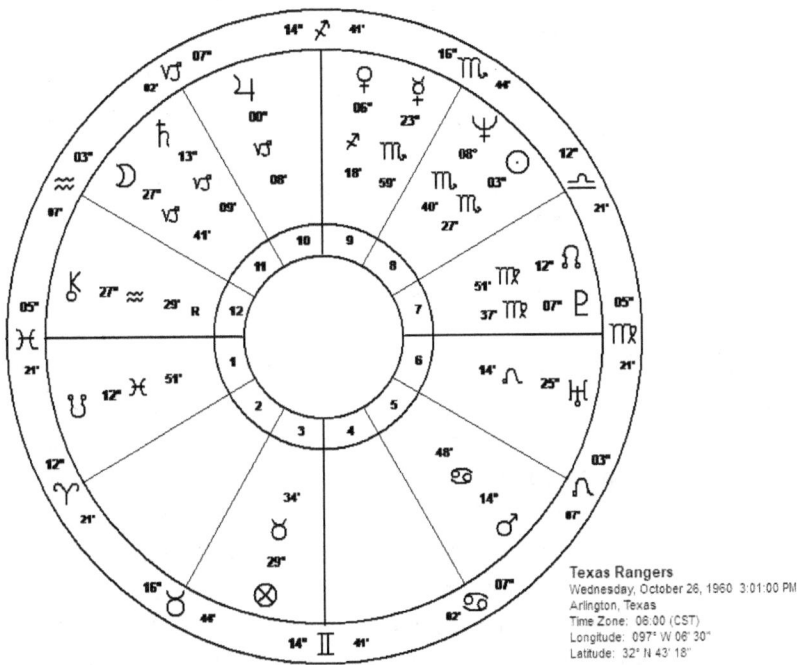

Texas Rangers
Wednesday, October 26, 1960 3:01:00 PM
Arlington, Texas
Time Zone: 06:00 (CST)
Longitude: 097° W 06' 30"
Latitude: 32° N 43' 18"

The Senators were born on October 26, 1960[440] at 4:01 pm EDT[441]. They lived in Washington from their birth through the 1971 season. In 1972, the Senators moved to Arlington, Texas, and changed their name to the Texas Rangers.

In the fall of 1960, four baseball teams were born. While the Sun was in Libra, the National League gave birth to the Mets and Astros. Nine days later, with the Sun in early Scorpio, the American League delivered the Angels and Senators.[442] The conditions for the American League births were not as benign as those enjoyed by the Mets and Astros. The American League was permitting a team to move from Washington, the country's seat of power. Without a team in the nation's capital, the politicians

---

440. *New York Times*, October 27, 1960.
441. Author's Note: I rectified the birthchart using solar arc progressions. When the team moved to Texas in 1972, a progressed MC-IC axis of 3 degrees Capricorn and Cancer would be conjunct the team's Mars-Saturn opposition.
442. There were other major league teams called the Washington Senators. In the 1880s, a team called the Washington Senators played in the National League. The original American League Washington Senators played in Washington from 1901 through 1960, before moving to Minnesota, where they are now called the Twins.

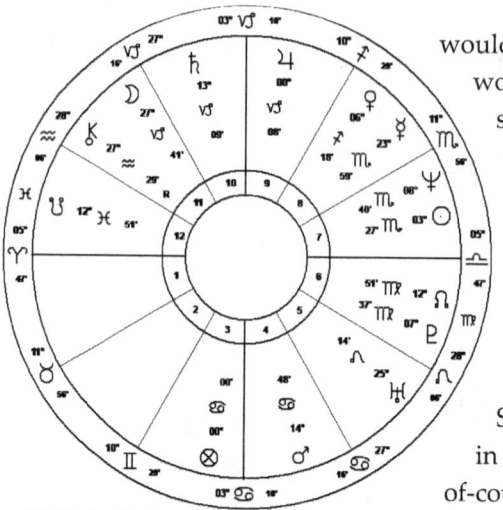

Washington Senators
Wednesday, October 26, 1960 4:01:00 PM
Washington, Dist of Columbia
Time Zone: 05:00 (EST)
Longitude: 077° W 01' 42"
Latitude: 38° N 53' 48"

would be angered. Congress would likely pass legislation to strip baseball of its anti-trust exemption. A new team needed to be quickly assembled. The "New Senators" were hastily assembled to appease the politicians and to protect the anti-trust exemption.[443] The rushed circumstances of the Senators' origin are discernible in its birthchart. The Moon is void-of-course. The Senators' Rising Sign is in the hasty sign of Aries, and its Sun is conjunct to the American League Mars in Scorpio.[444] One is likely to rush one's actions upon transits to a natal Mars.[445] With many of their personal planets in afflicted aspects, this team would endure severe growing pains.

The team's Venus in Sagittarius is square to Pluto in Virgo. When the team relocated to Arlington, Pluto became conjunct the Descendant, further intensifying this affliction. Venus square to Pluto brings extreme desires, as the attraction of Venus collides with the seductive power of Pluto. What one has is never enough, as he or she craves fulfillments that cannot be found. This affliction is especially challenging for a baseball team, as the game of baseball is slow-paced and can be mastered only through patience. In the 1970s, when the team should have allowed its homegrown talent to gradually mature, the Rangers made rash trades out of a desire for immediate success. Young players on the rise, such as Jim Bibby and Dave Righetti, were frequently traded for veterans past their prime, such as Bert Blyleven and Sparky Lyle. When the team did not achieve, managers were blamed and then fired. In 1977, the Rangers even traded the team's most popular player, outfielder Jeff Boroughs, for five players who never distinguished themselves.

The rushing of pitching prospect David Clyde exemplifies the Rangers' lack of patience. In June of 1973, the Rangers used the number one pick of the amateur draft to claim 18-year-old David Clyde from a Houston high

---

443. Dewey & Acocella, p. 582.
444. Author's note: I am using the Western League chart to represent the American League.
445. The new American League teams also rushed to take the field. They played their first season in 1961, while the expansion NL teams waited until 1962.

school. A left-handed pitcher with a blazing fastball, Clyde was also a local Texan. The Rangers organization hyped him as a can't-miss prospect and future star. David Clyde made his major league debut on June 27, 1973, the same month he was drafted. His opener appeared auspicious. A sellout crowd came to see the young man who would bring them to the Promised Land. David Clyde gave up only one hit in five innings and received the win. But his story ends tragically, as David Clyde soon developed arm problems and would win only a few games for Texas. The Ranger organization ruined the career of a young pitcher by rushing him into the majors.[446] The Rangers' Mercury in Scorpio is square to Uranus in Leo. This aspect can bring injuries to pitchers, as the suddenness of Uranus upends the delicate functioning of Mercury. Pitchers are fragile, as their signs, Gemini and Virgo, are mutable ones. Clyde's own birthchart[447] has an unlucky resonance with the birthchart of the Rangers. His Saturn in Scorpio is conjunct to the Rangers' Mercury, while his Pluto in Leo is conjunct the Rangers' Uranus.

The team's Moon resides at 28 degrees Capricorn, conjunct the Ascendant of the former Senators who moved to Minnesota in 1961. The Moon serves as a repository of one's past and antecedents. This conjunction between the New Senators' Moon and the former Senators' Ascendant reflects the heritage passed between the teams. An Ascendant corresponds to a name, and the New Senators would inherit their name from the departing team. They also inherited the political connections of the former team, as this Moon is also conjunct the United States Pluto of 27 degrees Capricorn. Fittingly, the Senators' first ownership group was headed by a high level bureaucrat, General Elwood "Pete" Quesada. His connections with the U.S. Pluto made him head of the Federal Aviation Authority. Although the team now resides in Texas, it still maintains connections to the nation's powerful. In the Lone Star State, the team has actually strengthened its political clout. An early owner of this team in Texas was Eddie Chiles, an oil tycoon and sponsor of right-wing radio commercials.[448] In 1989, Chiles sold the Rangers to a group that included future President George W. Bush, who was then the son of the Republican president. Although Bush sold his interest in the team when he became governor of Texas, he is still a frequent sight at Rangers' games.

---

446. Bjarkman, pp. 554-555; Dewey & Acocella, pp. 543-545.
447. David Clyde was born April 22, 1955 in Kansas City, Kansas.
448. Dewey & Acocella, p. 547: "Eddie Chiles, the Angry Man of Texas." *The Christian Science Monitor* July 10, 1980. http://www.csmonitor.com/1980/0710/071060.html

A Moon is afflicted when in the sign of Capricorn.[449] The earth sign of Capricorn instills structure and control, which are antithetical to the rhythms of the Moon. Emotional flows are repressed when the Moon is in Capricorn. A stoic attitude is often adopted, and depression is common. The troubles of the Rangers' Moon are worsened by Mars in the Moon's sign of Cancer in opposition to Saturn in Capricorn. Mars in Cancer increases the emotional pressure, which the opposition from Saturn attempts to control. The Capricorn Moon struggles to contain its emotions. Its frustration and depression are held by the fans who embody the team's Moon. The fans of this franchise have had much cause for sadness and frustration. In the eleven seasons they played in Washington, the Senators only once finished above .500. Four times they lost more than 100 games in a season. In four other seasons, they lost more than 90 games. In the end, the Senator, fans even suffered the scourge of abandonment when the team left them and moved.

The Senators fans let out all their emotions when they rioted during their final game. On September 30, 1971, the Senators were ready to win the last game in Washington. With two outs in the ninth inning, they were leading the Yankees 7-5. However, that afternoon, the Moon and Mars were conjunct in the libertine sign Aquarius. Together, these planets let loose an angry mob, as Mars brought out the anger of the lunar fans. The sign Aquarius gave the fans their licentious attitude. Just before the final out, fans jumped from the grandstands and stormed the field. They refused to disperse, and the game was subsequently forfeited.[450] Poetically, the Sun was in transit at 6 degrees Libra and conjunct to the Senators' Descendant. The Descendant represents the setting western sky. That afternoon, the Sun was symbolically set on Major League baseball in Washington.

In Texas, the fans still suffer, but in different ways. An odd incident occurred on Opening Day of 1984 that personified the struggles of the Rangers' Moon in Capricorn. Before the opener, the club announced that fans were no longer permitted to bring their own food into the ballpark. Nevertheless, when Opening Day arrived on April 3, the fans, as usual, brought their picnic baskets full of food. When they passed through the turnstiles, stadium personnel confiscated thousands of sandwiches and thermoses. Adding to this insult, as they exited the park, fans could actually

---

449. The Moon of the Rangers is also void-of-course, which contributes to its hardships.
450. Bjarkman, p. 551; Dewey & Acocella, p. 585.

observe stadium workers eating the food taken from them earlier.[451] That Opening Day, the Sun at 14 degrees Aries was square to the Rangers' Mars in Cancer. Food and nourishment are lunar-Cancer concerns. A Capricorn Moon is often deprived of emotional and nutritional sustenance.

The opposition between Mars and Saturn exists in the birthcharts of all four teams born in 1960: the Mets, Astros, Angels and Rangers. This opposition has brought the Rangers both the generational friction experienced by the Mets and the late season frustrations that curse the Angels and Astros. Bleak conflicts between Ranger managers and players have occurred, as they play out the archetypal drama of Saturn the father against Mars the son. The attack of Lenny Randle against manager Frank Lucchesi occurred against this backdrop. On March 28, 1977, as the Moon in transit through Cancer was conjunct to the Rangers' Mars, second baseman Lenny Randle attacked his manager. During Spring Training, Lenny Randle had been benched for weak hitting and mediocre play. After Randle complained, the manager said to reporters, "I'm tired of these punks saying 'Play me or trade me.' Anyone who makes $80,000 a year and gripes and moans all spring is not going to get a tear out of me." Randle's response was to beat his manager against the batting cage. Lucchesi required hospitalization and plastic surgery. After his release by the Rangers, Randle was signed by the Mets, another of the teams with the Mars-Saturn opposition.[452]

Billy Hunter, who followed Frank Lucchesi, was given the nickname of "Little Hitler" for his authoritarian personality. Hunter treated his players like children—even the veterans.[453] Doug Rader, who held the manager's reigns from 1983 until he was fired early in the 1985 season, regularly berated his players. Catcher Jim Sundberg was a target that Rader singled out. As the catcher, Sundberg embodied Mars in Cancer. Rader, as the manager, played the role of Saturn in Capricorn at the other pole of the opposition. Before Rader was hired, Sundberg had been mentioned as a possible manager. Apparently insecure in the catcher's presence, Rader openly questioned Sundberg's hustle and integrity.[454] After he was fired, team officials acknowledged that Rader's tongue lashes and caustic manner had harmed the development of their prospects.[455]

In the decades of the 1990s and 2000s, the Rangers Mars-Saturn

---

451. Bjarkman, p. 537.
452. Nash, Bruce & Zullo, Allan *The Baseball Hall of Shame*, p. 57.
453. Dewey & Acocella, p. 546.
454. Dewey & Acocella, p. 547.
455. Dewey & Acocella, p. 548.

opposition matured under the reigns of well-respected managers Johnny Oates, Buck Showalter, and Ron Washington. In contrast to previous Ranger managers who had left under clouds, Oats and Showalter earned manager-of-the-year awards, while Ron Washington guided the Rangers to the World Series.

The Mars opposition to Saturn has also brought the Rangers their struggles in the post-season. These difficulties are similar to those experienced by the Astros and Angels. For years, the Rangers had difficulty reaching the playoffs and World Series. Pundits speculated that the hot Texas Sun made the team tired by season's end. The Rangers did win the Western Division in 1994, but Saturn was cruel to them that year, as 1994 was the year of the strike when the playoffs and World Series were canceled. When the Rangers won the 1996 Western Division, they were the last of the teams born before the 1990s to reach the playoffs. The Rangers took a big step forward by fielding competitive teams in the 1990s. These teams, however, did not play well in the playoffs, as the Rangers lost to the Yankees in the first rounds of 1996, 1998, and 1999.

2010 was a watershed year for the Rangers. That year the Rangers were sold in bankruptcy court and they won their first pennant. In the previous year of 2009, the Tom Hicks ownership had borrowed money to meet its payroll. Their financial difficulty occurred soon after Pluto had entered the sign of Capricorn and formed a conjunction with the Rangers 10th House Jupiter of 0 degrees Capricorn. Planets in the 10th House correspond to executives. The bankruptcy sale was completed to a group led by Nolan Ryan and Chuck Greenberg on Aug. 5, 2010.[456] During the sale, the Rangers' Jupiter received many challenging transits, not only the conjunction from Pluto, but squares from Uranus and Jupiter in early

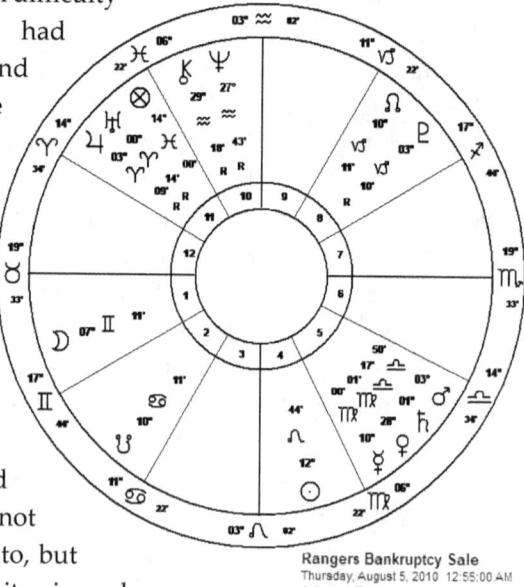

Rangers Bankruptcy Sale
Thursday, August 5, 2010 12:55:00 AM
Arlington, Texas
Time Zone: 05:00 (CDT)
Longitude: 097° W 06' 30"
Latitude: 32° N 43' 18"

---

456. ESPN reports that the sale was completed just before 1 a.m. on Aug 5. http://sports.espn.go.com/dallas/mlb/news/story?id=5436579

Aries, as well as squares from Saturn and Mars in Libra. The franchise proved extremely resilient, as it not only absorbed the multiple energies of these difficult aspects but channeled them toward a pennant victory. Indeed, the 2010 pennant was won under favorable aspects to their natal Jupiter. The Rangers beat the Yankees in the 2010 LCS on October 22, 2010 at 10:09 pm CDT, with the Moon at 0 degrees Taurus trine to their Jupiter and the Sun near 0 Scorpio sextile their Jupiter.[457] Enough of the dust has cleared from the drama of the bankruptcy. The post-season losses to the Yankees were exorcised, as well. The Rangers are a Scorpio team that ultimately regenerates under Pluto transits. The team transformed itself in 2010, shedding their post-season cobwebs and winning their first pennant.

In 2011, the Rangers repeated their effort to win the pennant, only to lose the World Series to St. Louis in seven games. The World Series included a classic Game Six, in which the Rangers twice came within one strike of winning the Series. The transits of these moments, when they nearly won the World Series but could not do so, are fascinating. Game Six occurred on October 27 in St. Louis. At 10:54 pm CDT[458], the Cardinals' David Freese was at bat in the ninth inning with two outs and two strikes. The Rangers were one strike away from winning the Series. The Descendant was positioned at 21 degrees Capricorn, conjunct the midpoint between the Rangers' Moon and Saturn.

Freese Ties Game
Thursday, October 27, 2011 10:54:00 PM
Saint Louis, Missouri
Time Zone: 05:00 (CDT)
Longitude: 090° W 16' 12"
Latitude: 38° N 38' 12"

There was a chance that perhaps the Moon would finally receive the ultimate fulfilment of a World Series win. The Descendant was also square to Saturn in transit near 22 degrees Libra. Perhaps Saturn was ready to crown them champions. But, no! The Rangers would not get to hold the trophy. David Freese hit a triple to tie the score. In the tenth inning, the Rangers again had the lead. Again, they needed only one more strike to

---

457. During the pennant-winning game, the Rangers' birthchart also experienced Mercury conjunct the natal Sun and Venus conjunct natal Neptune.
458. Fox Sports broadcast.

win the Series. At 11:23 pm CST[459], the Descendant was positioned at 27 degrees Capricorn, conjunct the Rangers' Moon in the sign of hard luck. Lance Berkman hit an RBI single that tied the score. The Rangers lost the game in the next inning and the World Series in the next game. The Rangers' Moon, built to endure so many somber autumns, would endure another.

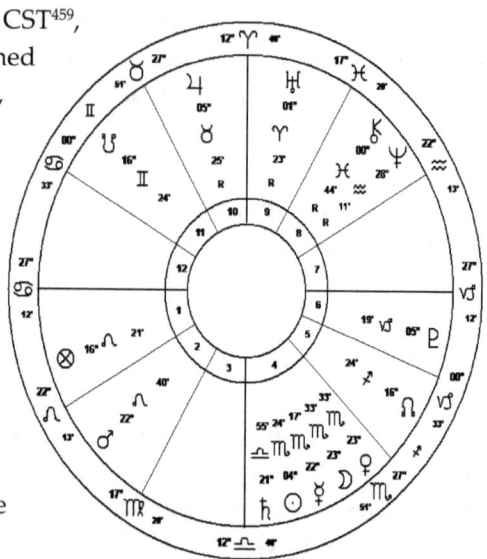

Berkman Ties Game
Thursday, October 27, 2011 11:23:00 PM
Saint Louis, Missouri
Time Zone: 05:00 (CDT)
Longitude: 090° W 16' 12"
Latitude: 38° N 38' 12"

---

459. Fox Sports broadcast.

The Angels

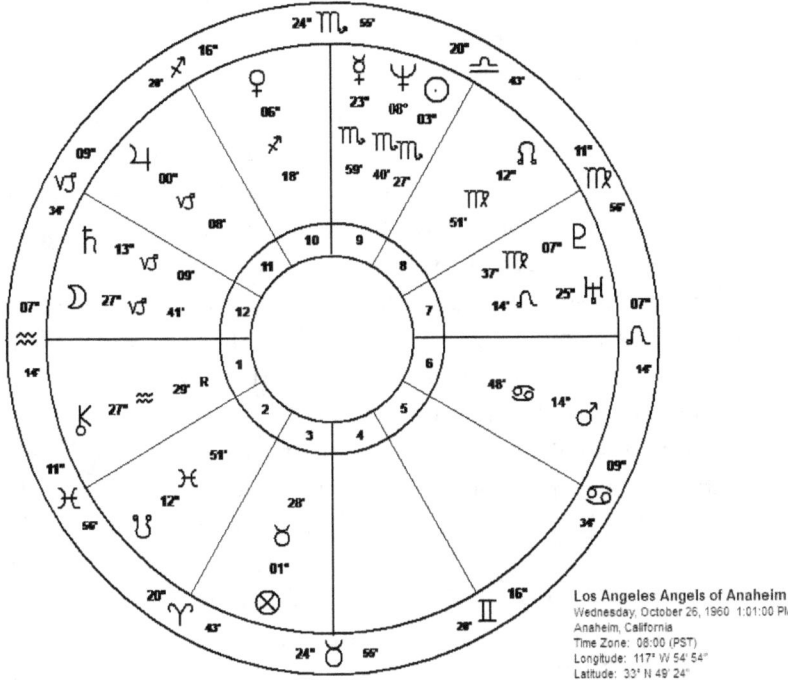

Los Angeles Angels of Anaheim
Wednesday, October 26, 1960 1:01:00 PM
Anaheim, California
Time Zone: 08:00 (PST)
Longitude: 117° W 54' 54"
Latitude: 33° N 49' 24"

The Angels were born on October 26, 1960[460] at 1:01 pm PST[461] together with the expansion Washington Senators, who are now known as the Texas Rangers. The birth of the Angels occurred under the same rushed circumstances as the birth of the expansion Senators. When the American League needed to quickly assemble a franchise for Washington D.C., it hurried the birth of the Southern California team alongside that of the Senators. The league's haste caused the Angels to be born under difficult aspects, including a void-of-course Moon in Capricorn. Their hard aspects include Mercury in Scorpio square to Uranus in Leo, and Venus in Sagittarius square to Pluto in Virgo. Much like their twin franchise, the Rangers, the Angels experienced severe growing pains. But unlike the Rangers or any other team, the Angels have suffered an uncanny number of tragedies.

As with the Rangers, the square between Venus in Sagittarius and Pluto

---

460. *New York Times Encyclopedia of Sports: Vol 2*, p. 128.
461. See Rangers' chapter for the rectification note.

in Virgo has brought the Angels an excess of desire. When Venus and Pluto are in such a challenging aspect, the dark urges of Pluto upset the patience and balance of Venus. The game of baseball requires waiting, not only in the course of an at-bat and the unfolding of a season, but through the growth cycle of a franchise. A team should allow its prospects to develop and its fortunes to emerge. The seductive power of Pluto disrupts the normal development processes. In the 1970s, the Angels rushed to buy a championship, paying big money for free agents. These expensive players underperformed and did not fulfill the team's expectations. Similarly, in the 2010s, the team overspent when it signed Albert Pujols and Josh Hamilton. Pluto's insistent desire was present early in the Angels' history. In their second season of 1962, the Angels were contenders, staying in the pennant race well into September. Their early success led them to neglect their farm system and long-term planning. The team also made too many trades.[462] Soon they fell to earth, and the Angels would only finish above .500 once more in the decade of the 1960s.

Lefthander Bo Belinsky, whose natal chart also includes a Venus-Pluto affliction, personified the flame-out of the Angels in their early years. A rookie pitcher in 1962, Belinsky shot to stardom by winning his first five decisions, including a no-hitter. Soon he became more famous for his life away from the diamond. A bon vivant, Belinsky's partying lifestyle and trysts with movie actresses were frequent copy for Los Angeles gossip columnists, making him an instant celebrity. Although his parties played on, life on the diamond stopped being as much fun for Belinsky. In spite of his meteoric start, he finished the 1962 season with only a 10-11 record. His wildness on the mound caused him to lead the league in walks, with 122. Frequently fined for his antics,

Bo Belinsky
Monday, December 7, 1936   12:00:00 PM
New York, New York
Time Zone: 05:00 (EST)
Longitude: 073° W 59' 30"
Latitude: 40° N 45' 00"

---

462. Dewey & Acocella, p.109.

The Angels

he was a bad influence on his teammates. Nevertheless, Belinsky was kept on the team because he drew crowds to the ballpark. In 1964, he got in a fight with a reporter, and poor press naturally followed. Management decided that Bo had gone too far and traded him to Philadelphia. Bo Belinsky never fulfilled his potential as a pitcher, and he became an alcoholic. His saga is one example of how Pluto's desire for immediate fulfillment overrode patience and balance within the organization. The perilous Venus-Pluto aspect, in the guise of Hollywood starlets, seduced Belinsky away from his potential as a baseball player.

The Angels, like the other teams born in 1960, have Saturn in opposition to Mars. This aspect has brought similar conflicts between players and managers as those experienced by the other teams. In 1971, the players' animosity against general manager Dick Welsh grew so bitter that, during batting practice, they aimed line drives in his direction. The opposition has also brought the Angels much late-season frustration, as the head-first efforts of their Mars collide against the barriers of their Saturn. The Moon's placement in the hard luck sign of Capricorn has also set them up for frustration. The planet Saturn, which rules the post-season, took a very long time before he finally awarded a pennant and a World Series win to the Angels in 2002. Like the Rangers and the Astros, the Angels experienced more than their fair share of late-season defeats. Angels' fans, braced by their Moon in the stoic sign of Capricorn, would endure many slings and arrows.

In 1982, the Angels were leading two games to none in a best-of-five League Championship Series against Milwaukee. Only one more win was needed to hold the pennant, but Pluto in Libra was square to the Angels' Capricorn Moon during the 1982 LCS. The Angels would suffer three losses in a row. In the 1986 League Championship Series, the Angels came even closer to winning the pennant. The Angels were not only ahead three games to one in the Series, they were one pitch away from the

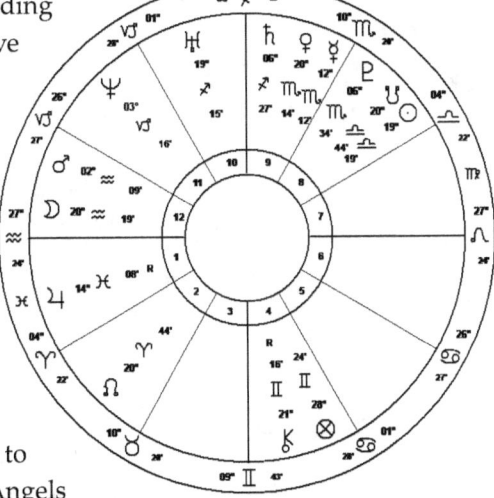

1986 LCS Game 5 Lost
Sunday, October 12, 1986 3:59:00 PM
Anaheim, California
Time Zone: 07:00 (PDT)
Longitude: 117° W 54' 54"
Latitude: 33° N 49' 24"

pennant. On the afternoon of October 12, Donny Moore had Dave Henderson in a 2 and 2 count before he surrendered the ninth-inning home run. The game was lost to Boston in the eleventh inning. A few days later, the pennant was lost. During the series, Saturn in transit at 6 degrees Sagittarius was conjunct the Angels' Tenth House Venus and square to the team's Pluto. If the 1986 Angels had been a more seasoned team, the conjunction from Saturn could have proved benefic. During the fateful Game 5, the Sun and South Node were conjunct near 20 degrees Libra, square to the midpoint between the Angels' Saturn and Capricorn Moon. This aspect further set them up to be thwarted.

Donnie Moore's Death
Tuesday, July 18, 1989 12:00:00 PM
Anaheim, California
Time Zone: 07:00 (PDT)
Longitude: 117° W 54' 54"
Latitude: 33° N 49' 24"

In the next year of 1987, Anaheim fans would boo Donnie Moore. Two years later, Moore was out of baseball. Then, on July 18, 1989, Donny Moore took his own life. Moore had never recovered from that fateful day when he played the goat.[463] His death took place during a Capricorn Full Moon conjunct to the Angels' own Moon in Capricorn.

In 2002, the Angels won their first pennant and first World Series. They did so under the transits of Neptune conjunct their Ascendant, Uranus opposite their natal Uranus, and Saturn quincunx their natal Saturn. Game 6 of the 2002 World

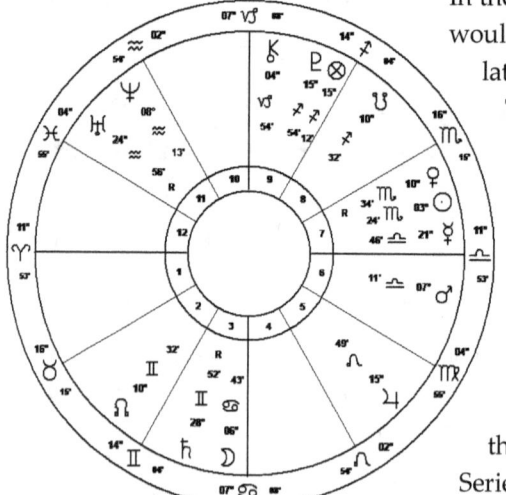

2002 World Series Game 6
Saturday, October 26, 2002 5:02:00 PM
Anaheim, California
Time Zone: 07:00 (PDT)
Longitude: 117° W 54' 54"
Latitude: 33° N 49' 24"

463. Beverage, p. 240

Series contained the stuff of a Hollywood movie about angelic intervention. The game occurred on October 26, a date which was also a solar return and the Angels' 42nd birthday. Behind 5-0 in the seventh inning, with the Rally Monkey[464] and the home crowd going wild, the Angels scored six runs in the next two innings. Scott Spezio, playing the Neptune position of first base, hit a 3-run homer in the seventh inning that changed the momentum in favor of the Angels. The transits for the game that set up a first baseman to be a hero included Neptune conjunct their Ascendant and Mars trine their Ascendant from 7 degrees Libra. The next day, the World Series was won with Venus conjunct the Angels' natal Neptune. Moreover, the Moon was in Cancer and opposite to the mid-point between the Angels' Saturn and their Moon in Capricorn. Upon their victory, the Moon in the watery sign of Cancer provided a valve for the Angels and their fans to release their years of pent-up emotions, which had been locked in their Capricorn Moon.

The Angels team has endured many horrible tragedies. A Scorpio organization is likely to experience death, but of the numerous teams in the American League with the Sun in Scorpio, the Angels have experienced more than an even share of tragic deaths. Many of the Angels' calamities have involved auto accidents. The Angels' birthchart has Mercury in Scorpio—the sign of death—in square to Uranus. This square is more pronounced with the Angels than with the Rangers because the Angels' Mercury is on an axis conjunct to the MC. Automobiles come under the rulership of Mercury. Driving an auto requires the Mercury skills of visual discernment and eye-hand coordination. Individuals with Mercury square to Uranus often have poor driving records. A hard aspect from Uranus to Mercury brings sudden changes in energy, jolts that upset one's perceptions and coordination. Eerily, Angel players were often not at fault in these auto fatalities but were rather the victims of hit-and-runs or a drunk driver. The accidents in which an Angel was at fault involved the player in his car colliding against a stationary object. On March 30, 1970, the station wagon of relief pitcher Minnie Rojas was crashed into by a hit-and-run driver. Rojas became paralyzed, while two of his children were killed. On Feb. 9, 1972, infielder Chico Ruiz died when he crashed his car against a sign post. On January 6, 1977, Mike Miley, a shortstop prospect, also died in a one-car accident when his car hit a culvert. Half of the team was involved in the bus accident that occurred at 1:47 AM on May 21, 1992.[465] The Angels were traveling from New York to Baltimore. One of the

---

464. The Rally Monkey is a mascot for the Angels team. Videos are shown of it at their home games when they are behind in late innings. *http://en.wikipedia.org/wiki/RallyMonkey*

465. *http://www.nytimes.com/1992/05/22/sports/baseball-a-frightening-jolt-interrupts-the-*

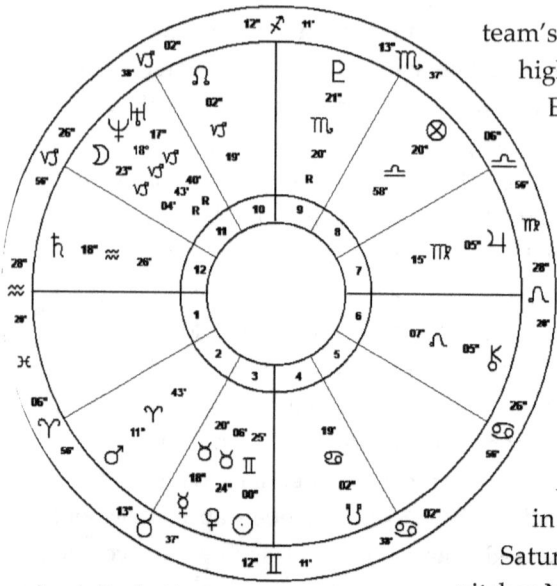

Angels Bus Accident
Thursday, May 21, 1992 1:47:00 AM
Dempford Township, New Jersey
Time Zone: 04:00 (EDT)
Longitude: 075° W 11'
Latitude: 39° N 40'

team's two buses swerved off the highway and into a grove of trees. Eleven players and Manager Buck Rodgers were injured. On the night of the bus crash, Pluto was conjunct the Angels' Mercury; and Venus, in transit at 24 degrees Taurus, was opposite to the Angels' Mercury and square to the Angels' Uranus. Then, on April 9, 2009, with the Sun in Aries square to the Angels' Saturn-Moon midpoint, rookie pitcher Nick Adenhart was killed by a drunk driver.

Not all the Angels' deaths have occurred by auto accident. Rookie pitcher Dick Wantz died of a brain tumor on May 13, 1965, while Mars, Pluto and Uranus were conjunct the Angels Pluto and North Node, as well as semi-square to their Mercury. At noon that day, the Moon was in Scorpio and conjunct the Angels' Sun in Scorpio. The death of Lyman Bostock did not occur by auto accident, but it did happen within a car. On the night of Sept. 23, 1978, Lyman Bostock was shot and killed by the estranged husband of a woman he was sitting beside in a backseat. The bullet was intended for the gunman's wife. Bostock's death occurred as Mars was

Lyman Bostock's Death
Saturday, September 23, 1978 9:00:00 PM
Gary, Indiana
Time Zone: 05:00 (CDT)
Longitude: 087° W 20' 12"
Latitude: 41° N 34' 06"

angels-season.html

The Angels

conjunct the Angels' Sun in Scorpio.

The name and persona of "Angels" corresponds with the team's Rising Sign of Aquarius[466] and the Ascendant's square from Neptune. Aquarius is the sign of the human being, but it also represents the best of human evolution. An angel is considered a class of evolved human being, one who has ascended to a divine position. Angels intercede in the affairs of humans on behalf of God. Angels also fall under the domain of Neptune, a planet associated with divine realms.

When Uranus entered its own sign of Aquarius in the 1990s, the planet brought a sudden interest in angels into the popular culture.[467] Depictions of angels appeared on jewelry, stickers, television shows, and movies. It became commonplace for people to talk about their own personal angels. The 1994 Walt Disney movie *Angels in the Outfield*[468] was a part of this Uranus-in-Aquarius angel phenomenon. The film dramatizes the Angels team and two children who are its fans. As the movie begins, the Angels are in last place, mired in a hopeless losing streak. The team is miserable, and the manager may soon be fired, but with the help of angels, who can only be seen by the two children, the team begins to win. The Angels rise in the standing. With one game left in the season, the Angels are a win away from winning the division.

The Angels' Ascendant of 7 degrees Aquarius is squared by Neptune, the planet of the film industry. Neptune is also conjunct the Angels' Sun. The Angels reside in Southern California, the home of the motion picture industry. The Angels baseball club would naturally be owned by Gene Autry, a Neptunian movie star and singer, and then by a film studio, the Walt Disney Company. Neptune's aspect to the Aquarius Ascendant also deepens the team's connection with divine realms. The deaths the Angels have endured also deepen their connections with divie realms.

---

466. Jocelyn, John, *Meditations on the Signs of the Zodiac*, pp. 218-221.
467. Jarvis, Mary E., "Angels, Aquarius, and the Age of Light," *Mountain Astrologer*, 12/94, p. 52.
468. *Angels in the Outfield* was a remake of a 1951 movie with the same name in which angelic intervention helped a last-place Pittsburgh Pirates team.

Seattle Pilots/ Milwaukee Brewers

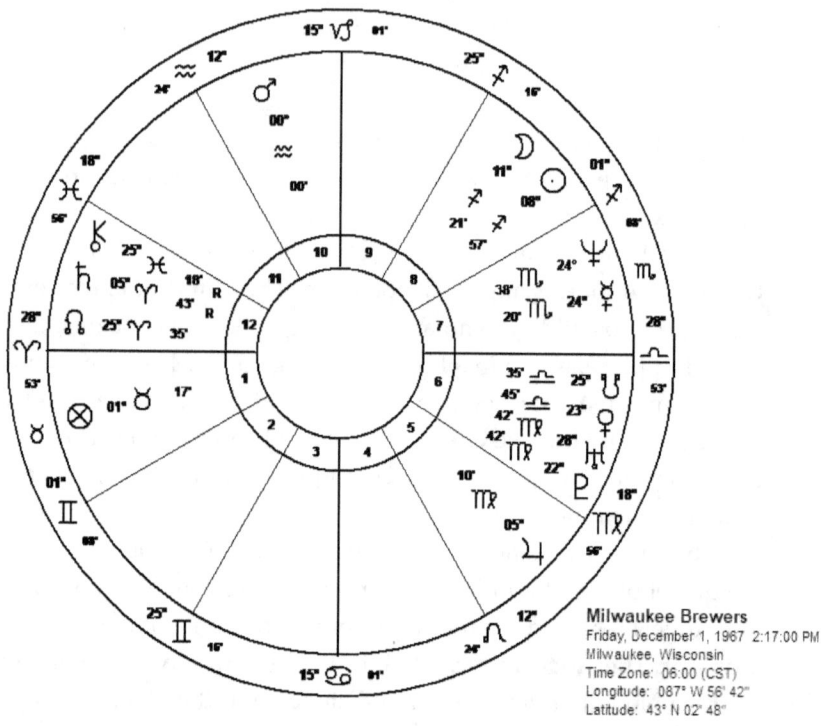

Milwaukee Brewers
Friday, December 1, 1967 2:17:00 PM
Milwaukee, Wisconsin
Time Zone: 06:00 (CST)
Longitude: 087° W 56' 42"
Latitude: 43° N 02' 48"

The current Milwaukee Brewers[469] were originally known as the Seattle Pilots. The team was born on December 1, 1967[470] at 12:17 PST[471] on a Sagittarius New Moon. They played the 1969 season in Seattle before moving to Milwaukee the following year.

In the Seattle chart, the Moon was in a very prominent position, conjunct to the MC. The issues of a planet conjunct an MC would be on public display for everyone to see. As the Moon rules stadiums, the

---

469. In 1891, a team called the Milwaukee Brewers played in the American Association. The current Baltimore Orioles played in Milwaukee in 1901 and were then called the Brewers.
470. bizofbaseball.com. See "Portland Baseball Club, Inc. v. Bowie Kuhn"
471. Rectification Notes: In the Milwaukee chart, the Moon progressed by solar arc becomes conjunct an MC of 15 Capricorn in 2001, the year that Miller Park opened. In 1982, the year the team won its first pennant, an MC of 15 Capricorn progressed by solar arc becomes conjunct the 10th House Mars of 0 Aquarius,

Pilots had unsolvable concerns with their home ballpark. The Pilots played in Sicks Stadium, a minor league park that could hold an attendance of only 15,000. The American League awarded the franchise to Seattle on the condition that Sicks Stadium would be expanded, but through the course of the 1969 season, the stadium was never adequately enlarged. Pilots' owner Dewey Soriano and Seattle mayor Floyd Miller traded accusations regarding the lack of progress on the stadium. The conflict boiled to a point at which the mayor even threatened to evict the Pilots from the city-owned ballpark. Sagittarius is the sign of the traveler, and a Moon is Sagittarius may indicate difficulty settling. The Pilots never grew roots in Seattle, playing there for only one year. Attendance was never large enough to keep the team financially viable. After the team declared bankruptcy in 1970, they were sold to a group led by Bud Selig, who moved them to Milwaukee. The team would establish roots in Wisconsin, but the legacy of its wayfarer Moon continues as the team has played in four different divisions and in both leagues. In 1970, the Brewers inherited the slot in the AL West that had been issued to the Pilots. They moved to the AL East in 1972, when the Texas Rangers were brought into the AL West. In 1994, they joined the newly established AL Central Division. After the 1998 realignment, the team moved to the NL Central Division.

In Milwaukee, the Brewers arrived as "the spiritual heirs"[472] of the Milwaukee Braves who had left Wisconsin after 1965. The Braves' most recognized player, Hank Aaron, ended his career as a Brewer in 1974, returning to the city where he had begun his career. The connections between the birthcharts of the Brewers and the Milwaukee Braves are striking. In Milwaukee, the Braves' MC was positioned at 24 degrees

Seattle Pilots
Friday, December 1, 1967 12:17:00 PM
Seattle, Washington
Time Zone: 08:00 (PST)
Longitude: 122° W 19' 12"
Latitude: 47° N 36' 48"

---

472. Dewey & Acocella, p. 309. The phrase "spiritual heirs of the Milwaukee Braves" is used by Dewey & Acocella.

Scorpio, the same degree held by the Brewers' Mercury and Neptune. Moreover, the Braves Sun of 0 degrees Aquarius is conjunct the Brewers prominent 10th House Mars of 0 Aquarius.

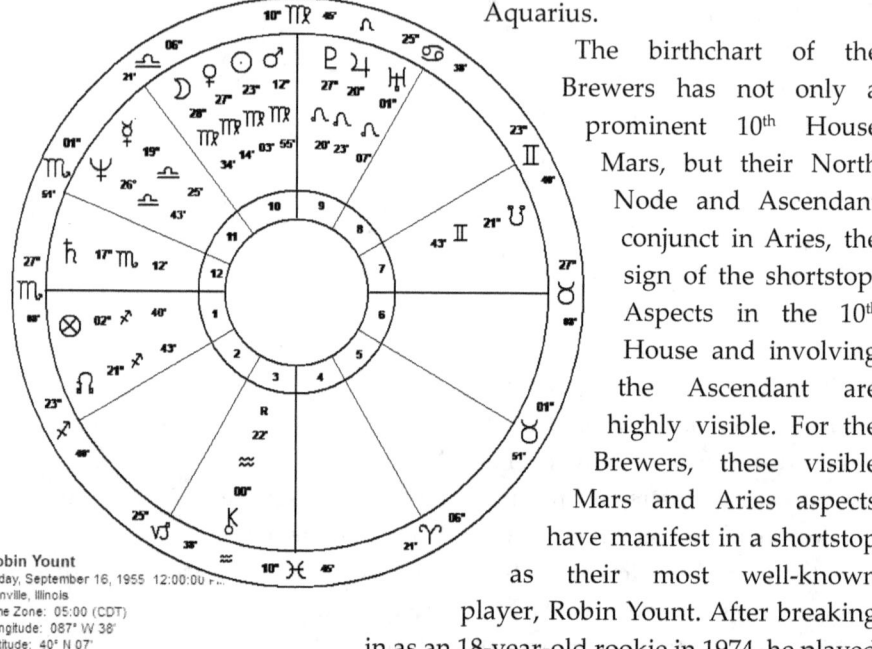

Robin Yount
Friday, September 16, 1955 12:00:00 P.M.
Danville, Illinois
Time Zone: 05:00 (CDT)
Longitude: 087° W 38'
Latitude: 40° N 07'

The birthchart of the Brewers has not only a prominent 10th House Mars, but their North Node and Ascendant conjunct in Aries, the sign of the shortstop. Aspects in the 10th House and involving the Ascendant are highly visible. For the Brewers, these visible Mars and Aries aspects have manifest in a shortstop as their most well-known player, Robin Yount. After breaking in as an 18-year-old rookie in 1974, he played his entire 20-year career in Milwaukee. When inducted into the Hall of Fame, Yount had collected 3142 lifetime hits.

With both the Sun and Moon in the batter's sign of Sagittarius, the Brewers are a strong offensive team. A square from Jupiter in Virgo to the Sun and Moon also bolsters their offense. This team consistently hits for power and average. In the 1970s, with sluggers such as Gorman Thomas and Cecil Cooper, they became known as Bambi's Bombers, a play on the name of Manager George Bamberger. In the 1980s, they were called Harvey's Wallbangers for their strong offense under manager Harvey Kuenn. Brewer hitters who have led the league in home runs include George Scott, Gorman Thomas, Ben Ogilvie, Prince Fielder, and Ryan Braun.

Mercury conjunct Neptune has manifested as an affliction for the Brewers pitching. The amorphous energy of Neptune is antithetical to that of precise Mercury. The planet Neptune can make pitchers prone to walks and control problems. In their history, the Brewers' staff has had only three pitchers with 20 or more victories in a season: Mike Caldwell, 22 wins in 1978; Jim Colborn, 20 wins in 1973; and Teddy Higuera, 20 wins in 1986.

Although the Mercury Neptune conjunction is an affliction for Brewers' pitchers, it proved an auspicious aspect for a writer on the team. Jim Bouton wrote *Ball Four* while playing for the Pilots. The book contains his diary of the 1969 season he played with Seattle. Bouton, then a knuckleball pitcher, secretly wrote his observations of fellow players and coaches. His furtive writings are an embodiment of the Neptune-Mercury conjunction in Scorpio. Neptune acts behind the scenes, and Scorpio is a secretive sign. Mercury rules writers and pitchers, and Bouton was both. The book breached the understood boundaries of baseball players, as Bouton exposed the private shenanigans of the locker room. Neptune will spring a leak in such conventions. A landmark in the history of sports literature, *Ball Four* was the first book to depict sports figures as flawed human beings, including exposing their drug use and womanizing. Previously, sports literature was largely meant as inspirational reading. Players were depicted as role models who had overcome adversities such as poverty and illnesses.[473] *Ball Four* led the way for books, such as *Juiced* by Jose Canseco, that expose the true lifestyles of sports figures.

Jim Bouton
Wednesday, March 8, 1939 12:00:00 PM
Newark, New Jersey
Time Zone: 05:00 (EST)
Longitude: 074° W 10' 42"
Latitude: 40° N 44' 18"

The Brewers are one of four teams in the expansion group of 1967 and 1968. All four teams were born under the Uranus-Pluto conjunction in Virgo, the aspect that led to the wider social upheaval of the 1960s. Interestingly, the birthcharts' of the other teams born in '67 and '68—the Royals, Padres and Nationals—have the Virgo and Gemini emphasis of pitching. Their birthcharts are aligned with baseball's *zeitgeist* from the late-1960s that highlighted pitching. The Brewers, in contrast, were born with a Sagittarian batting emphasis. Baseball teams are sometimes born in dialectical oppositions.[474] The strength of the Brewers' offense is a balance to the strong pitching of the other teams born in 1967 and 1968.

---

473. Kaplan, Ron, "The Legacy of Ball Four." *The Huffington Post*, Sept 9, 2010.
474. See Cubs and Tigers chapters. Planets within the birthcharts of the Cubs and Tigers have oppositions to planets within the birthchart of the Reds. These aspects mirror how the Cubs and Tigers were each born as a reaction to the Reds.

Kansas City Royals

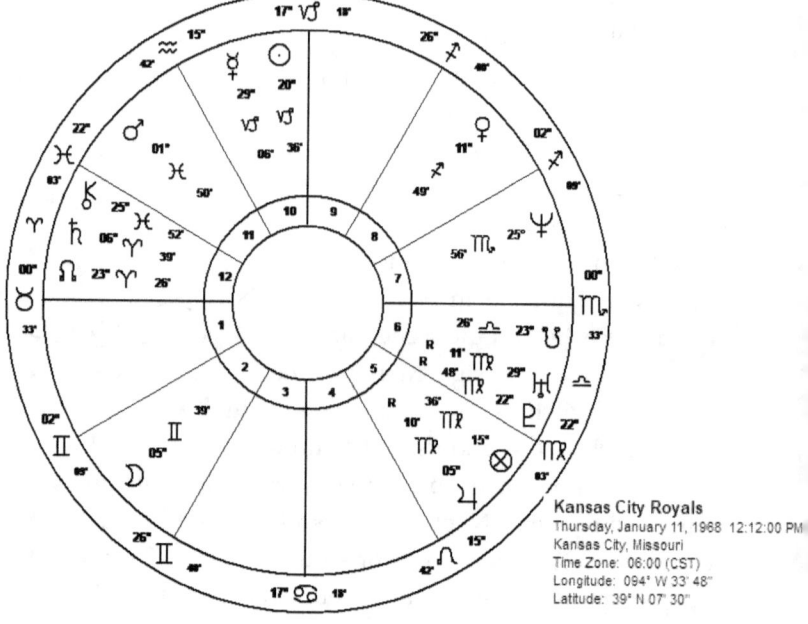

Kansas City Royals
Thursday, January 11, 1968 12:12:00 PM
Kansas City, Missouri
Time Zone: 06:00 (CST)
Longitude: 094° W 33' 48"
Latitude: 39° N 07' 30"

The Kansas City Royals were born on January 11, 1967[475] at 12:12 CST.[476] The birthchart of the Royals has a Sun in Capricorn and the Moon in Gemini. Their Capricorn Sun gave them a strong patriarchal owner, and their Gemini Moon has given them a tradition of strong pitching.

Although the sign of Capricorn is associated with royalty, the name "Royals" is not about kings and queens. Instead, the name honors the American Royal, a livestock show held annually in Kansas City.[477] The Royals have a Taurus Ascendant that corresponds to this name as livestock, especially cattle, comes under the rulership of Taurus.

The Royals are the only major league team with the Sun in the sign

---

475. Carle, Bill, "Kansas City Royals: Building a Champion from Scratch in America's Heartland," p. 185.

476. Rectification Note: An MC of 17 degrees Capricorn progressed by solar arc becomes conjunct the Royals Sun in 1971, the Royals' first winning season. The MC becomes conjunct Mercury in 1980, the year of the Royals' first pennant. In 1993, the year of Ewing Kauffman's death, a Descendant of 0 degrees Scorpio, progressed by solar arc, becomes conjunct the Eighth House Neptune.

477. Carle, p. 185.

of Capricorn. In other teams, the Sun is embodied in a position player, but the Royals' Sun is embodied in the sign of its executives, managers, and coaches. The Royals' first owner, Ewing M. Kauffman, personified the Capricorn role of benevolent patriarch. Kauffman, a self-made millionaire, generously invested in the team and took good care of the franchise. His birthchart shows his resonance with the Royals. Kauffman's birthchart has multiple aspects to the Royals' 10th House Mercury in Capricorn, including a conjunction from his North Node, a trine from his Sun in Virgo, and oppositions from his Moon and Saturn in Cancer. When his death became imminent, Kauffman even ensured that the Royals would remain in Kansas City by establishing a foundation for the team with explicit bylaws instructing that the team could not be moved from Kansas City.

Ewing Kauffman
Thursday, September 21, 1916 12:00:00 PM
Garden City, Missouri
Time Zone: 06:00 (CST)
Longitude: 094° W 11'
Latitude: 38° N 33'

The first number retired by the Royals belonged to a manager.[478] A Capricorn team would honor their manager before their position players. Dick Howser's number 10 was retired following his death in 1987. After he led the Royals to their first World Series victory in 1985, Howser would manage the American League in the All-Star Game the following July. His team won the All-Star Game, but broadcasters noticed something was wrong when he confused the signals as he changed pitchers. Howser's brain tumor was soon discovered, and he would leave his post to have surgery. The next year, Howser attempted to return as the Royals manager, but he managed only one game that spring before succumbing to fatigue. He would finally die on July 17, 1987.

Soon after the Royals began play in 1969, they established themselves as winners. Expansion teams usually take years to develop, but the Royals had a winning season in their third year, 1971, finishing second in the

---

478. Dewey & Acocella, p. 281; Carle, p. 199.

AL West. Throughout the 1970s and 80s, the Royals almost always had winning records. Capricorns succeed. They are the mountain goats that know how to climb to the top.

Early in their history, the Royals distinguished themselves for late-inning victories. Their very first official game lasted into extra-innings. On April 8, 1969, the Royals won 4-3 against the Twins in 12 innings. The following night, they would play 17 innings, winning by the same score of 4-3. A team with a Capricorn and Saturn emphasis wins games decided in the late innings. A team favored by Saturn also wins comebacks. The Royals' greatest achievement, as of this writing, is their comeback victory in the 1985 World Series. That year brought the I-80 World Series that matched the Royals against the cross-state St. Louis Cardinals. The Royals lost the first two games in their home ballpark, but recovered to win the Series in seven games. Prior to 1985, no team had lost the first two games at home and come back to win a World Series.

During their winning years in the 1970s and 1980s, the Royals thrived with a combination of good pitching, speed, and defense. The Royals' tradition of solid pitching emerges from both their Gemini Moon and their Sun conjunct with Mercury, the planet of pitchers. Royals' aces include Paul Splittorff, Dennis Leonard, and Dan Quisenberry. Steve Busby threw two no-hitters for the Royals in the 1970s. The Royals' Mercury emphasis has also manifest in their running game. Center fielder Willie Wilson led the league with 83 bases in 1979 and retired with a career total of 612 steals. Freddie Patek and Amos Otis would also lead the league in steals. A Royals catcher, John Wathan, set a base running record when he stole 36 bases, the most ever by a catcher in a season. Wathan set this mark in 1982, a season during which he had missed four weeks of play with a broken ankle.

The base running ability of the Royals also emerges from their Capricorn planets.[479] Like a goat on mountain path, a Capricorn is sure of its footing. A base stealer is similar to a goat on dangerous terrain. One stumble or hesitant step, and he is out. The theft of a base also involves timing, another domain of Saturn and Capricorn. A runner learns not to break too early or he will be picked off. Conversely, if one breaks too late, a runner is easily thrown out. A runner times the pitcher's delivery, discerning the precise moment to commit, the split second to enter a sprint to the next base. A team's running game is helped by a strong manager and a wise third base coach. The Royals, with the Sun in Capricorn, are

---

479. Holway, John "Diamond Stars: Baseball Astrology" Holway associates the sign of Capricorn with base stealers. He points out that Rickey Henderson has the Sun in Capricorn.

KANSAS CITY ROYALS

such a team. A seasoned manager knows when to put on the steal sign. A team with young and fast players is prone to baserunning mistakes. A steal is worth the risk only when it will help the team to win. Young players frequently lack the experience to analyze such game situations. They need to be told by the Saturnian figure in the dugout when to run and when to wait.

The Royals' speed game was enhanced by their stadium. Until 1995, Kauffman Stadium had an Astroturf surface that gave a quick bounce to balls hit on the ground. Many infield ground balls, which would have been outs on a slower grass field, reached the outfield for singles. Similarly, many balls that bounced on the outfield turf quickly skipped into gaps for extra bases. Rather than clubbing the ball over the fence, the Royals would win with sharp ground balls. The Royals do not hit a lot of homeruns. George Brett, who played his entire career with the Royals, is their all-time home run leader with only 317. Amos Otis hit only 193 homeruns, and Hal McRae hit just 169 while in a Royals uniform.

George Brett
Friday, May 15, 1953 12:00:00 PM
Glen Dale, West Virginia
Time Zone: 04:00 (EDT)
Longitude: 080° W 45'
Latitude: 39° N 56'

The early fortune of the Royals became reversed in the 1990s. The team was purchased by David Glass, a miserly owner who did not invest in the team.[480] But more to the Royals' misfortune, the style of the game changed when Uranus entered Aquarius, the aspect that brought steroids and the "juiced ball." As run totals increased, it became harder to win with a speed and defense strategy. The fans wanted to see home runs. Small-market teams such as Kansas City were at a disadvantage, since they could not afford to sign high-priced homerun hitters. In 1995, the Royals undermined their own chances of winning when they replaced the Astroturf of Kauffman Stadium with natural grass. That same year, the

---

480. Wikipedia

outfield fences were brought in ten feet to allow for more home runs.[481] These alterations conformed to the Aquarian current of the 1990s, and they diluted the Gemini qualities of the Royals' ballpark that had given them an advantage. The Royals fell on difficult times in the decade of the '00s, when they only once finished above .500 and would lose more than 100 games in four separate seasons.

In 2014, the Royals emerged out of baseball obscurity to claim the American League pennant. With Uranus out of Aquarius, the Royals were able to win a championship with a style of play that emphasized speed, defense, and pitching, just as they had done in their earlier years of glory. The 2014 Royals led both leagues in stolen bases, with 153. Interestingly, the steals were distributed throughout the roster, as no one Royal stole more than 40 bases. Jarrod Dyson led the team with 36 steals and was followed by Alcides Escobar with 31. The next year, the Royals would win the World Series against the Mets. The 2015 World Series featured a classic Game One in which the Royals showed off two of their Capricorn specials: outstanding base running and an extra-inning win and. On the first pitch thrown to a Royals batter, Alcides Escobar hit the ball hard and kept running, opening the World Series with an inside-the-park homerun.

A Capricorn team exists on an up-and-down path. The Royals' early success was followed by a steep and long fall. Then they returned to the top of the mountain.

---

481. In 2005, the Royals reversed course and moved the fences of Kauffman Stadium back to their original dimensions.

The San Diego Padres

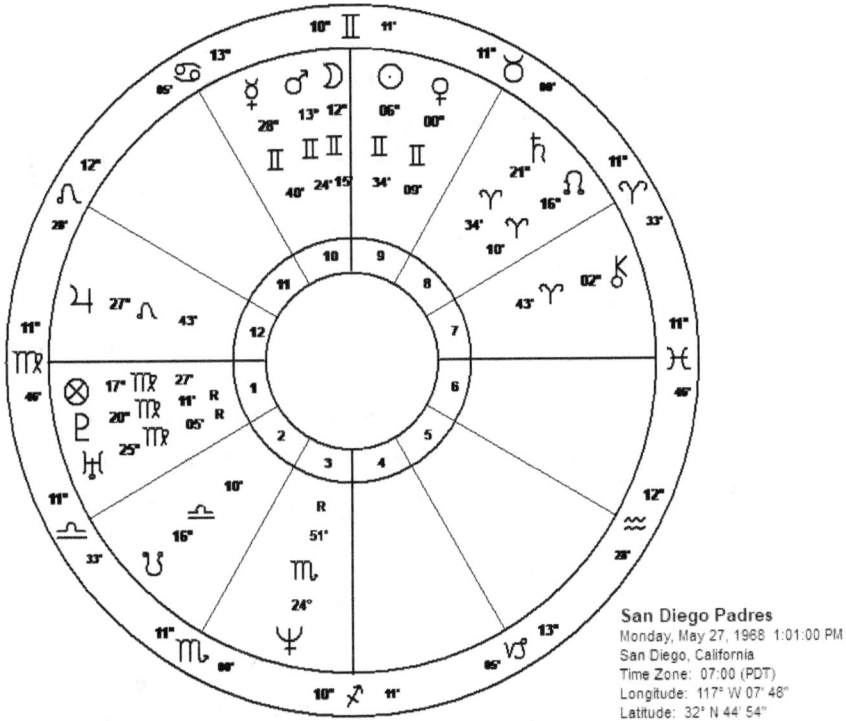

San Diego Padres
Monday, May 27, 1968 1:01:00 PM
San Diego, California
Time Zone: 07:00 (PDT)
Longitude: 117° W 07' 48"
Latitude: 32° N 44' 54"

The Padres were born on May 27, 1968[482] at 1:01 pm PDT[483] on a Gemini New Moon. The birthchart of the Padres has all five personal planets in the sign of Gemini. The Padres' Ascendant is Virgo, with Pluto and Uranus conjunct in the First House.

The Padres were born during the 1968 season. In baseball history, 1968 is remembered as "the Year of the Pitcher." That season, pitchers overwhelmed the batters. Games were very low-scoring, as both the National League ERA and the American League ERA were under 3.00.[484] Bob Gibson set the season ERA record with a 1.12 performance, and

---

482. Durso, Joseph, "National League adds Montreal and San Diego." *New York Times*, May 28, 1968.
483. Rectification Notes: Neptune in Scorpio, progressed by solar arc, becomes conjunct an IC of 10 degrees Sagittarius in 1984. That year, owner Roy Kroc died and the Padres won their first pennant. An Ascendant of 11 degrees Virgo, progressed by solar arc, becomes conjunct the South Node in 2004, the year the Padres moved into Petco Park.
484. Mead, William, *Two Spectacular Seasons*, p. ix

Don Drysdale set the record for consecutive scoreless innings with 58 1/3. Astrologically, 1968 experienced the Pluto-Uranus conjunction in the pitcher's sign of Virgo—the same aspect which brought much of the social and political turmoil of the 1960s brought power to the pitchers.[485] The expansion class of 1968,[486] which includes the Padres, features strong pitching as a legacy from the year they were born.

The Mercury emphasis of the Padres' birthchart is sweeping. All five of the Padres personal planets are in the sign of Gemini: the Sun, Moon, Mercury, Venus and Mars. The Padres' Rising Sign and two outer planets, Uranus and Pluto, are in Virgo, Mercury's other sign. The Padres' Neptune is located in the Third House, the house of Gemini. With such an abundance of planets in the Mercury's signs and houses, the Padres excel in pitching.

In spite of their Mercury emphasis and outstanding pitching, the Padres won their second pennant in 1998, a celebrated year within the "juiced ball" era. That year was baseball's "Summer of Love," a season when fan interest surged. Many baseball fans had become disillusioned after the 1994 strike, but their affections revived in 1998, as the nation followed the pursuit of Roger Maris's single season home run record by Mark McGwire and Sammy Sosa. That year, the Padres triumphed against the more Uranian teams. Their pitchers kept the team ERA at 3.63, second in the league, but they also took advantage of the Uranian energy in the air. They won the NL pennant as Uranus was trine their MC

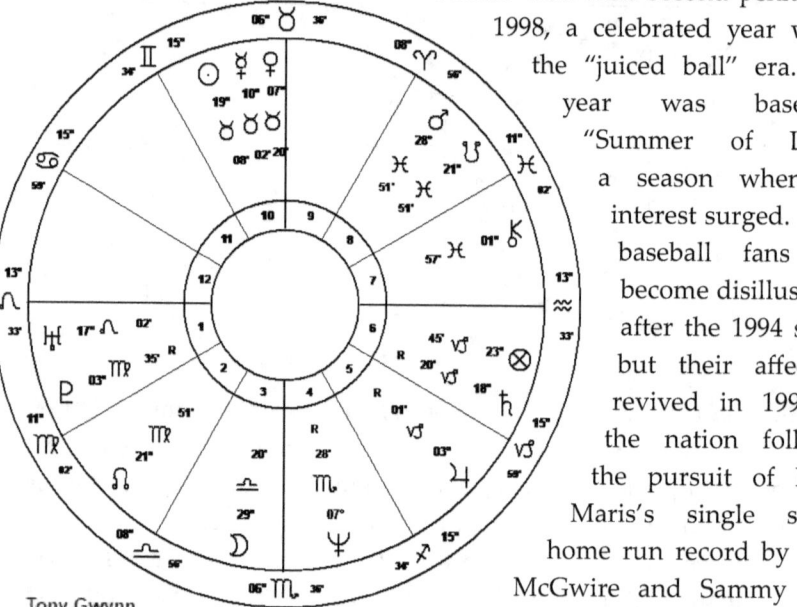

Tony Gwynn
Monday, May 9, 1960 12:00:00 PM
Los Angeles, California
Time Zone: 07:00 (PDT)
Longitude: 118° W 18' 54"
Latitude: 34° N 02' 48"

---

485. See Part III.

486. The expansion class of 1968 includes the Padres, Expos, Royals and Brewers. The Brewers were actually born in December of 1967, but still have the Uranus Pluto conjunction in Virgo. The Brewers, a hitting team with a Jupiter emphasis, are an antithesis to the other three Mercurial teams. The Brewers' Sun and Moon in Sagittarius are opposed to the Gemini Suns and Moons of the Padres and Expos.

that year. Padres left fielder Greg Vaughn rode the transit by hitting 50 home runs, third in the National League. The Padres have an abundance of Mercury energy, but they also have Uranus in the First House, which allows them to thrive under Uranus transits.

The Padres offense often has a strong speed component, another manifestation of their Mercury emphasis.[487] In their first winning season of 1978, then-Padre Ozzie Smith stole 40 bases, while Gene Richards stole 37 bases. When the Padres won the pennant in 1984, their offense was sparked by Alan Wiggins, who stole 70 bases. Wiggins, the leadoff hitter, was often on base, even walking 75 times. When Wiggins was traded the following year, the Padres' offense sputtered without a fast leadoff hitter as their catalyst. Batting averages near the top of the lineup sank. Even Tony Gwynn slumped, as he received fewer fastballs without Wiggens on base ahead of him.[488] In 1996, the Padres signed Rickey Henderson, the all-time stolen-base leader. Although Henderson was past his prime, his high on-base percentage helped solidify the offense that won the 1996 Western Division.

The Padres generally struggle. When they do win, they have difficulty sustaining their success. Their 1998 pennant capture was followed by five losing seasons. With so many planets in the signs of Gemini and Virgo, the birthchart of the Padres is very mutable, which makes achieving and sustaining stability difficult. Problematic squares exist between their Virgo and Gemini planets. The Virgo Ascendant is square to their Sun, Moon and Mars. Their Pluto and Uranus in Virgo are square to Mercury in Gemini. A square between Uranus and Mercury can bring devastating injuries.[489] The Padres also have a square between Pluto and Mars, which can also wreak havoc. Pitchers are fragile players who easily fall to injury. The Padres have had many outstanding pitching performances, including Cy Young award seasons by Randy Jones, Gaylord Perry, Mark Davis, and Jake Peavy. But they have lacked a franchise pitcher who would anchor the team for a succession of years. Randy Jones, who pitched two 20-win seasons in San Diego, is one of the most recognized pitchers in Padres history, but Jones played only eight seasons with San Diego. Trevor Hoffman stayed on the Padres staff for sixteen years, but as a closer rather than a starter.

---

487. When the Padres won the 1998 pennant, they stole only 79 bases, below that year's NL team average of 101 (http://www.baseball-reference.com/leagues/NL/1998.shtml. 1998 was an anomaly year because of Uranus in Aquarius.
488. Porter, David L., "San Diego Padres: The Saga of Big Mack and Trader Jack," p. 504.
489. See Rangers chapter.

Good pitchers on the Padres are usually traded, injured, or leave by free agency. Many pitchers have been traded after a good season. Dave Roberts held a 2.10 ERA through 270 innings for the last-place 1971 Padres, yet he was traded to Houston the following year. Fred Norman pitched six shut-outs for San Diego in 1972. The next season, Norman began slowly with a 1 and 7 record, then was traded to the Reds. Once in Cincinnati, he regained his form, posting a 12 and 6 record for the Big Red Machine. In 1976, reliever Butch Metzger won the Rookie of the Year award for the Padres. The following year, he was traded to St Louis. Mark Davis won the Cy Young award as the Padres' closer in 1989. The following year, Davis was in a Royals uniform.

It gets said that the good life of San Diego, with its sunshine and beaches, get in the way of competitive baseball.[490] The birthchart of the Padres suggests there is truth to this claim. The South Node is a realm of ease, a place of little challenge that one falls back upon. The Padres' South Node is in the Second House of material abundance. The South Node is also in the sign of Libra, a placement of congeniality and social grace. Together, these aspects breed a life of little hardship, as there is plenty of comfort and plenty of love. In contrast, the Padres' North Node, their point of growth, has very challenging aspects.

The Padres' North Node is in the Eighth House, the Sign of Aries, and conjunct to Saturn. Their North Node challenge is to embody the dark power of the Eighth House, the vigor of Aries, and the discipline of Saturn. With Saturn in this conjunction, it is the manager who steers the Padres on their path of growth. Saturn in Aries indicates an aggressive manager, either in strategy or personality. The Padres have performed best under aggressive managers. A team built around pitching and speed needs a manager who takes an active and hands-on role. Such a manager makes frequent pitching changes and dares to send his runners. But any planet conjunct to a lunar node will feel the pull from the sign of opposite node. The Padres' Saturn feels the pull from the South Node in easy-going Libra. So the manager's reins experience the duality of Aries and Libra. The personalities of San Diego managers swing between the politeness and agreeability of the team's Libra South Node and the Mars intensity of the Aries North Node. Steve Boros was a Libra-style manager who lasted only the one year. He was described as very kind man who treated his players well.[491] Yet, when he was fired after the 1986 season, he would

---

490. Dewey & Acocella, p. 520.
491. Porter, David, p. 505.

be criticized as "too passive."[492] Even Bruce Bochy, who managed the 1996 pennant winners, had been described in 1995 as too concerned with hurting his players' feelings.[493]

Some Padre managers have zealously embodied the aggression of Aries and the power hunger of the Eight House. Alvin Dark behaved as a tyrant when he managed the Padres for a part of the 1977 season. Dark was unwilling to delegate authority to his coaches, and he instituted unpopular rules, including no beer drinking.[494] Alvin Dark's game tactics included many signs and trick plays. The excess of signs and plays made the players nervous. Dark was fired during the Spring Training of 1978, after players complained about him to the front office.[495] The Padres had success under Dick Williams, whose natal Venus and Moon in Aries were conjunct the Padres' North Node and Saturn. Williams was aggressive on the field and also toward his players. A stern taskmaster who often stepped on people's toes, Williams had a win-at-all-cost attitude. Dick Williams, nevertheless, did win. The Padres' first pennant of 1984 came with him at the helm. Williams was also the first Padres manager to leave San Diego with a winning record.[496] Larry Bowa, who managed the Padres in 1987 and 1988, also had an Aries manner. A small and fiery Aries-shortstop personality, Bowa could not channel his Mars energy constructively. He was loud and intense, often venting his frustrations in clubhouse meetings. He expected his team to overachieve, and, when the Padres would lose, Bowa took it personally.[497]

Roger Craig managed the Padres in 1978, their first winning season. Craig was laid-back and congenial in personality. He was a positive motivator to his players.[498] However, Craig was aggressive on the field, often employing the hit-and-run and the squeeze play. A healthy balance of the Padres' South and North Node qualities, he treated his players with a Libran affability, yet he managed a game with Aries aggression.

A Gemini can talk too much or speak indiscreetly. A memorable moment of indiscretion occurred soon after the Padres were bought by McDonald's tycoon Ray Kroc. On April 9, 1974, the night of the Padres' home opener,

---

492. Dewey & Acocella, p. 525.
493. Krasovic, Tom: "Padres' Gains figure to be Encouraging their Flock" *The Sporting News Baseball Yearbook 1996*, p. 132. This observation was made the year before Bochy and the Padres won the 1996 Western Division.
494. Dewey & Acocella, p. 523.
495. Porter, David, p. 491.
496. Porter, David, pp. 504-505.
497. Porter, David, pp. 507-508.
498. Porter, David, p. 491.

the Padres were losing a sloppy error-filled game. In the 8th inning, with the Padres trailing the Astros 9-2, the new owner Ray Kroc addressed the crowd of 39,000 from the public address system. Kroc apologized to the fans for the Padres' poor play: "Ladies and gentlemen, I suffer with you," he told the fans. He also remarked, "I've never seen such stupid ballplaying in my life."[499] That night, the Padres were undergoing harsh transits. Their natal Mercury of 28 degrees Gemini suffered a conjunction from transiting Saturn and a square from transiting Mercury at 27 degrees Pisces. Saturn was embodied in the new owner, and his verbal excesses were a manifestation of the square from Mercury. A difficult square from Mercury, in transit to the Padres natal Mercury, triggered the new owner to criticize his team in public. The apologetic quality of Kroc's speech emerged from Mercury in the contrite sign of Pisces.

A Gemini can also sing in an uncouth manner—especially one with a Third House Neptune, the planet of music. Rosanne Barr sang an off-key rendition of the Star Spangled Banner before a Jack Murphy Stadium crowd on July 25, 1990. As she was booed, Rosanne made fun of baseball players by spitting and scratching her crotch. That day, Mercury at 24 degrees Leo was conjunct the Padres Jupiter and square to their Third House Neptune. Together, theatrical Jupiter in Leo and saucy Neptune in Scorpio pushed the boundaries of accepted taste. Additionally, the Padres' Pluto underwent a conjunction from the Moon. Pluto brought the iconoclasm that challenged the sanctity of the National Anthem.

With multiple squares between their Gemini and Virgo planets and axis points, the Padres are challenged to bring together the elements of air and earth. The mental brilliance of their Gemini air is challenged to ground within the humility and service of Virgo earth. The Padre mascot is a mendicant friar of the Franciscan order. The mascot is consistent with the team's Virgo Ascendant, as the Padre has the humble task of serving the poor and the less fortunate. The Padres were born in 1968, a year that planted energy for social change that included relief for the unfortunate. Expect the Padres to create more than a good pitching staff, as the ideas of their Gemini planets become one with the clay of their Virgo body.

---

499. Porter, David, p. 487.

Montreal Expos/ Washington Nationals

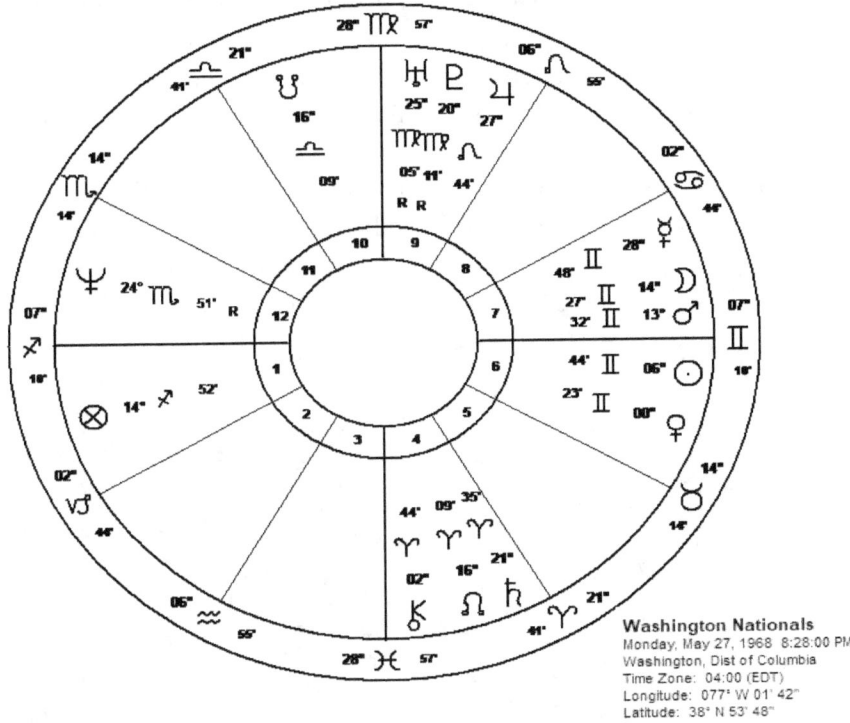

Washington Nationals
Monday, May 27, 1968 8:28:00 PM
Washington, Dist of Columbia
Time Zone: 04:00 (EDT)
Longitude: 077° W 01' 42"
Latitude: 38° N 53' 48"

The Washington Nationals of the National League were originally known as the Montreal Expos. They played in Montreal, Quebec, from their first season of 1969 until they moved to Washington in 2005. The Expos, like their twin franchise the Padres, were born on May 27, 1968,[500] but much later in the day. The Expos birthchart has a rectified time of 8:28 pm EDT.[501] The National League deliberated for 10 hours before making the surprise choice of placing a franchise in a city outside the United States.[502] The team has all its personal planets in the sign of Gemini: the Sun,

---

500. Durso, Joseph, "National League adds Montreal and San Diego," *New York Times*, May 28, 1968.
501. Rectification Notes: In 1977, the year the Expos moved into Olympic Stadium, natal Pluto progressed by solar arc became opposite an IC of 28 Pisces. In 1999, the year Jeffrey Loria solidified his control, natal Jupiter progressed by solar arc became conjunct an MC of 28 Virgo. When MLB bought control of the team in 2002, Neptune progressed by solar arc became square an MC of 28 Virgo.
502. Durso, Joseph, *New York Times*, May 28, 1968.

Moon, Mercury, Venus and Mars. The Moon is in a different degree[503] from the Padres' Moon, due to the team's birth later in the day.

When the team moved from Montreal to Washington, a relocated birth chart became active in D.C. Most teams experience radical changes in their birthcharts as the relocate, but this team's chart changed only slightly. The house placements of the planets remained, and the zodiac signs on the axes stayed the same. Both birthcharts have a concentration of planets near the Descendant, with the Gemini planets in the Sixth and Seventh Houses. In the Montreal chart, the Sun is exactly conjunct the Descendant within one degree.[504] Both charts have Virgo and Leo planets in the Ninth House, with Uranus conjunct the MC. In the Washington chart, Uranus is exactly conjunct the MC within one degree.

The Nationals have the legacy of being born in 1968 during the Uranus-Pluto conjunction, a time of intense social change. This legacy is on display in this team's birthchart, with Uranus conjunct the MC. The influence of a planet conjunct an MC becomes highly visible, and Uranus will bring the unusual. Many people scratched their heads at the Expos, as much of the team was a puzzle. The name and logo needed explaining.[505] The spirit of 1968 and the Uranus-

Montreal Expos
Monday, May 27, 1968 8:28:00 PM
Montreal, Quebec
Time Zone: 04:00 (EDT)
Longitude: 073° W 35'
Latitude: 45° N 33'

---

503. The Nationals' Moon is placed at 14 degrees, 27 minutes Gemini. When the team was born, the Moon has advanced beyond its Mars of 13 degrees 33 minutes Gemini. The Padres' Moon of 12 degrees, 14 minutes Gemini, meanwhile, is approaching Mars.

504. At the moment the Expos franchise was born, the Sun was setting in the city of Montreal. Oddly, their first stadium Parc Jarry, was set at such an angle that, when the Sun would set, the first baseman would become blinded. *https://en.wikipedia.org/wiki/Jarry_Park_Stadium*

505. The name Expos derived from the World Exposition held in Montreal in 1967. The design on the caps and uniforms contains a composite of three letters: an "E" for

Pluto conjunction involved experimentation with the new and unusual. This *zeitgeist* allowed Major League Baseball, a generally conservative institution, to place a team outside of the nation's borders rather than in Milwaukee or Dallas, middle-of-the-road American cities that were also vying for franchises in 1968. The Expos not only played in Canada, but in Quebec, a French-speaking province linguistically and culturally different from the United States. In Quebec, the Expos advanced the Uranian agenda that people from different nations and cultures acknowledge their shared humanity.

Like their twin the Padres, the Expos enjoyed the heritage of having been born in the "Year of the Pitcher." In 1968, the pitching was especially strong.[506] With the five personal planets in the sign of Gemini, the Expos succeeded with solid pitching. The Expos displayed their pitching excellence early in their history. In only their ninth game, an Expo pitcher threw a no-hitter. Bill Stoneman no-hit the Phillies on April 17, 1969 in Philadelphia. No team has featured a no-hitter so early in its existence.[507] The Expos had six no-hitters in their brief history, although two were unofficial. Bill Stoneman threw a second no-hitter in 1972. On May 10, 1981, Charlie Lau threw the first no-hitter in Olympic Stadium against the Giants. Two no-hitters, in oddball Expo style, would last only five innings. Although they were designated official games due to bad weather, they were unofficial as no-hitters. Dave Palmer pitched a "perfect game" in St. Louis on April 21, 1984, then Pascual Perez authored a 5-inning, no-hit novella on September 24, 1988 in Philadelphia.[508] Dennis Martinez threw a perfect game on July 28, 1991 against Los Angeles. Unlike the Padres, the Expos were able to maintain an ace pitcher for a number of years. Steve Rogers won 158 games with a 3.17 ERA in his 13 seasons with the Expos.

Like the other Mercury teams born in 1968, this franchise is a pitching, speed, and defense team. They score runs with daring base runners. A forgotten fact in Expo history is that the leadoff batter of their very first game was Maury Wills. It was Wills, the premier baserunner of the 1960s,

---

expos, a small "b" for baseball, and a large "M" for Montreal. The "e" and the "b" are inscribed in small lower-case letters. These two small letters are set within the perimeter of the large "M." The border of the entire design is the outline of the letter "M." (Bjarkman, Peter, "Montreal Expos: Bizarre New Diamond Traditions North of the Border," pp. 293-4.

506. See Royals and Padres Chapter.
507. Bjarkman, Peter, pp. 264, 267.
508. Oddly enough, Pascual Perez's brother, Melido Perez, also pitched a condensed no-hitter. Pascual pitched his no-hitter, while a White Sox, on July 13, 1990 against the Yankees. (Bjarkman, Peter, pp 290; 295. Gemini, the sign of pitchers and brothers, often does things in pairs.

who took the first Expo at-bat. Although the Hall of Fame shortstop spent almost all of his 14-year career with the Los Angeles Dodgers, he played 47 games for Montreal at the start of the 1969 season. Wills' Mars of 7 degrees Leo is trine to the Expos Ascendant of 7 Sagittarius. Ron LeFlore, another premier base stealer, also played for Montreal, stealing 97 bases in his only Expos season of 1980.[509] Tim Raines provided a consistent running threat for Montreal, stealing 634 bases in his 12 years with the Expos, including 90 in 1983 alone.[510]

This team, although Mercurial at its core, can, nevertheless, hit. Its Rising Sign is Sagittarius, the sign of the batter, and Jupiter, the planet of the batter, is at home in its own Ninth House. Uranus, the planet of the home run, is conjunct to the MC. Andre Dawson hit 225 homeruns in his 10 seasons with the Expos, including 32 in 1983. Gary Carter hit 7 grand slams in his Expos years.[511]

Like the Padres, this franchise has Saturn conjunct to the North Node in Aries. As it has in San Diego, this aspect has manifested in a series of aggressive managers. An Aries manager does not passively wait for a three-run-homer to win the game, but aggressively directs the running game to manufacture runs. One orders the sacrifice and the hit-and-run. The Expos first manager was Gene Mauch. At the time, Mauch had not yet acquired his reputation as a hard luck also-ran who would never win a pennant or manage in a World Series. Earlier, Mauch was known for transforming struggling young clubs into winners, a knack that corresponded with the Expos' Saturn in Aries. Aries represents

Gene Mauch
Wednesday, November 18, 1925 12:00:00 PM
Salina, Kansas
Time Zone: 06:00 (CST)
Longitude: 097° W 36'
Latitude: 38° N 49'

---

509. Bjarkman, Peter, p. 280.
510. Bjarkman, Peter, pp. 264, 285, 300.
511. Bjarkman, Peter, p. 300.

youth, and Saturn in Aries brings guidance to youth. The Expos under Mauch would contend for the National League East as early as 1973, their fifth season.[512] Mauch was described as a "one-run-at-a-time" manager with "rabbit-out-of-the-hat tactics."[513] An aggressive tactician, he would be criticized for over-managing.[514] Mauch's birthchart has the Sun and Saturn conjunct in the sign of Scorpio, with both planets conjunct to the Expos' Neptune.

Dick Williams managed the Expos from 1977 until he was fired during the strike-interrupted season of 1981. Williams managed the Expos the same has he would manage the Padres. He was aggressive both as a strategist and toward his players.[515] Williams left Montreal with a winning record, but the players bristled under his tyrannical rule.[516] In the 1990s, the Expos were managed by Felipe Alou, another Saturn-in-Aries-style manager. *The Sporting News* described him as "perhaps the most hands-on manager in the game."[517] Alou's birthchart has Mercury at 7 degrees Gemini conjunct to the Expos Sun.

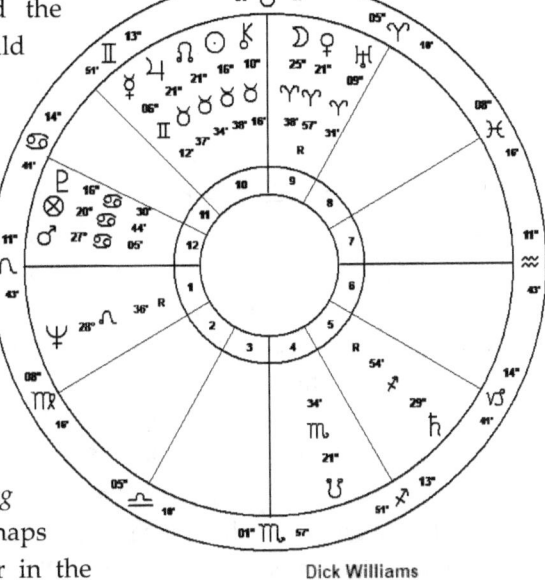

Dick Williams
Tuesday, May 7, 1929 12:00:00 PM
Saint Louis, Missouri
Time Zone: 05:00 (CDT)
Longitude: 090° W 16' 12"
Latitude: 38° N 38' 12"

In the 1990s, the Expos distinguished themselves as a small-market, financially strapped team that was able to remain competitive. They contended because of a superior farm system. The Expos excelled at the scouting, signing, and development of young talent. Their farm system was an embodiment of the conjunction between their Moon and Mars, as Mars rules youth. This Moon, conjunct to Mars, provided

---

512. The 1973 Expos finished 3 1/2 games behind the division and its pennant-winning Mets, but their won loss record was 4 games under 500.
513. Dewey & Acocella, p. 326.
514. Bjarkman, Peter, p. 274.
515. See Padres chapter.
516. Dewey & Acocella, p. 328.
517. Blair, Jeff, "The Expos' climb back will take longer than their fall," *The Sporting News Baseball Yearbook, 1996*, p. 102.

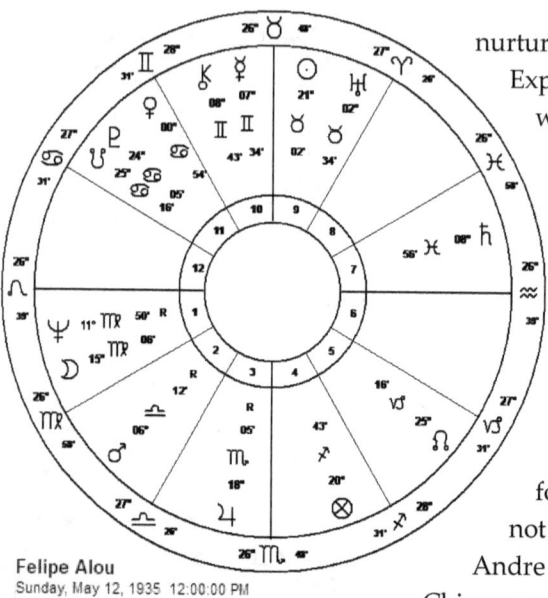

Felipe Alou
Sunday, May 12, 1935 12:00:00 PM
Bajos de Haina, Dominican Republic
Time Zone: 05:00 (EST)
Longitude: 070° W 02'
Latitude: 18° N 49'

nurturance to young men. The Expos Moon created a nest in which many prospects and rookies flourished.

Unfortunately, Saturn in the Fourth House also had its influence on the Expos' nest. Saturn often brings hardships to the Fourth House of home. Many players, uncomfortable with the foreignness of Quebec, did not feel at home in Montreal. Andre Dawson left Montreal for Chicago upon becoming a free agent after the 1986 season. Dawson signed with a team on U.S. soil, even though he was offered a larger paycheck to stay in Montreal. He was reportedly unhappy with the Astroturf stadium and the French-speaking fans.[518] In the 1990s, the Expos franchise had difficulty retaining its players because of their limited budget. The many stellar players who left Montreal in the 1990s included Marquis Grissom, Larry Walker, Andres Galarraga, John Wettland, and Moises Alou.

The Expos' Fourth House Saturn was further embodied in an uncomfortable home ballpark. When Olympic Stadium was built for the 1976 Summer Olympics, it required a wide field to enclose the running track. When the park opened for baseball, the stands were far away from the action.[519] The retractable roof was scheduled to be installed in 1976, but strikes and cost overruns delayed the doming of Olympic Stadium until 1989.[520] Then in September of 1991, a 50-ton beam collapsed inside the park, forcing the Expos to play the final stretch of games on the road. [521]

The Expos had many winning seasons, but they were obstructed from pennants by the strangest of ill fortune. In 1994, a year that Pluto was conjunct to their natal Neptune and square their Jupiter, the Expos finished with the best record in the National League. However, that season ended prematurely with the strike. The 2003 team was held in receivership by MLB

---

518. Bjarkman, Peter, p. 289.
519. Dewey & Acocella, p. 328.
520. Bjarkman, p. 278.
521. Dewey & Acocella, p. 328

and slated to be put to rest or relocated. Still, at the end of August, the team was contending for the NL wild card. Major League Baseball, however, refused to come up with the $50,000 needed to fund the September call-ups from the minor leagues. This disillusioned the players who had fought so valiantly under the cloud of the team's future. The League likely did not want the Expos in the 2003 post-season, where their presence would have undermined their plan for contraction or relocation.

When the Expos relocated to Washington D.C., they took on a conservative American persona. They adopted the colors and "W" logo of the previous Washington team, and the name of "Nationals," which had also been used by a previous Washington team. The team's Jupiter and Mercury form a yod to 28 Capricorn, the degree of the Ascendant of the original AL Senators and the degree of the New Senators' Moon.[522] Although the Nationals present a conservative image, Uranus is now conjunct their MC within one degree. How the National's Uranus and its legacy of 1968 will reveal itself in the nation's capital should prove very interesting. As the degrees of their axes are only one degree from those of the United States' birthchart,[523] the Nationals may have a strong influence upon American culture, and likely one that is more subversive than jingoistic. Indeed, Nationals' fans booed President Trump when he appeared at a World Series game in 2019.

---

522. See Senators/Twins and Senators/Rangers chapters.
523. See Chapter Two for the U.S. birthchart.

THE MARINERS

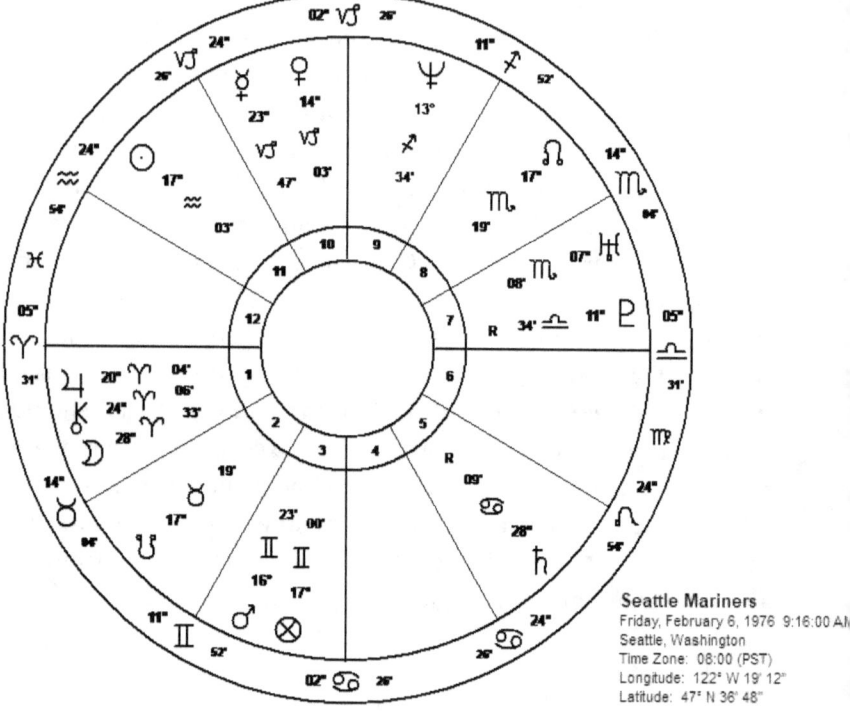

Seattle Mariners
Friday, February 6, 1976 9:16:00 AM
Seattle, Washington
Time Zone: 08:00 (PST)
Longitude: 122° W 19' 12"
Latitude: 47° N 36' 48"

The Seattle Mariners were born on February 6, 1976[524] at 9:16 am PST.[525] The birthchart of the Mariners has the Sun in Aquarius, which has brought homerun power. Their Moon and Jupiter are conjunct in Aries and square to Saturn in Cancer, the aspect that brought them growing pains.

The Mariners' birthchart has both the Sun in Aquarius and Uranus conjunct the North Node in Scorpio. A team with these aspects appears poised to hit a lot of homeruns. However, the fruits of a North Node are often obscure. Early in their history, the Mariners did not understand that the

---

524. O'Donnell, James "Waiting for a Winner in Baseball's Forgotten City," p. 394.
525. Rectification Note: An MC of 2 degrees Capricorn, progressed by solar arc, is conjunct the 10th House Venus in 1988, the year the team was sold to Jeff Smulyan. The team's natal Mars, progressed by solar arc, becomes opposite an MC of 2 Capricorn in 1992, the year the team was purchased by Nintendo. Natal Neptune, progressed by solar arc, becomes conjunct an MC of 2 degrees Capricorn in 1995, the "Refuse to Lose" season. An Ascendant of 5 degrees Aries, progressed by solar arc, becomes conjunct the Moon of 28 Aries in 1999, the year that Safeco Park opened.

homerun would be their path to success. When the Kingdome opened in 1977, the only other domed stadium was the Astrodome, where few homeruns were hit. The Mariners wrongly assumed that the air inside the Kingdome would have the same deadening effect on fly balls. Seattle's early rosters lacked power hitters, and the Mariners were actually out-homered in their own Kingdome by opposing teams in 10 of their first 12 seasons.[526] In 1979, Willie Horton joined the Mariners as an aging power hitter who had hit only eleven home runs the previous year, but that year, Horton hit 29 home runs and won the Comeback Player of the Year Award. It was Willie Horton who brought out the home run potential of the team. Center Fielder Ken Griffey Jr., one of the game's premier home run hitters, ended his career with 630 home runs, 417 of them in a Seattle uniform. In the 1990s, the Aquarian emphasis of their birthchart positioned them to take prime advantage of the Uranus in Aquarius transit. The juiced ball of Uranus

Ken Griffey Jr
Friday, November 21, 1969 12:00:00 PM
Donora, Pa
Time Zone: 05:00 (EST)
Longitude: 079° W 51'
Latitude: 40° N 11'

Jay Buhner
Thursday, August 13, 1964 12:00:00 PM
Louisville, Kentucky
Time Zone: 04:00 (EDT)
Longitude: 085° W 43' 24"
Latitude: 38° N 13' 18"

---

526. O'Donnell, p. 394.

in Aquarius brought leverage to Seattle. The 1997 Mariners set the record for home runs in a season, with 264, while transiting Uranus was square to the Mariners natal Uranus in Scorpio and Jupiter in Aquarius was conjunct their natal Sun. Right fielder Jay Buhner, who played alongside Ken Griffey Jr., hit more than 40 home runs in 1995, 1996 and 1997. Buhner is much loved by Seattle fans, and their emotional bond is mirrored in the synastry between his birthchart and that of the Mariners. Buhner's Venus, Mars and North Node are conjunct to the Mariners' Cancer MC, an indicator of the fans.

The Mariners Aquarian character extends beyond their homerun hitters. They play in Seattle, a high-technology city, home to Uranian businesses such as Boeing, Amazon, and Microsoft. The team was owned for several years by Nintendo, a computer game company. The Mariners also wear blue uniforms, the color associated with the planet Uranus. In 1995, a television commercial for the drink All-Sport exaggerated the high-tech feel of the Mariners. The ad featured Ken Griffey, Jr. and portrayed a futuristic version of baseball in which outfielders stood on power-spring platforms that projected them into the air to catch flies. Randy Johnson, who stands 6 feet, 10 inches tall, is another Uranian figure. Aquarius breeds large human beings.[527] His nickname, "the Big Unit," suggests a large machine such as a mainframe computer. Johnson's natal Saturn of 17 degrees Aquarius is conjunct the Mariners' Sun.

Randy Johnson
Tuesday, September 10, 1963   12:00:00 PM
Walnut Creek, California
Time Zone: 07:00 (PDT)
Longitude: 122° W 03' 24"
Latitude: 37° N 53' 54"

The Mariners' square between the Moon and Jupiter in Aries to Saturn in Cancer mirrors the difficult circumstances of the Mariners' founding. The American League gave birth to the Mariners franchise under threat

---

527. See Giants Chapter.

of litigation. Seattle had recently lost the Pilots baseball team. Millions of dollars in lawsuits were pending against organized baseball by the city of Seattle and the state of Washington over the loss of the Pilots.[528] The Mariners' Moon is conjunct to Jupiter, the planet of courts and litigation. The people of Seattle, represented by the Moon, had Jupiter and justice on their side. The Moon in the birthchart is separating from its conjunction with Jupiter, an aspect that reflects the lawsuits to be settled on the condition that Seattle was granted a franchise. The Moon is also in a very tight square with Saturn, an indicator of its struggles against the League. Although the Moon is separating from this square, it is also void-of-course. The Mariners' void-of-course Moon brought the difficulties of establishing a firm path once the franchise was born.

Unfortunately for the Mariners and the community of Seattle, the square between the Moon and Saturn remained active after the birth of the franchise. Fans and citizens interest groups, embodiments of the Moon, clashed with Mariners owners, representatives of Saturn. The Mariners' Moon is in Aries, the sign of war. For much of their history, Seattle fans were in a state of war with the team's owners. The ruthlessness of Mariners owners was emboldened by Venus in the Tenth House of ownership in square to Pluto. A square from Venus to Pluto can bring a severe desire for wealth.

The first conflict of note between Mariners owners and their fans occurred in 1978, their second season of play. The price of popular bleacher seats above left field was raised from $1.50 to a much higher one. A cheap ticket would now only get a fan into the third deck above right field. There, the view was so poor that fans couldn't see the nearby right fielder. That year, the franchise was still new and building its fan base. The owners needed to generate good will. Instead, they alienated the fans, who became suspicious of the owners' greed. Attendance steadily diminished in the Mariners early years, as ill will festered between fans and owners. Attendance was also hurt when the novelty of the new team wore off and the Mariners failed to play competitive baseball.

The most notorious owner in the Mariners' brief history was George Argyros, who owned the team from 1981 to 1989. Argyros had no home ties to the city and community of Seattle. Argyros committed an unpardonable act when he stated that, since the Mariners were his team, he could do whatever he wanted with them.[529] By making such a statement, Argyros

---

528. Dewey & Acocella, p. 537; O'Donnell, p. 394.
529. O'Donnell, p. 405.

betrayed the implicit trust between owners and fans that the owner is operating the franchise in the interest of the community. But his words were revealing of the Mariners' Saturn-Moon square.

In a much more positive vein, the Mariners Saturn-Moon square manifested in a father and son as teammates. On Aug. 30, 1990, Ken Griffey, Sr. and Ken Griffey, Jr., father and son, played in the same outfield. The Mariners' Moon is in Aries, the sign of youth, while Saturn is the planet of fathers. The Griffey outfield was a far nicer embodiment of the Saturn-Moon square than were the conflicts between owners and fans. Transits for the game included Saturn at 19 degrees Capricorn square to the Mariners' Jupiter in Aries, and Mars at 29 Taurus sextile the Mariners' Saturn.

With their challenging squares in their birthchart, the Mariners had many obstacles to overcome before they became competitive. Seattle did not have a winning season until their fifteenth year of 1991, a record for the longest wait before a baseball team broke the .500 mark. Seattle's fortune changed dramatically when Uranus entered Aquarius in 1995. With their Sun in Aquarius and Uranus conjunct the North Node, the Mariners were ready to thrive in the "juiced ball" era.

The Mariners had a spectacular season in 1995. That year, Neptune, progressed by solar arc, became conjunct the Mariners MC. Neptune brought the magical quality to the 1995 season. In mid-August, Seattle was 13 games behind the division-leading Angels. Then the Mariners got hot and would finish the regular season in a tie with the Angels. After winning the tie-breaker game against Anaheim, they beat the Yankees in the first round of the playoffs. The transits that assisted the 1995 Mariners included Uranus in Capricorn square to the Mariners' Moon and opposite their Saturn. During the month of September, the South Node was conjunct to the Mariners' Aries Moon. The Mariners' Moon and the lunar nodes embraced the fans. That year, fan interest reached floodgate proportions for the first time in Mariners' history.

The hit by Edgar Martinez known in Seattle as "the Double[530]" occurred on October 8, 1995 at 8:28 pm PDT.[531] The Double drove in the tying and winning runs in the 11th inning of Game 5 of the Division Series against the Yankees. A late-inning comeback was primed to happen with Venus at 28 degrees Libra square to the Mariners' Saturn. The stage was set for the Mariners DH to become the hero, as the Moon in Aries was conjunct

---

530. *http://en.wikipedia.org/wiki/The_Double_(Seattle_Mariners)*

531. *http://www.baseball-reference.com/boxes/SEA/SEA199510080.shtml*; author's note: the time that the game ended was calculated by adding the 4:19 time of game to the start time of 4:09.

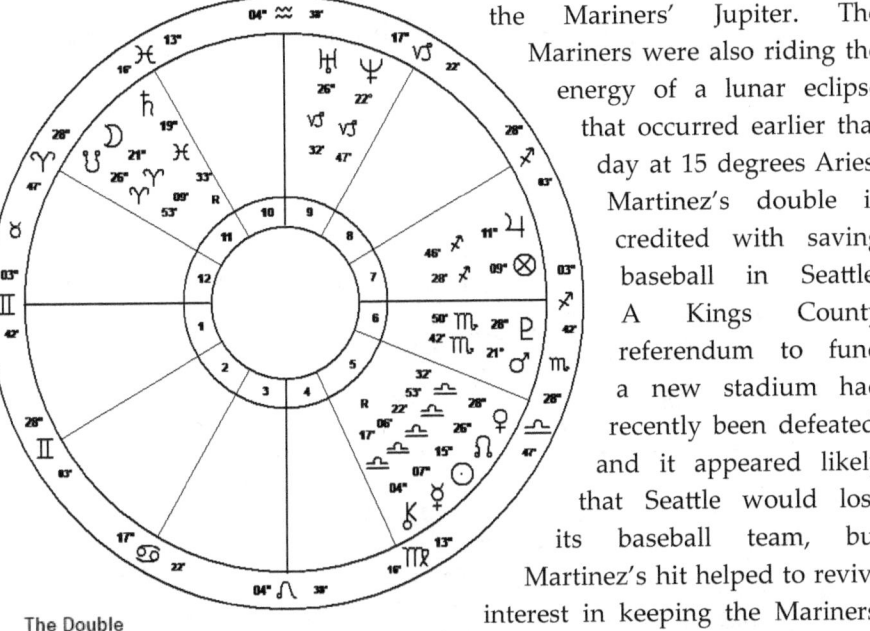

The Double
Sunday, October 8, 1995 8:28:00 PM
Seattle, Washington
Time Zone: 07:00 (PDT)
Longitude: 122° W 19' 12"
Latitude: 47° N 36' 48"

the Mariners' Jupiter. The Mariners were also riding the energy of a lunar eclipse that occurred earlier that day at 15 degrees Aries. Martinez's double is credited with saving baseball in Seattle. A Kings County referendum to fund a new stadium had recently been defeated, and it appeared likely that Seattle would lose its baseball team, but Martinez's hit helped to revive interest in keeping the Mariners. Edgar Martinez is credited with saving Seattle baseball and even has a street named for him alongside Safeco Field. However, the lunar eclipse, which occurred with the South Node at 26 Aries conjunct the Mariners' Moon, also did its share to save the Mariners.

The Mariners' tradition of strong pitching emerges from Mars in Gemini in the Third House. Seattle's Mars is in both a pitcher's sign and a pitcher's house. In addition to ace pitchers such as Randy Johnson and Felix Hernandez, their collective staff is often near the league leaders in ERA. Surprisingly, Safeco Field, which opened in 1999, turned out to be a park that favored pitchers and a difficult place to hit homeruns. This was unexpected for the team that had played in the homerun-happy Kingdome. A pitcher's park, however, is part of the unfolding of the Mariners' Moon, which has a square from Mercury, the planet of pitchers.

In 2013, the outfield fences of Safeco Park were brought closer to homeplate in order to encourage more homeruns. In true Aquarian fashion, the organization thoroughly cogitated the decision. They conducted an exhaustive scientific study of every ball hit at Safeco Field from 2009 to 2011. They also consulted former and present players, including pitchers. In conclusion, the franchise decided it would be "fair" to the hitters to bring in the fences.[532]

---

532. Stone, Larry, "Safeco Field changes aren't expected to turn ballpark into a launching

The Toronto Blue Jays

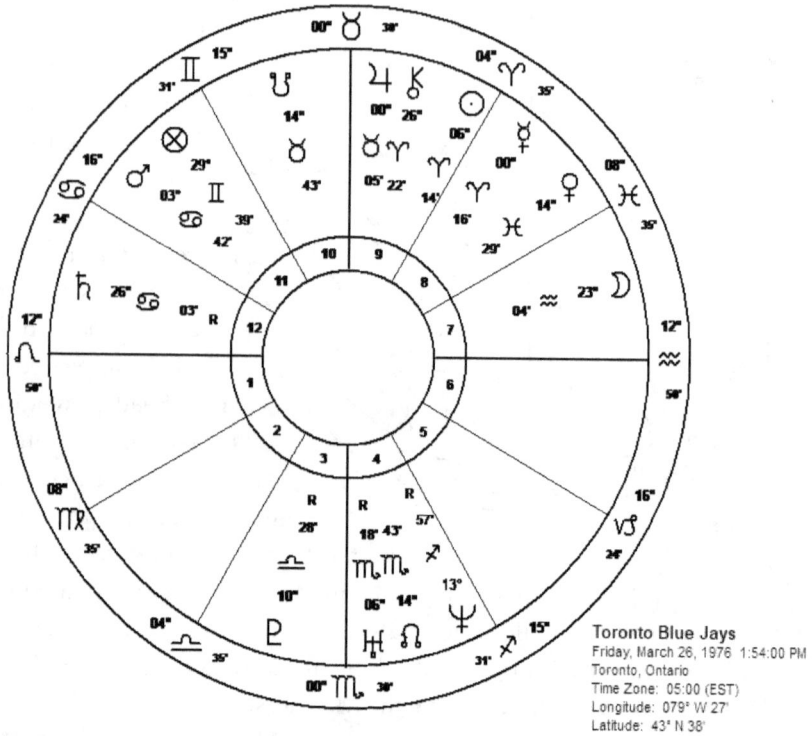

Toronto Blue Jays
Friday, March 26, 1976 1:54:00 PM
Toronto, Ontario
Time Zone: 05:00 (EST)
Longitude: 079° W 27'
Latitude: 43° N 38'

The Toronto Blue Jays were born on March 26, 1976[533] at 1:54 pm EST.[534] Their birthchart has the Sun and Mercury conjunct in Aries and square to Mars in Cancer, an aspect that has given them a tradition of strong shortstops. The international quality of the Blue Jays emerges from their Moon in Aquarius.

The Aquarian placement of the Moon is reinforced by Uranus, the dispositor of Aquarius, in the Moon's Fourth House, and by the conjunction of Uranus to the Moon's North Node, which is also in the Fourth House. The Blue Jays, following the path blazed by the Expos, were the second major league team to reside outside the United States. It is an Aquarian

---

pad for home runs—but should make it 'fair,'" *The Seattle Times*, April 2, 2013.
533. New York Times *Encyclopedia of Sports: Vol. 2 Baseball*, p. 186.
534. Rectification note: An IC of 0 degrees Scorpio, progressed by solar arc, becomes conjunct to the Fourth House North Node in 1989, the year the Skydome opened. Natal Saturn, progressed by solar arc, became conjunct an Ascendant of 12 Leo in 1992, the year the team won its first World Series. The natal Sun, progressed by solar arc, becomes conjunct an IC of 0 Taurus in 2000, the year the team was sold to Rogers Communications.

agenda to bring people from diverse cultures and nationalities together and to have them accept their differences. When the Blue Jays beat Atlanta in the 1992 World Series, they demonstrated the international scale of the game. Not only had they made a Canadian city their home, but the Blue Jays would win the World Series with a large number of players from Latin American countries.

The first Blue Jay inducted into the Hall of Fame was a Latin American. Second baseman Roberto Alomar, from Puerto Rico, was inducted in 2011. The second baseman's birth chart shows his affinity with the Blue Jays, as Alomar's Saturn of 8 degrees Aries is conjunct to the Blue Jays' Sun. His Sun of 16 degrees Aquarius is conjunct the Jays' Moon. It is also conjunct the Jays' Descendant, an indicator of the second base position.

Roberto Alomar
Monday, February 5, 1968 12:00:00 PM
Ponce, Puerto Rico
Time Zone: 04:00 (AST)
Longitude: 066° W 37'
Latitude: 18° N 00'

The Aquarian Blue Jays brought a steady stream of players from Latin America into the major leagues. In the 1980s, they placed a network of scouts into Latin America, a move unrivaled in the majors. The fruits of their work were abundant by 1989, a year in which the Jays had 16 Latin players on their 40-man roster. Espy Guerrero is the scout credited with finding the many quality Dominican players who played for Toronto. Guerrero's keen eye scouted George Bell, Tony Fernandez, and Manuel Lee.[535]

A stunning manifestation of the Blue Jays' Moon in Aquarius is their gargantuan futuristic stadium, the Skydome.[536] As the Moon rules ballparks, a Moon in Aquarius would build a modern futuristic park. When the Skydome opened in June of 1989, it was the first stadium to have a retractable roof.[537] The Skydome complex encompasses restaurants, a

---

535. Dewey, p. 554; Bjarkman, pp. 452, 461.
536. The Skydome was renamed the Rogers Centre in 2005.
537. The retractable roof of Olympic Stadium in Montreal was completed earlier but did not function.

shopping mall, a hotel with hundreds of suites, and a scoreboard that is nine stories high.[538] Its many decks above the playing field give the stadium an atmosphere of a futuristic city. In the early 1990s, Toronto was drawing gargantuan crowds at the Skydome. The Blue Jays were the first team to have an attendance of over 4 million in a season.[539] Four million human beings passing through turnstiles is another awesome manifestation of the Aquarian Moon. Such a mass of humanity is both an Aquarian and a lunar phenomenon. The name "Skydome" also has Aquarian meaning. Aquarius is an air sign, and the sky is where an Aquarius resides. One can occupy the sky, literally, through the Aquarian pursuits of air travel and space exploration, or symbolically by warming oneself with knowledge or humanistic ideals.

The Moon in Aquarius also manifested itself in the Blue Jays' first stadium, Exposition Stadium, where they played from 1977 until the Skydome opened in 1989. On April 30, 1985, a game at Exposition Stadium was postponed due to heavy wind. The air sign of Aquarius can bring extremes of wind. In keeping with the Aquarius rulership of the homerun, Exposition Stadium, like the Kingdome, was a launching pad for the longball. There, the Blue Jays set the record for the most homeruns in a single game. On September 14, 1987, the Jays hit 10 homeruns to beat the Orioles 18-3. The transits for that game included Uranus at 22 degrees Sagittarius and sextile to the Blue Jays' natal Moon. Uranus was opposed by the Moon, in transit at 22 degrees Gemini and trine to the Blue Jays' natal Moon. Exposition Stadium was also the only ballpark where a homerun was hit in its very final at-bat. Its curtain closed on May 28, 1989, as George Bell hit a 10th inning homerun to win the final game.[540] Many seagulls made Exhibition Stadium their home. In the late-innings, these birds would descend on the empty seats and eat food left by the departed fans.[541] Winged creatures such as seagulls and blue jays are associated with the air signs. A team with an air sign Moon such as Toronto would naturally have a home that welcomed birds. In fact, the seagull had become the unofficial mascot for the team. All this set the stage for the strange arrest of Dave Winfield on August 4, 1983. That day, Winfield was a visiting player for the Yankees. During the fifth inning, Winfield was warming up by playing catch with the Toronto bat boy. A ball thrown by Winfield struck and killed a seagull. Soon Winfield was

---

538. Dewey, p. 558; Bjarkman, p. 470.
539. Dewey & Acocella, p. 558.
540. Bjarkman, p. 467.
541. Bjarkman, p. 468.

arrested by a local police officer and charged with cruelty to animals.[542] An Aquarius rarely takes things personally. Instead, one rationalizes the other's offending behavior. But this Aquarius Moon was offended when its unofficial mascot was killed by a Yankee. The charges were dropped when the absurdity of the situation was acknowledged. More in keeping with the character of an Aquarius, Winfield was forgiven and would even join the Blue Jays in 1992, playing on their World Series winning team. Transits for the incident placed stress on the Blue Jays' Saturn in Cancer. Pluto at 26 Libra and Saturn at 28 Libra were square to the Jays' Saturn, while Mars at 24 Cancer was conjunct to their Saturn. Planets in Cancer will zealously guard the home and family, including the pets.

J. P. Aricibia made his debut as the Blue Jays' catcher on August 4, 2010. Representing the Jays' Moon, the young catcher would hit a home run on the very first pitch he faced. The transits for the game included a t-square with Pluto at 3 degrees Capricorn, Uranus at 0 Aries, Jupiter at 3 Aries, and Mars at 3 Libra. These four planets completed a Grand Cross with the Blue Jays' Mars of 3 degrees Cancer. The Blue Jays' Mars is appropriately in the sign of the catcher.

With the Sun in Aries, the Blue Jays have excelled at the Aries position of shortstop. Their first pick in the expansion draft was for a shortstop. On Nov 5, 1976, the Jays would pick shortstop, Bob Bailor,[543] who would bat .310 in 1977. In 1979, the Blue Jays' Alfredo Griffith would win the Rookie of the Year Award as their

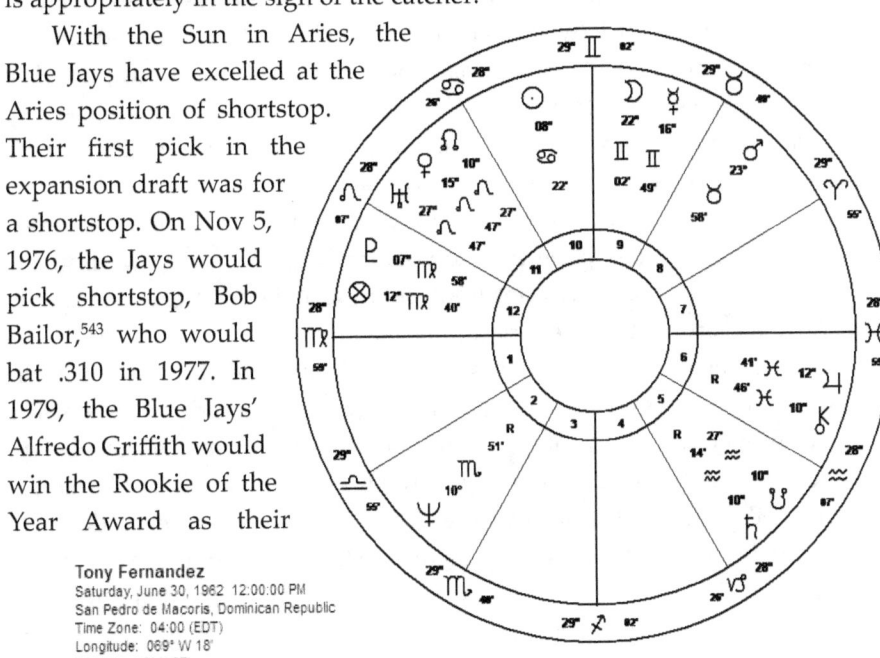

Tony Fernandez
Saturday, June 30, 1962 12:00:00 PM
San Pedro de Macoris, Dominican Republic
Time Zone: 04:00 (EDT)
Longitude: 069° W 18'
Latitude: 18° N 27'

---

542. Bjarkman, p. 468; Bluejayhunter.com "Acid Flashback Friday: Dave Winfield Hits a Seagull," Sept. 9, 2011.
543. The pick is documented by Peter Bjarkman to have occurred at 10:31 AM in New York on Nov 5, 1976 (Bjarkman, p. 448). A chart for the moment shows the Sun and Mercury conjunct at 13 degrees Scorpio, square to the Blue Jays' Ascendant.

shortstop. But it was Tony Fernandez who anchored the position for the Blue Jays through the 1980s. Fernandez was acquired by the Blue Jays on April 24, 1979[544] with Mercury at 6 degrees Aries conjunct to the Blue Jays' Sun in Aries. Fernandez's own birthchart has the Sun in Cancer, unusual for a shortstop, yet his Sun is conjunct to the Jays' own Mars in Cancer. His Venus and North Node are in Leo and conjunct to the Jays' Ascendant, which made Fernandez a very visible member of the team.

A square between Mars and the Sun can breed hyperactive or aggressive youth. With this aspect, the energy of Mars has difficulty finding an appropriate outlet. Interestingly, the Blue Jays' square between Mars in Cancer and the Sun in Aries did not give the team a rambunctious childhood or misfired adolescence. Instead, the Blue Jays' Mars energy was consciously channeled toward player development. As Mars rules youth, the early days of the franchise had an emphasis on player development. The franchise did not expect to win in its expansion days. The attention given to young players did upset some of the older players. Outfielder Rick Bosetti accused the Blue Jays' first manager, Roy Hartsfield, of spending all his time with rookies and ignoring the rest of the team.[545] Years later, Pat Gillick, who would enter the Hall of Fame as an executive, admitted that the organization had formulated a thought-out plan. The plan began with the stockpiling of young players. During this stage, Roy Hartsfield was maintained as manager. The second stage called for a different manager. When Bobby Mattick became manager in 1980, his role was to accelerate player development with lengthy instruction. However, he also gave more playing time to young players than they would have normally received. It was not until Bobby Cox became the manager in 1982 that Toronto became serious about winning.[546]

The development plan was successful, and the Blue Jays became competitive in less time than had most expansion teams of their era. The plan was obvious and rational, and one that new teams and businesses should emulate. But this kind of plan requires a patience that is difficult in an age that demands immediate results. The Jays were able to stick with their plan, and they successfully channeled their Mars and Aries energy to that end. The plan was bolstered by their Aquarian nature, as an Aquarius looks toward the future and also has the tenacity and integrity that come from being a fixed sign.

---

544. Topps 1990 baseball card.
545. Dewey & Acocella, pp. 555-6.
546. Bjarkman, p. 458.

The Colorado Rockies

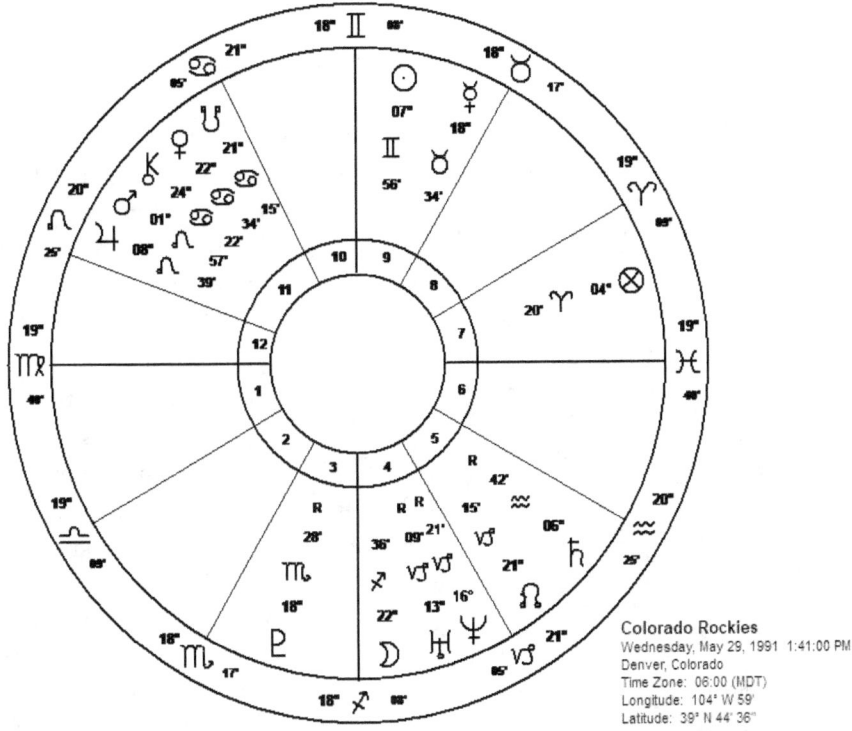

Colorado Rockies
Wednesday, May 29, 1991 1:41:00 PM
Denver, Colorado
Time Zone: 06:00 (MDT)
Longitude: 104° W 59'
Latitude: 39° N 44' 36"

The Rockies were born on May 29, 1991[547] at 1:41 pm MDT.[548] The birthchart of the Rockies has the Moon in Sagittarius, the aspect that makes the Colorado offense so strong. Although their Sun is in the pitcher's sign of Gemini, their pitchers suffer because of the opposition of Pluto to Mercury.

When they began play in 1993, Eric Young hit a home run in the first at-bat by a Rockies player in their home ballpark.[549] Also in their first year,

---

547. The decision by the NL's expansion committee to approve franchises for Colorado and Florida was made on May 29 in New York. Their decision was subsequently approved by the major league owners on June 10, 1991. (*San Francisco Chronicle*, June 11, 1991). The May 29 date has proven active for Colorado, while the June 10 date has proven active for the Marlins.
548. Author's Rectification Note: This is a relatively young franchise. Since it has relatively few historical moments to ground a rectification, I am only tentatively proceeding with this birth time. An IC of 18 Sagittarius progressed by solar arc becomes conjunct the natal Moon in 1995, the year the team moved into Coors Field. The Sun in Gemini progressed by solar arc becomes conjunct an MC of 18 Gemini in 2002, the year the humidified ball became introduced.
549. The first home game was played on April 9, 1993 at Mile High Stadium.

Andres Galaraga hit .370 and won the batting title. The Rockies quickly established an identity as a hitting team. Their high batting averages and many home runs are embodiments of their Moon in Sagittarius and their Fourth House Uranus. Rockies' bats have done amazing things. In 2000, the team batted .294. On July 30, 2010, they batted eleven consecutive hits[550] in an inning against the Cubs.

With the Moon in Sagittarius, the sign of the batter, the Rockies not only have a strong offence but play in a park that greatly favors hitters. The Rockies Fourth House of stadiums, which holds the Moon, Uranus, Neptune and the North Node, is very friendly to hitters. Uranus in the Fourth House manifests in the many homeruns hit in Denver. In 1999, the home and away teams combined to hit 303 homeruns at Coors Field. The dimensions of Coors Field are actually quite spacious. The foul lines are 347 feet, and straight away center field is 415 feet. But the wide and deep dimensions do not compensate for the thin and dry air of Denver. Many batted balls that would be simple fly-ball outs at regular altitudes become home runs in the Mile-High City. Moreover, the dimensions of Coors Field create a lot of grass for outfielders to cover. Many balls fall for hits before the outfielders can get to them.

The Rockies' home park is also influenced by Neptune in the Fourth House. Neptune brings alcohol, particularly beer. The Rockies' home park has the same name as a brand of beer. It also has a microbrewery within its confines.

Dante Bichette
Monday, November 18, 1963 12:00:00 PM
West Palm Beach, Florida
Time Zone: 05:00 (EST)
Longitude: 080° W 06' 12"
Latitude: 26° N 43' 30"

---

550. Transits for the game include the Moon, Uranus, and Jupiter conjunct in Aries opposite to Mars and Saturn conjunct in Libra. These planets made trine and sextile aspects to the Rockies Mars in Leo.

The Rockies' Sun is in Gemini, a pitcher's sign. Normally, the Sun in Gemini breeds a team with strong pitching, but Mercury, the despositor of the Rockies' Sun and the pitcher's planet, is in a difficult opposition with Pluto. This aspect is intensified by Pluto's placement in the pitcher's Third House. Like any team, the Rockies need pitching to win championships, regardless of its potent offense. The Rockies, with the Sun in Gemini, also need pitchers to ground the franchise. However, pitchers have a very challenging time in Denver, as a typical afternoon in Coors Field can greatly inflate an earned-run average. Pitchers have particular difficulty throwing breaking pitches in the thin air. Top line, veteran pitchers such as Denny Neagle and Mike Hampton, when signed by the Rockies, have met their demise in the Colorado altitude.

The Rockies, with their high-octane offense, were well-positioned to take advantage of the Juiced Ball Era of Uranus in Aquarius. When they won the Western Division in 1995, they had been playing for only three years. That year, the team had a team ERA of 4.97, the worst in the NL. Still they slugged their way to the top of the division by leading the league in runs, with 785, and homeruns, with 200.

In 2002,[551] the Rockies' organization helped its pitchers by introducing humidified baseballs. The team ERA lowered afterwards. The humidified balls are easier for pitchers to grip and cannot be hit as hard as the previously used dry ones. The Rockies won the National League pennant in 2007. That year, their pitching staff had an ERA of 4.32, eighth in the 16-team National League, demonstrating that Colorado only needs its pitchers to have middle-of-the-pack statistics. In 2009, the Rockies won the NL Wild Card with a 4.22 ERA, which was also eighth in the National League.

It will be interesting to witness how Colorado pitchers perform as the franchise matures. Pluto's opposition to Mercury will lead the staff through creative transformations.

---

551. In 2002, Uranus exited the sign of Aquarius, and the juiced ball era began to wane. The humidified baseballs at Coors Field coincided with the diminishment of Uranian energy.

The Marlins

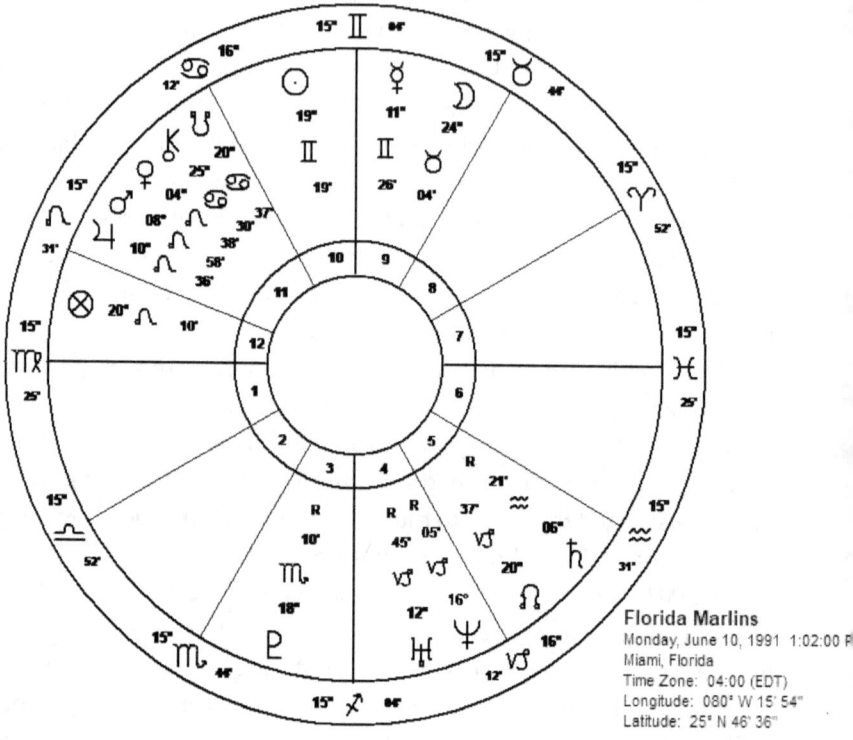

Florida Marlins
Monday, June 10, 1991 1:02:00 PM
Miami, Florida
Time Zone: 04:00 (EDT)
Longitude: 080° W 15' 54"
Latitude: 25° N 46' 36"

The Marlins were born on June 10, 1991[552] at 12:02 pm EDT.[553] The birthchart of the Marlins has the Sun and Mercury in the sign of Gemini, which has given them strong pitching. Their Moon in Taurus is opposed by Pluto in Scorpio, an aspect that has brought them extremes of both abundance and deprivation.

With the Sun, Mercury and MC conjunct in Gemini and the Ascendant in Virgo, the Marlins are strongly represented by the two pitcher's signs. As a result, the Marlins have excelled in pitching. In their brief history, four Marlins pitchers have thrown no-hitters: Al Lieter, on May 11, 1996; Kevin Brown, on June 10, 1997; A. J. Burnett, on May 12, 2001; and Anibal

---

552. The National League expansion committee awarded franchises to Colorado and Florida was made on May 29, 1991, in New York. Then their decision was approved by the Major League owners on June 10, 1991. (*San Francisco Chronicle*, June 11, 1991) The May 29 date of birth has proven active for Colorado, while the June 10 birth date has proven active for the Marlins.

553. Rectification Note: The Moon progressed by solar arc to 2012 becomes conjunct an MC of 15 Gemini in 2012, the year the team moved into a new stadium and was featured on The Franchise, a reality TV show.

Sanchez, on Sept 6, 2006. Kevin Brown also had a 1.89 ERA in 1996, a remarkably low ERA for a pitcher in the Juiced Ball Era.

The journey of the Marlins has taken them to the peaks of victory and abundance followed by fast slides into sinkholes of poverty and loss. These highs and lows are manifestations of the opposition between their Moon in Taurus and Pluto in Scorpio. The Marlins' Moon is in Taurus, a sign of wealth and abundance, but it is opposed by Pluto in Scorpio, which can scorch the earth. The Marlins are infamous for their "fire sales" in which ownership trades away players of their championship teams. Rash and impetuous owners react to the Pluto energy by razing their own teams. In only their sixth year, the Marlins won the 1997 World Series. That year, their natal Pluto of 18 Scorpio progressed by solar arc became exactly opposite their Moon of 24 Taurus. The burst of Pluto energy that brought them the World Series trophy would also drop them to the cellar the following year. The 1997 World Series championship was followed by Wayne Huizenga's fire sale, which left few of the starters from the championship team. The sale jettisoned closer Rob Nen, right hander Kevin Brown, catcher Charles Johnson, center fielder Devon White, right fielder Gary Sheffield[554] and others. The gutted 1998 team lost 108 games and finished in last place. The 2003 Marlins' World Series win was followed by the fire sale of 2005. The Marlins cut loose third baseman Mike Lowell and pitcher Josh Beckett. They also let go centerfielder Juan Pierre and second baseman Luis Castillo, the speedsters at the top of the lineup who had sparked the offence. With all the trades and free agent departures, the 2006 Marlins had only one starter left from their 2005 opening day line-up.[555] In 2012, the team did not win a World Series, but it opened a new stadium. Expectations were high, but the team floundered. In July, the team began trading players. By the next year, ownership had cut loose many of its starters, including shortstop Jose Reyes, third baseman Hanley Ramirez, and pitchers Mark Buehrle and Josh Johnson.

Before their first fire sale, the Marlins had an even darker manifestation from the Pluto-Moon opposition. Pluto is the planet of death, and even before their first game, death came calling to the Marlins. During the 1992 winter meetings, team president Carl Barger died of a ruptured abdominal aortic aneurism. Barger collapsed while a meeting was in progress.

---

554. The trade that sent catcher Charles Johnson and right fielder Gary Sheffield to Los Angeles occurred on May 15, 1998, with the Sun and Mars at 24 Taurus, conjunct the Marlins' Moon.

555. Jong, Michael: "Miami Marlins Fire Sale Comparison, 2012 vs. 2005." (Nov. 29, 2012 Fish Stripes.htm).

American League president Bobby Brown applied cardiopulmonary resuscitation to no avail. Barger's death took place on Dec. 9, 1992, while Pluto opposed the Marlins' Moon within one degree, and the Moon was conjunct to the Marlins' MC,[556] an indicator of executives.

The Marlins' birthchart has Venus, Mars and Jupiter in the sign of Leo. These three Leo planets are in opposition to Saturn in Aquarius. Planets in the sign of Leo, especially Mars, often bring ego-driven personalities. Such players can be entertaining show-offs, but they can also become me-first players more concerned with their individual statistics than the good of the team. The opposition of these Leo planets to Saturn brings such ego-driven players into conflict with managers. In the 1990s, right fielder Gary Scheffield played the role of the unhappy ego-driven player who didn't get along with management. In 2010, All-Star shortstop Hanley Ramirez would embody the self-centered Leo player. Ramirez was considered a selfish player by his teammates.[557] He also clashed with manager Fredi Gonzalez. On May 17, 2010, with Mercury at 3 degrees Taurus square to the Marlins' Mars, the planet of shortstop, Gonzalez removed the shortstop from a game for a lax effort pursuing a ball. A little more than a month later, the impatient Marlins owner Jeff Loria fired the manager because the team was not contending. Gonzalez's natal Sun and Mars in Aquarius are conjunct to the Marlins' Saturn. When he

Karl Barger Collapses
Wednesday, December 9, 1992 10:55:00 AM
Louisville, Kentucky
Time Zone: 05:00 (EST)
Longitude: 085° W 43' 24"
Latitude: 38° N 13' 18"

---

556. Barger reportedly collapsed just before 11:00 AM. At 10:55 AM in Louisville, Kentucky, Pluto was exactly conjunct the MC, and the Moon, in transit at 13 degrees, 43 minutes Gemini, was approaching an exact conjunction to the Marlins' MC, an indicator of executives. By the time Carl Barger was pronounced dead at 2:34 PM, the Moon had advanced to 15 degrees, 49 minutes Gemini, conjunct to the Marlins' MC within one degree. https://www.orlandosentinel.com/news/os-xpm-1992-12-10-9212100055-story.html

557. Associated Press: "Ramirez Won't Apologize to Teammates," May 19, 2010. http://sports.espn.go.com/mlb/news/story?id=5197935

was fired on June 23, Venus at 10 degrees Leo was conjunct the Marlins' Leo planets.

At times, the opposition has manifested in ego involvement by an owner, manager, or coach, rather than by a position player. The birthchart of Jeffrey Loria, who purchased the team in 2002, has aspects similar to those in the Marlins' birthchart. His Moon and Pluto are conjunct in Leo. They are also conjunct to the Marlins' Leo planets. The opposition between his Sun in Scorpio to Uranus in Taurus is superimposed upon the Marlins Pluto-Moon opposition in the team's birthchart. Loria would play the role of the egotistical owner who made reckless decisions when his team did not perform to his expectations. He kept the team payroll near the lowest in the league, yet he regularly fired managers when they did not meet his post-season expectations.

Jeffrey Loria
Wednesday, November 20, 1940 12:00:00 PM
New York, New York
Time Zone: 05:00 (EST)
Longitude: 073° W 59' 30"
Latitude: 40° N 45'

Ozzie Guillen, whose Mars in Aquarius is conjunct the Marlins' Saturn, was hired in 2012 as the charismatic manager who would guide the Marlins in a year of high expectations. That year, the Marlins opened a new stadium and were featured on The Franchise, a reality TV show. Soon, the outspoken Guillen alienated Miami's Cuban community when he expressed his admiration for Fidel Castro. Eventually, Guillen was criticized by his own players, and the reality show was cancelled. After only one year, Guillen was fired.

In 2013, Tino Martinez resigned as the Marlins' batting coach. Martinez verbally abused his players and reportedly assaulted one of them. Interestingly, when Martinez explained his side, he criticized the egotistical Leo side of the Marlins. Martinez claimed that the players were too self-centered to do humble tasks such as pick up balls in the batting cage.[558] Like Guillen, Martinez's natal Mars in Aquarius is conjunct to the

---

558. Rosenthal, Ken: "Martinez Speaks out about Incidents" (Fox Sports, July 30, 2013). Martinez resigned on July 28, 2013, a day when the opposition was triggered by the Sun at 5 Leo in square to Saturn at 5 Scorpio.

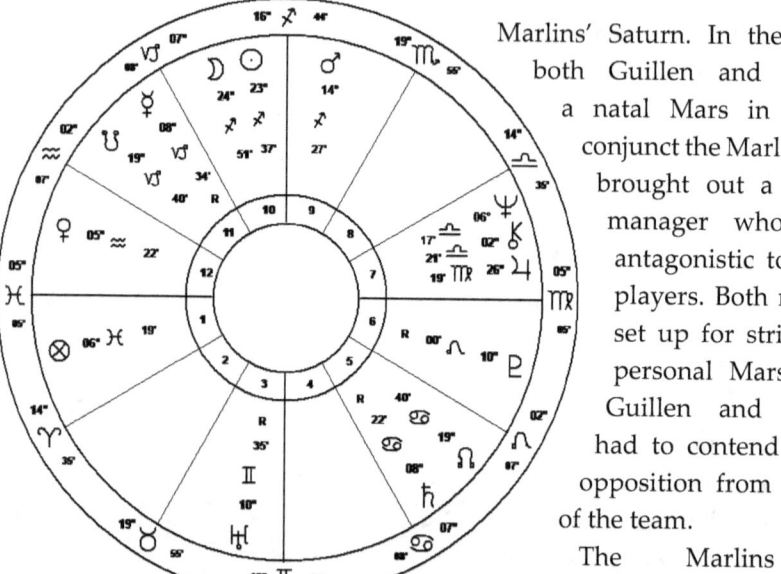

Jim Leyland
Friday, December 15, 1944 12:00:00 PM
Perrysburg, Ohio
Time Zone: 05:00 (EST)
Longitude: 083° W 38'
Latitude: 41° N 33'

Marlins' Saturn. In the cases of both Guillen and Martinez, a natal Mars in Aquarius conjunct the Marlins Saturn brought out a coach or manager who became antagonistic toward his players. Both men were set up for strife, as the personal Mars of both Guillen and Martinez had to contend with the opposition from the Mars of the team.

The Marlins have succeeded with wise and seasoned managers who were able to negotiate the opposition of its Leo planets against Saturn. These managers contained the selfish side of the players' egos, but also allowed their talents to flourish. In 1997, manager Jim Leyland brought out the best from the volatile Gary Sheffield. The birthchart of Jim Leyland, who managed the Marlins to their 1997 World Series victory, also has an opposition between Leo and Aquarius planets. His birthchart contains Venus in Aquarius opposite to Pluto in Leo. In 2003, Jack McKeon guided the team to their second World Series win. McKeon was credited with getting his players to disarm their egos.[559] The oldest manager to ever win a World Series at age 72, McKeon personified the crusty Saturnian baseball sage. Interestingly, McKeon's own birthchart contains Mars in Leo, a placement on the players' side of the Aquarius and Leo polarity. Still, McKeon was able to channel the Marlins' excess of Leo energy into a World Series winner.

---

559. Pitcher Carl Pavano said this about Jack McKeon: "He was able to disarm a lot of our egos, so we were able to put them aside, and that's tough to do throughout a season." (Morgan, Joe "McKeon, Marlins' 2003 Squad Back in Miami" Aug. 4, 2013, MLB.com)

The Tampa Bay Rays

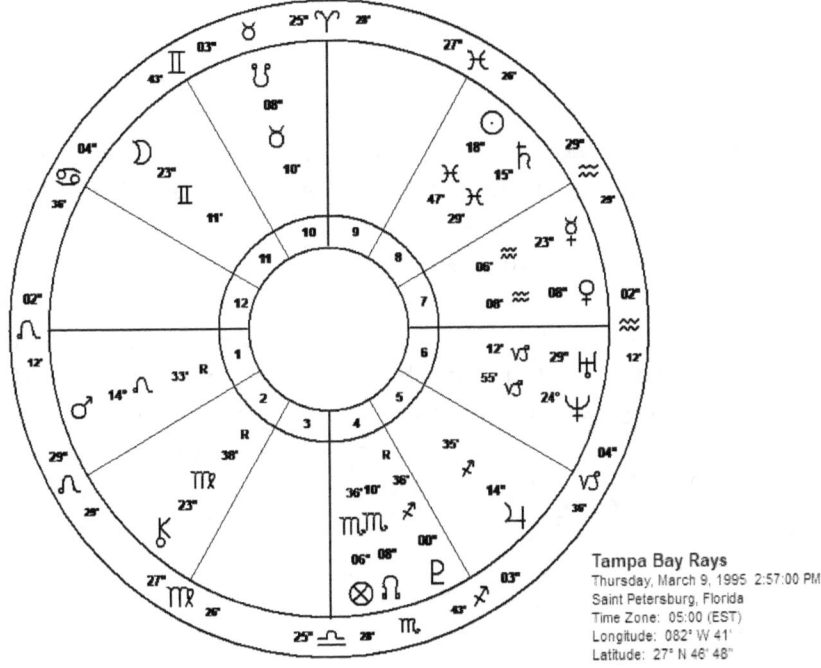

Tampa Bay Rays
Thursday, March 9, 1995 2:57:00 PM
Saint Petersburg, Florida
Time Zone: 05:00 (EST)
Longitude: 082° W 41'
Latitude: 27° N 46' 48"

Along with their twin, the Diamondbacks, the Tampa Bay Rays were born on March 9, 1995[560] at 2:57 pm EST.[561] The franchise was called the Devil Rays until 2008, when they changed their name to the Rays. Their birthchart has the Sun and Saturn conjunct in the sign of Pisces, an aspect that mired them in their early years. The Moon in Gemini is trine to Mercury in Aquarius, a trine of air energy that generates bold ideas.

The Devil Rays were born under difficult conditions. On the day of their birth, Major League Baseball was mired in a very long strike. Players and owners had dug into uncompromising positions, and the previous year's World Series had been cancelled. The conjunction of the Sun and Saturn in Pisces reflects the moribund energy surrounding baseball that

---

560. http://en.wikipedia.org/wiki/Tampa_Bay_Rays
561. Rectification Note: An Ascendant of 2 degrees Leo, progressed by solar arc, becomes conjunct the First House Mars in November of 2007, when the franchise changes its name and uniforms. An MC of 25 Aries becomes loosely conjunct the South Node of 6 Taurus in October of 2005, when Stuart Sternberg becomes the majority owner.

spring. A Pisces can succumb to depression when surrounded by negative circumstances. With Saturn blocking the Sun, there was little sunshine on the baseball world when the Rays were born. Also, the region of Tampa Bay had begun litigation against Major League Baseball. The city of St Petersburg was suing over the aborted move of the Giants to their city in 1993. In addition, Congress was again debating whether to revoke baseball's antitrust exemption.[562] As the strike wore on, there was little sympathy for organized baseball. Beneath these storm clouds, Major League Baseball gave birth to the Devil Rays to mollify the politicians and the city of St. Petersburg. The square from Jupiter in Sagittarius to the Rays' Sun and Saturn mirrors the legal challenges that helped midwife the team.

Unlike their twin, the Diamondbacks, the Rays had a long road to travel before their first winning season. The Rays finished almost all of their first ten years in last place. Only in 2004 did they finish above the cellar, and that year they finished only fourth in the five-team AL East. In many ways, the early Rays resembled the Cubs.[563] Both teams have the Sun in Pisces. Like the Cubs, the early Rays would finish a lopsided number of years in last place. Pisces, the last sign of the zodiac, rules last place. Oddly, in its early days, the franchise was looking backward rather than forward. The early rosters of the Devil Rays were stacked with established players on the downsides of their careers, such as Wade Boggs, Mo Vaughn, and Jose Canseco. Most expansion teams emphasize prospects and youth rather than fading veterans. But the Rays are a Pisces, and the last sign prefers to look back.

Vince Naimoli
Thursday, September 16, 1937 12:00:00 PM
Paterson, New Jersey
Time Zone: 04:00 (EDT)
Longitude: 074° W 09' 54"
Latitude: 40° N 55' 18"

---

562. Jackson, Robert L. "Threat to Antitrust Exemption: Baseball Congressional Committee Approves Legislation that would partly Remove Protection of Owners from Suits by Players." (*Los Angeles Times*, Sept. 30, 1994.)

563. The Cubs Sun of 17 degrees 49 minutes Pisces is conjunct to the Devil Rays' Sun of 18 degrees Pisces within one degree. Similarly, the Cubs Mercury of 21 degrees, 55 minutes Aquarius is conjunct to the Rays' Mercury of 23 degrees Aquarius.

The Sun conjunct Saturn also brought an oppressive owner. Vince Naimoli, the Rays' earliest owner, ran the team without an understanding of the business of baseball. Notorious for his tyrannical and penny-pinching ways, he did not allow fans to bring their own food to Tropicana Field. He would even fire ushers who had allowed food to be sneaked into the ballpark. Naimoli's birthchart shows uneasy aspects with the Rays' Sun-and-Saturn conjunction. His Sun, Mercury and Neptune in Virgo are opposite the Rays' Sun and Saturn in Pisces, while his Mars in Sagittarius is square to the Rays' Pisces planets. The square from Mars brought out his anger and aggression. Niomoli's Virgo planets, when placed within the Rays' birthchart, occupy their Second House of finance. Virgo planets in a Second House can manifest in a nitpickiness and severity over money. Niomoli's unwillingness to provide an adequate payroll did not help the team rise from the cellar.

A lot changed for the Devil Rays in 2005. That year, their IC progressed by solar arc became conjunct their Part of Fortune and the North Node. Stuart Sternberg bought a controlling share of the franchise in 2005.[564] That same year, Joe Maddon was hired as the field manager. Maddon's Sun and Venus in Aquarius are conjunct the Rays' Mercury. Maddon's Aquarian energy brought fresh air to a franchise accustomed to the dark waters of last place. In 2006, Madden declared he wanted to be around free thinkers. He wore a t-shirt that stated, "Tell me what you think, not what you've heard."[565] The Aquarian Maddon used elaborate computer models to determine his defensive shifts, bringing alignments to a more sophisticated level.[566] At times,

Joe Maddon
Monday, February 8, 1954 12:00:00 PM
Hazletown, Pennsylvania
Time Zone: 05:00 (EST)
Longitude: 075° W 58'
Latitude: 40° N 58'

---

564. Sternberg took control on Oct. 6, 2005 while Jupiter & Mercury were conjunct the Rays' IC.
565. Atkins, Hunter: "Rays' Joe Maddon: King of Shifts," *New York Times*, May 7, 2012.
566. These elaborate shifts, invented by the Rays, were soon copied by the rest of the

he daringly used four outfielders. These shifts tightened his defense. Soon the Ray's pitching improved as well. Under Madden, the Rays were able to manifest the outstanding pitching latent in the trine of their Gemini Moon to their Mercury in Aquarius.

Joe Maddon lifted the Rays with his unorthodox strategy. He also inspired them with his odd Aquarian persona. His thick-rimmed glasses made him look like a scientist in addition to a baseball man. Maddon welcomed original thinkers and listened to his players.[567] In 2008, he used a quirky math equation as an inspirational slogan for the team. The equation 9=8 was a head-scratcher, yet it inspired his team. Maddon's slogan meant: nine players playing together for nine innings become one of eight teams in the playoffs.[568] Inspirational slogans generally contain Neptunian language about the power of believing. Maddon's slogan was odd in its use of the Uranian language of math.

The year 2008 was a watershed year for the franchise. That year, their Ascendant, progressed by solar arc, became conjunct their First House Mars in Leo. The team that had been lethargic for many years suddenly found its vitality when its Ascendant progressed to Mars. Tampa Bay received new logos and a new mascot. The name Devil Rays was let go. Devil Rays had been a good name for a Pisces team, as Devil Rays are fish that swim in deep waters. Unfortunately, deep waters for Tampa Bay had corresponded to the deep end of the standings. Their name was changed to "The Rays," and the new uniforms contained a sunburst logo. Stuart Sternberg stated that the team had become "a beacon that radiates throughout Tampa Bay and across the entire state of Florida."[569] This is justified language for the progression of a Leo Ascendant to a Leo planet. Leo rules the Sun. One may even say Leo rules beacons and light.

In 2008, the Rays not only had their first winning season, but they won their first pennant. Transits for 2008 included Uranus in Pisces conjunct to the team's Sun and Saturn, and Neptune in Aquarius conjunct with the team's Mercury. First baseman Carlos Peña channeled the Neptune energy with 102 RBIs.

In 2018, the Rays again made use of their inventive Aquarius planets when they began the practice of a closing pitcher starting a game. With

---

League.
567. Stark, Jayson: "Manny Ramirez's voice being heard" (espn.com. March 22, 2011).
568. Ghiroli, Brittany "Maddon uses 9=8 slogan to motivate." (MLB.com, 07/03/08)
569. Tampabay.rays.mlb.com: "Time to shine: Rays introduce new name, new icon, new team colors and new uniforms" (Nov. 8, 2007)

this strategy, the reliever pitches only one inning and then hands the ball to a regular starter. Sometimes the game is pitched entirely by relievers. The strategy proved effective and was soon copied by other baseball teams. It began when Sergio Romo, normally a closer, began a game in Anaheim on May 19, 2018. Transits for the game include a t-square of Uranus in Taurus, Mars in Aquarius, and the Moon in Leo. Uranus, the planet of innovation, was positioned at 0 degrees Taurus, while Mars in Aquarius was conjunct to the Rays' Descendant from 1-degree Aquarius. The Moon, meanwhile, was positioned at 1-degree Leo and conjunct the Rays' Ascendant.[570]

The brief history of the Rays demonstrates how a team mired in a swamp of losing energy can suddenly emerge a winner when the qualities of its birthchart unfold.

---

570. At times, the Ascendant corresponds to a lead-off hitter. This game suggests that the Ascendant may also correspond to a starting pitcher.

The Arizona Diamondbacks

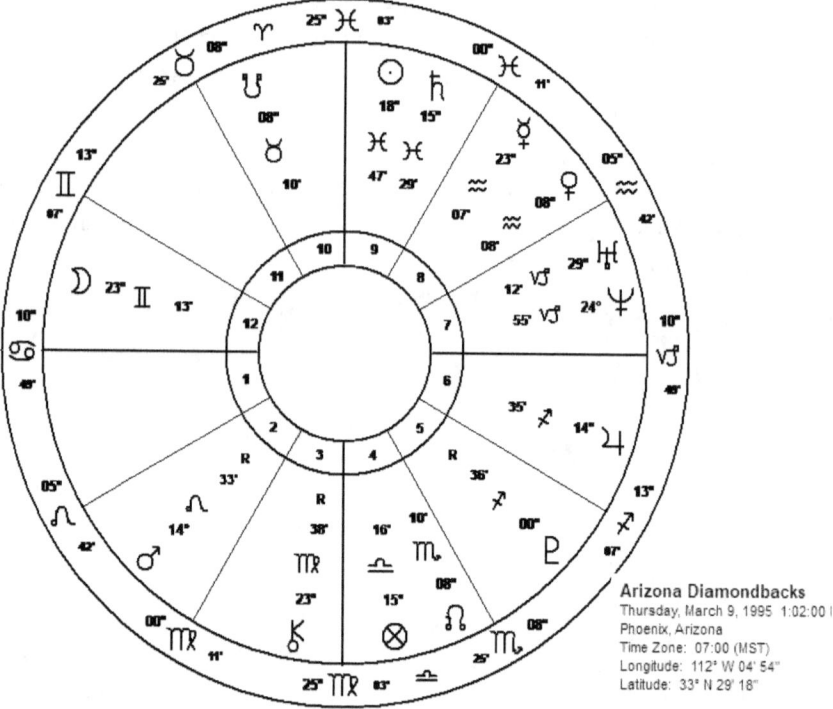

Arizona Diamondbacks
Thursday, March 9, 1995 1:02:00
Phoenix, Arizona
Time Zone: 07:00 (MST)
Longitude: 112° W 04' 54"
Latitude: 33° N 29' 18"

The Arizona Diamondbacks were born on March 9, 1995[571] at 1:02 pm[572] MST, a few minutes after their twin franchise, the Rays. Their birthchart has the Sun and Saturn conjunct in the sign of Pisces, bringing them strength at the first base position. Their Second House holds Mars in Leo, the aspect that has made them aggressive spenders.

The Diamondbacks quickly established themselves as contenders. In their second season of 1999, the team won 100 games. In their fourth season of 2001, the team won the World Series. Much of their success was due to

---

571. http://en.wikipedia.org/wiki/History_of_the_Arizona_Diamondbacks
572. Author's rectification note: Twin franchises are usually born simultaneously, but it appears the Diamondbacks were born a few minutes after the Devil Rays. Their Sun progressed by solar arc becomes conjunct an MC of 25 Pisces near November of 2001, when they won their first World Series. Their Saturn progressed by solar arc becomes conjunct an MC of 25 Pisces in 2004, the year of financial problems and ownership changes.

the financing of owner Jerry Colangelo, who spent lavishly on free agents. In their first year, the Arizona roster included frontline players such as third baseman Matt Williams, second baseman Jay Bell, and right-hander Andy Benes. In their second year, the spending continued as Arizona signed center fielder Steve Finley and left-hander Randy Johnson. The Diamondbacks have Mars in the Second House of finances, an aspect which manifests in an intense desire to have. Indeed, the Diamondbacks' strong desire was to have a World Series trophy. The Diamondbacks' Mars is also in the sign of Leo, an aspect that can bring forcefulness and arrogance. Not content to wait through the losing seasons, which is the usual cycle of an expansion team, Arizona pushed to become an instant contender.

The payroll of the 2001 team was ostensibly $85 million, but behind that figure was much more in deferred compensation. The Diamondbacks were able to finance their World Series team by backloading contracts with payments to be made at future dates. In 2004, the chickens came home to roost, when Neptune, in transit through Aquarius, formed an opposition to the Diamondbacks' free-spending Mars. Similarly, the Diamondbacks' Mars had progressed by solar arc to an opposition with Mercury in the Eighth House. Planets in the Eighth House can bring profound financial changes. Here, Mercury the Messenger served as the bill collector. Arizona was paying bucketfuls of money to players no longer on the team, and the franchise found itself in deep financial trouble. Soon Jerry Colangelo was ousted by the minority owners.[573] The team on the field lost 111 games and fell to last place.

Jerry Colangelo
Monday, November 20, 1939 12:00:00 PM
Chicago Heights, Ill
Time Zone: 06:00 (CST)
Longitude: 087° W 38'
Latitude: 41° N 30'

---

573. Colangelo was ousted in Aug. 6, 2004, with the Sun at 14 Leo conjunct Arizona's Mars and Neptune at 14 Aquarius opposite to Arizona's Mars.

A Sun and Saturn conjunction is normally a challenging aspect. The Diamondbacks were born during the strike of 1994 and 1995, but the early Arizona team did not succumb to the mired Saturnian energy of the strike as the Rays did. Instead, the early Diamondbacks were at the center of a league realignment controversy. Saturn rules structures such as the divisions within the leagues. When the expansion class of 1995 was born, Major League Baseball specified that Arizona would join the NL West, yet in 1997, then Acting-Commissioner Bud Selig proposed "radical realignment," which would place Arizona in the American League. Arizona stayed stubborn in its intent to join the NL West, and it got its way. The newborn team's ability to maintain its integrity in this conflict against established teams reflected the strength of the team's Sun-Saturn conjunction.

With the Sun in Pisces, it is poetic that the first Diamondback to establish himself would be a first baseman, the Pisces position. In their first game on March 31, 1998, first baseman Travis Lee claimed the first Diamondbacks hit, a single in the first inning. He also hit their first homerun and first RBI. Unlike the many free agents signed, Lee was a homegrown Diamondback from their farm system who made his rookie debut that day. Lee's birthchart has Mercury in Gemini conjunct Arizona's Moon. The Diamondbacks' first game is also notable for the two disc jockeys with scuba tanks at the bottom of the centerfield pool. The two had sworn they would remain underwater until the first Diamondbacks' homerun.[574] Fortunately, Lee hit his home run in the sixth inning. The game began[575] with Neptune conjunct the IC and square the Ascendant, as Neptune rules swimming pools.

There is an interesting affinity between the Diamondbacks and the

Travis Lee
Monday, May 26, 1975 12:00:00 PM
San Diego, California
Time Zone: 07:00 (PDT)
Longitude: 117° W 07' 48"
Latitude: 32° N 44' 54"

---

574. Gloster, Rob: "In Ariz., Swim While Watching a Game." (*Associated Press*, April 1, 1998, www.apnewsarchive.com
575. March 31, 1998, 8:22 pm MST in Phoenix.

Chicago Cubs.[576] Not only is Arizona a region to which many people from Chicago have relocated, but the Cubs and the Diamondbacks both have the Sun in Pisces and Mercury in Aquarius.[577] First baseman Mark Grace was an important part of both teams at the Pisces position. The Diamondbacks' Cancer Ascendant is conjunct within one degree to the Cubs' IC of 11 degrees Cancer. Interestingly, the idea that led to the Diamondbacks was born at Wrigley Field. It was at a Cubs game that Jerry Colangelo thought to acquire a baseball franchise.[578]

The Diamondbacks' outstanding pitching is an embodiment of their Moon in Gemini trine to Mercury in Aquarius. Randy Johnson won four consecutive Cy Young awards from 1999 to 2002 in a Diamondbacks uniform. Brandon Webb won the Cy Young for Arizona in 2006. Then, in 2011, Ian Kennedy nearly won the award while posting a 2.88 ERA and a 21-4 record.

The first Diamondbacks player to have his number retired was Luis Gonzalez. The left fielder drove home the winning run in the 2001 World Series. A fan favorite, Gonzalez's birthchart shows his affinity with the team. His natal Uranus, the planet of left fielders, is positioned at 23 degrees Virgo, which is conjunct the Arizona IC, an indicator of the fans.

Luis Gonzalez
Sunday, September 3, 1967 12:00:00 PM
Tampa, Florida
Time Zone: 04:00 (EDT)
Longitude: 082° W 27' 54"
Latitude: 27° N 58' 12"

Although the Diamondbacks and Rays are twin franchises, the differences in their character and their paths are striking. These dissimilarities mirror their distinct Rising Signs and house placements.

---

576. Such strong affinities between teams born in different eras are rare. The other examples are the synastries between the Braves with the Brewers; and the original AL Senators with the Rangers.
577. The Cubs' Sun of 17 degrees 49 minutes Pisces is conjunct to the Diamondbacks' Sun of 18 degrees Pisces within one degree. The Cubs Mercury of 21 degrees, 55 minutes Aquarius is conjunct to the Diamondbacks' Mercury of 23 degrees Aquarius.
578. http://en.wikipedia.org/wiki/Jerry_Colangelo

It will be interesting to observe whether their paths, which diverged so sharply at their teams' births, become parallel in the future.

PART III

Transits

This section provides the lenses with which to witness the manifestations of astrological transits within baseball games. The ideas of Part I and the birthcharts of Part II are employed to analyze specific games. Famous games are examined.

Each baseball game unfolds as a manifestation of the transits and aspects that occur as the game is played. When a planet in transit forms an aspect to a sensitive degree in a baseball team's birthchart, an effect is manifest on the field of play. A baseball team is a vessel that absorbs and channels planetary energies. Each baseball team reacts to the energy of the planets in transit according to the features of its birthchart. The team usually channels the transits in a positive manner, harnessing the planets to its benefit. Certain transits, however, are disruptive. A transit from a disharmonious angle may interfere with a team's regular operations. Likewise, a transit from a planet that is antithetical to a team's general energy often proves disruptive. For example, teams with a Mercury emphasis often respond poorly to Neptune transits.

Seemingly random things happen in baseball games. A weak hitter will hit three homeruns. A gold glove fielder makes a costly error. A disproportionate number of balls are hit to a specific position. Such supposedly random events have a logic that is understood by an analysis of the transits. An astrological chart cast for a game contains keys to the ensuing drama. Such a chart points to which players will become the main actors for that game. Most players are not called to center stage every day. Even Hall-of-Fame players who are consistent over the course of years are not the primary actors of every game. Supporting players, such as utility infielders and number nine hitters, are placed into center roles when the transits call them.

Transits in Games

Within the long baseball season—which includes Spring Training, 162 regular-season games, the post-season and the World Series—numerous players will be key actors in the outcomes of many different games. Star players affect the course of games more often than others, but different players will move into the lead roles on different days. In one game, the center fielder will hit for the cycle, while the next day he or she will do little of note, yet the third baseman will hit a three-run homer and make a game-saving catch. It is the planetary transits that influence which players will be the most significant players within a specific game. Those players who are central to that day's drama are the ones whose positions correspond to the planets involved in that day's most prominent transits, specifically the transits that occur during the two or three hours of game time. Such players make the key hits or provide critical defensive plays.

When a planet within a team's birthchart undergoes a transit, the player that represents the team's planet is affected. Players also embody the planets making the transits. When a transiting planet makes an aspect to a sensitive degree within a team's birthchart, the player who embodies the planet in transit is also affected. Thus, the key players in a game are both those that represent the planets in the team's birthchart undergoing the transit and those players who represent the planets making the transits. For example, when the Sun in transit is conjunct to a team's natal Neptune, the right fielder, as a representative of the Sun, and the first baseman, as a representative of Neptune, receive the transit. The right fielder and first baseman will be main actors in the game. When the Moon, in transit, is square to a team's natal Pluto, that team's catcher and third baseman are affected. When transiting Mars is trine to a team's natal Venus, the shortstop, second baseman, and center fielder are affected.

Baseball players who are affected by transits usually enjoy a marked improvement in their play. The effects of the transit are noticeable in both a player's hitting and fielding. If the aspect is a disruptive one, however, the players may commit errors or bat poorly. A quality player is more likely to respond positively to transits than is an average or Mendoza-line player. Sometimes, the effects of a transit are too subtle and not discernable. A dominant pitcher may overpower an entire team, making a day's transits to the other team's members unnoticeable on the field. Nevertheless, if one has access to the clubhouse or dugout, one could likely witness the emotional effects of transits on particular players. Also, a team may be so mired in a slump that a given day's favorable transits cannot penetrate its doldrums. Such prolonged slumps are caused by outer-planet transits in challenging aspects to points in a team's natal chart.

ORBS

A planet in transit that is near enough to a natal planet to cause an effect is said to be "within orb." An "orb" is the distance, measured in degrees of the zodiac, from which a transiting planet will affect a natal planet. The widths of orbs vary according to their aspects. Most astrological textbooks describe an orb of 8 degrees as operational for transits. If the Sun or Moon is involved, the orb increases to 10 or 12 degrees. Orbs are smaller, however, for the minor aspects of the sextile and semi-square, which are 5 or 6 degrees width. The orbs of transits to the birthcharts of baseball teams, however, are much smaller than the orbs of transits to the birthcharts of individuals. The widths of a team's orbs are usually only 1 degree. If the transiting Moon is involved, the orb can be slightly larger, as wide as 2 or 3 degrees.

The Aspects

The aspects that cause the most discernable affects to a baseball game are the conjunction, square, trine, opposition and quincunx. Sextiles are less noticeable. However, any aspect that is a multiple of 15 degrees, such as the semi-sextile of 30 degrees, the semi-square of 45 degrees, and the sesquiquadrate of 135 degrees, can bring an observable effect.

Squares and oppositions are not likely to be malefics to a baseball team. A team can thrive off of such challenging aspects. A square or opposition, however, is more likely to manifest in poor play or an injury when formed to a planet in a mutable sign. Similarly, if a square or opposition is formed to a planet of a mutable nature such as Mercury and Neptune, it will more likely manifest as a malefic.

Examples of Transits from History

Transits involving the Sun affect the right fielder. On June 10, 1959, Mercury, in transit at 28 degrees Gemini, formed a quincunx to the Cleveland Indians' natal Sun of 28 degrees Scorpio. Right fielder Rocky Colavito hit four home runs against Baltimore.[579] On April 13, 1965, the Sun, in transit at 23 degrees Aries, formed a square to the Tigers' natal Venus in Capricorn. Right fielder Al Kaline had 5 RBIs in an 11-4 Tiger win over the Athletics.[580] On May 17, 1995; the Sun, in transit at 27 degrees Taurus, formed a trine to the Texas Rangers' Moon of 27 Capricorn. Rangers' right fielder Jack Voigt had two hits that included a home run.

Transits involving a team's either natal Moon or IC and transits from the Moon usually result in a significant day for the team's catcher. On July 1, 1948, the Sun, in transit at 9 degrees Cancer, formed a square to the Dodgers natal Moon of 9 degrees Libra. Catcher Roy Campanella

---

579. *Day by Day in Cleveland Indians History*, p. 90.
580. *This Date in Tiger's History*, p. 22.

made his rookie debut, hitting a double and two singles.[581] On June 7, 1970, the Sun, in transit at 16 degrees Gemini, was conjunct to the Reds' natal Moon. Johnny Bench had 5 RBIs as the Reds beat the Mets 10-2 at Crosley Field.[582] On October 3, 1993, the Sun, in transit at 10 degrees Libra, formed a conjunction with the Dodger's natal Moon. Mike Piazza, then a rookie catcher, hit two home runs and had four RBIs against the Giants.[583] Watch for a play at the plate on days with strong lunar aspects. If the team undergoing a lunar transit is playing at home, the stadium crowd may become a factor in the game. Fans can run on the field. The crowd may be extra large or rowdy.[584]

Transits from Mercury affect the player representing the planet receiving the aspect in the natal chart. On July 31, 1956, Mercury, in transit at 20 degrees Leo, formed a square to the Dodger's Pluto. Jackie Robinson, playing third base, had all three Dodger RBIs in a 3-2 win over the Braves.[585] On May 9, 1967, Mercury, in transit at 16 degrees Taurus, was conjunct to the Cubs' Pluto. Third Baseman Ron Santo had 5 hits in 5 at-bats as Chicago beat San Francisco 10-2.[586] On Sept. 25, 1997, Mercury, in transit at 19 degrees Virgo, was conjunct to the Houston Astros' Moon. Brad Ausmus, the Astros' catcher, hit a three-run homer as the Astros clinched the NL Central Division, beating the Padres 9-1.

Transits to the natal Mercury of a team's birthchart affect a team's pitchers.[587] Such an aspect will affect not only of the starting pitcher, but the relievers as well. A transit from a favorable angle will likely enhance the pitchers' performances. A transit from a difficult angle often proves disruptive. A natal Mercury is sensitive and easily affected. Since Mercury has a mutable nature, it is very receptive to transits. A Mars transit from a challenging aspect to a team's Mercury will likely disrupt the pitchers. When Mercury becomes retrograde, the first day of this period is often marked by players making errors. Certain pitchers have Mercury retrograde in their birthcharts. These pitchers generally improve their performances when Mercury is retrograde.

Transits involving Venus affect the center fielder and the second

---

581. Gewecke, Cliff, *Day by Day in Dodgers History*, p. 42.
582. *Day by Day in Cincinnati Reds History*, p. 49.
583. *Los Angeles Times*, Oct. 4, 1993: The Dodgers won the game 11-1, knocking the Giants out of first place in the NL Western Division on the last scheduled game of the seson.
584. See Chicago White Sox Chapter and Disco Demolition Night.
585. Gewecke, Cliff: *Day by Day in Dodgers History*, p. 52.
586. *This Date in Cubs History*, p. 21.
587. See section on no-hitters.

baseman. On April 24, 1931, Venus, in transit at 28 degrees Pisces, formed a square to the Cubs' natal Saturn in Sagittarius. Cubs' second baseman and player-manager Rogers Hornsby hit three consecutive home runs and had eight RBIs in a 10-6 Cubs victory over Pittsburgh.[588] On August 15, 1919, Venus, in transit at 26 degrees Virgo, formed a trine to the White Sox' Jupiter in Taurus. Center fielder Happy Felsch set a record with four outfield assists.[589] On June 9, 1912, Venus, in transit at 11 degrees Gemini, formed a square to the Red Sox' natal Mars in Virgo. Tris Speaker, playing center field for the Red Sox, hit for the cycle.[590] On September 16, 1974, the Sun in transit at 23 degrees Virgo formed a conjunction to the Pirates natal Venus. Second baseman Rennie Stennett hit 7 for 7 against the Cubs.[591]

Mars transits affect the shortstop. On July 25, 1908, Mars, in transit at 11 degrees Leo, formed a square to the Pirates' natal Saturn. Shortstop Honus Wagner went 5 for 5. On September 23, 1936, Mars, in transit at 28 degrees Leo, was square to the White Sox' Sun. Shortstop Luke Appling not only hit a home run, a double and two singles, but overtook Cleveland's Earl Averill for the AL batting title.[592] On July 7, 1978, Mars, in transit at 13 degrees Virgo, was conjunct the Tigers' natal Uranus. Tiger shortstop Alan Trammell went 5-for-6 against the Rangers.[593] Game Six of the 1997 World Series occured on October 25, 1997. That night, the Sun, in transit at 2 degrees Scorpio, was conjunct to the Indians' Mars. Shortstop Omar Visquel hit a double and stole two bases against the Marlins. With the bases loaded, Visquel made a diving stop of a ground ball to the hole, preventing two runs from scoring.

The transits from the middle and outer planets are less discernible in particular games. The effects of the middle and outer planet transits are more strikingly observed in the statistics for the duration of the transit. The player representing the outer planet in transit and the player representing the natal planet undergoing the transit will experience significant changes in their batting averages in the course of the transit. For their energy to be harnessed in a specific game, middle and outer-planet transits generally need an additional aspect from an inner planet. For example, Pluto in transit may conjunct to a team's natal Sun within a one-degree orb, but its effect on a particular day's game will likely not be seen unless an inner

---

588. *This Date in Cubs History*, p. 16.
589. *This Date in White Sox History*, p. 58.
590. *Triumphs and Tragedies in Red Sox History*, p. 19.
591. www.baseball-reference.com
592. *This Date in White Sox History*, p. 70.
593. *This Date in Tigers' History*, p. 49.

planet such as the Moon is also making an aspect to the team's natal Sun. However, the transits to the middle and outer planet within a team's birthchart are easily observed, when the inner planets of the sky make aspects to them.

Games with aspects to a natal Jupiter are favorable to hitters, often bringing high scores.[594] In the American League, the designated hitter is specifically affected. In the National League, Jupiter aspects affect the team's offense as a whole. On September 23, 1997, the Sun, in transit at 0 degrees Libra, formed a square to the Rangers' natal Jupiter of 0 degrees Capricorn. The Rangers scored 14 runs against the A's in Oakland, defeating them 14-6. Designated hitter Juan Gonzalez had four RBIs and a home run, while right fielder Alex Diaz had three RBIs and a home run.

Games with aspects to a natal Saturn bring a variety of manifestations that include injuries. On May 2, 1970, the Sun and Saturn, conjunct at 12 degrees Taurus, formed an opposition to the Phillies' Moon of 12 degrees Scorpio. Two Phillies' catchers, Tim McCarver and Mike Ryan, broke their hands in the sixth inning of a 3-1 loss in San Francisco.[595]

Saturn, the ruler of time, will often wait until late in the game to make his entrance. On Saturn-aspected days, extra-inning games are likely. Saturn also rules comebacks. On June 12, 1967, the Sun, in transit at 21 degrees Gemini, formed a trine to the White Sox' Saturn; The White Sox would play a game that lasted six hours and 38 minutes, ultimately defeating the Senators 6-5 in a game that took 22 innings.[596] On May 4, 1973, Venus, in transit at 20 degrees Taurus, was conjunct to the Phillies' Saturn. The Phillies played a 20-inning game against Atlanta, beating them 5-4.[597]

Saturn transits also bring grand slams.[598] On July 29, 1915, Saturn in transit at 9 degrees Cancer, formed a conjunction with the Pirates' Mars. Shortstop Honus Wagner, then a 41-year-old Saturnian veteran, hit a grand slam.[599] On October 3, 1997, Saturn was in transit at 17 degrees Aries. At 7:04 pm PDT in San Francisco, while Saturn was rising and conjunct the Ascendant, the Marlins' Devon White hit a grand slam to win the last

---

594. See Famous Games Chapter: Cubs 26 - Phillies 23 and Blue Jays 15 - Phillies 14
595. *This Date in Phillies History* p. 30
596. *This Date in White Sox History*, p. 39.
597. *This Date in Phillies History*, p. 30.
598. Saturn rules the grandslam. The adjective "grand" signifies "old" and "before," Saturnian qualities. Four runs score in a grandslam. The number four is a manifestation of Saturn. (See Chapter 5.)
599. *This Date in Pirates History*, p. 51. (Another significant transit for July 29, 1915 was Mars at 17 degrees Gemini square to the Pirates' Uranus. Mars rules shortstops.)

game of the 1997 Division Series against the Giants. The most grand slams ever hit on a single day occurred on Aug. 9, 1999.[600] That day, 5 grand slams were hit in both leagues, as Saturn at 16 degrees Taurus was part of a grand cross that included the Sun at 16 degrees Leo, Mars at 16 degrees Scorpio, and Uranus at 14 degrees Aquarius. Saturn transits also bring comebacks, clutch performances, and championship wins.[601]

Games with Uranus transits highlight the left fielder. On July 20, 1961, Mars, in transit at 13 degrees Uranus, formed a conjunction to the Tigers' natal Uranus. Left fielder Rocky Colavito hit 2 home runs and 5 RBIs in a 15-8 Tiger win against the Orioles.[602] On July 18, 1969, Venus in transit at 13 degrees Gemini formed a square to the Tigers' natal Uranus in Virgo. Left fielder Willie Horton had 11 putouts, which tied a record for putouts by an outfielder. Horton also hit a two-run homer.[603] On May 9, 1995, Mercury, in transit at 9 degrees Gemini, formed an opposition to the Athletics' natal Uranus. Geronimo Beroa, playing left field for Oakland, had four hits that included a home run.

Neptune-aspected days emphasize the first basemen. On June 3, 1951, the Sun, in transit at 12 degrees Gemini, formed a conjunction to the Indians' Neptune. First baseman Luke Easter hit three home runs as the Indians swept the Yankees in a double header.[604] On September 14, 1957, Mercury in transit at 12 degrees Virgo formed a square to the Indians' natal Neptune. First baseman Vic Wertz had seven RBIs in two innings in a 13-10 loss to the Red Sox.[605]

Days in which Neptune is heavily aspected can also bring lost concentration and errors to a team. Such errors are likely to occur at the hand of the first baseman and the position representing the planet in aspect with Neptune. When slow-moving Neptune makes transits of a lengthy duration at difficult angles, it can bring long periods of lost focus and diminished intensity to a team.[606]

Pluto-aspected days feature third basemen. On September 2, 1918, Mars, in transit at 10 degrees Scorpio, was conjunct to the White Sox' MC. Mars also formed a quincunx to the White Sox Pluto of 10 degrees Gemini. In a Sox double header, third baseman Buck Weaver would have 8 hits in

---

600. http://articles.latimes.com/1999/aug/10/sports/sp-64493
601. See "Saturn in the Post Season" Chapter.
602. *This Date in Tigers' History*, p. 53
603. *This Date in Tigers' History*, p. 52.
604. *Day by Day in Cleveland Indians History*, p. 85.
605. *Day by Day in Cleveland Indians History*, p. 168.
606. See Reds' Chapter

10 at-bats. On June 2, 1950, Mars, in transit at 27 degrees Virgo, formed a trine to the Tigers' natal Pluto. Third baseman George Kell hit for the cycle against the Athletics. [607] On July 3 and 4 of 1977, Mars, in transit at 20 and 21 degrees Taurus, formed a conjunction to the Dodgers' natal Pluto. Third baseman Ron Cey had five hits on July 3, and he would have three more hits on July 4.[608]

AXES CONJUNCT TO THE PLANETS

Most of the scoring in a baseball game occurs when an axis is conjunct to a planet. When the Ascendant, Descendant, MC or IC is conjunct to a planet, batters are much more likely to get hits or reach base. This orb of opportunity is usually one degree, the same as the orb of transits to planets. Only a small window exists as the degrees rapidly change on the axes. Indeed, it usually takes 7 minutes for a degree on an axis to change. Nevertheless, when the Moon is conjunct an axis, the orb expands to 2 or 3 degrees. If a planet is square or trine an axis, such an aspect can also result in base runners, but these aspects are not as consistently productive as the conjunction.

Baseball is a game of lulls, long periods where little of significance appears to happen. No one gets a hit or reaches base. Then, suddenly, a team erupts for multiple hits and scores runs. A team's batting average is usually in a range between .230 and .280. With such an average, a team would likely get a little less than one hit an inning. Yet teams generally string their hits together in the same inning in order to score. They are able to string their hits because, in certain innings, the rotation of the zodiac wheel brings planets into conjunction with the Ascendant, Descendant, MC or IC. Usually, an axis is conjunct a planet for about the length of a half inning, long enough for a team to score.

If a player is at bat while his representative planet is conjunct an axis: rising, setting, or conjunct the MC or IC, his chances of getting a hit or providing a dramatic moment greatly increase. Catcher Mike Piazza hit a clutch two-out RBI single with the Moon conjunct to the IC on Sept 18, 1997 at 2:55 pm, in San Francisco. Piazza's hit scored two runs to tie a game against the Giants. On Sept 27, 1997 at 3:45 pm in San Francisco, Venus, in transit at 18 degrees Scorpio, was exactly conjunct to the IC. Darryl Hamilton, playing the Venus position of center field for the Giants, hit an RBI single. The next batter up was first baseman J. T. Snow. Neptune, in transit at 27

---

607. *This Date in Tigers' History*, p. 37.
608. Gewecke, Cliff: *Day by Day in Dodgers History*, p. 44.

degrees Capricorn was conjunct to the Ascendant. Snow responded to his planet on the Ascendant by hitting a double that drove in two runs.

If you are following a game and a dramatic event occurs, cast an astrological chart for the moment. There will generally be an aspect from one of the axes to a planet in transit. At other times, an axis will form an aspect to a natal planet in the birthchart of the team or to the birthchart of the player involved. Newspapers and books rarely give the times that events within a baseball game occur. The history books do tell us that Bobby Thomson hit the home run that won the 1951 pennant at 3:58 pm EDT,[609] but rarely are such times easily available. Still, astrological charts for walk-off games can be deduced. Many box scores are available on the Internet. Additionally, libraries have microfilm of old newspapers that include decades of box scores. When you find the box score for a game you wish to study, it will include a time of game. This is the duration in hours and minutes between the first pitch and the final out. Then, find the announced start time for the game.[610] Add the duration of the game to the start time. The sum will give you the time that the game ended. Keep in mind that announced start times are not always accurate. Delays are frequent, especially in bad weather, but games usually begin within five minutes of the scheduled time.

Transits to a Season

Lieb and Baumgartner's history of the Philadelphia Phillies includes the following passage:

> *The bad breaks of 1911 were intensified in 1912. Believers of astrology insisted that the Phillies were under a bad sign from April to December. Or, as Jimmy Hagen's Irish grandmother would have it, "Some bad little people are sitting on their backs."*[611]

The "bad sign" that the 1912 Phillies were under was a Saturn return. Pluto in transit was also conjunct the Phillies' natal Jupiter.

Middle and outer planets move slowly enough that their transits can last for an entire baseball season. In addition, even if an outer planet has

---

609. Stein, Fred: "New York Giants-San Francisco Giants: A Tale of Two Cities" *Encyclopedia of Major League Baseball: National League*, p. 319. (See Giants Chapter in Part II for the analysis of this game.)
610. If the start time is not listed with the box score, go to microfilm of the previous day's newspaper, which will include start times with the list of that day's games.
611. Lieb & Baumgartner, *The Philadelphia Phillies*, p. 97.

completed its transit and moved out of orb, it may have caused an injury or a trade that influences the remainder of the season. If a team can take favorable advantage of a transit from an outer or middle planet, the result is a marked improvement in play at the position represented by the outer planet. There is also an improvement at the position represented by the planet in the birthchart that receives the transit.

New Moons also have discernable effects on a team. On June 1, 1992, the New Moon occurred at 11 degrees Gemini. The San Francisco Giants experienced this New Moon as an opposition to their natal Mercury of 10 degrees Sagittarius. As Mercury rules pitchers, the following lunar cycle proved devastating to their pitching staff. The 1992 Giants began the month of June in first place, but the Gemini New Moon in opposition to their Mercury triggered a collapse of their pitching. The Giants fell into a slump and finished the 1992 season under .500. On September 16, 1993, the New Moon occurred at 23 degrees Virgo, conjunct to the Giants' Uranus of 23 degrees Virgo. The Giants had been playing poorly, losing first place to the Atlanta Braves, but the New Moon conjunct to their Uranus revived them from their slump. Left fielder Barry Bonds, representing Uranus, channeled the energy of this lunar cycle and greatly improved his play.

Hitters' Years and Pitchers' Years

Some years bring an unusual increase in home runs. Batting averages also rise in these years. When this has happened in the past, the ball was said to be "juiced." Pundits would speculate that league officials had directed the manufacturers of baseballs to wind the yarn tighter to make the ball tighter, springier, and easier to hit a long way. The motive behind juicing the ball is that, with increased offense, more fans will attend games and the owners will make more money.

In the late-1990s and the first years of the 21st Century, the ball was said to be juiced. Roger Maris's single-season home run record of 61, which had stood for 37 years, was broken in 1998 by both Mark McGwire and Sammy Sosa. Barry Bonds then surpassed McGuire's record in 2001. Pundits of the era not only credited the juiced ball, they also said that smaller ballparks and pitching weakened by the expansion of teams had led to the increase in home runs. Now, that period of baseball history is referred to as "the Steroid Era."[612] Mark McGwire, Sammy Sosa, and Barry Bonds would all become associated with steroid use. Nevertheless, there is a deeper astrological explanation to the many homeruns that occurred

---

612. See Giants Chapter.

in that period. In 1996, Uranus entered the sign of Aquarius, where it remained until 2003. Uranus rules the home run. When Uranus entered its own sign of Aquarius, the home run totals naturally increased.

In the 1960s, pitching was unusually strong. 1968 is remembered as "the Year of the Pitcher." In 1968, Bob Gibson set a record with an ERA of 1.12. Only one hitter in the American League would bat over .300, Carl Yastrzemski who managed to reach .301. The primary astrological transit of 1968 was the conjunction between Pluto and Uranus in Virgo, a pitcher's sign. This transit would also bring much of the social liberation and feminist energy of the 1960s. The game of baseball is a vessel for both the male energy of offense and the female energy of defense.[613] Overall the game is more feminine in nature than masculine, since the defense has more control over the game than the offense. Baseball is generally low-scoring, in contrast to basketball and football, sports that are more masculine in nature. The Uranus-Pluto conjunction of the 1960s occurred in the feminine sign of Virgo. For the United States as a whole, the conjunction in the sky brought social change and strength to the Women's Movement. For baseball, it brought increased power to the pitchers, whose sign is Virgo.

The Months

The baseball season is very long. It lasts from late-winter into fall. During a baseball season, the Sun will travel through more than half of the zodiac. As the Sun moves through the different signs of the zodiac, the tone of the season changes. The Sun in Pisces brings the dreaminess of Spring Training. The Sun in Aries brings enthusiasm and optimism and the new beginning of Opening Day. Six months later, the season ends with the Sun in Scorpio. Shadows of the light towers hang across the diamond. In the crisp fall air, veterans announce their retirement. The end of a baseball season is an aftermath of planets in Scorpio, the sign of death.

As a season closes, a few teams remain in the pennant races or reach the post-season. The games of these teams are especially exciting. The heightened tension is a measure of our awareness that time is running out. Saturn, the ruler of time, makes his presence conspicuous at season's end. The aspects of Saturn become most important at the close of a season.

---

613. See Section One, Chapter One.

Saturn in the Post-Season

It is Saturn that crowns the champions at the end of the season. Teams win pennants and World Series under transits from Saturn. Baseball commentators often say that a good indicator that a team will win a pennant is that it has the ability to come from behind to win games. Another indicator that a team will likely win the pennant is its ability to get clutch hits. Come-from-behind victories and clutch hits are both functions of Saturn. A team winning by such means is operating under a favorable transit of Saturn. Indeed, pennant-deciding games and World Series victories have the distinct Saturn tension and atmosphere.

When the last out is recorded that ends a championship game, there is a precise aspect involving Saturn. This aspect occurs from an axis to the planet Saturn or from the Moon to Saturn. Either the axis or the Moon makes these aspects to Saturn in transit, or to Saturn in the birthchart of the championship team. These aspects bring the baseball season to its close. These aspects also crown the champions.

The following observations are from pennant and World Series victories. The times listed are from the author's notes.

The 1993 World Series was won on October 23, 1993, when Joe Carter hit a ninth-inning homerun off Mitch Williams. The homerun that ended the 1993 season was hit at 11:45 pm EDT in Toronto. At that moment, Venus, in transit at 10 degrees Libra, was exactly conjunct to the IC. Moreover, the Ascendant was positioned at 28 degrees Cancer, conjunct to the Blue Jays' natal Saturn of 26 degrees Cancer. Saturn, in transit at 23 degrees Aquarius, had been conjunct to the Blue Jays' Moon through the 1993 season, and the Moon at 21 degrees Aquarius was conjunct to Saturn at 23 degrees, 40 minutes Aquarius. Both these

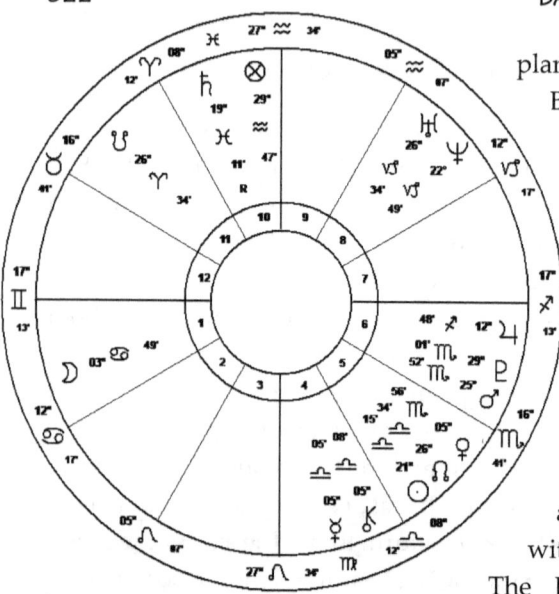

Braves Win 1995 NL pennant
Saturday, October 14, 1995 10:04:00 PM
Atlanta, Georgia
Time Zone: 04:00 (EDT)
Longitude: 084° W 23' 06"
Latitude: 33° N 46' 24"

planets were conjunct to the Blue Jays' natal Moon of 23 Aquarius. With Saturn in the sign of Aquarius, it was poetic that the 1993 season would finish on an Aquarian coda, a home run. Joe Carter also played the Aquarius position of left field.

The 1995 World Series and pennants were played with Saturn in the sign of Pisces. The Braves won the National League pennant by defeating the Reds on October 14, 1995, at 10:04 pm EDT in Atlanta. At that moment, the Moon, in transit at 3 degrees, 49 minutes Cancer, formed an opposition to the Braves natal Saturn of 4 degrees, 15 minutes Capricorn. Three nights later, on October 17, the Indians won the American League at 8:03 pm PDT in Seattle. While no significant aspect from an axis to Saturn occurred in Seattle on that occasion, above the city of Cleveland, the MC stood at 19 degrees Pisces, exactly conjunct to Saturn, in transit at 19 degrees Pisces. The Braves would defeat the Indians in the sixth game of the 1995 World Series on October 28, 1995, at 10:27 pm EDT in Atlanta. At that moment, the MC of 18 degrees Pisces was exactly conjunct to Saturn.

The Yankees won the 1996 American League pennant on October 13, 1996 at 7:22 pm EDT in Baltimore, with the

Cleveland Wins 1995 AL pennant
Tuesday, October 17, 1995 11:03:00 PM
Cleveland, Ohio
Time Zone: 04:00 (EDT)
Longitude: 081° W 40' 42"
Latitude: 41° N 28' 24"

TRANSITS

South Node of 8 degrees Aries conjunct to Saturn at 2 degrees, 39 minutes Aries. In Baltimore, there occurred no significant aspect from an axis to Saturn at 7:22 pm. In New York, however, an Ascendant of 17 degrees Taurus formed a semi-square to Saturn. Also in 1996, the Braves would win the National League pennant against the Cardinals on October 17 at 10:40 pm EDT in Atlanta. The Braves came back from a 3-games-to-1 deficit in the LCS to beat St. Louis in a seventh game. At 10:40, the Moon was positioned at 3 degrees 31 minutes Capricorn, square to transiting Saturn in Aries, and conjunct within 1 degree to the Braves' natal Saturn of 4 degrees, 15 minutes Capricorn.

Braves Win 1995 World Series
Saturday, October 28, 1995 10:27:00 PM
Atlanta, Georgia
Time Zone: 04:00 (EDT)
Longitude: 084° W 23' 06"
Latitude: 33° N 46' 24"

The Yankees won the 1996 World Series against the Braves on October 26, with Saturn at 2 degrees Aries conjunct to the South Node of 7 degrees Aries. The last out of the Series was recorded at 10:56 pm EDT in New York, with the MC at 6 degrees Aries, conjunct to both the South Node and Saturn. The 1997 pennants and World Series were

Yankees Win 1996 AL pennant
Sunday, October 13, 1996 7:22:00 PM
Bronx, New York
Time Zone: 04:00 (EDT)
Longitude: 073° W 52' 12"
Latitude: 40° N 50' 36"

played with Saturn retrograde between 17 and 15 degrees Aries. The 1997 American League LCS is an especially interesting astrological study since it matched the Indians and Orioles, both Western League teams that have identical planetary degrees in their birthcharts. While their MC-IC and Ascendant-Descendant axes are different, the natal planets of the Orioles and Indians receive transits at the same planetary degrees. During the 1997 LCS, Saturn in Aries was conjunct to the Moon and North Node of both the Indians and the Orioles.

Braves Win 1996 NL Pennant
Thursday, October 17, 1996 10:40:00 PM
Atlanta, Georgia
Time Zone: 04:00 (EDT)
Longitude: 084° W 23' 06"
Latitude: 33° N 46' 24"

With Saturn conjunct to the Indians' Moon, catcher Sandy Alomar, Jr. responded with an outstanding 1997 season, batting .321 and hitting 21 homeruns. Alomar also performed in the clutch, even hitting the home run that won the All-Star game for the American League. However, more important for the Indians, on October 5, Alomar hit an 8th inning home run in Game Four of the Division Series against the Yankees to tie the game. In the next inning, the Indians scored again and won the game, preventing elimination. On October 12, one week later, Sandy Alomar would be the hero of Game Four of the League Championship Series when he

Yankees Win 1996 World Series
Saturday, October 26, 1996 10:56:00 PM
Bronx, New York
Time Zone: 04:00 (EDT)
Longitude: 073° W 52' 12"
Latitude: 40° N 50' 36"

hit a ninth-inning RBI to win the game 8-7.[614]

While Sandy Alomar Jr. was savoring the fruit of the Saturn transit, Baltimore's catcher Lenny Webster would suffer its bitterest dregs. In the same Game Four in which Alomar was the hero, Webster was involved in a play in which two runs scored on a wild pitch. One day earlier, Lenny Webster allowed the game-winning run to score on a pass ball. The error involved a failed squeeze play. Since Webster missed the ball, Marquis Grissom would score the winning run, ending a twelve inning 2-1 pitcher's duel.

The Indians eventually won the 1997 AL pennant on October 15, 1997 at 8:09 EDT in Baltimore. The pennant was won in extra-inning Saturnian fashion by second baseman Tony Fernandez. Tony Fernandez hit a home run in the top of the 11th inning at 7:53 with the MC conjunct to Uranus. When the game ended at 8:09, the Moon was positioned at 20 degrees, 33 minutes Aries, conjunct to Saturn in transit and exactly opposite to the natal Saturn in Libra of both the Indians and the Orioles.

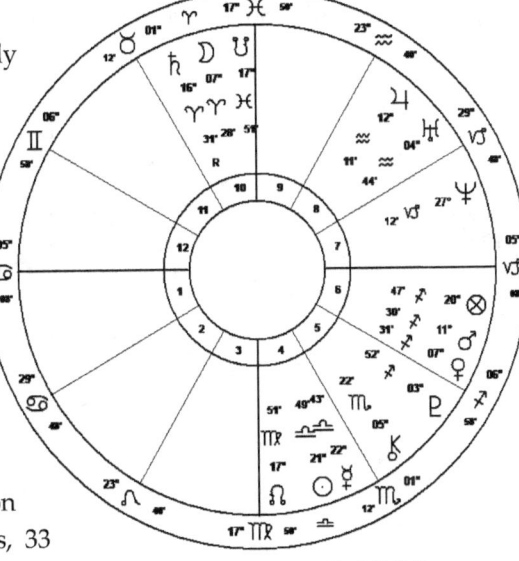

Cleveland Wins 1997 AL Pennant
Wednesday, October 15, 1997 8:09:00 PM
Baltimore, Maryland
Time Zone: 04:00 (EDT)
Longitude: 076° W 37' 12"
Latitude: 39° N 18' 48"

Marlins Win 1997 NL Pennant
Tuesday, October 14, 1997 11:18:00 PM
Atlanta, Georgia
Time Zone: 04:00 (EDT)
Longitude: 084° W 23' 06"
Latitude: 33° N 46' 24"

---

614. The hit occurred at 11:07 pm EDT with the Ascendant at 8 degrees Cancer and trine to the Moon, the planet of catchers.

The Marlins defeated the Braves for the 1997 National League pennant on October 14, 1997, at 11:18 pm EDT in Atlanta. At that moment, the IC of 18 degrees Virgo was conjunct to the North Node in transit at 19 degrees Virgo. Both the IC and the North Node were in a quincunx aspect to Saturn, positioned at 17 degrees Aries.

The 1997 World Series between the Marlins and the Indians would end in extra innings of a seventh game, which was played on October 26. In the ninth inning, Cleveland was ahead 2-1 and poised to win the Series. Saturn was even conjunct to the MC, but he would not crown Cleveland. Instead, he allowed a rally by the Marlins. Moises Alou led off the inning with a single, then scored the tying run on a sacrifice fly by Craig Counsell at 11:08 pm EST. When Counsell scored, the MC was conjunct to Saturn in transit from 19 degrees Aries, while the Libra IC was conjunct to the Indians' natal Saturn of 20 degrees Libra. Saturn, which had blessed Cleveland in the League Championship Series, would forsake them in the World Series.

In 1997, Cleveland's second baseman Tony Fernandez would have the distinction of embodying opposite roles of Saturn, both the hero and the goat.

Counsell RBI Ties Game 7
Sunday, October 26, 1997 11:08:00 PM
Miami, Florida
Time Zone: 05:00 (EST)
Longitude: 080° W 15' 54"
Latitude: 25° N 46' 36"

Marlins Win 1997 World Series
Monday, October 27, 1997 12:05:00 AM
Miami, Florida
Time Zone: 05:00 (EST)
Longitude: 080° W 15' 54"
Latitude: 25° N 46' 36"

This is striking, since Cleveland has Saturn in Libra, the sign of the second baseman. Fernandez, who had hit the home run to win the pennant just 12 nights earlier, would allow a ground ball to get by him that should have started a double play. Two batters later, the 1997 World Series was won as Edgar Renteria, the Marlins' shortstop, hit a single to drive in Craig Counsell. The Series-winning hit occurred just past midnight, 12:05 am EST on October 27, 1997. The Ascendant at that moment was 7 degrees Leo, conjunct to the Marlins' Mars of 9 degrees Leo and opposite the Marlins Saturn of 6 degrees Aquarius.

With a Mars-Saturn opposition in the Marlins' birthchart, it is relevant that a shortstop would make the clutch-Saturnian hit to win the World Series. It is also poetic that the transit of Saturn in Aries manifested in a Series-winning hit by a shortstop, much as Saturn in Aquarius had manifested in the Series-winning hit by a left fielder in 1993.

Transits to the Birthcharts of Pitchers

Pitchers have obvious good and bad outings. Even a dominant pitcher will have a few games a year in which he doesn't have his stuff. A below-average pitcher, meanwhile, has occasional games where he commands all his pitches, even throwing a shutout or a no-hitter. Then there are games in which a pitcher is throwing fine, but, without warning, loses his control and can't throw the ball over the plate. Such sudden losses of control can be explained through transits. Although the transits to a pitcher's birthchart are not as vital to a game's outcome as the transits to his team's birthchart, they are worth observing. Pitchers, ruled by Mercury, are of a mutable nature. This makes them highly sensitive to the fluctuations of transits.

To cast a birthchart for a pitcher, locate the pitcher's date of birth.[615] Dates of birth are found in various sources, including websites, team yearbooks and baseball magazines such as *Street and Smith's*. Since times of birth are usually unavailable, cast a noon birthchart for the day a player was born. A noon chart will not give you enough information to thoroughly analyze a pitcher's character or nuances, since the house positions and an accurate degree of the Moon will be lacking. Yet many of a pitcher's strengths and weaknesses will still be discernible. The birthcharts of

---

615. Keep in mind the possibility of an incorrect birthdate when casting a pitcher's birthchart. Some players lie about their date of birth. They may wish to considered older to be able to sign a contract, or younger to increase their contract value.

pitchers have well-aspected Mercurys. They also have personal planets in the pitcher's signs of Gemini and Virgo. If a time of birth is available, notice the planets in the Third and Sixth Houses.

The most important transits for a pitcher involve the planet Mercury. Favorable transits from Mercury improve a pitcher's performance. Likewise, favorable transits to a pitcher's natal Mercury improve a pitcher's performance. Conversely, challenging transits to a pitcher's natal Mercury will adversely affect one's performance. If a planet in transit forms a challenging angle to a pitcher's natal Mercury, the pitcher will likely have a rough outing. A challenging angle, however, is tricky to define. Squares and oppositions are not necessarily malefics for pitchers. Major league pitchers are competitive individuals who have usually overcome adversity in their lives. Such competitors commonly have challenging aspects in their natal charts. Since difficult aspects are not new to them, they have the ability to channel a transit from a difficult angle. Seasoned players who are comfortable under pressure excel under challenging aspects. Veteran pitchers are especially able to thrive under squares and oppositions. Young pitchers are more likely to be undone by difficult transits, but do not assume that a young pitcher will wilt under a challenging square. Observe the starting pitchers of your local team and note how each of them performs under squares and oppositions.

Transits from Mars or to a pitcher's natal Mars bring added energy and strength. Such a Mars transit will assist a fastball power pitcher. A pitcher who relies on speed will be even swifter under a Mars transit. But a finesse pitcher, one who relies on refined control and a command of breaking pitches, will likely have difficulty under a Mars transit. A Mars transit will disrupt a finesse pitcher's feel for his pitches. He may become uncommonly wild.[616] A Mars transit functions like an adrenaline rush. Certain pitchers are able to absorb adrenaline by channeling it in a manner that assists their pitching, but other pitchers are undone by adrenaline. It makes them wild and disrupts their control or concentration. Successful pitchers are also able to control their emotions, especially anger. Mars transits often bring anger. They may involve an umpire making a call against a pitcher or a teammate committing a costly error, events that can derail the concentration one needs to get the batters out. A successful

---

616. Relief pitchers often have the problem of being "too strong." A bullpen pitcher lacks the regular rhythm of a starter who pitches every fourth or fifth day in a rotation. A pitcher who has not recently thrown is storing excess energy. If he is stronger than he is used to being, he can lose control and become wild. A starting pitcher can have the same problem when a team's rotation is disrupted. If a pitcher has gone an extra day between starts, he may be too strong and experience wildness.

pitcher has the emotional steel to continue through adversity and to pitch through such difficulties.

The transits that a pitcher experiences from the slow-moving outer planets will affect a pitcher for a long span. The effects may last longer than a season. If a pitcher is experiencing a difficult transit from Saturn, he may suffer an injury that affects his play or his career for months or years to follow. A pitcher who experiences a difficult transit from Uranus will likely give up an increased number of home runs. A difficult Uranus transit can ruin a pitcher's entire season as he surrenders home runs on a regular basis. Similarly, if a pitcher receives a transit from a planet to his natal Uranus, he is likely to yield home runs. A pitcher who undergoes a difficult Neptune transit will experience a loss of control and walk batters. The energy of Neptune is antithetical to that of Mercury, the pitcher's planet. A pitcher needs to concentrate and focus on the job at hand. Neptune brings a dreaminess that undermines pitchers.

In a game of three-hour length, the degrees of the Ascendant, Descendant, MC, and IC will shift through about 45 degrees of the zodiac. When degrees of the zodiac form conjunctions to sensitive degrees within a pitcher's birthchart, unexpected things can happen. A sure-handed pitcher may suddenly lose control and walk the bases full of runners. When a pitcher loses control without warning, a degree on the MC-IC axis or the Ascendant-Descendant axis is often conjunct to the pitcher's natal Neptune. Similarly, when an axis degree is conjunct to a pitcher's natal Uranus, the pitcher can surrender homeruns without warning. Back-to-back home runs are rare, but they are more likely to occur when the degree of an axis makes a conjunction to a pitcher's natal Uranus.

NO-HITTERS

Most no-hitters are the results of favorable transits to the birthcharts of individual pitchers. Sometimes a no-hitter is pitched under favorable transits to both the

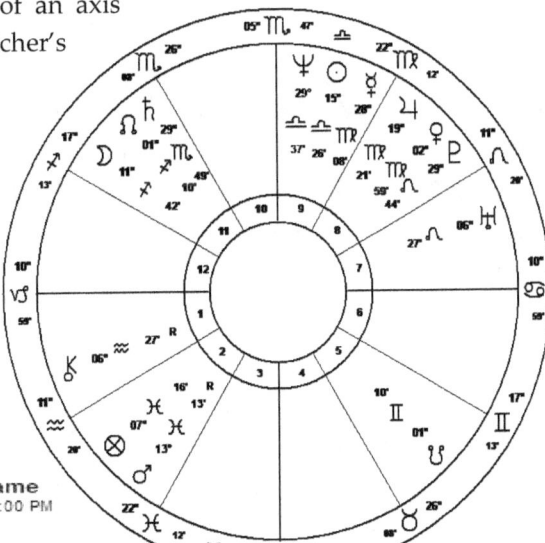

Don Larson's Perfect Game
Monday, October 8, 1956 2:00:00 PM
Bronx, New York
Time Zone: 04:00 (EDT)
Longitude: 073° W 52' 12"
Latitude: 40° N 50' 36"

Don Larson
Sunday, August 7, 1927 12:00:00 PM
Michigan City, Indiana
Time Zone: 04:00 (EDT)
Longitude: 086° W 53'
Latitude: 41° N 42'

Hideo Nomo's No Hitter
Tuesday, September 17, 1996 7:05:00 PM
Denver, Colorado
Time Zone: 06:00 (MDT)
Longitude: 104° W 59'
Latitude: 39° N 44' 36"

birthchart of the pitcher and the birthchart of his team.

Don Larsen's World Series perfect game occurred on October 8, 1956. The Yankees' Neptune of 29 degrees Gemini was active that day. The planet Neptune is antithetical to the pitcher's energy of Mercury, but it is in the pitcher's sign of Gemini within the Yankees' birthchart. That day, Mercury, in transit at 28 degrees Virgo, was square to the Yankees Neptune in Gemini. Mercury was also conjunct Larsen's natal Mars of 21 degrees Virgo. Three transiting outer and middle planets were in tight alignment: Pluto at 29 degree Leo, Neptune at 29 degrees Libra, and Saturn at 29 degrees Scorpio. Pluto and Saturn were in a powerful square, and Saturn was conjunct the North Node. The Sun, at 15 degrees Libra, was positioned in the exact mid-point of the Pluto-Saturn square and semi-square to both planets. Don Larsen's birthchart shows he was primed to harness the energy of these planets. Larsen's Mercury of 23 degrees Leo and his Neptune of 0 degrees Virgo received a conjunction from Pluto and a square from Saturn. His Sun, positioned at 15 degrees Leo, received a sextile from the transiting Sun.

Hideo Nomo's no-hitter occurred on Sept. 17, 1996 against the Colorado Rockies. Nomo's performance occurred on a night so filled with Mercury energy that a no-hitter was even possible at Coors Field, a notorious hitter's park. Mercury and the Sun were conjunct at 24 and 25 degrees Virgo, a pitcher's sign. Both planets formed a conjunction to the midpoint between Nomo's natal Pluto of 22 degrees Virgo and his natal Venus-Uranus conjunction at 28 degrees Virgo. Nomo's natal Mercury, positioned nearby at 29 degrees Virgo, also harnessed the energy of the transit. The Sun and Mercury also made a conjunction to the Dodgers' natal Jupiter of 25 degrees Virgo. Dodger pitchers are receptive to transits to their team's natal Jupiter, not only because of its placement in Virgo but because its opposition to the Dodgers' Mercury in Pisces.

Kevin Brown's no-hitter occurred on June 10, 1997, in San Francisco. Venus, in transit at 8 degrees Cancer, formed a square to Brown's natal Mercury of 10 degrees Aries and a trine to his natal Saturn of 9 degrees Pisces. However, even more interesting was the fact that Brown's team, the Marlins, experienced a solar return on the day of his no-hitter. The Marlins' Sun in the pitcher's sign of Gemini received a conjunction from the Sun, in transit at 19 degrees Gemini. The no-hitter on the Marlins' birthday proved a harbinger for the rest of the season. The 1997 Marlins continued to play well and ended the season with their World Series win against Cleveland.

Kevin Brown
Friday, May 14, 1965 12:00:00 PM
Milledgeville, Georgia
Time Zone: 04:00 (EDT)
Longitude: 083° W 13' 30"
Latitude: 33° N 04'

THE DOUBLE NO-HITTER OF 1917

The greatest pitchers' duel in major league history occurred on May 2, 1917 in Chicago. That day, the Moon was in Virgo and Mercury made a station[617] at 29 degrees Taurus. The game matched the Reds' Fred Toney against the Cubs' Jim "Hippo" Vaughn. Both pitchers threw no-hitters.

"Hippo" Vaughn was a fastball pitcher with a Sun in Aries. Vaughn's natal Mercury was in the sign of Pisces and conjunct to Venus. Fred

Double No-hitter Of 1917
Wednesday, May 2, 1917 2:00:00 PM
Chicago, Illinois
Time Zone: 05:00 (CDT)
Longitude: 087° W 39' 42"
Latitude: 41° N 51' 54"

---

617. Mercury was moving slowly and would turn retrograde in a few days.

Toney's Mercury was in the sign of Scorpio with an opposition to natal Neptune. Toney had a variety of pitches in his arsenal, including the spitball.[618]

The birthcharts of both Vaughn and Toney have natal Neptune very close to 29 degrees Taurus, the degree of the zodiac where Mercury was positioned that afternoon. Vaughn's Neptune is located at 28 degrees Taurus, and Toney's Neptune is positioned at 0 degrees Gemini. Neptune is generally a malefic for pitchers, but the particulars of the natal charts of these two pitchers allowed each to excel under this transit. The placement of Vaughn's Mercury in the sign of Pisces made his Neptune the despositor of his Mercury. While Neptune rules walks and often brings a poor outing for a pitcher, a pitcher with Mercury in Pisces or natal Mercury-Neptune aspects is ready to harness a Neptune transit.[619] That day, a transit to Vaughn's Neptune would assist his Mercury. Toney, meanwhile, would undergo both

Hippo Vaughn
Sunday, April 8, 1888 12:00:00 PM
Weatherford, Texas
Time Zone: 06:00 (CST)
Longitude: 097° W 47'
Latitude: 32° N 45'

Fred Toney
Tuesday, December 11, 1888 12:00:00 PM
Nashville, Tennessee
Time Zone: 06:00 (CST)
Longitude: 086° W 46' 54"
Latitude: 36° N 09' 18"

618. Spitball pitchers commonly have natal aspects between Mercury and Neptune or Mercury in the sign of Pisces. See Dodgers' chapter.

619. Greg Maddox is another pitcher with Mercury in Pisces and the Sun in Aries. Transits to Maddox's Neptune were generally favorable for him.

the conjunction from Mercury to his natal Neptune and an opposition from Mercury to his natal Mercury in Scorpio.

The transits to the team birthcharts in this game are also striking. The game would be won by the Reds in the tenth inning, when Vaughn surrendered a hit to Reds' shortstop Larry Kopf. Mars, in transit at 28 degrees Aries, had formed a quincunx to the Reds' natal Mercury that day, bringing the Reds' shortstop into a key role. On the play, Kopf would reach third base on an outfielder's error. Soon afterwards, the game was lost on a mental error by the Cubs' catcher Art Wilson. Jim Thorpe, hitting for the Reds, dribbled a ball up the third base line. Vaughn fielded the ball and threw it to the catcher in time to prevent Kopf from scoring, but Wilson let the ball bounce off his chest protector. Saturn, in transit at 25 degrees Cancer, had been conjunct to the Cubs South Node in Cancer. Both the Lunar Nodes and planets in Cancer manifest in a team's catcher, and this transit they received from Saturn would conscript the Cubs' catcher into making the error that lost the double no-hitter.

COMBINED NO-HITTERS

Combined no-hitters occur when more than one pitcher contributes to a team's no-hit performance. These no-hitters occur under transits to a teams' birthchart rather than to the birthchart of an individual pitcher.

On September 28, 1975, four Oakland Athletics pitchers contributed to a no-hitter against the Angels.[620] Vida Blue pitched the first five innings. Glen Abbott pitched the sixth inning. Paul Lindblad pitched the following seventh inning, and Rollie Fingers pitched the final two innings. The game occurred on the A's final regular season game of 1975. Since the A's had already clinched the AL Western Division,

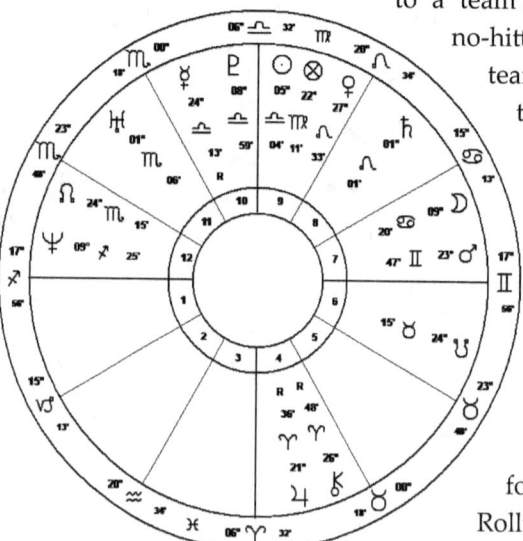

Athletics Combined No-hitter
Sunday, September 28, 1975 1:05:00 PM
Oakland, California
Time Zone: 07:00 (PDT)
Longitude: 122° W 14'
Latitude: 37° N 47' 36"

---

620. Coberly, Rich: *No-hit Hall of Fame*. Triple Play Publications. Newport Beach, Ca. 1985. *San Francisco Chronicle*, Sept. 29, 1975, p. 39.

they were content to let Vida Blue rest after 5 innings. The afternoon's major aspect involved Mercury, in transit at 24 degrees Libra and trine to Mars at 24 degrees Gemini. Mercury, the pitcher's planet, was strengthened by the favorable trine from Mars in the pitcher's sign of Gemini. The Athletics' Ascendant of 24 degrees Libra received the aspect as a conjunction from Mercury and a trine from Mars. The 4-0 Athletics victory occurred on Fan Appreciation Day at the Oakland Coliseum on a Sunday afternoon. The Moon was in Cancer, the sign of the fans and conjunct to the A's natal Moon in Cancer. By game's end, the transiting Moon was exactly conjunct to the A's natal Moon. When the game started, the Moon was positioned at 9 degrees Cancer and square to Pluto in transit at 9 Libra. The Moon was also quincunx to transiting Neptune at 9 degrees Sagittarius. Neptune had been conjunct to the A's Uranus and Jupiter of 9 degrees Sagittarius and trine to the A's Mars. The A's Mars of 10 degrees Leo would channel the energy of these transits. Reggie Jackson, playing the Leo position of right field, hit two home runs that game.

The Angels, meanwhile, were under a bad sign. They were playing poorly and would finish the season in last place. Saturn at 1 degree Leo was quincunx to their natal Jupiter of 0 degrees Capricorn. This aspect to their Jupiter had left their hitters in a slump. Their team batting average of .246 would be the lowest that year in the American League.

A bizarre combined no-hitter occurred in an unofficial game in the pre-season of 1995. The Major League players had been on strike since the previous August. That spring, the owners fielded "replacement players" in case the strike lasted into the regular season. With the replacement players on the field, the birthcharts of the Major League teams were still

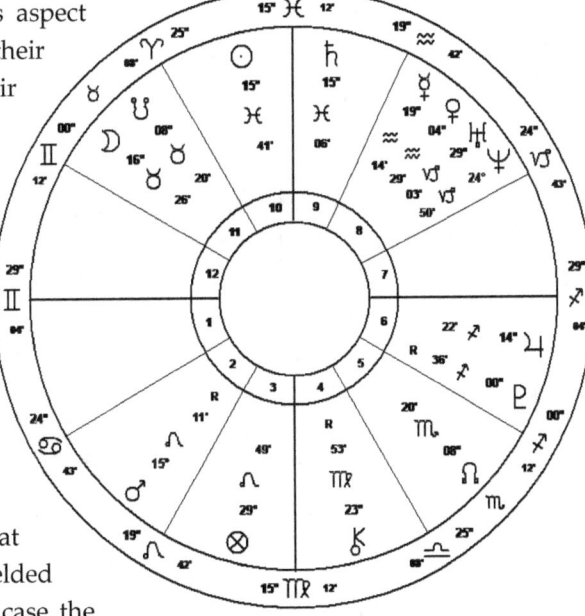

Braves Combined No-hitter
Monday, March 6, 1995 12:30:00 PM
West Palm Beach, Florida
Time Zone: 05:00 (EST)
Longitude: 080° W 06' 12"
Latitude: 26° N 43' 30"

responsive to transits. On March 6, 1995, the replacement Atlanta Braves threw a combined no-hitter against the New York Mets. Five pitchers in Braves uniforms contributed to the feat, and the Braves won the game 5-0. Jose Alvarez, Phil Harrison and Eric Moran each pitched two innings, while Keith Brown and Daren Brown pitched one inning each. None of the five pitchers would play for the Braves when the official season began, yet that day they channeled the transits to the Braves' birthchart. As the game began, the Moon, in transit at 16 degrees, 43 minutes Taurus, was conjunct to the Braves Third House[621] Pluto of 17 degrees Taurus. Transiting Neptune at 24 degrees, 50 minutes Capricorn had been conjunct the Braves natal Twelfth House Mercury of 24 degrees, 22 minutes Capricorn.[622] Mercury, in transit at 19 degrees Aquarius, had formed a sextile to the Braves' natal Neptune of 19 Aries. "Typical Braves pitching," remarked Braves' Manager Bobby Cox afterwards.[623]

On June 24, 1917, two Red Sox pitchers, Babe Ruth and Ernie Shore, pitched a combined no-hitter against the Washington Senators. Babe Ruth would start the game and walk the first batter, Ray Morgan.[624] Ruth didn't like the umpire's call and argued. Soon he was ejected, after hitting the umpire on the ear. Ernie Shore entered the game with the runner on first base. Morgan, who had received the walk, tried to steal second base and was caught.

Red Sox Combined No-hitter
Sunday, June 24, 1917 3:00:00 PM
Boston, Massachusetts
Time Zone: 04:00 (EDT)
Longitude: 071° W 05' 42"
Latitude: 42° N 20' 48"

---

621. Natal planets in a Third House correspond to pitching.
622. The Braves' Mercury, which resides in the 12th House, responds positively to transits of Neptune.
623. Associated Press, *San Francisco Chronicle*. March 7, 1995.
624. A starting time for this game is not available. Most games of that era began at 3:00 pm. This game, however, was the opener of a double header, so it may have begun earlier than 3:00. If the game did begin at 3:00, at that hour Neptune was exactly conjunct to the MC. Neptune brings walks, and the game began with Babe Ruth walking the Senators' leadoff hitter, Ray Morgan.

Ernie Shore then retired the next 26 batters.

This game occurred under significant aspects to both the Red Sox' birthchart and the birthcharts of Babe Ruth and Ernie Shore. Mercury, in transit at 12 degrees Gemini, was conjunct to the mid-point between the Red Sox' Moon of 9 degrees Gemini and Pluto of 15 degrees Gemini, both of which are in the pitcher's sign of Gemini. The no-hitter was the opening game of a double-header. In the second game that afternoon, the Red Sox beat Washington 5-0 as "Dutch" Leonard pitched a shutout. The transit from Mercury to the Red Sox Moon-Pluto midpoint drew 18 innings of outstanding pitching from the Red Sox staff.

Babe Ruth's natal Neptune, located at 13 degrees Gemini, also received a conjunction from transiting Mercury at 12 degrees Gemini. Since Neptune rules bases on balls, it is poetic that Ruth would walk the only batter he faced while a planet was conjunct his Neptune. My rectified birthchart for Babe Ruth has an MC of 29 degrees Cancer.[625] During this game, Saturn, in transit at 29 degrees, 55 minutes Cancer, was conjunct to Babe Ruth's MC. Saturn, the planet of umpires and authority, ejected Ruth. His subsequent suspension may have cost the Red Sox the 1917 pennant.[626] At the start of the game, the Moon was in transit at 19 degrees Leo, forming squares to Ruth's natal Uranus of 20 degrees Scorpio and to his Mars of 17 degrees Taurus and his Ascendant of 19 degrees Taurus. The Moon was also opposite to his Sun of 18 degrees Aquarius. The Moon found Ruth's trigger, his volatile Uranus-Mars opposition. The Moon further provoked him with an opposition to his libertine Aquarian Sun.

Astros Combined No-hitter
Wednesday, June 11, 2003 7:05:00 PM
Bronx, New York
Time Zone: 04:00 (EDT)
Longitude: 073° W 52' 12"
Latitude: 40° N 50' 36"

---

625. See Red Sox and Yankees chapters.
626. The Red Sox finished the 1917 season with a 90-42 record, in second place and 10 games behind the White Sox.

The birthchart of Ernie Shore has a Sun-Mercury conjunction at 4 degrees Aries and Pluto positioned at 6 degrees Gemini. That afternoon, Mars was in transit at 6 degrees Gemini, exactly conjunct Shore's Pluto. A transit from Mars to Pluto often proves malefic as injuries are likely, but an Aries pitcher such as Shore, intimate with Mars energy, has a sound capacity to channel a Mars-Pluto conjunction. Ernie Shore's birthchart also has a trine between Mars at 12 degrees Taurus to Saturn at 12 degrees Virgo. Mercury, in transit at 12 Gemini, formed a square to Shore's Saturn and a semi-sextile to his Mars. Shore completed the no-hitter under an aspect that many astrologers would consider malefic, not only a square but a square to his Saturn.

On June 11, 2003, six pitchers of the Houston Astros pitched a combined no-hitter at Yankee Stadium. Starter Roy Oswalt was removed after one inning due to an injury. Five Astro pitchers followed to secure the no-hitter. The transits for the game included a hard square from Mercury at 28 Taurus and the North Node at 29 Taurus to Mars at 28 degrees Aquarius. These planets made 15-degree and 105-degree aspects, respectively, to the Astros' Descendant of 12 degrees Gemini, a pitcher's sign. The Sun, in transit at 20 degrees Gemini, on that date formed a square to the Astros' Moon in Virgo. Both pitcher's signs of Gemini and Virgo were energized that day. Meanwhile, catcher Brad Ausmus responded to the transit to the Astros' Moon with three hits.

BIRTHCHARTS OF POSITION PLAYERS

When a player is having a significant day, it is most often the result of a transit to the planet representing his position in his team's birthchart. However, a significant day can also be accounted for by transits to a player's individual chart. Unless a time of birth is available, cast a noon birthchart for a player. All of a player's planets are sensitive to transits, but, in general, hitting feats are the result of Jupiter transits, and homeruns come from Uranus transits. Cast a chart for the moment a player makes a key hit or an outstanding defensive play. Charts for such moments show that a player's natal planets are sensitive not only to the planets in transit, but also to the rapidly changing degrees of the axes. Remember that the birthcharts of players have many individual distinctions. A transit that would be a benefic to one player will prove to be a malefic for another. Follow the transits to the birthchart of your favorite player to discover its nuances. Batting streaks and slumps are especially interesting to follow through the lens of a player's transits.

INJURIES

An injury to a key player occurs when a planet in his team's birthchart absorbs an excess of energy. These injuries happen when the energy from the transit of a planet or of multiple planets is more than the natal planet can safely hold. Players of the positions representing the natal planets are vulnerable to injuries under such transits. Uranus and Mars are often involved. The birthcharts of an injured individual players are similarly aspected.

The right foot of Giants' Third Baseman Matt Williams was broken on the afternoon of June 3, 1995. A very vital planet within the Giants' birthchart is Pluto at 29 degrees Taurus. The Giants have the Moon in Scorpio, making Pluto their Moon's despositor. Their third baseman became injured when the Giants' natal Pluto was undergoing an opposition from retrograde Pluto at 29 degrees Scorpio and a quincunx from Uranus at 0 degrees Aquarius. These aspects were from challenging angles, but third baseman Matt Williams had responded well to them in the early months of 1995. Williams was on a hitting rampage, leading the National League in homeruns, RBIs, and batting average. Nevertheless, on June 3, the Sun was at nearly 13 degrees Gemini and Mercury was retrograde near 15 degrees Gemini. Together their midpoint was 15 degrees from the Giants' natal Pluto. Meanwhile, the Moon was approaching 14 degrees Leo, 75 degrees from the Giants' Pluto. These disharmonious aspects added to the weight of retrograde Pluto in opposition to the Giants' natal Pluto. The excess weight of all these planets were too much for the Giants' Pluto to carry. Their embodiment of Pluto would become injured. Williams fouled a ball off his right foot and soon left the game in pain. At the time of his injury, the Giants were leading the NL West, but Williams' injury would

Matt Williams Injury
Saturday, June 3, 1995 3:00:00 PM
San Francisco, California
Time Zone: 07:00 (PDT)
Longitude: 122° W 25' 12"
Latitude: 37° N 46' 24"

be devastating. He remained on the disabled list until very late in the 1995 season, and the Giants finished the year in last place.

Mariners' center fielder Ken Griffey Jr. suffered a broken left wrist on May 26, 1995.[627] That night, Mars at 0 degrees Virgo was inconjunct to Uranus of 0 degrees Aquarius. Both planets formed disharmonious aspects to the Mariners' Venus of 14 Capricorn. Uranus formed a 15-degree aspect to Seattle's Venus, while Mars formed a 135-degree sesquiquadrate to their Venus. Griffey, who played the Venus position of center field, received the blow from the transit to the Mariners' Venus. Junior's own birthchart, which has the Sun of 29 degrees Scorpio conjunct Mercury of 2 Sagittarius, received the Mars transit as a square to his Sun and Mercury. Junior's Mercury received the worst of it, as Mercury rules wrists. Mars-Uranus aspects are notorious for spurring accidents. When the suddenness of Uranus combines with the aggression of Mars, the blend is unpredictable and disruptive.

Danny Tartabull had just joined the Athletics when he re-injured a rib on Aug. 2, 1995. The A's and

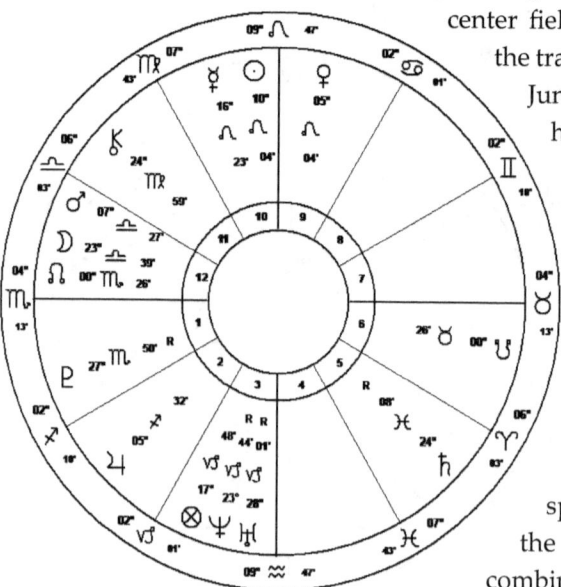

Ken Griffey Jr. Injury
Friday, May 26, 1995 8:00:00 PM
Seattle, Washington
Time Zone: 07:00 (PDT)
Longitude: 122° W 19' 12"
Latitude: 47° N 36' 48"

Danny Tartabull Injury
Wednesday, August 2, 1995 1:14:00 PM
Oakland, California
Time Zone: 07:00 (PDT)
Longitude: 122° W 14'
Latitude: 37° N 47' 36"

627. http://seattletimes.com/html/mariners/2012145723_griftimeline20a.html

Yankees had traded Danny Tartabull for Ruben Sierra, who both played the Leo position of right field. The injury occurred as Tartabull was batting at 1:14 pm PDT.[628] At this moment, the MC was exactly conjunct the Sun at 10 degrees Leo, while both the MC and the Sun were conjunct to the A's natal Mars of 10 degrees Leo.[629] That afternoon, the Sun was in a sesquiquadrate aspect to Saturn in transit at 24 degrees, 8 minutes Pisces, and it made a 165-degree aspect to Neptune at 23 degrees 44 minutes Capricorn. In addition, the Moon at 23 degrees Libra was square to Neptune and exactly conjunct the A's Ascendant, adding further stress to the A's Mars.[630] The A's new right fielder would succumb to the excess energy of these transits and injure his rib. Fittingly, ribs are ruled by the sign of Libra. The sign of Libra was heavily emphasized that afternoon. Not only was the Moon conjunct to the A's Ascendant in Libra, but the A's natal Sun is in the sign Libra.

Danny Tartabull's own birthchart[631] has an interesting synastry with the Athletics birthchart. His Mars of 9 degrees Leo is conjunct to the A's Mars within 1 degree. His Mercury of 21 degrees, 39 minutes Libra is conjunct the Athletics' Sun. Although Danny Tartabull played less than one full season with the A's, the connections between his chart and the A's right field planets are uncanny. It is also notable that his father, Jose Tartabull, made his debut with the A's in 1962. Jose Tartabull[632] also played the outfield, and his Mars of 21 degrees Libra is conjunct the A's Sun.

---

628. KFRC radio broadcast
629. The Sun and planets in Leo correspond to the right fielder.
630. The Ascendant can be a dispositor of Mars.
631. Danny Tartabull's date of birth is Oct. 30, 1962
632. Jose Tartabull's date of birth is Nov. 27, 1938

Famous Games:

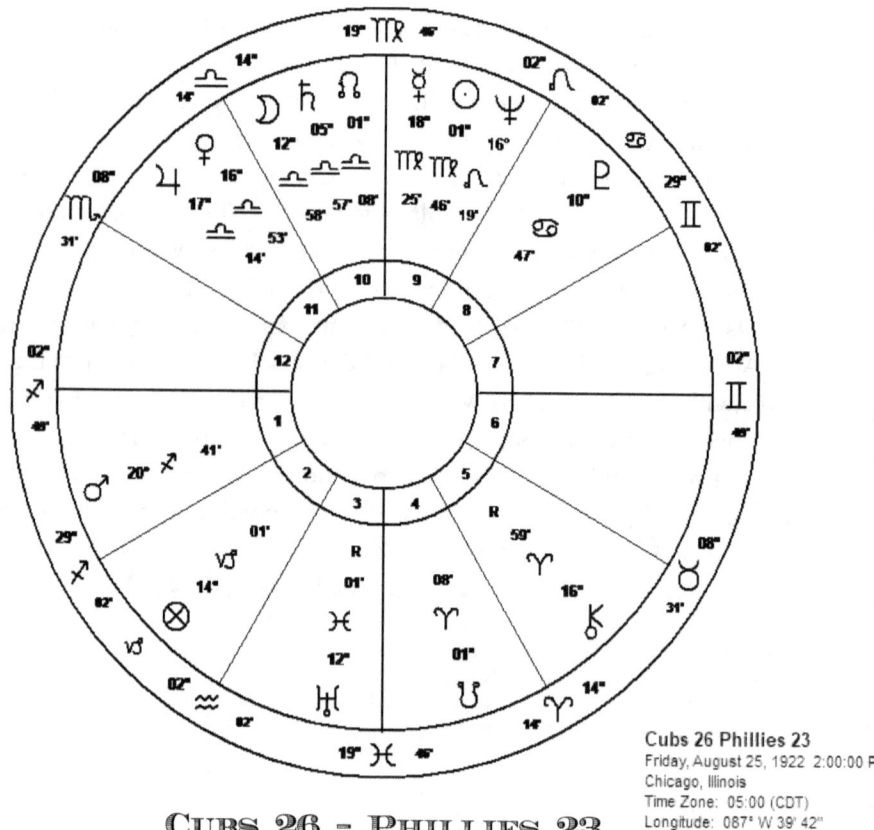

Cubs 26 — Phillies 23

Cubs 26 Phillies 23
Friday, August 25, 1922 2:00:00 PM
Chicago, Illinois
Time Zone: 05:00 (CDT)
Longitude: 087° W 39' 42"
Latitude: 41° N 51' 54"

It is a freak occurrence when a team scores over 20 runs. It is even more extraordinary for two teams to score over 20 runs in the same game. The highest scoring official game ever played in major league baseball occurred on August 25, 1922, when the Cubs beat the Phillies 26 to 23.[633] A record was also set for the most hits in a game by two teams, as the Cubs and Phillies combined for 51 hits. Although the Phillies lost the game, they would out-hit the Cubs 26 to 25. Both the Cubs and the Phillies had below-average pitching in 1922, but the pitchers were not at fault that afternoon.[634]

---

633. *New York Times*, Aug 26, 1922.
634. The Phillies team ERA for 1922 was 4.64, and the Cubs team ERA was 4.34. Neither was excessively higher than the National League average of 4.10 in 1922.

The main aspect for this game involved Jupiter, the planet of hitters. Venus and Jupiter were conjunct at 17 degrees Libra. Both Venus and Jupiter were sextile to Neptune, in transit at 16 degrees Leo. The Sun at 2 degrees Virgo was semi-square to Venus and Jupiter and 15 degrees from Neptune. These planets—Jupiter, Venus, Neptune, and the Sun—were in tight aspects to each other. It is rare for multiple planets to be in such a tight formation. Their combined power would be channeled by the Phillies and the Cubs, manifesting as a deluge of hits and runs.

The birthcharts of the Cubs and the Phillies both have features that enabled them to channel that day's alignment of planets. The Cubs have multiple planets in the 16th, 17th and 18th degrees of the zodiac. The Cubs' birthchart has the Sun at 17 degrees, 49 minutes Pisces conjunct to Mars at 18 degrees, 43 minutes Pisces. The Cubs' Jupiter and Pluto are conjunct at 16 degrees Taurus. Neptune at 18 degrees Aries is square to Uranus at 18 degrees Cancer. These natal planets are aligned to each other within tight orbs. The transits for the game formed tight aspects to the closely aligned planets within the Cubs' birthchart. These Cubs planets became highly energized, enabling players at every position to harness the day's transits. The box score shows that at least two hits and two runs were generated from every position in the Cubs' lineup.

The Phillies' birthchart has an Ascendant of 17 degrees Aries and a Descendant of 17 degrees Libra. That afternoon's Jupiter and Venus conjunction would occur exactly conjunct to the Phillies Descendant. The Phillies chart also has Neptune positioned at 16 degrees, 40 minutes Taurus quincunx to Mars at 16 degrees, 31 minutes Sagittarius. Their natal planets in these degrees and the degrees of the Phillies Ascendant and Descendant enabled the Phillies to channel the planets in transits.[635]

Most of the scoring occurred in big innings. The Cubs scored 10 runs in the second inning, then followed with 14 runs in the fourth inning. The fourth inning likely occurred as the MC formed conjunctions to the Moon, Jupiter, and Venus. The Phillies scored most of their runs in the final two innings: 8 runs in the eighth inning, and 6 runs in the ninth inning. The box score indicates that the game lasted 3 hours and 1 minute. If the game began at 2:00 pm, the standard start time for games in the 1920s, it would have ended at 5:01 pm. Pluto[636] would have been setting in this last inning

---

635. Interestingly, the New York Giants, whose chart is almost identical to that of the Phillies, scored only 4 runs this day. Although the Phillies and Giants share the same planets, their axes differ. The New York Giants had a Descendant of 19 degrees, 41 minutes Libra. The Jupiter-Venus conjunction did not energize the Giants' birthchart as it did the Phillies' birthchart.

636. The Phillies, with a natal Moon in Scorpio, make good use of Pluto transits.

when the Phillies scored 6 runs and almost tied the game.

One would think that a high-scoring game at Wrigley Field would have many home runs. Remarkably, only three homeruns were hit in this game. The Cubs' right fielder Hack Miller hit two home runs. The Cubs' catcher Bob O'Farrell hit the other home run. The Moon at 12 degrees Leo formed a quincunx to Uranus at 12 degrees Pisces, bringing home-run energy to the catcher. Aspects between the Moon and Uranus often result in a home-run hit by the catcher.

WHIZ KIDS WIN THE PENNANT

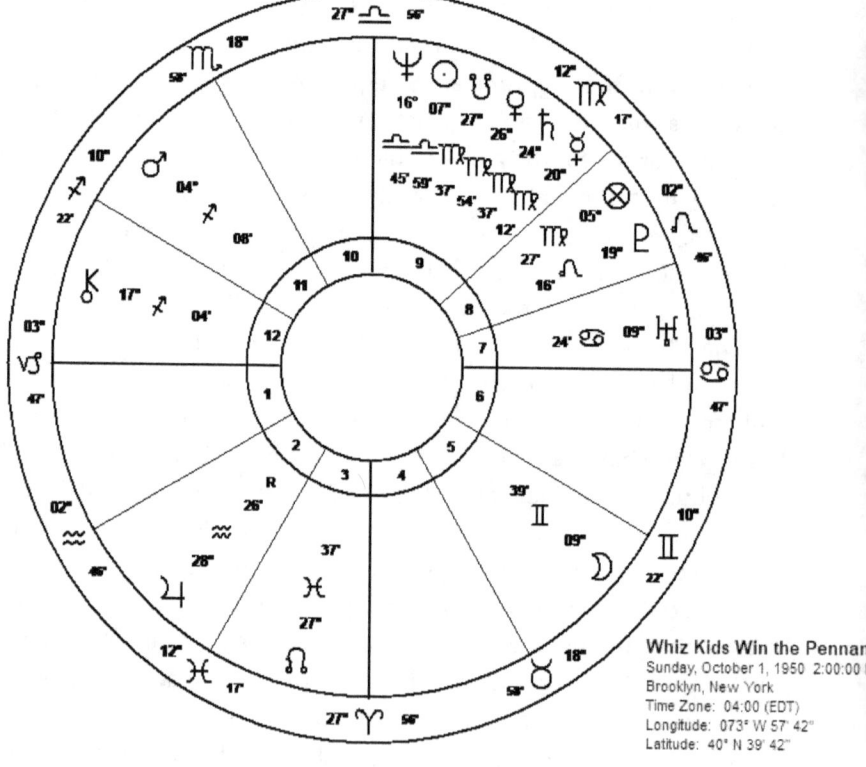

Whiz Kids Win the Pennant
Sunday, October 1, 1950 2:00:00
Brooklyn, New York
Time Zone: 04:00 (EDT)
Longitude: 073° W 57' 42"
Latitude: 40° N 39' 42"

On October 1, 1950, the Phillies[637] beat the Dodgers 4-1 in a ten-inning game to clinch the National League pennant[638] on was the last regular season game of the year. One month earlier, Philadelphia was enjoying a substantial lead in the standings and coasting towards the pennant.

---

637. The 1950 Phillies were known as the "Whiz Kids" for the many young players on their team.
638. McGowen, Roscoe *New York Times* October 2, 1950. pages 1, 27.

However, on the first of October, the Phillies were stumbling to cross the finish line, winning only 2 of their previous 11 games. The Dodgers, meanwhile, were in a sprint, having won 13 of their last 15 games.

The game began at 2:00 at Ebbett's Field and ended at 4:35. Robin Roberts of the Phillies and Don Newcombe of the Dodgers would each pitch the entire ten innings. At the start of the game, the Moon was approaching 10 degrees Gemini and was semi-sextile to Uranus, in transit at 9 degrees Cancer. Uranus had been conjunct the Phillies' IC within one degree since late August. Both the Moon and Uranus were in minor aspects[639] to transiting Saturn at 25 degrees Virgo. Saturn was conjunct the Dodgers' natal Jupiter of 25 degrees Virgo. The Moon was trine to the Dodgers' natal Moon of 10 degrees Libra, bringing a sizable crowd of 35,073 fans to Ebbett's Field, the largest gathering of Dodgers fans to attend a game in the 1950 season. The Moon's influence on Dodgers catcher Roy Campanella was also clear. Campanella would have only one hit, but he had a key defensive play, throwing out a Phillie attempting to steal, the fleet Ralph Caballero who pinch-ran for Andy Seminick in the ninth inning.

The Moon in Gemini also formed an opposition to the Phillies' natal Mercury of 10 degrees Sagittarius. An opposition to a team's Mercury usually brings challenges to a team's pitcher. The pressure was clearly on Robin Roberts. The Phillies pitcher had nineteen wins coming into the game, but when seeking the twentieth win, Roberts had failed his previous six starts. This game would be Robin Roberts' last chance for the elusive twentieth win. Far more important, it was his mission to save the pennant for Philadelphia. In the most important game of his life, Robin Roberts responded marvelously to the pressure. With the Moon opposite to the Phillies' Mercury, he held the Dodgers to 5 hits in 10 innings.

Mercury, in transit at 20 degrees Virgo, formed a similar challenging opposition to the Dodgers' Mercury of 20 degrees Pisces. Don Newcombe was also seeking his twentieth win of 1950. Through the first nine innings, he allowed only 1 run and 8 hits. Newcomb would be assisted with outstanding defensive plays: a ninth-inning leaping catch by Cal Abrams at the left-field wall and Campanella's throw to nail Caballero. Newcombe pitched valiantly, but, in the end, he was not as effective as Roberts.

Mercury at 20 degrees Virgo also formed a trine to the Phillies' natal Saturn of 20 degrees Taurus, bringing the windfalls of Saturn in a championship and extra-inning game. Mercury, the planet of pitchers,

---

639. Uranus at 9 Cancer formed a 75-degree aspect to Saturn. The Moon at 9 Gemini formed a 105-degree aspect to Saturn.

found its anchor in this aspect to the Phillies' Saturn. The transit solidified Phillies pitching, assisting Roberts in the pennant-deciding game. The Phillies' Saturn in Taurus, the sign of the center fielder,[640] would also manifest in a game-saving throw from center fielder Richie Ashburn.

The Sun, in transit at 8 degrees Libra, formed an inconjunction to the Dodgers' Mars in Taurus. The Dodgers, who have the Sun in Aries, are especially sensitive to Mars transits. Shortstop Pee Wee Reese would have three of the Dodgers' five hits, including a home run that accounted for the Dodgers' only score. But the inconjunction is a challenging aspect, and the Dodgers' right fielder Carl Furillo, embodying the Sun's transit, did not respond well to it. In the bottom of the ninth, Furillo had his chance to be the hero, when he came to bat with a runner on third and one out. But Furillo could only fly out to first base, failing to bring the runner home.

Venus and the South Node were conjunct to each other at 27 degrees Virgo and loosely conjunct to the Phillies' Uranus of 23 degrees Uranus. Both were exactly square to the Phillies natal Jupiter of 27 degrees Gemini. These planets also formed inconjunctions to the Dodgers' Neptune of 27 degrees Aries and a 165 degree aspect to the Dodgers' Saturn of 12 degrees Aquarius. Center fielder Richie Ashburn, embodying Venus, would play a hero under this transit. In the bottom of the ninth, Dodger Cal Abrams was poised to score the pennant-winning run. Abrams was on second base with no outs when Duke Snyder singled to center field. Ashburn somehow knew to play shallow. He fielded the ball perfectly and threw Abrams out at the plate. Dodger third base coach Milton Stock had directed Abrams to round third and head for the plate, a decision that would be questioned. *The New York Times* reported was thrown Abrams was out by fifteen feet. Saturn, in transit at 24 degrees Virgo, was conjunct to the Dodgers' Jupiter. Saturn is

Whiz Kids Pennant Final Out
Sunday, October 1, 1950 4:35:00 PM
Brooklyn, New York
Time Zone: 04:00 (EDT)
Longitude: 073° W 57' 42"
Latitude: 40° N 39' 42"

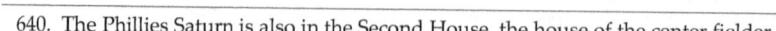

640. The Phillies Saturn is also in the Second House, the house of the center fielder.

represented by coaches and managers, while Jupiter is embodied in batters and runners. Saturn's conjunction to the Dodger's Jupiter manifested in ill advice from the third base coach.

The Phillies' natal square of Jupiter in Gemini to Uranus in Virgo has an orb of a little more than 4 degrees. Jupiter and Uranus, although generally malefic to pitchers, are in the pitchers' signs within the Phillies' birthchart. Transits to either Jupiter or Uranus affect Phillies pitchers. In this game, the transit from Venus and the lunar nodes came to the aid of Robin Roberts. Transits to the Phillies' Jupiter and Uranus also affect the Phillies left fielder, the position of Uranus. On this day, these transits to the Phillies' Uranus set up the classic home-run ending. The stage was also set by the Moon's trine with Uranus and Saturn's near conjunction to the Phillies' Uranus. In the top of the tenth inning, left fielder Dick Sisler hit a three-run home run. When the game ended at 4:35 pm, the Descendant of 18 degrees 54 minutes Leo was conjunct to Pluto at 19 degrees Leo. Both were square to both the Phillies' South Node[641] and Saturn, the planet that crowns pennant winners.

THE SIXTH GAME

When Boston fans refer to "The Sixth Game," they mean the sixth game of the 1975 World Series in which the Boston Red Sox played the Cincinnati Reds.[642] The Sixth Game took place in Boston on the evening of October 21, 1975. It began at 8:32 pm EDT. An astrological chart cast for the start of the game has the same degrees on the MC-IC and Ascendant-Descendant axes as the birthchart of the Boston Red Sox. Significant moments for a team occur when the axes in transit are aligned in such exact conjunctions to the axes of the team's birthchart.[643] The Sixth Game took place under three significant multi-planet transits: Venus semi-square the Sun, Mercury conjunct Pluto, and Saturn square Uranus.

The semi-square is an ambiguous aspect, one that can be either fortunate or malefic. The semi-square of October 21, between Venus at 13 degrees Virgo and the Sun at 28 degrees Libra, would prove beneficial and

---

641. The Phillies Mean Node is 19 degrees 15 minutes Scorpio. Their True Node is 20 degrees, 29 degrees Scorpio. There are two methods for measuring the location of the Lunar Node. The location of the Mean Node is measured with an average rate of motion, while the True Node is measured in its exact location. Both methods are used by astrologers.
642. Thorn, John *Baseball's Ten Greatest Games* (p. 153-171) Four Winds Press. New York 1981.
643. On September 27, 1997 at 4:17 pm PDT in San Francisco, a game ended in which the Giants clinched the NL Western Division title. When the game ended, the axes were exactly conjunct to the axes of the San Francisco Giants' birthchart.

adversarial to both the Red Sox and the Reds. The aspect proved uncomfortable for the Reds' Mercury of 28 degrees Virgo as it received the Sun from a semi-sextile and Venus from 15 degrees. Reds pitchers would combine for seven walks, three home runs, and seven earned runs. However, the position players that represented Venus and the Sun excelled. Center fielder César Geronimo had two hits, including a rare home run. Second basemen Joe Morgan had only one hit, yet he was robbed of an extra-base hit in an amazing play by Dwight Evans. Right fielder Ken Griffey, Sr., would have two RBIs and two hits that included a triple.

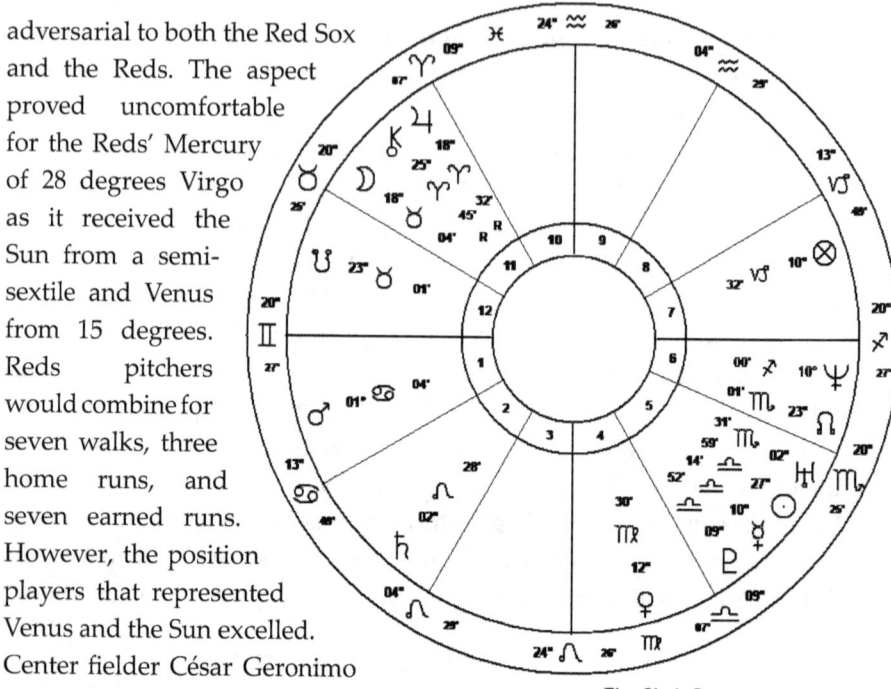

The Sixth Game
Tuesday, October 21, 1975 8:32:00 PM
Boston, Massachusetts
Time Zone: 04:00 (EDT)
Longitude: 071° W 05' 42"
Latitude: 42° N 20' 48"

For the Red Sox, the semi-square between the Sun and Venus formed aspects to their North Nodes of 28 degrees Scorpio.[644] Their North Node received the Sun as a semi-sextile, and Venus from a 75-degree aspect. Red Sox players at the Venus and Sun positions would also experience the good and the bad of the semi-square. Center fielder Fred Lynn hit a three-run homer in the first inning. Unfortunately, in the fifth inning, the semi-square proved painful for Lynn as he collided against the center field fence while attempting to field a drive by Ken Griffey, Sr. Second baseman Denny Doyle would also become humbled by the semi-square. In the bottom of the ninth inning, with the score tied, Doyle attempted to score from third base on a shallow fly ball to left field. Doyle ran through the hold sign from the third base coach and was thrown out. In the tenth inning, right fielder Dwight Evans made what Sparky Anderson would say was the best catch he had ever seen. Joe Morgan had hit the ball into deep right field and over Evans' head. But Evans sprinted to the wall,

---

644. Mean Node

lunged with his arm fully extended, caught the ball, then threw it quickly to first base, doubling up Griffey.

The Mercury and Pluto conjunction at 10 degrees Libra formed a square to the Reds' Ascendant. The Reds' Capricorn Ascendant is embodied in their manager. This aspect to the Reds' Ascendant brought the manager into a very active role in this game. The object of the manager's attention would be his pitching staff, a manifestation of the Mercury's aspect to the Ascendant. Sparky Anderson employed eight different pitchers in the Sixth Game, which would set a record for the most pitchers used by one team in a World Series game. Pete Rose, playing third base, would embody the transit from Pluto. Rose would have two hits and score one run. He was also the Reds' lead-off hitter, another manifestation of Pluto's aspect to the Reds Ascendant, as the Ascendant of a birthchart can correspond to the leadoff hitter.

For the Red Sox, the Mercury-Pluto conjunction formed a trine to their Moon of 9 degrees Gemini. Since the Red Sox' Moon is in Gemini, it is especially receptive to transits from Mercury. Carlton Fisk, the Red Sox catcher, became the major channel of this trine. Fisk would, of course, hit the game-winning home run in the bottom of the twelfth inning that won the game 7-6. The Mercury-Pluto conjunction also formed a square to the Red Sox natal Saturn of 11 degrees Capricorn. Transits involving Saturn set the stage for late-inning comebacks and extra-inning games, especially in post-season games.[645]

Fisk's home run occurred past midnight, at 12:33 am EDT. At that moment, the IC had reached 29 degrees Libra, conjunct to the Sun. The Moon had reached 20 degrees Taurus and was conjunct to the North Node. With the Moon and the IC in

Carleton Fisk HR
Wednesday, October 22, 1975 12:33:00 AM
Boston, Massachusetts
Time Zone: 04:00 (EDT)
Longitude: 071° W 05' 42"
Latitude: 42° N 20' 48"

---

645. See Saturn in the Post Season.

such powerful aspects, the script was written for a catcher to be the hero. Also at 12:33 am, the Ascendant was positioned at 11 degrees Leo and quincunx the Red Sox natal Saturn of 11 degrees Capricorn. Saturn makes an appearance in walk-off games.

The most powerful aspect that occurred during the 1975 post-season was the square between Saturn at 2 degrees Leo and Uranus at 2 degrees Scorpio. These planets had been locked within a very tight orb, less than 1 degree, since the second week of September. When an intense transit involving Saturn occurs in the fall, the teams who survive to the post-season will be winning under its influence. During the 1975 post-season, the Red Sox' Jupiter of 2 degrees Capricorn received the transit as a sextile from Uranus and a quincunx from Saturn, but Saturn and Uranus would form stronger aspects to the birthchart of the Reds. Saturn was exactly conjunct to the Reds' Venus of 2 degrees Leo,[646] while Uranus was exactly conjunct to the Reds MC of 2 degrees Scorpio. The MC is the marker of highest achievement, and the Reds would win the 1975 World Series in the seventh game.

Blue Jays 15 – Phillies 14

The highest scoring World Series game occurred on the evening of October 20, 1993 in Philadelphia. The game began at 8:12 pm EDT and would end 4 hours and 14 minutes later. Like the highest-scoring regular season game, this game also involved the Phillies. Philadelphia would lose this one, too, but, unlike the 1922 game, in which they were behind in the late innings and almost caught up, the Phillies had led most of Game Four of the 1993 World Series. When the eighth inning began, the Phillies were winning 14-9, but Toronto would score 6 runs in the top of the eighth to take the lead for good. The important transits of the game were Venus semi-square Mercury, the Sun conjunct to Jupiter, and Saturn square to Pluto.

Venus, in transit at 6 degrees Libra formed a semi-square to Mercury at 21 degrees Scorpio. As in the Sixth Game, a semi-square involving Mercury and Venus led the pitchers to perform poorly.[647] Both starting pitchers walked a batter with the bases loaded. Phillies starter Tommy Greene

---

646. The next day, October 22, 1975, Joe Morgan hit a clutch two-out RBI single in the ninth inning, which drove in the Series-winning run for the Reds. On this final day of the season, second baseman Morgan, manifested the Saturn transit to the Reds' natal Venus with the final and most important RBI of 1975.

647. In the Sixth Game, which is analyzed in the preceding pages, the Sun and Venus in semi-square to each other formed an aspect to the Reds' Mercury.

lasted only 2 1/3 innings while surrendering 7 runs. Blue Jays starter Todd Stottlemyre would last only two innings and give up 6 runs. The semi-square to Mercury also caused a problem with the manager's communication to the bullpen, as the phone line that connected the Blue Jays' dugout with their bullpen would malfunction. Mercury rules communication devices.

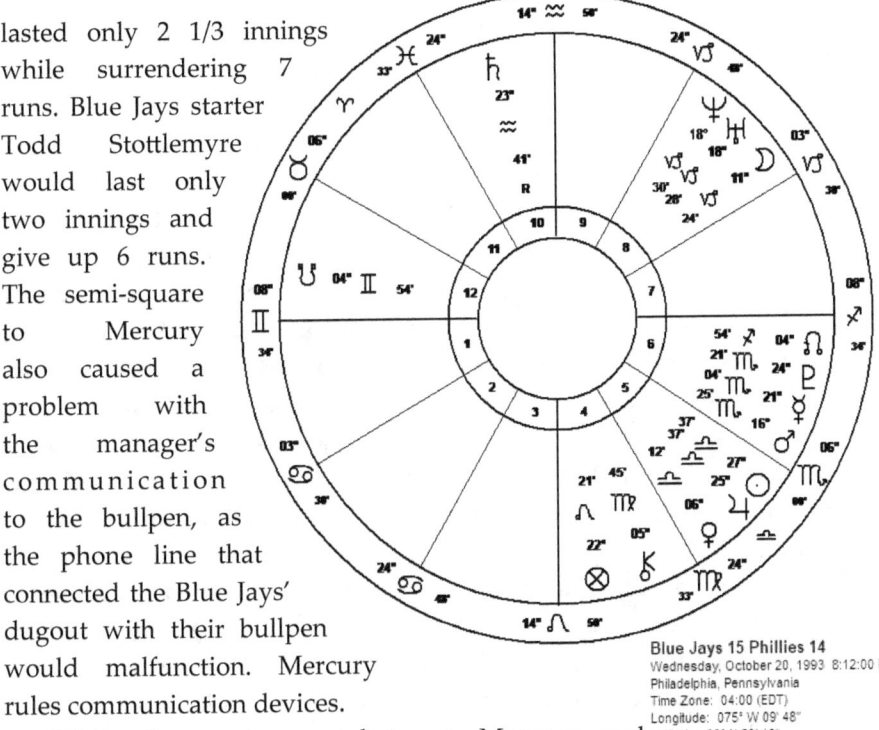

Blue Jays 15 Phillies 14
Wednesday, October 20, 1993 8:12:00 PM
Philadelphia, Pennsylvania
Time Zone: 04:00 (EDT)
Longitude: 075° W 09' 48"
Latitude: 39° N 59' 18"

While the semi-square between Mercury and Venus disrupted the pitchers, it did assist the Venus position players: the center fielders and second basemen. Venus and Mercury both formed aspects to the Phillies' Saturn of 21 degrees Taurus. Mercury formed a tight opposition to the Phillies' Saturn, while Venus made a 135-degree sesquiquadrate to it. The Phillies' Saturn in Taurus is represented in the Taurus position of center field. Lenny Dykstra, playing center field, responded to the transits by hitting two home runs. Dykstra would finish the game with four runs, three hits and four RBIs, while second baseman Mariano Duncan would have three hits and one RBI.

The Blue Jays would channel the Mercury-Venus semi-square through their natal Sun and Uranus. Transiting Venus, positioned at 6 degrees Libra, opposed the Blue Jays natal Sun of 6 degrees Aries. Venus also formed a semi-sextile to the Jays' natal Uranus of 6 degrees Scorpio. Center fielder Devon White had 4 RBIs and 3 hits, including a double and a triple; while Blue Jays' second baseman Roberto Alomar had two hits. Right fielder Joe Carter, embodying the Sun, had three hits. Left fielder Rickey Henderson, representing Uranus, had two hits and two RBIs.

Jupiter, the planet of the batter, is regularly involved in high-scoring games. This night, Jupiter received aspects from both the Sun and the

Moon. The Sun was conjunct to Jupiter with an orb of two degrees. At the start of the game, the Sun, in transit at 27 degrees, 27 minutes Libra, was separating from a conjunction with Jupiter at 25 degrees, 27 minutes Libra.[648] Usually, a 2-degree orb is too wide to have a discernible effect in a baseball game, but the Moon, in transit through Capricorn, this time added an extra aspect that brought the outpouring of Jupiter offense. At the start of the game, the Moon was positioned at 11 degrees, 24 minutes Capricorn, forming a 105-degree aspect to Jupiter. When the game ended, 4 hours and 14 minutes later, the Moon would be positioned at 13 degrees, 43 minutes Capricorn, forming a 105-degree aspect to the Sun.

The Sun at 28 degrees Libra formed an exact trine to the Phillies' natal Jupiter of 28 degrees Gemini. The Phillies Third House Jupiter in Gemini is embodied in both their pitchers and their batters. A trine to the Phillies' Jupiter is usually auspicious for the pitchers, as well as for the batters. Phillie batters did respond positively to the transit of the Sun to their natal Jupiter. Even a pitcher had a hit, as Tommy Greene singled and scored in the second inning—but Phillie pitchers were not assisted in their pitching by the trine from Jupiter. Six Phillie pitchers would allow the 15 runs. Mitch Williams, who played the goat in the 1993 World Series, took the loss. Williams was charged with three runs. He also allowed two inherited runners to score.

For the Blue Jays, the Sun and Jupiter both formed squares to their natal Saturn. The midpoint between the Sun and Jupiter was 26 degrees Libra, exactly square to the Blue Jays' natal Saturn of 26 degrees Cancer. A natal Saturn is embodied in a team's manager, and the transiting square to the Jays' natal Saturn brought manager Cito Gaston a very active role that night. In the fifth inning, the Blue Jay manager was forced to cope with the breakdown of his bullpen's telephone. Gaston had intended reliever Tony Castillo to pitch in the fifth inning. However, since the phone to the bullpen was not working, the wrong pitcher, Mike Eichhorn, warmed up. When Gaston called for the bullpen pitcher to enter the game, Mark Eichhorn walked to the mound and started his warm-up throws. After two throws, Eichhorn was stopped by Gaston, who then explained to the umpire the problem of the broken telephone. Tony Castillo was then brought to the mound and allowed all the time he needed to warm up. Although Castillo's line would not be impressive, allowing 2 runs in 2 1/3 innings, he would receive the win. Oddly, in a move that would be

---

648. Two days earlier on October 18, 1993, when the Sun was exactly conjunct to Jupiter within 1 degree, there was no World Series game as the team traveled from Toronto to Philadelphia. Jupiter rules travel, particularly international and long-distance travel.

criticized, Gaston allowed Castillo to bat. With the Blue Jays trailing 13-9, Castillo led off the seventh inning. Castillo, an American League pitcher not accustomed to batting, could only strike out.

The Blue Jays' Saturn is placed in the Twelfth House, the house of things hidden from view. A secretive manager corresponds with a Twelfth House Saturn, and Cito Gaston had a reputation for secrecy against the media. A post-game comment from Gaston further exemplified the placement of the Blue Jays' Saturn in Cancer. After the game, Gaston told reporters, "Maybe I want your stomach to bother you—the way you bother mine."[649] Cancer rules the stomach, and Saturn brings pain. That night, the Jays' manager felt the transits to the Jays' Saturn in Cancer right in his stomach.

The Blue Jays came from behind in the eighth inning to win the game. Saturn aspects regularly bring comebacks, and the square of the Sun and Jupiter to the Jays' natal Saturn allowed their rally of 6 runs to win the game. Two nights later, the Blue Jays won the World Series when Joe Carter hit a three-run homer off Mitch Williams. A defining transit of the 1993 season was the square between Saturn and Pluto. The Blue Jays were in perfect position to take advantage of this aspect. As the season came to a close, Pluto at 24 degrees Scorpio was square to Saturn at 24 degrees Aquarius. This powerful aspect would be channeled by the Blue Jays Moon of 23 degrees Aquarius.[650]

Following a Game

Cast a "game chart" for the scheduled start time of a baseball game. You can do this with many computer programs. Have in hand the birthcharts of both teams. Analyze the transits that will be made to each teams' natal planets. Pay special attention when the players corresponding to planets involved with that game's transits come to bat. These players will be keys to the game's outcome. You can also cast birthcharts of the starting and closing pitchers, or of any players whose individual transits you wish to observe. Transits to managers' charts are especially interesting to witness, especially in championship games.

Calculate the times that the Ascendant, Descendant, MC and IC will become conjunct to any planets. These are the same times that a planet will rise, set, and be conjunct to an axis. Pay extra attention to the game at these moments. Most of the scoring will occur when these axes points

---

649. *San Francisco Chronicle* Oct 21, 1993. p. D4
650. See" Saturn in the Post-Season" for a discussion of Game Six of the 1993 World Series. Also, see the Phillies Chapter for a discussion on Mitch Williams.

form conjunctions with planets.

Remember that the degrees of the zodiac are in continuous motion. These degrees repeat themselves every 24 hours. One degree of the zodiac passes an axis about every eight minutes. Since an a nine-inning baseball game usually lasts around 3 hours, the sky will shift enough to proceed through an average of 45 degrees of the zodiac during the course of a game. Not every planet will have an opportunity to cross an axis in a game of average length. In a typical day game, most of which begin at 1:05 pm daylight savings time, the sun crosses the MC in the first inning. In night games, which usually begin at 7:05 pm daylight savings time, the Sun crosses the Descendant in the first or second inning. Mercury's distance from the Sun is always within 28 degrees—and Venus is always within 47 1/2 degrees—of the Sun. These planets often cross an axis just before or soon after the Sun. The Moon, the middle planets, and the outer planets can be anywhere in the zodiac band and cross an axis at any time.

Post-season games are generally scheduled near 8pm Eastern Daylight Time to increase the national television audience. In the month of October, the Sun, Mercury, and Venus will already have crossed the Descendant by 8 pm for a game held on the East Coast. Nevertheless, a planet does not need to be conjunct an axis for a playoff team to respond to its energy. Barring an end-of-the-season or post-season slump, a playoff team is highly responsive to transits. Teams that reach the post-season are more likely to channel a planet into hits and runs without its being conjunct to an axis.

Follow the transits to the birthchart of your favorite team. You will learn the riches of your team's birthchart by observing its transits on a daily basis. If you do not have a favorite team, choose a team whose birthchart has synastry with your own by searching through Section II.

If you are inclined, follow the transits to the birthcharts of every Major League team. Each morning, analyze the box scores of the previous day's game and witness how the transits influenced the games. Why is one team playing hot? Why is another team mired in a slump? Why did a certain player go four-for-four? Why did a center fielder make two outfield assists? Defensive gems are generally overlooked in wire service reports. Similarly, putouts and assists are not regularly listed in box scores. But perhaps in the future, putouts and assists will be listed in the morning box scores, along with astrological notes.

SELECTED BIBLIOGRAPHY

PART I

Block, David. (2006). *Baseball before we knew it: A search for the roots of the game.* Lincoln, NE: University of Nebraska Press.

Campbell, Joseph. (1949). *The hero with a thousand faces.* Princeton, NJ: Princeton University Press.

Corrado, Gini. (1981). *Rural ritual games in Libya (Berber baseball and shinny).* Retrieved from *Our Game,* https://ourgame.mlblogs.com (2012. (Original source: *Rural Sociology, 4*(3). Columbia, Mo.: *Rural Sociological Society,* September 1939, pp. 283–299.)

Doczi, Gyorgy. (1981). *The power of limits: Proportional harmonies in nature, art and architecture.* Boston, MA: Shambala.

Feather, Norman. (1959). *An introduction to the physics of mass, length and time.* London, UK: Edinburgh University Press.

Frobinius, Leo. (1913). *Voices of Africa (Vol. II).* London, UK: Hutchinson.

Kahn, Roger. (1973). *The boys of summer.* New York, NY: Signet Books of the New American Library, Inc.

Kinsella, W. P. (1986). *The Iowa baseball confederacy.* New York, NY. Houghton Mifflin Harcourt.

Giamatti, A. Bartlett. (1989). *Take time for Paradise: Americans and their games.* New York, NY: Simon and Schuster.

Halberstam, David. *Summer of '49.* (1989). New York, NY: Avon Books.

Henderson, Robert W. (1947). *Ball, bat and bishop: The origin of ball games.* New, NY: Rockport Press.

Huizinga, Johan. (1950). *Homo ludens: A study of the play elements in culture.* Boston, MA: The Beacon Press.

Kherdian, David. *Monkey: A journey to the West: A retelling of the Chinese folk novel by Wu Cheng-en.* Boston, MA.: Shambala (distributed by Random House).

Lawlor, Robert. (1982). *Sacred geometry: Philosophy and practice.* London, UK: Thames & Hudson, Ltd.

Nichols, Sally. (1984). *Jung and Tarot: An archetypal journey* York Beach, ME. Samuel Weisner, Inc.

Mack, Connie. (1950). *My 66 years in the Big Leagues: The great story of America's national game.* Philadelphia, PA: The John C. Winston Company.

Malamud, Bernard. (1952). *The natural.* New York, NY: Dell Publishing.

Nucciarone, Monica. (2009). *Alexander Cartwright: The life behind the baseball legend.* Lincoln, NA: University of Nebraska Press.

Oken, Alan. (1974). *The horoscope, the road and its travelers.* New York, NY: Bantam.

Peterson, Harold. (1973). *The man who invented baseball.* New York, NY: Charles Scribner's Sons.

Rudhyar, Dane. (1972). *The astrological houses: The spectrum of individual experience.*

Garden City, NY: Doubleday.

Tedlock, Dennis. (1996). *Popol Vuh: The definitive edition of the Mayan Book of The Dawn of Life and The Glories of Gods and Kings.* New York, NY: Touchstone.

Thorn, John. (2011). *Baseball in the Garden of Eden: The secret history of the early game.* New York, NY: Simon & Schuster.

Vlasich, James. (1990). *A legend for the legendary: The origin of the Baseball Hall of Fame.* Bowling Green, Ohio: Bowling Green State University Popular Press.

Will, George. (1990). *Men at work: The craft of baseball.* MacMillan Publishing Company. New York 1990

Witold, Kula. (1986). *Measures and men* (Translated by Robert Szreter). Princeton, NJ: Princeton University Press.

PART II

Adomites, Paul. (1993). *Pittsburgh Pirates: The art of the comeback.* In *Encyclopedia of major league baseball: National League team histories.* New York, NY: Carrol & Graf.

Adomites, Paul. (1993). *Seattle Pilots – Milwaukee Brewers: The bombers, the bangers and the burners.* In Peter Bjarkman (Ed.), *Encyclopedia of Major League Baseball: American League.* New York, NY: Carroll & Graf.

Ahrens, Art. (1993). "Sic Transit Gloria Mundi." In *Encyclopedia of Major League Baseball: National League Team Histories.* New York, NY: Carroll & Graf.

Alexander, Charles C. (1988). *John McGraw.* New York, NY: Viking Penguin.

Alexander, Charles C. (1984). *Ty Cobb.* New York, NY: New York University Press.

Allen, Lee. (1948). *The Cincinnati Reds.* New York, NY: G. P. Putnam's Sons.

Allen, Lee. (1961). *The National League story: The official history.* New York, NY: Hill &Wang.

Appel, Marty. (1993). "New York Yankees: Pride, tradition and a bit of controversy." In *Encyclopedia of Major League Baseball: American League,* (Peter Bjarkman, Ed.). New York, NY: Carroll & Graf.

Asinof, Eliot. (1963). *Eight men out: The Black Sox and the 1919 World Series.* New York, NY: Holt, Reinhart & Winston.

Associated Press. (2010, May 19) *Ramirez Won't Apologize to Teammates.*

Atkins, Hunter. (2012, May 7) "Rays' Joe Maddon: King of shifts" *New York Times.*

Benson, Michael. (1989). *Ballparks of North America: A comprehensive historical reference to baseball grounds.* Jefferson, N C: McFarland.

Beverage, Richard E. (1993). Los Angeles Angels – California Angels: A cowboy's search for another champion." In *Encyclopedia of Major League Baseball: American League* (Peter Bjarkman, Ed.). New York, NY: Carroll & Graf.

Bisher, Furman. (1972). *Strange but True Baseball Stories.* New York, NY: Random House Children's Books.

Blair, Jeff. (1996). The Expos' climb back will take longer than their fall. In *The Sporting News Baseball Yearbook (1996).*

Bjarkman, Peter C. (1993). *Encyclopedia of major league baseball: National League team histories.* New York, NY: Carrol & Graf.

Bjarkman, Peter C. (1993). "Washington Senators – Texas Rangers: There are no dragons in baseball, only shortstops." In *Encyclopedia of Major League Baseball: American League* (Peter Bjarkman, Ed.). New York, NY: Carroll & Graf.

Bjarkman, Peter C. (1993). "Toronto Blue Jays: Okay, Blue Jays! From worst to first in a Decade." In *Encyclopedia of Major League Baseball: American League* (Peter Bjarkman, Ed.). New York, NY: Carroll & Graf.

Bluejayhunter.com (2011, Sept. 9). *Acid Flashback Friday: Dave Winfield hits a Seagull*.

Bouton, Jim. (1990). *Ball four*. New York, NY: Macmillan USA.

Bryson, Bill. (1951). *Through the years with the Western League since 1885*. Western League.

Canseco, Jose. (2005). *Juiced: Wild times, rampant 'roids, smash hits & how baseball got big*. New York, NY: Regan Books.

Caple, Jim. (2009, January 6th). *Pohlad was good, bad for Twins*. (ESPN.com)

Carle, Bill. (1993). "Kansas City Royals: Building a champion from scratch in America's Heartland." In Peter Bjarkman, (Ed.), *Encyclopedia of Major League Baseball: American League*. New York, NY. 1993

Carlson, Stan. (1993). St. Louis Cardinals: Baseball's perennial gas house gang. In *Encyclopedia of Major League Baseball: National League Team Histories*. New York, NY: Carrol & Graf.

Carroll, John M. (1991). *Houston Colt .45's—Houston Astros: From showbiz to serious baseball business*. In Peter Bjarkman (Ed.), *Encyclopedia of Major League Baseball: National League*. New York, NY: Carroll & Graf.

Cava, Pete. (1993). New York Mets from Throneberry to Strawberry: Baseball's most successful expansion franchise. In Peter Bjarkman (Ed.), *Encyclopedia of Major League Baseball: National League*. New York, NY: Carroll & Graf.

Chass, Murray. (1992, Dec. 10). "Those Tumultuous Winter Meetings Conclude under a Cloud." In *New York Times*.

Christian Science Monitor. (1980, July 10). "Eddie Chiles: The Angry Man of Texas."

Dewey, Donald, & Acocella, Nicholas. (1993). *Encyclopedia of Major League Baseball Teams*. New York, NY: HarperCollins.

Durso, Joseph. (1968, May). "National League adds Montreal and San Diego." In *New York Times*.

Eckhouse, Morris. (1993). Boston Braves – Milwaukee Braves – Atlanta Braves: More woes than wahoos for baseball's wanderers." In Peter Bjarkman (Ed.), *Encyclopedia of Major League Baseball: National League*. New York, NY: Carroll & Graf.

Eckhouse, Morris. (1993). "Cleveland Indians: Reent Wahoo woes overshadow Cleveland's baseball tradition." In Peter Bjarkman (Ed.), *Encyclopedia of Major League Baseball: American League*. New York, NY: Carroll & Graf.

Eckhouse, Morris. (1993). *Day by Day in Cleveland Indians History*. New York, NY: Leisure Press.

Eckhouse, Morris. (1993). "Detroit Tigers: The cornerstone of Detroit baseball is stability." In Peter Bjarkman (Ed.), *Encyclopedia of Major League Baseball: American League*. New York, NY: Carroll & Graf.

Ellard, Harry. *Baseball in Cincinnati: A History*. BaseballChronology.com edition

(originally published in Cincinnati 1907)

Eskenazi, Gerald. (1988). *Bill Veeck: A Baseball Legend*. New York, NY: McGraw-Hill.

espn.com news services. "Barry Bonds Steroids Timeline." sports.espn.go.com

Felber, Bill. (1993). "St. Louis Browns – Baltimore Orioles: One of the Very Worst and One of the Very Best." In Peter Bjarkman (Ed.), *Encyclopedia of Major League Baseball: American League*. New York, NY: Carroll & Graf.

Garnet, Vance. (2011, Oct. 10). "The Washington Monument and Baseball: Related icons." The Washington Times Communities. (communities.washingtontimes.com)

Gewecke, Cliff. (1984). *Day by Day in Dodgers History*. New York, NY: Leisure Press.

Ghiroli, Brittany. (2008). "Maddon uses 9=8 slogan to motivate." MLB.com 07/03/08

Gloster, Rob. (1998/April 1). "In Ariz., Swim While Watching a Game." *Associated Press* (www.apnewsarchive.com).

Golenbock, Peter. (2000). *Spirit of St. Louis: A History of the Cardinals and Browns*. New York, NY: HarperCollins.

Greene, Liz. (1983). *The Outer Planets and Their Cycles: The Astrology of the Collective*. Sebastopol, CA

Green, Jerry. (1969). *Year of the Tiger: The Diary of Detroit's World Champions*. New York, NY: Coward-McCann.

Guntze, Jeff Severns. (2010: Sept. 8). *Racial Justice for the Minnesota Twins: The Forgotten Battle*." (Minnesota Post).

Halberstam, David. (1995). *October 1964*. New York, NY: Barnes & Noble.

Halberstam, David. (1989). *Summer of '49*. New York, NY: Avon Books.

Hall, Donald, with Dock Ellis. (1989). *Dock Ellis in the Country of Baseball*. New York, NY: Fireside Books.

Hazacha, Andrew. (2008). "Educating Wrigley: The Failed Experiment of the College of Coaches." In *Northsiders: Essays on the History and Culture of the Chicago Cubs*.

Hoch, Bryan. (2008: Oct. 28). "In a First, World Series Game Suspended" MLB.com

Holway, John B. (1993). "Diamond Stars: Baseball Astrology." In Peter Bjarkman (Editor), *Baseball & The Game of Ideas: Essays for the Serious Fans*. Delhi, NY: Birch Brook Press.

Hurte, Bob. *Sabre Baseball Biography Project: Steve Blass*. http://sabr.org

Ivor-Campbell, Frederick. (1994, Sept. 30). "Their Foot Shall Slide… Baseball's Most Potent Myth." In *Encyclopedia of Major League Baseball: American League* (Peter Bjarkman, Ed.). New York, NY: Carroll & Graf.

Jackson, Robert L. (1994, Sept. 30) "Threat to Antitrust Exemption: Baseball Congressional Committee Approves Legislation that Would Partly Remove Protection of Owners From Suits by Players." *Los Angeles Times*

Jarvis, Mary. "Angels, Aquarius and the Age of Light." (1994: Dec.). In *The Mountain Astrologer*. Cedar Ridge, CA.

Jocelyn, John. (1970). *Meditations on the Sign of the Zodiac*. Blauvelt, New York: Rudolf Steiner Publications.

Jefferson City Post-Tribune. (1961, Mar. 9). "St. Petersburg Denies Snubbing Negro Players," p. 9.

BIBLIOGRAPHY

Jong, Michael. (2012, Nov. 29). "Miami Marlins Fire Sale Comparison 2012 vs. 2005." Fish Stripes.

Kaplan, Ron. (2010, Sept. 9) "The Legacy of Ball Four." In *The Huffington Post*.

Kaese, Harold. (1948). *The Boston Braves*. New York, NY: G. P. Putnam's Sons.

Kahn, Roger. (1971). *The Boys of Summer*. New York, NY: Harper & Row.

Krasovic, Tom. (1996). "Padres' Gains figure to Be Encouraging Their Flock." In *The Sporting News Baseball Yearbook*.

Lewis, Franklin. (1949). *The Cleveland Indians*. New York, NY: G. P. Putnam's Sons.

Libby, Bill. (1975) *Charlie O. and the Angry A's*. Garden City, New York: Doubleday.

Lieb, Frederick. (1945). *Connie Mack: Grand Old Man of Baseball*. New York, NY: G. P. Putnam's Sons.

Lieb, Frederick G. (1945). *The Detroit Tigers*. New York, NY: G. P. Putnam's Sons.

Lieb, Frederick G. (1948). *The Pittsburgh Pirates*. New York, NY: G. P. Putnam's Sons.

Lieb, Frederick G. (1956). *The Baltimore Orioles*. New York, NY: G. P. Putnam's Sons.

Lieb, Frederick G. (1955). *The Pittsburgh Pirates*. New York, NY: G. P. Putnam's Sons.

Lieb, Frederick, & Baumgartner, Stan. (1953). *The Philadelphia Phillies*. New York, NY: G. P. Putnam's Sons.

Lieb, Frederick. (1945). *Connie Mack: Grand Old Man of Baseball*. New York, NY: G. P. Putnam's Sons.

Lindberg, Richard. (1983). *Who's on 3rd?: the Chicago White Sox Story*. South Bend, Indiana: Icarus Press.

Lindberg, Richard. (1993). "Chicago White Sox: Second Class in the Second City." *Encyclopedia of Major League Baseball: American League*, (Peter Bjarkman, Ed.). New York: NY: Carroll & Graf.

Macht, Norman L. (1993). "Philadelphia Athletics—Kansas City Athletics—Oakland A's: Three Families and Three Baseball Epochs." In *Encyclopedia of Major League Baseball: American League Team Histories*, Bjarkman, Peter C. (Editor). New York, NY: Carrol and Graf.

Macmullan, Jackie. (2011, Sept. 30). Unlikeable Red Sox flunked chemistry. ESPN Boston.com

Mandel, Mike. (1979. *SF Giants: An oral history*. Santa Cruz, CA: Author.

Mead, William B. (1978). *Even the Browns: The zany, true story of baseball in the early forties*. Chicago, Il.: Contemporary Books.

Mead, William B. (1990). *Two spectacular seasons*. New York, NY: Macmillan.

Morgan, Joe. (2013, Aug. 4). "McKeon, Marlins' 2003 squad back in Miami." MLB.com

Nack, William. (1990: Aug. 20) "Hey, Hey, Hey, Good Bye!" In *Sports Illustrated*.

Nash, Bruce, & Zullo, Allan. (1985). *The Baseball Hall of Shame*. New York, NY: Pocket Books.

New York Times Encyclopedia of Sports. Volume 2: Baseball. (1979). Gene Brown, (Ed.). New York, NY: Arno Press.

New London Conn. (1953, Jan. 29, p. 12). "Fred Saighn, Cardinal Owner, Gets 15

Months in Jail for Tax Evasion."

NPR.org (2013, Sept. 5). "The Boston Red Sox and Racism."

O'Donnell, James. (1993). "Seattle Mariners: Waiting for a winner in baseball's forgotten city." In *Encyclopedia of Major League Baseball: American League*. Peter Bjarkman, Ed. New York, NY: Carroll & Graf.

Okkonen, Marc. (1991). *Baseball uniforms of the 20th Century*. New York, NY: Sterling.

Okrent, Daniel. (1985). *Nine innings*. New York, NY: McGraw-Hill.

Onigman, Mark. (1982). *This Date in Braves History*. Briarcliff Manon, NY: Stein & Day.

Pace, Eric. (1993, Aug. 2). "Ewing M. Kauffman, 76, Owner of the Kansas City Baseball Team." New York, NY: *New York Times*.

Parker, Dan. (1959). "The Los Angeles Dodgers." In *The National League*. (Ed Fitzgerald, Ed.). New York, NY: Grosset & Dunlap.

Petrusza, David. (2005). *Major Leagues: The formation, sometimes absorption and mostly inevitable demise of 18 professional baseball organizations, 1871 to present*. Jefferson, NC: McFarland.

Porter, David L. (1993). "San Diego Padres: The saga of Big Mac and Trader Jack." In *Encyclopedia of Major League Baseball: National League*. Peter Bjarkman, Ed. New York, NY: Carroll & Graf.

Povich, Shirley. (1954). *The Washington Senators*. New York, NY: G.P. Putnam's Sons

Rose, Pete, & Kahn, Roger. (1989). *Pete Rose: My Story*. New York, NY: Macmillan.

Rosenthal, Ken. (2013, July 30*). Martinez speaks out about incidents*." Los Angeles, CA: Fox Sports.

Reach, A. J. (1894) *Reach's Official Base Ball Guide*. Philadelphia, PA: A. J. Reach.

Shaughnessy, Dan. (1990). *Curse of the Bambino*. New York, NY: E. P. Dutton.

Shaughnessy, Dan. (2006). *Reversing the curse: Inside the 2004 Boston Red Sox*. New York, NY: Mariner Books

Stark, Jayson. (2011, Mar. 22). "Manny Ramirez's voice being heard." In espn.com.

Stein, Fred, & Peters, Nick. (1987). *Giants Diary*. Berkeley, CA: North Atlantic Books.

Stone, Larry. (2013, Apr. 2). "Safeco Field changes aren't expected to turn ballpark into a

launching pad for home runs—but should make it 'fair.'" Seattle, WA: *Seattle Times*.

Tampabay.rays.mlb.com. (2007, Nov. 8). "Time to shine: Rays introduce new name, new icon, new team colors and new uniforms."

Tarnas, Richard (2007) *Cosmos and Psyche: Intimations of a New World View*. New York: Plume Penguin Books.

Thompson, Dick, & The Society of American Baseball Research, No. 20. (2015). *"In Name Only": The National Pastime: A Review of Baseball History*.

Updike, John. (1960, Oct. 22). "Hub Fans Bid Kid Adieu." In *The New Yorker*.

Voight, David Quintin. (1993). *American baseball: Volume I*. Pennsylvania State University Press: University Park and London.

Whitford, David. (1993). *Playing hardball: The high-stakes battle for baseball's new *franchises*. New York, NY: Doubleday.

Work Project Administration. (1939). *Baseball in Old Chicago: Federal Writers Project of Illinois*. Chicago, IL.: A.C. McClerg & Co.

PART III

Ahrens, Art, & Gold, Eddie. (1982). *Day by day in Chicago Cubs history*. New, NY: Leisure Press.

Berke, Art, & Schmitt, Paul. (1982). *This date in Chicago White Sox history*. New York, NY: Stein & Day.

Coberly, Rich. (1985, Sept. 29). *No-hit hall of fame* (Triple Play Publications). Newport Beach, CA. In *San Francisco Chronicle*, p. 39.

Conner, Floyd, & Snyder, John. (1983). *Day-by-day in Cincinnati Reds history*. New York, NY: Leisure Press.

Eckhouse, Morris. (1980) *This date in Pittsburgh Pirates history*. New York, NY: Stein & Day.

Eckhouse, Morris. (1984). *Day-by-day in Cleveland Indians history*. New York, NY: Leisure Press.

Gewecke, Cliff. (1984). *Day-by-day in Dodgers history*. New York, NY: Leisure Press.

Hawkins, John. (1981). *This date in Tiger's history: A day-by-day listing of the events in the history of the Detroit Tigers Baseball Team*. New York, NY: Stein & Day.

Lewis, Allen, & Shenk, Larry. (1979). *This date in Philadelphia Phillies history*. New York, NY: Stein and Day.

Lieb & Baumgartner (1993, Oct. 4). *The Philadelphia Phillies*. G. P. Putnam's Sons.

Thorn, John. (1981). *Baseball's ten greatest games*. New York, NY: Four Winds Press.

Walton, Edward H. (1980). *Triumphs and tragedies in Red Sox history: A continuation of day-by-day listings and events in the history of the Boston American League Baseball Team*. New York, NY: Stein & Day.

INDEX

4-F players 171
1919 World Series 67, 137, 160, 161, 163, 168, 356

A

Aaron, Hank 41, 83, 84, 89, 96, 133, 142, 259
Abbot, Jim 38
Adenhart, Nick 256
Aeneas 47
Affinities 29
Alcoholics Anonymous 46
Alexander, Grover Cleveland 121, 122, 147, 148
Allen, Dick 149
Alomar, Jr., Sandy 324
Alomar, Roberto 287, 351
Alou, Felipe 140, 277
Alou, Jesus 140
Alou, Matty 140
Alou, Moises 79, 80, 278, 326
Alston, Walter 100
American Association 112, 113, 114, 119, 258
Anderson, Greg 142
Anderson, Sparky 104, 348, 349
Andrews, Mike 205
Angelos, Peter 177
Angels 156, 243, 251, 335
Angels in the Outfield 257
Anheiser-Busch 121
Anson, Cap 71, 73, 74, 76
Aparicio, Luis 165
Appling, Luke 35, 165, 314
Aquarius 21
Aquarius and home run 41
Aquarius and left field 41
Argyros, George 283
Aricibia, J. P. 288
Aries 18
Aries and shortstop 35
Arizona Diamondbacks 156, 177, 180, 186, 187, 188, 243, 251, 336
Aspects 31,
Astrodome 237, 239, 240, 281
Astroturf 240, 265, 278
Athletics 156, 177, 180, 186, 187, 188, 243, 251, 336
Atlanta Braves. See Braves
Axes Conjunct to the Planets 317

B

Baez, Javiar 80
Baker, Frank 187
Baker, William 148
Ball, Bat and Bishop 156

Ball Four 260, 261
Ball of the Mother of the Pilgrim 11, 14
Baltimore Orioles 60, 169, 325
Bancroft, Dave 148
Banjo Players 114
Banks, Ernie 74, 174
Barger, Carl 295, 296
Barr, Rosanne 272
Bartholomay, William 87, 90
Bartman, Steve 79, 80
Baseball Before We Knew It 10
batter and Sagittarius 39
Belinsky, Bo 252, 253
Bench, Johnny 313
Bennett, Charley 108
Bennett, Charlie 85
Bennett Park 108
Berber 11, 14, 355
Bergen, Marty 86
Berra, Dale 117
Bierbauer, Lou 112
Biggio, Craig 239
Big Red Machine See Cincinnati Reds
Billyball 207
Birthcharts 25, 59, 327, 338
Birthcharts of Position Players 338
Black Cat Incident 79
Black Sox 161, 162, 164, 165
Blass, Steve 111, 117
Block, David 10, 11
Blue Jays 15 - Phillies 14 350
Blue, Vida 334, 335
boating accident 192, 193
Bonds, Barry 41, 115, 133, 140, 141, 142, 319
Bonds, Bobby 141
Boone, Aaron 215, 216
Bostock, Lyman 256
Boston Braves. See Braves
Boston Red Sox 156, 177, 180, 186, 187, 188, 243, 251, 336
Boston Red Stockings National League. See Braves
Bottomley, Jim 121
Boudreau, Lou 35, 184, 194
Bouton, Jim 260
Boyd, Dennis "Oil Can" 227
Boyer, Ken 126, 129
Boys of Summer 36, 98
Brady, Laurie 210
Brainard, Asa 65
Braves 82, 105, 108, 206, 220, 241, 259, 306, 319, 322, 323, 336
Brennan, Ad 148
Brett, George 265
Briggs Stadium 108
Briggs, Walter O. 108
Brock, Lou 127

Brooklyn Dodgers. See Dodgers
Broun, Heywood 136
Brown, Kevin 294, 295, 331
Brush, John 137
Buckner, Bill 219, 220, 229
Buhner, Jay 37, 282
Burns, Ken 210
bus accident 255
Busch Jr., August "Gussie" 121
Busch Stadium 121

C

Cadore, Leon 91
California Angels. See Angels
Calovito, Rocky 191
Calypso 47
Camili, Dolf 148
Campanella, Roy 37, 98, 99, 100, 203, 312, 345
Campbell, Joseph 44, 54
Cancer 19
Cancer and catcher 36
Candlestick Park 138
Canseco, Jose 207, 208, 261, 300
Capricorn 21
Capricorn and the manager 40
Cardinal farm system 124
Carew, Rod 39, 188
Carey, Harry 161, 167
Carlton, Steve 128, 147
Carter, Gary 37, 276
Carter, Joe 112, 153, 321, 322, 351, 353
Cartwright, Alexander 10, 11, 51, 54, 355
Cash, Norm 108
Castor and Pollux 222
Cat 10
catcher 36
center fielder 35
Champion, Aaron 64
Chance, Frank 73, 74, 76, 213
Chapman, Ray 191, 192
Chase, Hal 67, 68, 161, 214
Chavez Ravine 98
Chicago Cubs 51, 59, 70, 306
Chicago Daily News 75
Chicago Tribune Media Group 75
Chicago White Sox 60, 159
Chicago White Stockings (National League). See Chicago Cubs
Chief Yellowhorse 115
Christopher, Mayor George 138
Cincinnati Reds 59, 63, 161, 213, 216, 313, 347
Cincinnati Red Stockings. See Cincinnati Reds
Citizen's Bank Park 145
Civil Rights 90, 129
Clarke, Fred 114
Clarkson, John 71
Clark, Will 42

Clemens, Roger 225, 227, 242
Clemente, Roberto 37, 115
Cleveland Indians 156, 190, 243, 251, 325, 326
Clyde, David 244, 245
Cobb, Ty 40, 69, 102, 104, 105, 106, 107, 108, 109, 110, 165
Cochran, Mickey 200
Colangelo, Jerry 304, 305, 307
Colorado Rockies 231, 291
Comiskey, Charles 121, 160, 164, 191
Comiskey Park 159, 160, 161, 164, 166, 167, 191
Commissioner Kenesaw 'Mountain' Landis 109, 124, 130
Conigliaro, Tony 220
conjunction 31
Conner, Roger 133
Continental League 233, 237
Cosmos and Psyche 158
Counsell, Craig 326
Craig, Roger 135, 271
Crawford, Sam 105
Cronin, Joe 138, 184, 185
Cubs 26 - Phillies 23 315, 342
Curse of Rocky Calovito 191
Curse of the Bambino 219, 223
Curse of the Goat 77, 78

D

Dahlen, Bill 139
Damn Yankees 8, 180
Dark, Alvin 140, 271
DaVinci, Leonardo 53
Dawson, Andre 276, 278
Dead Ball Era 133, 167, 168, 207
Dean, Dizzy 121, 123
Delahanty, Ed 184, 185
Delehanty, Ed 147
Dent, Bucky 215, 229
Detroit Tigers 60, 63, 82, 83, 84, 85, 86, 87, 88, 89, 90, 91, 99, 100, 102,
Detroit Wolverines 108
DiMaggio, Joe 40, 215
Disco Demolition Night 160, 165, 166, 313
Dodgers 91, 92, 334
Dodger Stadium 98, 100
Doescher, Herman 107
Doheny, Ed 116
Dominican Republic 140, 287
Donlin, Mike 136
Doolan, Mickey 148
Doubleday, Abner 9, 10, 11
The Double 284, 285
Double No-Hitter 332
Dravecky, Dave 139
Dreyfuss, Barney 111, 113
Drysdale, Don 101, 267
Durocher, Leo 76, 77, 123

E

Easter 13
Ebbets Field 92, 94, 345
Eckersley, Dennis 205, 209
Edison, Thomas 21
egg 14
Egypt 12, 53, 56
Elements 8, 22, 152
Ellis, Doc 111, 117, 118
Evers, Johnny 73
Ewing, Buck 66, 151
Expansion Era 156, 177, 180, 186, 187, 188, 231, 243, 251
Exposition Stadium 288

F

Famous Games 342
fan interference 79
father's side 14
FDR 183
Fear Strikes Out 225
Federal League 147, 148
Feller, Bob 171, 191, 196
Fernandez, Tony 287, 289, 325, 326
Fewster, Chick 95
Fielder, Prince 108, 260
Field of Dreams 8, 51
Fingers, Rollie 209, 334
Finley, Charlie 201, 205, 207
first ball 180, 181, 182
first baseman 41
Fisk, Carlton 349
Flood, Curt 130
Florida Marlins. See Marlins
foot, unit of 55
Foxx, Jimmy 138, 207, 227
Freedman, Andrew 137
Freese, David 126, 249
Frobenius, Leo 15

G

Gaedel, Eddie 172, 173, 174
gambling 63, 68, 69, 213
Gandil, Chick 161, 163
Gas House Gang 123, 126
Gaston, Cito 352, 353
Gebel Nefusa 11, 14, 355
Gehrig, Lou 42, 138, 177, 178, 217, 220
Gemini 19
Gemini and pitcher 36
Giamatti, A. Bartlett 51, 223
Giants 132
Gibson, Bob 121, 267, 320
Gibson, Kirk 205
Gini, Corrado 11, 355
Glass, David 265
Glavine, Tom 88
Go-Go Sox 168

Golenbock, Peter 125
Gore, George 73
Grandstand Managers' Day 174
Gray, Pete 171, 172
Greenberg, Hank 108, 196
Greene, Liz 238
Green Monster 226
Griffey Jr., Ken 281, 282
Griffey, Sr., Ken 284, 348
Griffith, Calvin 184, 187, 188
Griffith, Clark 182, 183, 184, 185, 187, 188, 200, 201, 213
Grimes, Burleigh 96, 116
Grimm, Charlie 114
Guerrero, Pedro 95
Guillen, Ozzie 165, 297

H

Hades 13, 14, 47, 222
Haines, Jesse 121
Halberstam, David 127, 215
Hanged Man of the Tarot 46
Harmony Conference 113
Harris, Bucky 184
Heilman, Harry 106
Henderson, Krazy George 203
Henderson, Rickey 207, 210, 264, 269, 351
Henderson, Robert 10, 12
Herman, Babe 95
Hernandez, Keith 121
The Hero with a Thousand Faces 44, 54
Hershiser, Orel 38
Higham, Dick 107
Hilltop Park 211
Hitters' Years 319
Hobbs, Roy 41, 152
Hodges, Gil 235, 236
Horton, Willie 281, 316
Houses 26, 28, 62, 106, 138, 274, 328
House System 27
Houston Astros 156, 187, 188, 237, 243, 338
Houston Colt .45s. See Houston Astros
Howser, Dick 263
Hoy, William "Dummy" 66
Hubbel, Carl 138
Hubbell, Carl 36
Huizenga, Wayne 295
Hurst, Don 146

I

inconjunction 32
Industrial Revolution 50, 64
Injuries 6, 339
The Iowa Baseball Confederacy 51
Isis 12

J

Jack Murphy Stadium 272

Jackson, Joe 163, 165
Jackson, Reggie 37, 207, 214, 335
Jacobs, Eli 177
Jadum 11, 14, 355
Jason and the Argonauts 48, 222
Jennings, Hughie 105
Jenson, Jackie 226
Jesus 13
Jethro, Sam "Jet" 88
Johnson, Ban 40, 156, 157, 183, 184, 212, 221, 225
Johnson, Randy 38, 282, 285, 305, 307
Johnson, Walter 184, 186, 187, 195
Jonah Old Testament 45
Jones, Cleon 236
Jones, Randy 269
Joseph Old Testament 45
Joyce, Robert 93
juiced ball 141, 265, 268, 281, 284, 293, 319
Jupiter 24
Jupiter and the batter 39

K

Kaline, Al 106, 312
Kansas City Athletics. See Athletics
Kansas City Royals 262
Kauffman, Ewing M. 263, 360
Keane, Johnny 126
Kelly, Mike "King" 37, 71, 85
Killebrew, Harmon 188
Killefer, Bill 148
Kingdome 280, 281, 285, 288
Kings County 285
Kinsella, W. P. 51
Klein, Chuck 145, 146, 148
Knabe, Otto 148
Koufax, Sandy 36, 101
Kroc, Ray 271
Kuhn, Bowie 205, 258

L

Lajoie, Napolean 197
Lajoie, Napoleon 147, 186, 193, 197, 203
Larsen, Don 330
LaRussa, Tony 200, 209
Lasorda, Tommy 95, 100
Latham, Arlie 125
Lawlor, Robert 53
Lazzeri, Tony 122
Leach, Tommy 114
left fielder 41
Leo 19
Leo and right fielder 37
Leyland, Jim 104, 298
Libra 20
Libra and second base 3Libya 10
Lieb, Frederick 105, 108, 148
Loma Prieta Earthquake 142
Long Ball 11
Loria, Jeffrey 296

Los Angeles Angels of Anaheim. See Angels
Los Angeles Coliseum 100
Los Angeles Dodgers. See Dodgers
Louisville Colonels 114
Luque, Adolfo 66

M

Mack, Connie 12, 40, 51, 52, 87, 135, 191, 199, 200, 201, 202
Maddon, Joe 80, 301, 302
Maddox, Greg 88, 333
Magee, Lee 67
Maigaard, Per 11
Malamud, Bernard 152
manager 40
Mantle, Mickey 214
Maranville, Rabbit 114
Marichal, Juan 139, 140
Maris, Roger 41, 126, 141, 209, 215, 268, 319
Marlins 294, 325-327
Mars 24
Mars and shortstop 35
Martin, Billy 105, 188, 207
Martinez, Edgar 284, 285
Martin, Pepper 123, 126
Mathewson, Christy 67, 134
Mauch, Gene 41, 276
Mayan twins 47
Mays, Carl 192, 225
Mays, Willie 36, 90, 133, 135, 136, 140, 141, 192, 225, 228
Mazeroski, Bill 39, 111, 112
McCormick, Jim 73
McCovey, Willie 42, 133
McGinnity, Joe "Iron Man" 138
McGraw, John 86, 105, 113, 132, 134, 136, 139, 150, 175, 184, 212
McGwire, Mark 121, 126, 141, 207, 268, 319
McKeon, Jack 298
McKnight, Denny 113
McLain, Denny 107
Medwick, Joe 109
Mercer, Win 107
Mercury 23
Mercury and pitcher 36-38
mergers 113
Messersmith, Andy 90
Miami Marlins. See Marlins
Mills Commission 10
Milwaukee Braves. See Braves
Milwaukee Brewers 156, 258,
Minnesota Twins 156, 179, 243
Minute Maid Park 240
Miracle Mets 76, 234, 235
Miracle of Coogan's Bluff 144
Mize, Johnny 121
Modalities 22
Moneyball 208
Months 320

Montreal Expos 273
Moon 23
Moon and catcher 36
Moon, Wally 100
Moore, Donny 254
Moran, Pat 148
Morgan, Joe 39, 238, 348
Moses 48
Mota, Manny 140
mother's side 14
Moultrie, Jim 139
Murakami, Masanori 140
Murtaugh, Danny 111
Musial, Stan 124, 129

N

National League 60, 64, 66, 75, 87, 102, 103, 112, 113, 114, 124, 131
National League Date of Birth 131
The Natural 41, 152
Navin Field 108
Navin, Frank 107, 108
Neptune 25
Neptune and first base 41
Newcombe, Don 345
New Senators 179, 231, 244, 245, 279
Newsom, Bobo 185
New York Cubans 239
New York Daily News 235
New York Game 10
New York Giants. See Giants
New York Highlanders. See New York Yankees
New York Mets 232
Nimick, William 124
Nintendo 280, 282
No-hitters 329
Nomo, Hideo 38, 101, 140, 331
Northwestern League 113
Nucciarone, Monica 10, 54, 355
Nugent, Gerald 148

O

Oakland Athletics. See Athletics
O'Doul, Lefty 145
Oeschger, Joe 91
Oken, Alan 25, 32
Old Testament 45
Olympic Stadium 273, 275, 278, 287
O'Malley, Peter 100
O'Malley, Walter 97, 100
Opening Day 35, 180, 181
Orbs 32, 311, 317
O'Rourke, Jim 84
Orpheus 47
Osiris 12, 13
Osteen, Claude 101
Ott, Mel 133
Owen, Marv 109

P

Pacific Bell Park 138
Parker, Dave 115, 117
Payson, Joan 233
Perry, Gaylord 269
Persephone 13
Pesky, Johnny 220, 229
Peterson, Harold 9, 10, 11, 14, 355
Philadelphia Athletics. See Athletics
Philadelphia Phillies 5, 60, 105, 145 241, 315, 342, 344
Piasecki, Eugene 14
Piazza, Mike 99, 100, 313, 317
Piersall, Jimmy 225
pilgrim 14
Pisces 22
Pisces and first base 41
pitcher 36-38
Pitchers' Years 319
Pittsburgh Drug Trials of 1985 117
Pittsburgh Pirates 111, 315
Players League 112
Players Protective Association 183
Pluto 25
Pluto and third base 39
Pohlad, Carl 188
Poison Ball 10
Polo Grounds 133
Popol Vuh 47
Powers, Mike "Doc" 202
Preacher Roe 96
progressions 32
Providence Grays 84
Pujols, Albert 121, 252
Pythagoras 52, 56

Q

quincunx 32

R

Raines, Tim 276
Ramirez, Hanley 295, 296
Ramirez, Manny 226, 228, 302
Raymond, Bugs 135
Renteria, Edgar 143, 327
reserve clause 84, 85, 130
Reuss, Jerry 128
Rickey, Branch 96, 123, 124, 126
right fielder 37
Ripken Jr., Cal 177, 178
Rizzuto, Phil 224
Roberts, Robin 147, 151, 345, 347
Robinson, Brooks 39, 176
Robinson, Frank 176, 196
Robinson, Jackie 92, 96, 97, 228, 313
Roseboro, Johnny 100
Rose, Pete 25, 26, 31, 33, 62, 66, 67, 68, 69, 149, 153, 349
Rothstein, Arnold 137, 161

Rudhyar, Dane 26, 355
Rulerships 29
Rusie, Amos 137, 138
Ruth, Babe 41, 83, 89, 90, 109, 133, 138, 196, 197, 207, 209, 211, 214, 215, 219, 225, 226, 336, 337
Ryan, Nolan 36, 186, 235, 248

S

Sacred Geometry 52, 53
Sacred Geometry: Philosophy and Practice 53
Safeco Field 285
Sagittarius 21
Sagittarius and the batter 39, 44
Saigh, Fred 124
San Diego Padres 231, 267
San Francisco Giants. See Giants
Sanguillen, Manny 115
Santo, Ron 77, 79, 313
Saturn 24
Saturn and the manager 40
Saturn in the Post-Season 216, 320
Sax, Steve 95
Schmidt, Mike 39, 145, 149, 152
Schotz, Marge 65, 66
Scocia, Mike 100
Score, Herb 192
Scorpio 20
Scorpio and third base 39
Seaton, Tom 147
Seattle Mariners 231, 280
Seattle Pilots 258
Seaver, Nancy 235
Seaver, Tom 235
second baseman 38
Selig, Bud 259, 306
semi-square 32
September 11 attacks 189
Seth 12, 13, 14
sextile 32
Shannon, Mike 126
Shea Stadium 79
Shibe Park 199, 202, 203, 204
Shore, Ernie 225, 336, 337, 338
shortstop 35
Sianis, Billy 78
Sicks Stadium 258, 259
signs 18
Simmons, Al 138, 200, 207
Sisler, George 175
The Sixth Game 347
Skydome 286, 287, 288
Slaughter, Enos 126, 220, 229
Smith, Mayo 107
Smith, Ozzie 35, 269
Smoltz, John 88
Smulyan, Jeff 280
Snider, Duke 36
Sockalexis, Louis 197
Soden, Arthur 84
Somers, Charles 190, 191, 221
Sosa, Sammy 268, 319
Sotomayor, Sonia 177
South End Grounds 82, 85
Spaulding, Albert 9, 10, 72, 73, 75
Speaker, Tris 107, 196, 197, 228, 314
spitball 96, 116, 333
Sportsman's Park 127, 171, 173, 174, 175
square 31
Stahl, Chick 220, 221
Stahl, Jake 221, 223, 228
Stallings, George 105
Stargell, Willie 118
Stengal, Casey 148, 234
steroids 41, 140, 141, 208, 265
St. Louis Browns 119, 119
St. Louis Cardinals 119, 249, 250
Stoneham, Charles 137
Stoneham, Horace 135, 137
Stoolball 10
Stovey, Harry 112
St. Petersburg Yacht Club 128
Strange but True Baseball Stories 170
Strawberry, Darryl 234
streakers 166
Street, Gabby 181, 182
Strike of 1994 and 1995 177, 299
Sullivan, Sport 161
Sun 23
Sun and right fielder 37
Sutton, Don 101
The Sybil 47

T

Taft, William Howard 180, 181
Take Time for Paradise 51
Ta kurt om el mahag 11, 14, 355
Tammany Hall 137, 212
Tampa Bay Devil Rays. See Tampa Bay Rays
Tampa Bay Rays 231, 154, 299
Tarnas, Richard 158
Tartabull, Danny 340, 341
Taurus 19
Taurus and center field 35
Tebbetts, Birdie 224
Tenney, Fred 87
Tesla, Nikola 21
Texas Rangers 179, 231, 243, 251, 315
theater 49
Thelma's deal 185
third baseman 39
Thompson, Sam 105, 145
Thompson, W. G. 107
Thomson, Bobby 91, 144, 318
Thorpe, Jim 334
Throneberry, Marv 234
Tierney, Jim 115
Tiger Stadium 102, 108
Tinker, Joe 73

Toney, Fred 65, 332
Toronto Blue Jays 231, 286, 350
Transits 33, 310
Transits in Games 310
Transits to the Birthcharts of Pitchers 327
trine 31
Tripartide Agreement 113
Tripitaka 48
Tripolitania 11
Tucker, Tommy 86
Turner, Ted 84, 90

U

Ulysses 47
umpire 12 49, 56, 107, 134, 174, 180, 225, 328, 336, 352
United States 8, 9, 26, 41, 85, 121, 177, 180, 181, 182, 232, 234, 238, 245, 275, 279, 320
Updike, John 223
Uranus 24
Uranus and home run 41
Uranus and left field 41

V

Valenzuela, Fernando 101
Vance, Dazzy 95
Van der Meer, Johnny 64
Vaughn, Jim "Hippo" 332
Veeck, Bill 157, 158, 166, 167, 174, 175, 194, 207
Venus 24
Venus and center field 35
Venus and second base 38
Versalles, Zoilo 187
Veteran's Stadium 151
Vindemiatrix 97, 98
Virden, Bill 115
Virgo 20
Virgo and pitcher 37, 38
Von der Ahe, Chris 120, 124, 126, 127

W

Waddell, Rube 114, 116
Wagner, Honus 35, 114, 184, 314, 315
Waitkus, Eddie 152
Walker, Harry 126
Walsh, Runt 148
Walters, Bucky 148
Washington Monument 181, 182
Washington Nationals 231, 273
Washington, Ron 248
Washington Senators 156, 177, 179, 243, 251, 336
The Wave 203
Weaver, Buck 163, 165, 316
Webster, Lenny 325
Western League 60, 155
WGM 75

White, Bill 121, 128, 129
Whitehead, George 115
Whitney, Pinky 146
Whiz Kids 151, 152, 344
Will, George 41, 50, 64, 227
Williams, Dick 41, 229, 271, 277
Williams, Matt 305, 339
Williams, Mitch 149, 153, 321, 352, 353
Williams, Ted 223, 224, 225, 226
Wills, Maury 127, 275
Wilson, Hack 73, 74
Wolverines 103
World Series 320-327
Wright, George 84, 88
Wright, Harry 40, 64, 66, 88
Wrigley Field 70, 74, 75, 78, 307, 344

Y

Yankees 157, 211, 323, 324
Yastrzemski, Carl 226, 229, 320
Yeager, Steve 100
Year of the Pitcher 267, 275, 320
Yost, Eddie 187
Young, Dick 235

Z

Zimmerman, Henry 135, 136
Zobrist, Ben 81
Zodiac Belt 18, 23, 31

www.ingramcontent.com/pod-product-compliance
Lightning Source LLC
Chambersburg PA
CBHW072146070526
44585CB00015B/1018